Thailand

An Apsonsi, Grand Palace, Bangkok

B. Régent-PHOTONONSTOP

Published in association with the SIAM CEMENT GROUP

MICHELIN

Travel Publications

Hannay House, 39 Clarendon Road
Watford, Herts WD17 1JA, UK
☎ 01923 205 240 - Fax 01923 205 241
www.ViaMichelin.com
TheGreenGuide-uk@uk.michelin.com

Manufacture française des pneumatiques Michelin
Société en commandite par actions au capital de 304 000 000 EUR
Place des Carmes-Déchaux – 63 Clermont-Ferrand (France)
R.C.S. Clermont-Fd B 855 200 507

© Michelin et Cie, Propriétaires-éditeurs, 2002
Dépôt légal mars 2002 – ISBN 2-06-000894-8 – ISSN 0763-1383
Printed in France 03-02/2.1

Typesetting: Le Sanglier, Charleville-Mézières
Printing: I.M.E., Baume-les-Dames
Binding: I.M.E., Baume-les-Dames

Cover design: Carré Noir, Paris 17ᵉ arr.

Discovering Thailand

Thailand, formerly the Kingdom of Siam, is an exotic destination which fires the imagination and fosters a desire to explore. Its appeal ranges from the verdant mountain scenery of the north peopled by proud hill-tribes to the sparkling beaches and idyllic islands in the south, from ancient cultural sites to the teeming capital with its golden spires crowning the royal palace and temples. Festivals celebrated with great verve break the serene ryhthm of the Buddhist way of life. The mouthwatering Thai food is a feast for the senses, a subtle blend of many flavours.

The Green Guide Thailand, a valuable companion on your travels, will help you to make the most of your holiday. The challenging task of compiling the guide was undertaken by Sybille Bouquet, who as well as coordinating the contributions of valued specialists in Thailand and the United Kingdom, made eight visits to the country and wrote the major part of the text. The information contained in the guide is based on extensive research into the history and art of the country. Essential features of this publication are extracts from a map and an atlas of Thailand compiled by the Michelin Cartography department. The whole project which took three years to complete was sponsored by the Siam Cement Group, the commercial partner of Michelin Siam in Thailand.

The Green Guide is attractively presented with many illustrations; the quality of the cartography reflects the accuracy for which Michelin is renowned. The maps and plans were produced by an expert team who covered the territory.

In this revised edition of The Green Guide Thailand the practical information section for the main tourist destinations features hotels and restaurants, shopping, entertainment and excursions. The information is checked regularly but we welcome readers' comments on any discrepancies or changes which may have occurred since publication. As publishers of travel publications for over a hundred years Michelin aims to offer the best guide on the market.

Thank you for choosing The Green Guide. Enjoy your trip to Thailand, the Land of Smiles.

H. Deguine
International Director – The Green Guide
The GreenGuide-uk@uk.michelin.com

Contents

Fruit vendor afloat

Paper parasols

Sights 82

A roaring dragon

Mythical figures

5

Using this guide

● The summary maps on pages 10-17 are designed to assist at the planning stage: the **Map of Principal Sights** identifies the major attractions according to their star ratings; the Map of Touring Programmes outlines regional motoring itineraries and places to stay.

● The **Practical Information** chapter includes useful travel advice, addresses, services, information on recreational facilities and a calendar of events.

● It is worth reading the Introduction before setting out as it gives background information on history, the arts and traditional culture.

● The main natural and cultural attractions are presented in alphabetical order in the **Sights** section; excursions to places in the surrounding district are attached to many of the town chapters.

● The clock symbol ⊘ placed after the name of a sight refers to the Admission times and charges chapter at the end of the guide.

● This guide is designed to be used in conjunction with the Michelin road **Map 965** and the **Michelin Tourist and Motoring Atlas Thailand**. Cross references to these maps appear in blue print under the chapter headings in the Sights section.

● To find a particular place or historic figure or event or practical information, consult the **Index**.

We greatly appreciate comments and suggestions from our readers. Contact us at :

Michelin Travel Publications,

Hannay House

39 Clarendon Road, Watford WD17 1JA, UK

Tel 01923 205 240

Fax 01923 205 241

TheGreenGuide@uk.michelin.com

TheGreenGuide@us.michelin.com

www.ViaMichelin.com

J. de Boisberranger/ HEMISPHERES

Novices at leisure

Key

★★★ **Highly recommended**

★★ **Recommended**

★ **Interesting**

Tourism

⊙	Admission Times and Charges listed at the end of the guide	►►	Visit if time permits
	Sightseeing route with departure point indicated	AZ B	Map co-ordinates locating sights
	Ecclesiastical building	🛈	Tourist information
	Synagogue – Mosque		Historic house, castle – Ruins
	Building (with main entrance)		Dam – Factory or power station
■	Statue, small building		Fort – Cave
✝	Wayside cross		Prehistoric site
◎	Fountain		Viewing table – View
	Fortified walls – Tower – Gate	▲	Miscellaneous sight

Recreation

	Racecourse	🚶	Waymarked footpath
	Skating rink	♦	Outdoor leisure park/centre
	Outdoor, indoor swimming pool		Theme/Amusement park
	Marina, moorings		Wildlife/Safari park, zoo
	Mountain refuge hut	⊕	Gardens, park, arboretum
	Overhead cable-car		Aviary, bird sanctuary
	Tourist or steam railway		

Additional symbols

	Motorway (unclassified)		Post office – Telephone centre
❶ ❶	Junction: complete, limited		Covered market
	Pedestrian street		Barracks
	Unsuitable for traffic, street subject to restrictions		Swing bridge
	Steps – Footpath		Quarry – Mine
	Railway – Coach station	B F	Ferry (river and lake crossings)
	Funicular – Rack-railway		Ferry services: Passengers and cars
	Tram – Metro, Underground		Foot passengers only
Bert (R.)...	Main shopping street	③	Access route number common to MICHELIN maps and town plans

Abbreviations and special symbols

H	Town Hall		Thai Boxing Stadium
J	Law Courts		Market
P	Provincial Office		Scenic road
POL.	Police		National Park – Zoo
T – U	Theatre – University		Marshland – Rice fields
	Historical Park		Beach – Hotel
	Buddhist Temple		Embassy, consulate
	Long-tail boat	★★KRABI	Title of chapter describing a region

9

Principal sights

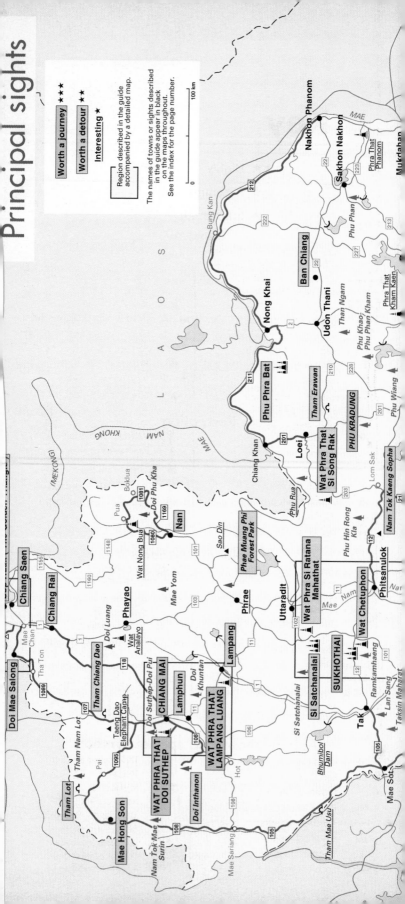

Worth a journey ★★★

Worth a detour ★★

Interesting ★

The names of towns or sights described in the guide appear in black on the maps throughout. See the index for the page number.

Region described in the guide accompanied by a detailed map.

0   100 km

Doi Mae Salong

Chiang Saen

Chiang Rai

Tham Chiang Dao

Tham Nam Lot

Tham Lot

Mae Hong Son

Doi Luang

Wat Analayo

Phayao

Doi Phu Kha

Wat Nong Bua

Nan

Phae Muang Phi Forest Park

Phrae

Sao Din

Doi Suthep-Doi Pui

CHIANG MAI

Lamphun

Doi Khuntan

Lampang

WAT PHRA THAT LAMPANG LUANG

WAT PHRA THAT DOI SUTHEP

Doi Inthanon

Taeng Dao Elephant Camp

Nam Tok Mae Surin

Uttaradit

Wat Phra Si Ratana Mahathat

Si Satchanalai

Si Satchanalai

SUKHOTHAI

Wat Chetuphon

Phitsanulok

Nam Tok Kaeng Sopha

Phu Hin Rong Kla

Phu Kradung

Wat Phra That Si Song Rak

Loei

Chiang Khan

Phu Rua

Tham Erawan

Phu Phra Bat

Nong Khai

Ban Chiang

Udon Thani

Than Ngam

Phu Khao Phu Phan Kham

Phu Phan

Phra That Kham Kaen

Phu Wiang

Sakhon Nakhon

Phra That Phanom

Nakhon Phanom

Mukdahan

Tak

Taksin Maharat

Lan Sang

Ramkamhaeng

Bhumibol Dam

Mae Sot

Tham Mae Usu

Bung Kan

Bukiua

Pua

Pai

Hot

Lom Sak

Lan Sang

Mae Sariang

NAM KHONG

MEKONG

NAM MAE

MAE

MAE

L A O S

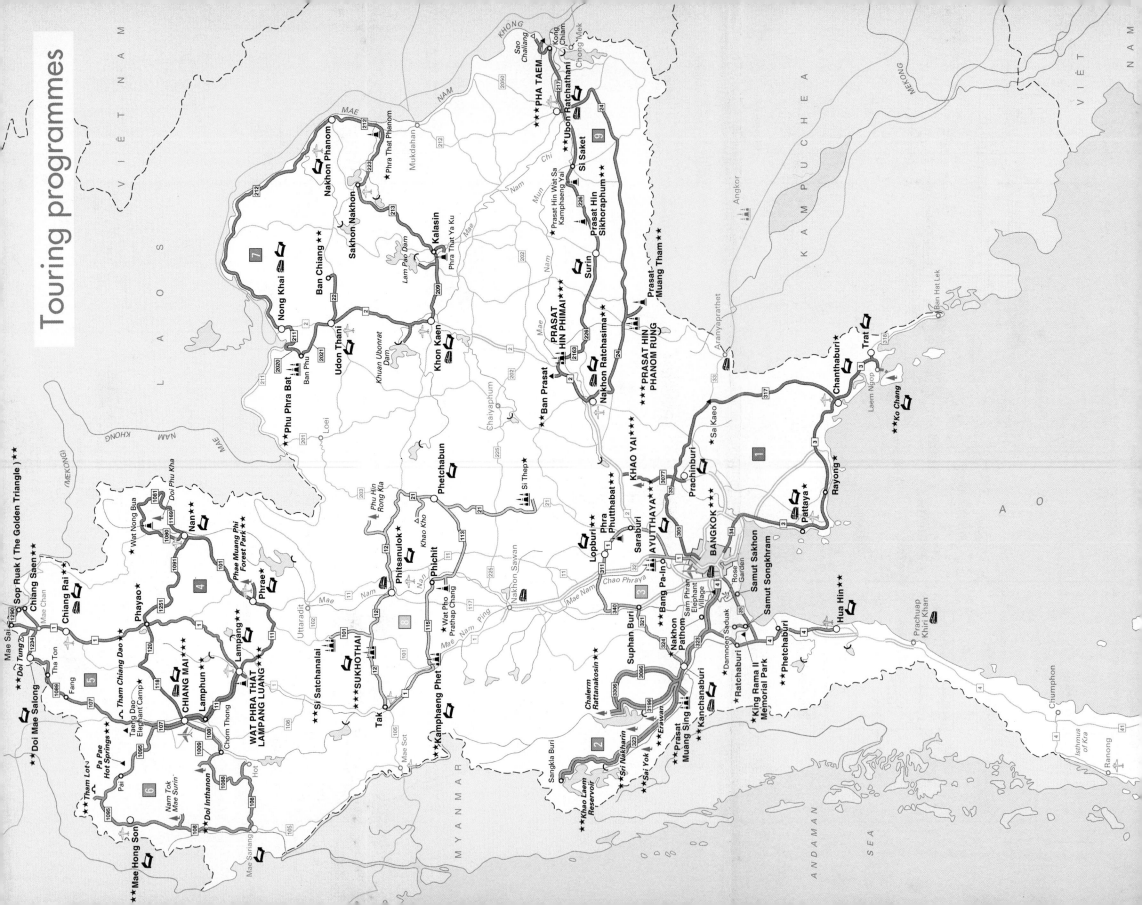

Touring programmes

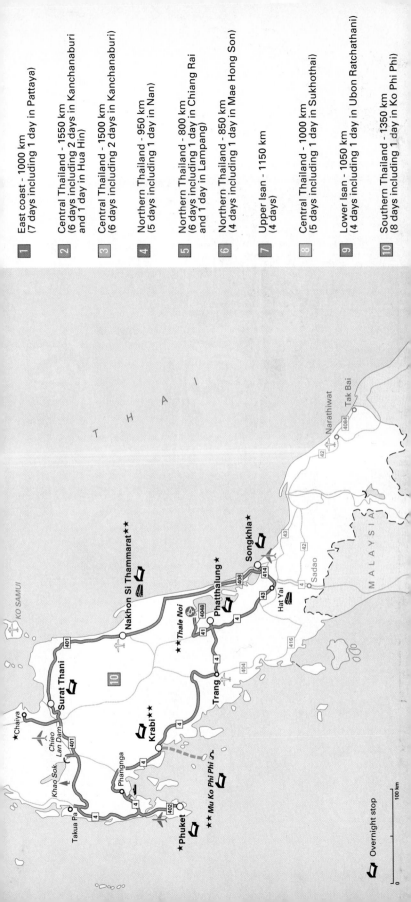

1 East coast - 1000 km
(7 days including 1 day in Pattaya)

2 Central Thailand - 1550 km
(6 days including 2 days in Kanchanaburi
and 1 day in Hua Hin)

3 Central Thailand - 1500 km
(6 days including 2 days in Kanchanaburi)

4 Northern Thailand - 950 km
(5 days including 1 day in Nan)

5 Northern Thailand - 800 km
(6 days including 1 day in Chiang Rai
and 1 day in Lampang)

6 Northern Thailand - 850 km
(4 days including 1 day in Mae Hong Son)

7 Upper Isan - 1150 km
(4 days)

8 Central Thailand - 1000 km
(5 days including 1 day in Sukhothai)

9 Lower Isan - 1050 km
(4 days including 1 day in Ubon Ratchathani)

10 Southern Thailand - 1350 km
(8 days including 1 day in Ko Phi Phi)

Overnight stop

0   100 km

Traditional marionnettes on display, Chiang Mai

Practical
information

Planning your trip

When to go – Thailand has a tropical climate with three distinct seasons and the best time to visit is from October/November to February/March to avoid the hot and rainy seasons.

Time – The time difference is 7 hours ahead of Greenwich Mean Time (GMT + 7).

Climate – The average annual temperature is 26° and the humidity is relatively high. The cool, dry season is from November to February when it can be misty and quite chilly at night in the mountains in the north. From March to June temperatures can rise above 40° during the day. The rainy season lasts from July to October with heavy downpours lasting one to two hours and occasional blue skies and sunshine. The worst months are September and October at the equinox when flooding is likely in Bangkok and in the central plain, as high tides in the Gulf of Thailand threaten the Chao Phraya delta already awash from the rains.
The south has a varied climate; Ko Samui and the Gulf of Thailand may be sunny while Phuket is under rain. Temperatures remain high with little seasonal variation.

Dress – Light, cotton clothing is the most comfortable all year round. A light jacket or pullover may be necessary in the evening in the north. Modest dress – avoid shorts and bare shoulders – is required for visiting temples. Swimwear is appropriate only at the beach. Hats should be worn as protection from the sun and comfortable slip-on shoes are best for visiting monuments and walking in the countryside.

National holidays

1 January	New Year's Day
February – full-moon day	Makha Bucha
6 April	Chakri Day
12-14 April	Songkran
5 May	Coronation Day
May – full-moon day	Visakha Bucha
July – full-moon day	Asaraha Bucha
12 August	HM the Queen's Birthday
23 October	Chulalongkorn Day
5 December	HM the King's Birthday
10 December	Constitution Day
31 December	New Year's Eve

Documents – Foreign visitors travelling to Thailand must be in possession of full **passports** valid at least six months beyond the date of arrival at the destination. Loss or theft should be reported to the local police and to the relevant embassy. It is advisable to make photocopies of passports and visas as documentary proof to facilitate issue of replacement documents. After new passports have been obtained, apply to the Immigration Division, Old Building, Soi Suan Plu, Sathon Tai Road, Bangkok 10120. ☏ 02 287 3101-10 for new visas.

Visas – Nationals of all European countries and Australia, Canada, Japan, New Zealand, USA, Singapore, Malaysia, Indonesia and Myanmar may enter the country for a maximum period of 30 days without a visa provided they hold a return ticket. Nationals of other countries should enquire about visa requirements from travel agents and Thai embassies or consulates abroad. Although visas may be obtained at the four international terminals on arrival, it is advisable to obtain visas in advance to avoid lengthy delays.
Thai embassies and consulates issue tourist visas valid for 60 days for which a fee is charged. Apply for visas in good time. Except in exceptional circumstances, extensions for not more than 30 days may be granted on application to the Immigration Bureau. Fee: 500 Baht. Application for re-entry permit: 1 000 Baht.
Visitors exceeding the period of stay stamped on arrival face a fine of 100 Baht per excess day on departure.

Inoculations – No vaccinations are required unless passengers have visited a yellow fever infected area within ten days of travelling to Thailand. However it is wise to ask for medical advice before departure. *See Health recommendations below.*

Travel Insurance – It is essential to have adequate comprehensive insurance cover for any medical or other emergencies.

Customs – Amounts in excess of $US 10 000 in foreign currency must be declared in writing on arrival. On departure travellers must obtain authorisation to take out amounts in excess of 50 000 Baht. Duty free allowances amount to 1 litre of wine or spirits, 200 cigarettes or 250g of tobacco.
One still-camera or one movie-camera and 5 rolls of still-camera film or 3 rolls of movie-camera film are allowed free of duty. It is wise to list valuable equipment (photographic and video cameras) and serial numbers separately. The list can be handed in on arrival and this will speed up customs clearance on departure.
Drugs and pornographic material are prohibited as well as certain species of fruits, vegetables and plants.

Tourist Information

Tourism Authority of Thailand (TAT) – For information, brochures, maps and assistance in planning a trip to Thailand contact TAT offices abroad *(addresses below)*.

Local offices *(addresses in the chapter Times and Charges)* also provide maps and information on sights, activities, travel, local events, festivals, listings of accommodation, and assistance in solving any problems. There is usually an English-speaking member of staff.

TAT Head Office

Tourism Authority of Thailand, Le Concorde Building, 202 Thanon Ratchadaphisek, Huai Khwang, Bangkok 10310, Thailand. ☎ (66) 02 694 1222; Fax (66) 02 694 1220/1; center@tat.or.th; www.tat.or.th; www.tourismthailand.org

Open Mondays to Fridays, 8.30am to 4.30pm. Closed weekends. Information Desk: open daily.

Some **TAT Offices** overseas cover several countries:

Australia
2nd Floor, 75 Pitt Street, Sydney 2000, Australia. ☎ (61) 2 9247 7549; Fax (61) 2 9251 2465; info@thailand.net.au
Australia, New Zealand, South Pacific.

France
Office National du Tourisme de Thaïlande, 90 Avenue des Champs-Elysées, 75008 Paris, France. ☎ (33) 1 5353 4700; Fax (33) 1 4563 7888; tatpar@wanadoo.fr
France, Belgium, Luxemburg, The Netherlands.

Germany
Thailandisches Fremdenverkehrsamt, Bethmannstr 58 D-60311 Frankfurt/M., Germany. ☎ (49) 69 1381 390; Fax (49) 69 281 468; tatfra@t-online.de
Austria, Switzerland and Eastern Europe.

Hong Kong
401 Fairmont House, 8 Cotton Tree Drive, Central, Hong Kong. ☎ (852) 2868 0732, 2868 0854. Fax (852) 2868 4585; tathkg@hk.super.net
Hong Kong, Macau, China.

Italy
Ente Nazionale per il Turismo Thailandese, Via Barberini 68, 4th Floor, 00187 Rome, Italy. ☎ (39) 6 487 3479, 481 8927; Fax (39) 6 487 3500; tat.rome@iol.it
Italy, Spain, Greece, Portugal, Israel, Egypt, Turkey.

Japan:
Tokyo
Yurakucho Denki Building, South Tower 2nd Floor, Room No 259, 1-7-1 Yurakucho, Chiyoda-ku, Tokyo 100, Japan. ☎ (81) 3 3218 0337/0355/1077; Fax (81) 3 3218 0655; tattky@crisscross.com

Osaka
Technoble Yotsubashi Bldg, 3rd Floor, 1-6-8 Kitahorie, Nishi-ku, Osaka 550-0014, Japan. ☎ (81) 6 6543 6654/6655; Fax (81) 6 6543 6660; tatosa@ca.mbn.or.jp

Malaysia
Suite 22.01, 22nd Floor, Level 22, Menara Lion, 165 Jalan Ampang, 50450 Kuala Lumpur, Malaysia. ☎ (60 3) 262 3480; Fax (60 3) 262 3486; sawatdi@po.jaring.my
Malaysia, Brunei.

Singapore
c/o Royal Thai Embassy, 370 Orchard Road, Singapore 238870. ☎ (65) 235 7694/7901, 735 0637; Fax (65) 733 5653; tatsin@mbox5.singnet.com.sg
Singapore, Indonesia, The Philippines.

UK
49 Albemarle Street, London W1X 3FE, UK. ☎ (44) 020 7499 7679; Fax (44) 020 7629 5519; info@tat-uk.demon.co.uk; www.thaismile.co.uk
UK, Ireland, Finland, Scandinavia.

USA:
Los Angeles
611 North Larchmont Blvd, 1st Floor, Los Angeles, CA 90004, USA. ☎ (1 323) 461 9814; Fax (1 323) 461 9834; tatla@ix.netcom.com

New York
1 World Trade Centre, Suite no 3729, New York, NY10048, USA. ☎ (1 212) 432 0433/0435; Fax (1 212) 912 0920; tatny@aol.com

Export restrictions apply to statues of the Buddha including fragments, antiques and art objects as well as reproductions. A licence must be obtained from the Department of Fine Arts and takes up to two weeks to process. For further information apply to the Fine Arts Department, Bangkok. ☎ 02 221 7811. Permits must be shown to Customs on departure. Customs officials make spot baggage checks and heavy fines are imposed for infringements.

Embassies and Consulates

Australia	37 Thanon Sathorn Tai, Bangkok. ☎ 02 287 2680.
Canada	15th floor, Abdularhim Place, 990 Thanon Rama iV, Bangkok. ☎ 02 636 0560.
France	29 Thanon Sathon Tai. ☎ 02 285 6104/7.
Ireland	United Flour Mill Building, Soi Sampeng, Thanon Ratchawong, Bangkok. ☎ 02 223 0876.
Japan	9th Floor, 159 Sermit Tower, Sukhumvit 21, Bangkok. ☎ 02 259 0444.
New Zealand	93 Thanon Witthayu, Bangkok. ☎ 02 254 2530.
UK	1031 Thanon Phloenchit, Bangkok. ☎ 02 253 0191.
USA	95 Thanon Witthayu, Bangkok. ☎ 02 205 4000.

Getting there

By air – Scheduled airlines operate direct flights to Don Muang International Airport, Bangkok, from all over the world. Other international airports are Phuket, Hat Yai and Chiang Mai.

A passenger tax is levied on all international passengers passing through Don Muang or other international airports and must be paid for at check-in counters on departure: 500 Baht.

Departure information: ☎ 02 535 1254, ☎ 02 535 1386. Arrival information ☎ 02 535 1149.

Transfer from the airport to Bangkok – Apply to the Public Taxi Counter for authorised taxis which carry a yellow licence plate and a TAXI-METER sign. Fares to various destinations are posted at the taxi stand as a guideline.

There is also an Airport Taxi Counter which is more expensive and a private Limousine Service.

A train service *(45min)* runs from Don Muang. Fares 5 to 70 Baht depending on class of train.

Buses (regular and air-conditioned) can be boarded at the bus-stop on Viphavadi Rangsit Highway. Fares: 5.50 Baht (any distance) in regular buses (nos 29, 59, 95), 8-18 Baht in air-conditioned buses (nos 4, 10, 13, 29). Private air-conditioned buses: 70 Baht.

By train – Services operate from Singapore, Kuala Lumpur and Butterworth in Malaysia to Bangkok. The Eastern and Oriental Express runs a luxury trip from Singapore to Bangkok stopping at various stations on the way and from Bangkok to Chiang Mai.

By road – Overland border points are at Songkhla, Yala and Narathiwat (south); Mae Sai, Chiang Khong (by ferry), Nong Khai, Mae Sot (north); Three Pagodas Pass (west); Nakhon Phanom, Mukdahan and Chong Mek (by ferry), Aranyaprathet (east). Some of the sensitive border posts may be closed at short notice because of border conflicts. Travellers must ensure that they have the necessary visas which must be obtained in advance as few border posts issue visas on arrival.

Getting around

By air – Many airlines operate flights to several destinations. Information and reservations from authorised Thai Inter travel agencies.

Thai Airways International, 485/2-3 Thanon Silom. ☎ 02 232 8000.

Bangkok Airways, Queen Sirikit National Convention Center, Zone C, 60 Thanon New Ratchadapisek, Klongtoey, Bangkok 10110. ☎ 02 229 3456-63.

PB Air, 17th floor, UBC Building, Thanon Sukhumvit, Soi 33. ☎ 02 261 0220-5.

Angel Air, 499/7 Thanon Viphavadi Rangsit, Chatuchak. ☎ 02 535 6287/8.

By sea – Apply to travel agencies for information on cruise ships plying coastal waters.

By train – The State Railway of Thailand runs an excellent rail service with fast, comfortable trains to long-distance destinations. There are four types of train: Ordinary (ORD), Rapid (RPD), Express (EXP) and Sprinter (SPR) and three classes. Third class is not recommended if there is an alternative. There is an Advance Booking Service in Bangkok Railway Station: 8.30am-4pm. ☎ 02 225 0300. Apply at least 90 days in advance.

Rail passes valid for 2nd or 3rd class travel for 20 days: 750 Baht (child) to 3 000 Baht. ☎ 02 225 6964 (information)

The State Railway organises 1-2 day economy tours to various destinations on Saturdays, Sundays and holidays. ☎ 02 223 7010, 02 223 7020.

Bangkok is served by two stations: **Hua Lamphong**, Thanon Rama IV, ☎ 02 223 0341 for most destinations; **Bangkok Noi** Thonburi Station to Kanchanaburi ☎ 02 411 3102, 02 465 2017.

By road – There is an excellent road network and an efficient bus service covering the whole country. Air-conditioned buses afford more comfort.

Northern/Northeastern Bus Terminals, Thanon Phahonyothin and Thanon Kamphaeng Phet. ☎ 02 936 3660 (air-conditioned buses), 02 271 0101-5 (regular buses).

Southern Bus Terminal, Thanon Pinklao-Nakhon Chaisri. ☎ 02 435 1199, 02 435 1200 (air-conditioned buses), 02 434 5538 (regular buses).

Eastern Bus Terminal, Sukhumvit. ☎ 02 391 2504 (air-conditioned buses), 02 392 2521 (regular buses).

Route planning – The whole of Thailand *(see Contents page)* is covered by the **Michelin map 965** (scale 1:1 370 000 – 1cm:13.70km) and the **Michelin Tourist and Motoring Atlas Thailand** (scale 1:1 000 000 – 1cm:10km). In addition to the usual detailed road information, they indicate features such as beaches or bathing areas, golf courses, race courses, scenic routes, tourist sights, national parks etc.

Motoring – Vehicles drive on the **left**. Driving in Bangkok is not recommended because of the dense traffic. Outside Bangkok it is strongly advisable to hire a car or minibus with a local driver as road conditions and driving habits are unpredictable, with buses and trucks racing on the highway and innumerable hazards (pedestrians, children playing, motorcycles, tractors, animals, vehicles with no lights) on the road. Road signs are in both Thai and English and traffic signs conform to international standards with a few exceptions.

The speed limit is 60km/h in built-up areas and 120km/h on country roads and motorways but these restrictions are often ignored.

Car hire should only be through reputable rental agencies. For overseas bookings contact:

> **Avis**, 2/12 Thanon Wittayu. ☎ 02 254 6716, Reservation ☎ 02 252 1131/2; Fax 02 254 6718/9. Don Muang Airport ☎ 02 535 4031/2; Fax 02 535 4055. www.avisthailand.com
>
> **Hertz**, 420 Soi Sukhumvit. ☎ 02 711 0574/8. Fax 02 381 4572. Don Muang Airport ☎ 02 535 3004/5.
>
> **Budget**, 19/23 Building A, Royal City Avenue, Thanon New Petchburi. ☎ 02 203 0225, 203 0250; Fax 02 203 0249; www.budget.co.th

Rates include insurance but very high deposits are demanded except if booking by international credit card. A valid international driving licence is required. Check the roadworthiness of the vehicle and the insurance cover. Air-conditioning is recommended.

Motorcycles – There are rental agencies in large towns and holiday resorts. Motorcycles are convenient for exploring the countryside and remote areas. However, check the insurance cover and ensure that the vehicle is roadworthy. Helmets are compulsory but the rule is often ignored outside Bangkok. Take great care on the road.

Hitch-hiking – This is not a common practice in Thailand.

Local transport – Prices should be agreed in advance in all cases unless using a metered taxi.

Tuk-tuk

Hang yao, long-tail boats, are the most common means of transport on the waterways. They are fast and noisy.

In country towns *Song Tao*, pick-up trucks fitted with two benches, run on fixed routes and have set fares. They can often be hired for excursions.

P. de Wilde/ HOA QUI

Motorbike taxis are the quickest way to get about but safety is an important consideration. Riders wearing coloured vests are usually found at road junctions; they are often a useful source of local information.

Samlors are a type of tricycle found in any town. The *Tuk-Tuk* is a motorised scooter version found in Bangkok and other large towns.

Bicycles are a safe and pleasant way to explore towns such as Chiang Mai and Chiang Rai. Taxis are also available in some towns; some may have meters and air conditioning.

Places to stay

The major cities and the inland and coastal resorts offer a wide range of accommodation from luxury hotels to simple guest houses.

To find a place to stay turn to the blue pages in selected chapters in the Sights section and consult the list of addresses – hotels, guest houses, resorts – chosen to suit a variety of tastes and budgets.

The map on pages 14-17 indicates places for overnight stays.

The Tourism Authority of Thailand (TAT) publishes current lists of accommodation and rates ranging from luxury hotels and guesthouses to bungalows, simple Chinese-style hotels and beach huts which are available from local Tourist Offices.

The Thai Hotels Association counter at Don Muang Airport, Bangkok and other provincial airports will make bookings at its member hotels.

Large hotels offer postal, telephone and fax services.

Youth Hostels – They offer simple, inexpensive accommodation and accept persons of all ages as well as families. Advance booking is advisable. Make sure personal possessions are securely stored.

Bangkok   YMCA, 27 Thanon Sathon Tai. ☎ 02 287 2727.
                YWCA, 13 Thanon Sathon Tai. ☎ 02 286 1936.

Chiang Mai YMCA International House, Thanon Mengrai-Rasami. ☎ 053 221 819.

Chiang Rai YMCA International House, 70 Thanon Phahonyothin. ☎ 053 713 785/6, 053 714 336.

Services

Currency – The Thai currency unit is the **Baht** which equals 100 satang. Coins are in denominations of 25 and 50 satang (copper), 1, 5 baht (silver) and 10 baht (composite silver and copper). Bank notes are valued at 10 (brown), 20 (green), 50 (blue), 100 (red), 500 (mauve) and 1000 (khaki) bahts. $US 1 is worth about 45 bath, £1 is worth about 60 baht. Coins and bills of different sizes are in use and this can be confusing.

Credit Cards – Major international credit cards, such as American Express, Diners, Carte Blanche, Mastercard and Visa are widely accepted but cash is better for bargaining. Visitors should be aware of fraud risks. Make sure amounts tally on both copies of the voucher and destroy the carbon. When paying by credit card, check that no surcharge is added to the price of the merchandise. If there is a surcharge contact the card company.

Foreign Exchange – Banks and authorised money changers will readily cash travellers cheques in US dollars. Cheques in other currencies are best changed in Bangkok where better rates prevail. Many hotels provide exchange facilities but rates are generally lower.

Banks – The main Thai banks have branches all over the country for the usual transactions and can also organise bank transfers from abroad. Opening times are Mon-Fri, 9.30am-3.30pm. Closed Sat, Sun and public holidays. Some banks also provide currency centres in tourist areas which open daily from 07.00 to 21.00.

Post – Outside Bangkok most post offices open Mon-Fri, 8.30am-4.30pm and only larger ones open on Sat, 8.30am-noon. Fax services are also available in most towns.

Telephone – Direct dialling to most countries is possible from phone booths in tourist areas. In remote areas it is best to use the Overseas Telephone Service at post offices. For international calls, dial 001, followed by the country code and the number. To make a national call simply dial the regional code and number.

A Subscriber Indentity Module Card (SIM Card) for use with digital mobile phones (GSM within 900mhz range or PCM within 1800mhz range) is available in Thailand. Information (24 hours) from Advanced Info Service Public Co Ltd, 1291/1 Shinawatra Tower, 2 Thanon Phahonyotin, Bangkok 10400. ☎ +662 271 9000; callcenter@ais900.com

Internet – Services are available at leading hotels.

Electricity – The electric current is 220 volts AC (50 hertz). There are many plugs and sockets in use; adaptors are recommended.

Chemists – There are many pharmacies (Green Cross sign) in tourist centres which stock almost all medicines in common use in the West. To avoid confusion or if a proprietary brand is required take along the original packaging or check the availability with the Bangkok branch of the relevant pharmaceutical company (see Yellow Pages).

Shopping – Many stores open 12 hours a day all week. Thailand is a paradise for shoppers. Bangkok, Chiang Mai and Pattaya are the best centres with amazing markets and stores, and all regions boast typical crafts. Bargaining is a common practice and prices may be reduced by as much as 30%. Courtesy is appreciated.

Some travellers arrive with very little luggage as ready-to-wear and made-to-measure garments at bargain prices are available at markets and stores all over the country. For made-to-measure outfits ensure at least one fitting.

Colourful Thai silks, cottons and folk handicrafts (embroidery, dolls, silver jewellery) are typical; silver, bronze and pewter ware is of excellent quality. Jewellery and precious stones should be acquired only from reputable dealers. Leather goods and luggage are good value. Other tempting items include fine wood carving, lacquer, mother-of-pearl, cloisonné and niello ware. Dealers will arrange for export of cane and carved wood furniture.

Thai silk

An export licence is required for statues of the Buddha and art objects including reproductions *(see Customs above)*. Certificates of authenticity for antiques can be obtained from the Fine Arts Department in Bangkok or the regional divisions.

Shoppers should be aware that clothing and watches which carry famous and designer labels may not be the genuine article, and counterfeits may be confiscated by customs in their home country. Visitors should also refrain from purchasing ivory and items from protected species (crocodile skin, butterflies).

To claim VAT refund on goods taken out of Thailand within 60 days of purchase ask the sales assistant to fill in Form P.P.10 (for purchases to a value of 2 000 Baht or more including VAT on any day). Refunds can only be claimed on a minimum amount of 5 000 Baht including VAT. Submit the form, original invoices and goods for inspection at the Customs desk and allow plenty of time for processing.

Duty-free shopping in Bangkok is convenient: Thailand Duty Free Shops Co., 7th Floor, World Trade Centre, 4 Thanon Ratchadamri, Patumwan, Bangkok 10330. ☏ 02 252 3407. There are also pre-order points at the Imperial Queen's Park Hotel and the River City Complex in Bangkok, at Samphran Park in Nakhon Pathom and at the Alcazar in Pattaya. Purchases are delivered at the airport.

Tipping – It is customary to tip porters and hotel staff and to give a 10-15% tip in restaurants.

Smoking – Smoking is prohibited in cinemas and public buses. Offenders are fined.

Tourist Police

A special police unit with English-speaking officers provides assistance to tourists and can be reached on **1155**. The Tourist Police are attached to TAT offices in the main tourist centres.

Useful numbers: Ayutthaya 035 242 352, 035 241 446; Bangkok 1155, 02 281 5051; Chiang Mai 053 248 130, 053 242 966; Chiang Rai 053 717 779/796; Kanchanaburi 034 512 668/795 Pattaya 038 425 937, 038 429 371; Phuket 076 217 517, 076 225 361; Songkhla 074 246 733.

Recommendations

Health Precautions – Although there are no compulsory inoculations, medical advice should be sought on vaccinations against tetanus, poliomyelitis and Hepatitis A. Those travelling in rural areas should take the recommended course of anti-malaria tablets and be vaccinated against Japanese encephalitis. At night protective clothing (long-sleeved shirts and trousers) should be worn to avoid mosquito bites (moquitoes are active between dusk and dawn). Mosquito coils, electric gadgets with tablets, insect repellents and nets are all useful precautions.

A good first aid kit as well as pain killers, antiseptic ointment, medicines for gastric problems and travel sickness, sun creams with a high filter factor are necessities.

Allow time for acclimatisation to the tropical climate as heat exhaustion and dehydration can cause problems. Avoid over-exertion in the debilitating heat and over-exposure to the sun; drink lots of water and take salt to make up for loss of fluid.

Tap water is not recommended for drinking. Bottled water is widely available and should be used even for cleaning teeth.

Avoid cut fruit and uncooked vegetables from roadside stalls. Freshly cooked hot food presents no risks.

Turn off the air-conditioning at night to avoid catching cold.

Medical facilities are of good standard in most tourist centres. Medical practitioners and hospitals are listed in the Yellow Pages. Hotel staff and local tourist offices will give advice in emergencies.

Sex-tourism – Prostitution and massage parlours are social issues which may disturb some visitors. However, it is vital to be aware that infection with AIDS and other sexually transmitted diseases are real dangers; condoms are essential.

Sexual abuse of children is a crime and offenders face prosecution in their home country.

Drugs – Possession of drugs and trafficking are serious offences punishable by long prison sentences. Dealers are rumoured to report foreign drug users to the police. Never agree to carry parcels out of the country as a favour for anyone, especially recent acquaintances.

Safety – Thailand has a good reputation for safe travel but special care should be taken in sensitive border areas. Common sense and watchfulness against petty crimes are the rule. Lock hotel rooms and place valuables in room safes or safe deposit boxes or keep them in your possession. To avoid the risk of fraud or rip-offs, beware of people offering incredible bargains especially precious stones, and of invitations from strangers to visit places of entertainment off the beaten track.

Etiquette – The Royal Family is revered by the Thai people and visitors must show respect for royal portraits and other symbols as well as for the National Anthem.

Statues of the Buddha, even in ruins, are sacred. Never clamber over statues or religious monuments for photographs.

Dress in suitable attire (no shorts or bare shoulders) for visits to religious shrines. Shoes should always be removed on entering Thai homes, Buddhist temples, and mosques. Women must not touch or hand anything directly to Buddhist monks.

Never pat anyone on the back or point your foot at a person or object. The Thai are very respecful of older people and of figures of authority. A cool head and a sense of humour achieve better results than rudeness and angry outbursts; public displays of affection between men and women should be avoided.

Language – Thai is the official language although in tourist areas most shops, hotels and restaurants have English-speaking staff. Local people are full of good will and a smile and sign language will help in most situations. It is also useful for visitors to ask someone to write out their requirements in Thai.

Useful expressions

Hello, goodbye – *Sawadee kap* (man), *sawadee ka* (woman)
Yes – *Kap* (man), *ka* (woman)
No – *Maï*
Thank you – *Kop khun kap* (man), *kop khun ka* (woman)
How much ? – *Taorai ?*
Where is … ? – *Yu tinnaï … ?*
What is this ? – *Nee arai ?*
The bill please – *Kep tang*
I don't speak Thai – *Mai kap chai*
I don't understand – *Mai kao chai*
Excuse me, I beg your pardon – *Ko thot*

Entertainment

Thailand's English language newspapers publish daily listings on cultural events – Thai dance and puppet shows, concerts, exhibitions, cinemas. Complimentary weekly tourist publications such as Bangkok Dining and Entertainment, This Week, Explore Pattaya etc. give useful information on restaurants and nightlife attractions.

Theatre – In Bangkok the main venues for shows are the National Theatre, Thailand Cultural Centre (Thanon Ratchadapisek), Alliance Française Auditorium (Thanon Sathon Tai), AVA Language Centre Auditorium (Thanon Ratchadamri), British Council Centre (Siam Square), Goethe Institute (Soi Attakarnprasit, off Thanon Sathon Tai).
In Chiang Mai: National Theatre, Old Chiang Mai Cultural Centre, Thanon Wualai and KAD Performing Arts Centre.

Nightlife – There are bars, cabarets, jazz clubs, nightclubs and discotheques to suit all tastes as well as karaoke clubs which are very popular. Most are respectable places with loud music and good food. Some areas in Bangkok, Pattaya, Phuket have a reputation for licentious entertainment.

Thai Boxing – The rules of this traditional sport allow boxers to use feet, legs, elbows, shoulders and fists to overcome their opponents. Events take place at Ratchadamnoen Stadium (Mon, Wed, Thur and Sun) and Lumphini Stadium (Tues, Fri and Sat) in Bangkok.

Recreation

The topography of Thailand provides the natural environment for a variety of activities.

Golf – This popular sport can be enjoyed all year round. The major golf courses, many of which are up to professional standard, are located around Bangkok, Pattaya, Hua Hin, Nakhon Pathom, Chonburi, Phuket and Chiang Mai.

Trekking – Trekking is very popular for exploring the remote mountain areas of the north, experience the simple life and visit hilltribe villages. The trip usually includes spending the night in a modest hut in a village. Opium is often on offer but this is not recommended because the after-effects combined with the high altitude and the strenuous effort of trekking may be harmful. The Tourist Offices in Chiang Mai and Chiang Rai publish lists of reputable agencies and advise on cost. Deposit valuables in a safety deposit box at a bank. Make sure the guide speaks the language of the tribe. Contact The Trekking Collective Company, 25/1 Thanon Ratchawithi, Chiang Mai 50200. ☏/Fax (66) 053 419 080.

Rafting – This exciting activity is often combined with trekking trips when visiting the north. For ecological considerations, the rafts are more likely to be made of rubber than bamboo. Apply to the Tourist Offices in Chiang Mai and Chiang Rai for lists of reputable operators. Wear life belts and helmets.

The impact of foreign visitors on hill-tribes is a controversial issue. Certain rules of behaviour should be observed in order not to cause offence. It is advisable to dress modestly; request permission before entering a house or taking photographs of anyone; refrain from stepping on door sills, touching or photographing spirit shrines. Visitors should also offer suitable gifts to children such as pencils and writing paper rather than sweets.

Sea Canoeing – Sea canoeing offers great sport and the opportunity to explore limestone islands and sea caves in the Andaman Sea and the Gulf of Thailand. Contact Sea Canoe Thailand Co., 367/4 Thanon Yaowarat, Phuket, 83000 Thailand. ☏ (66) 76 212 252. Fax (66) 76 212 172.

Game Fishing – The seas around Thailand teem with all kinds of gamefish from marlin to sailfish and barracuda. The main centres for big game fishing are Pattaya, Phuket, Chumphon and Ko Samui.

Sailing – Enthusiasts will find excellent facilities at all resorts along the coast. The sheltered Ao Phangnga with its spectacular limestone islands offers calm seas all year round. Phuket is the yachting centre with regattas held in early December. Hobbie cats, lasers and prindles are available in Hua Hin and Phuket.

Scuba Diving/Snorkelling – The marine parks, tropical islands and sheltered bays around the coast offer clear waters, coral reefs, sunken wrecks and exotic marine life to delight amateurs all year round, either in the Andaman Sea or in the Gulf of Thailand depending on the season. There are qualified instructors at most resorts.

Windsurfing – This popular sport can be practised at all resorts. The warm climate and clear waters with long open stretches are ideal for both beginners and experienced windsurfers. Jomtien Beach in Pattaya is the major windsurfing centre.

Motor Sports – Local and international motor and motorcycle racing events are regularly held at the 2.4km Bira International Circuit in Pattaya.

Go-karting – There are circuits at Chiang Mai, Pattaya, Phuket, and Ko Samui.

National Parks – These are major conservation areas which offer wonderful scenery and abundant wildlife and are ideal havens of solitude with varied scenic attractions including caves, waterfalls and hiking trails. Some parks have basic accommodation. There are also some 50 wildlife sanctuaries. Contact National Parks Division, Royal Forestry Department, Reservations Department, Thanon Phahonyothin, Bangkok. ☏ 02 579 7223, 02 579 5734.

The most popular national parks are:
  – Khao Yai National Park (200 kilometres northeast of Bangkok)
  – Doi Inthanon National Park in Chiang Mai province
  – Ko Samet in Rayong province
  – Erawan and Chalerm Rattanakosin National Parks in Kanchanaburi province
  – Sam Roi Yot National Park in Prachuap Khiri Khan province
  – Khu Khut Waterfowl Park in Songkhla province
  – Ao Phang Nga National Park in Phang Nga province
  – Mu Ko Tarutao Marine National Park in Satun province
  – Ko Samui and Mu Ko Ang Thong Marine National Park in Surat Thani province

---

Special interests

Buddhist meditation – Meditation temples attract large numbers of devotees.
The main centres in Bangkok are Wat Mahathat, Wat Pak Nam, Wat Chonprathan Rangsarit, Wat Phra Dhammakayaram and Wat Boworniwet where English language instruction is available.
Wat Suan Mokkha Phalaram, a 120-acre forest temple in Chaiya, Surat Thani, Wat Pa Nanachat and Wat Nong Pa Phong in Ubon Ratchathani are also well known.

Traditional Thai Massage – Courses and sessions are available at Wat Po, Wat Mahathat and Wat Parinayok in Bangkok. Thai massage is also on offer at health centres of good hotels and at beach resorts.

Calendar of events

The lunar calendar regulates rural and religious life in Thailand although the Western calendar is used in daily and business life. Exact dates of religious festivals can be obtained from TAT offices while national holidays are fixed.

February – full-moon day

Countrywide   Makha Bucha commemorating the Buddha's first sermon (1250) to his disciples – candle-lit processions at all temples

Early February

Chiang Mai   Flower Festival – flower-decked floats, orchid displays, beauty contests

Late February-early March

Bangkok, Phuket, Nakhon Sawan   Chinese New Year

Yala   ASEAN Singing Bird contest

Pattaya   Festival – beauty parades, floats, special events, firework display

Mae Hong Son   Buat Luk Kaeo Festival – ordination of young Shan novices

Countrywide   Songkran Festival – the Water Festival celebrating the Thai New Year. Chiang Mai festivities (13-15 April) are renowned. The exuberant revellers enjoy a good soaking

Bangkok   Royal Ploughing Ceremony presided over by His Majesty the King at Sanam Luang to mark the beginning of the rice-planting cycle and ensure abundant harvests

Yasothon   Rocket Festival – giant rockets are fired to ensure plentiful rain in the monsoon season

Countrywide   Visakha Bucha – the holiest Buddhist holiday celebrates the birth, enlightenment and entry into nirvana of the Buddha

Countrywide   Fruit Fairs at Rayong, Chanthaburi, Chachoengsao, Surat Thani

Ubon Ratchathani   Khao Phansa – the beginning of the Buddhist period of fasting. Procession of beautifully-carved giant wax candles

Rocket Festival

B. Davies

October

Nationwide   Ok Phansa & Thot Kathin – the end of rains retreat intro-
duces´ the Kathin period when new robes are offered to
monks

Phuket   Vegetarian Festival – parade of white-clothed devotees and
ascetic displays

Chonburi   Water-buffalo races

Late October-early November

Nan, Nakhon Phanom,
Phichit, Pathum Thani   Boat races mark the Kathin period

November – full-moon night

Countrywide   Loi Krathong – the Festival of Lights. Lotus or banana leaf
rafts adorned with lighted candles, incense sticks and flow-
ers are set adrift on waterways. Wonderful displays at
Sukhothai and Chiang Mai

November

Surin   Elephant Round-Up – demonstrations of intelligence,
strength, gentleness and obedience. Wild-elephant hunts and
war parade.

Nakhon Pathom   Pilgrimage to Phra Pathom chedi, the oldest chedi in Thailand. Temple festival

Late November, early December

Kanchanaburi   River Kwai Bridge Week – Son et Lumière

Mae Sariang   Sunflower festival

December

Bangkok   HM the King's birthday (5 December). On 3 December the
Royal Guards swear allegiance to His Majesty King Bhumibol
in a colourful ceremony. On 5 December, festivities are held
throughout Thailand.

Further reading

Titles which are out of print may be obtained from specialist bookshops and libraries
in the UK.

The Kingdom and People of Siam – Sir John Bowring 1857. Oxford University Press,
Singapore 1987
South East Asia – An Illustrated Introductory History – Milton Osborne – Allen & Unwin
1991
A Short History of Thailand – David K Wyatt – Yale University Press 1994
Studies in Thai History – David K Wyatt – Silkworm Books, Thailand 1994
Ancient Capitals of Thailand – Elizabeth Moore, Philip Stott, Surivarudh Sukhasvasti –
Photographs Michael Freeman – Asia Books 1996
Palaces of the Gods – Khmer art and architecture in Thailand – Smitthi Siribhadra,
Elizabeth Moore – Photographs Michael Freeman – Asia Books 1992
Art and Architecture of Thailand – Steve Van Beek and Luca Invernizzi Tettoni – Thames
& Hudson, 1991
Isaan – Ben Davies – Luna Publications, Bermuda 1996
Thai Temples and Temple Murals – Rita Ringis – Oxford University Press 1990
Old Bangkok – Michael Smithies – Oxford University Press 1993
Journal du voyage de Siam fait en 1685 et 1686 – Abbé de Choisy, adapted by M Dassé
– DK Books, Thailand 1976
Description du Royaume Thai ou Siam – Monseigneur Pallegoix, adapted by M Dassé
– DK Books, Thailand 1976
*Journals of an Embassy from the Governor-General of India to the Courts of Siam and
Cochin-China* – John Crawfurd 1828 – Oxford University Press 1971
Travels in Siam, Cambodia and Laos 1858-60 – Henri Mouhot 1862 – Oxford Univer-
sity Press, Singapore 1989
An Asian Arcady – Reginald Le May – White Lotus, Bangkok 1986
The English Governess at the Siamese Court – Anna Leonowens 1870 – Oxford Uni-
versity Press, Singapore 1988
The Legendary American – William Warren – Houghton Mifflin, Boston 1970

The Gentleman in the Parlour – Somerset Maugham 1930 – Mandarin Paperpacks 1966
The Shadow-Line – Joseph Conrad – Penguin Books 1986
The Temple of Dawn – Yukio Mishima – Alfred Knopf, New York 1973
To the River Kwai – John Stewart – Bloomsbury Publishing 1988
The Great Railway Bazaar – Paul Theroux – Penguin Books 1977
Behind the Painting and other stories – Siburapha – Oxford Paperbacks 1990
Katia and the Prince of Siam – Eileen Hunter and Narisa Chakrabongse – River Books 1994
Wild Thailand – Belinda Stewart-Cox, Photographs G Cubitt, New Holland
The Thai Song – Don Townsend
The Dragon's Pearl – Sirin Phathanothai – Simon & Schuster 1995
The Bangkok Secret – Anthony Grey – Pan 1990
Thailand – Culture Shock – Robert and Nanthapa Cooper – Kuperard (London) Ltd 1991
The Beach – Alex Garland – Penguin 1999
The Food of Thailand – Asia Books 1994

Films

Two great films in particular and a recent success are popularly associated with Thailand:

The King and I – Walter Lang 1956
The Bridge over the River Kwai – David Lean 1957
The Beach – Danny Boyle 2000

Thailand's spectacular tropical and mountainous scenery has provided exotic locations for many successful films:

The Man with the Golden Gun – G Hamilton 1974
The Killing Fields – R Joffe 1984
Air America – R Spottiswoode 1990
Good Morning Vietnam – B Levinson 1987
Casualties of War – B de Palma 1989
Heaven and Earth – O Stone 1993
Rambo Part III – P McDonald 1988
The World is Not Enough – M Apted 1999

The Bridge over the River Kwai

House on stilts in Ko Panyi, Ao Phangnga

Introduction

Landscape

Thailand is situated in the heart of Southeast Asia bordered to the north by Myanmar (Burma) and Laos, to the east by Kampuchea (Cambodia) and to the south by Malaysia. Its largely flat terrain, tropical climate and abundant rivers have made it one of the most fertile countries in the world. The topography has favoured migrations that have had a profound impact on its history.

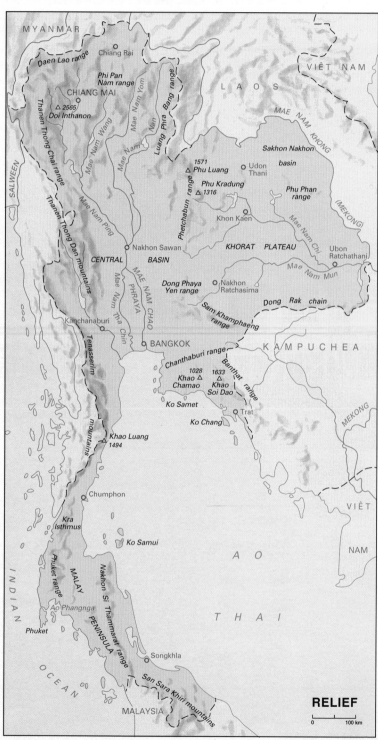

MYANMAR

Daen Lao range

Chiang Rai

Phi Pan Nam range

VIÊT NAM

CHIANG MAI

△ 2565
Doi Inthanon

L A O S

Thanen Thong Chai range

Mae Nam Wang

Mae Nam Yom

Nan

Luang Phra Bang range

MAE NAM KHONG

SALWEEN

Thanen Thong Dan mountains

Mae Nam Ping

Phetchabun range

Sakhon Nakhon basin

1571
△ Phu Luang

Udon Thani

Phu Kradung
△ 1316

Phu Phan range

(MEKONG)

Khon Kaen

KHORAT PLATEAU

Ubon Ratchathani

Nakhon Sawan

CENTRAL   BASIN

Mae Nam Chi

Kanchanaburi

Mae Nam Tha Chin

PHRAYA

Dong Phaya Yen range

Nakhon Ratchasima

Mae Nam Mun

MAE NAM CHAO

Sam Khamphaeng range

Dong Rak chain

BANGKOK

K A M P U C H E A

Chanthaburi range

Banthat range

1028
△ Khao Chamao

1633
△ Khao Soi Dao

Ko Samet

Tenasserim   mountains

Ko Chang

Trat

MEKONG

△ Khao Luang
1494

VIÊT

Chumphon

NAM

Kra Isthmus

Ko Samui

A O

Phuket range

MALAY

Nakhon Si Thammarat range

T H A I

Ao Phangnga

PENINSULA

INDIAN

Phuket

Songkhla

OCEAN

San Sara Khiri mountains

RELIEF

0   100 km

MALAYSIA

TOPOGRAPHY

From the air, the Thai landscape resembles a vast and intricate canvas of rice fields criss-crossed by rivers and canals that stretch to an endless horizon. On closer view, however, the country has distinctive topographical features that vary from region to region.

The central region is composed of a vast plain cut by the limestone ridges of river valleys and incorporates the Mae Nam Chao Phraya Basin also known as the Mae Nam Basin, and its fertile delta.

The northern region is more mountainous with forests and deep valleys and is delineated by the Burmese and Lao borders. The northeast is largely made up of the arid Khorat Plateau that juts out towards Cambodia and Laos.

The Gulf region, which stretches southeast from Bangkok to the narrow Cambodian border is more tropical with beaches and islands. The south is the region best known for its palm-fringed beaches and turquoise seas set against a largely mountainous interior.

The central basin – Lush, green and flat, the central region is one of the most bountiful areas on earth, producing up to three rice crops every year. Irrigated by the Chao Phraya the Mae Nam Basin constitutes a giant delta covering a total of 12 424km. Delineated to the west by the rugged Thanen Thong Dan mountains and to the east by the Dong Phaya Yen mountain range, it is home to some 30% of the population. The people have evolved a distinctive way of life with houses on stilts and waterborne transport along an extensive network of canals. Barges carry rice and sand downstream to Bangkok.

Thailand's mightiest river the **Chao Phraya** (352km) starts out at the confluence of the Mae Nam Ping, Yom and Nan in Nakhon Sawan. From this city, it runs due south irrigating the fertile central plains before flowing into the Gulf of Thailand. Known as Mae Nam "mother of waters", this is the historic and symbolic lifeline of the country celebrated by poets and monarchs alike.

Favourable geographic and geological factors have made this region the cradle of Thailand's three successive capitals: Ayutthaya, Thonburi and Bangkok. Besides the countless villages and rice fields, the area also provides a variety of landscapes from the floating market of Damnoen Saduak, to the salt plains near Samut Sakhon and, further to the west, the tropical forest of the Sai Yok National Park.

To the south of the Mae Nam Basin, sediment carried by the Mae Nam Chao Phraya has altered the topography of the region. Originally Bangkok was at the mouth of the river. Today it is separated by a giant mass of sediment that continues to expand into the Gulf of Thailand. High tides reach up to 30km upriver and during the rainy season the low-lying areas are liable to flooding in spite of the building of dykes and dams.

To the west lies Kanchanaburi, a vital watershed and a region of spectacular waterfalls, caves and forested conservation areas. The Mae Nam Mae Klong and Tha Chin are the main waterways.

The mountainous north – The northern region is Thailand's most mountainous region sweeping down from the foothills of the Himalayas: a land of valleys, forests and hills which offers some of the most dramatic scenery in the country. Its highest mountain **Doi Inthanon** culminates at 2 565m and overshadows the canyoned headwaters of the Mae Nam Mae Ping. Varying amounts of rainfall and higher elevations make this area less suitable for rice farming than the Central Plain, although agriculture, including temperate fruits and vegetables, remains the cornerstone for the people. Once forested with teak, redwood and evergreen, the north now boasts extensive conservation areas, notably the Doi Inthanon and Lan Sang National Parks.

B. Davies

Rice fields

Hill-tribe village

This is also a region of great ethnic contrasts. Around Chiang Mai, Chiang Rai and Mae Hong Son districts, some 500 000 hill-tribe people inhabit the generally higher areas practising slash-and-burn agriculture. Along the eastern border with Laos are other groups of hilltribes including the elusive Mrabri.

Geologically the area has limestone mountains and precipitous rocks, especially around Doi Inthanon and the village of Pai in Mae Hong Son District. Numerous rivers including the Mekong, the Nan, the Yom, the Ping and the Wang, run across this spectacular landscape which is renowned for its waterfalls and caves. The rich soil supports rhododendrons as well as almost 1 000 species of orchid.

The **Mae Nam Khong (Mekong)**, the world's 12th-longest river, enters Thailand at Chiang Saen, at the centre of the infamous Golden Triangle at Sop Ruak. The river then wends its majestic course round north and northeastern Thailand on its 4 022km journey from Tibet to the Mekong Delta in Vietnam. Another important waterway, the **Salween**, forms part of the border with Myanmar.

During the cool months from November to January, early morning mist clings to the landscape with temperatures falling as low as 5°C (40°F). In the centre of the region lies Chiang Mai, which is the major hub and capital of the north.

The Khorat Plateau – The northeast is dominated by a vast plateau that rises to an average height of 200m above sea-level and slopes gently towards the Sakhon Nakhon and Mekong basins. It is cut by the Mekong tributaries (Mun, Chi) rising in the **Phetchabun** range and is delimited in the south by the **Dong Rak** chain on the Cambodian border. For the most part the Mekong is the natural border with Laos.

It is the poorest, the most arid and least visited region in Thailand. Its terrain is made up largely of red sandstone and laterite. This makes it less water-absorbent and less able to support traditional rice crops. Despite countless dams including the giant Ubonrat Dam at Khon Kaen and the Sirinthon Reservoir near Ubon Ratchathani, tapioca, sweet corn, tobacco and carrots have proved to be better suited to the soil. In summer months, temperatures can soar as high as 40°C (103°F). In the rainy season, parts of the countryside are prone to flooding.

The northeast region, which is known as **Isan** after the Kingdom of Shiva, is made up predominantly of small villages that have changed little in recent times. None the less the region also boasts major cities like Khorat, Khon Kaen and Udon Thani which were used as major US air bases during the Vietnam war. It has benefited from programmes for the improvement of agriculture, transport and general living conditions.

In the upper region of the northeast, a change to higher elevations occurs with the vast parks dominated by the imposing peaks of **Phu Kradung** (1 316m), **Phu Luang** (1 571m) and **Phu Rua** (1 365m) and covered in pine and evergreen. To the north and east where the Mekong marks the border with Laos, the land is more fertile, its rich alluvial silt nourishing mulberry plantations and vegetable gardens.

In the northeast several archaeological sites (Phu Wiang, Sahat Sakan, Chaiyaphum) have revealed amazing evidence of species of dinosaurs and other prehistoric animals *(Siamosaurus sutheethorni, Siamotyrannus isanensis, Phuwiangosaurus sirindhornae)*, some previously unknown, which raise many interesting issues in the field of palaeontology. The region's Khmer legacy comprises exceptional temples ranging from Prasat Hin Phimai to Prasat Hin Phanom Rung and Prasat Muang Tham. As its population is largely of Khmer and Lao origin, the cultural flavour is akin to neighbouring Laos and Cambodia.

The Gulf Region – Tropical fruits, fish and rubies are the major products of this fertile region squeezed between the Gulf of Thailand, the northeast and the border with Cambodia. Predominantly flat to the west, the winding valley parallels the **Khao Soi Dao** mountain range (1 633m) eventually tapering down to Hat Lek in the south. Here evergreen forests combine with mountainous granite country to create the spectacular scenery of **Khao Chamao** (1 024m) and the Nam Tok Phliu. The deep sea port of Laem Chabang has attracted new industries to the region which is undergoing rapid development.

Along the coast, there are countless small fishing villages hugging the narrow coves. Other towns like Bang Saen, Pattaya and Rayong have developed into major tourist destinations. The prosperity of the country has also resulted in a building boom with condominiums springing up along the coast.

The area around Chanthaburi in the centre of the region was once known for its rubies and sapphires, traditionally mined using pans and ladders. Nowadays these precious stones are mainly smuggled in from over the border from Cambodia.

Off the coast lie some of the kingdom's most magnificent island national parks: **Ko Chang** with its 52 islands dotted around the Gulf of Thailand, and the better known **Ko Samet** with its white sandy beaches and turquoise sea.

The peninsular area – Shaped like the trunk of an elephant, this narrow sliver of land that stretches all the way down the Malay Peninsula comprises some 2 080km of coastline bounded by the Gulf of Thailand to the east and the Indian Ocean to the west. This area is best known for its pristine beaches, idyllic islands and turquoise waters.

The inland area is characterised by mountainous foothills rising as high as 2 000m. The tropical climate and fertile soil make this region better suited for rubber trees and palm oil than rice. Along the coast, coconut plantations are numerous, while in Phuket tin mining was until recently the primary motor of the economy.

To the west, the **Tenasserim** Mountains form a natural frontier with Myanmar rising to 1 494m at **Khao Luang**. Further south, the **Kra Isthmus** measures just 22km across the neck of land which separates the two countries. Various governments have proposed building a canal here which would cut nearly 1 000 kilometres off shipping routes between ports on the Indian Ocean and the Gulf of Thailand. To date, it remains a pipe dream.

The two coastal regions of the south have striking geological differences. On the west coast, magnificent limestone formations and towering rocks erupt out of the sea in **Ao Phangnga** and **Ao Phra Nang**. To the east, extensive mangrove forests grow along much of the coast, although areas have been partially cleared to make way for shrimp farming.

The secluded islands of Ko Samui, Ko Phangan and Ko Tao are sited off the east coast in the Gulf of Thailand. Off the west coast lie Phuket and Ko Phi Phi which are popular destinations, as well as the archipelagos of Mu Ko Similan, Mu Ko Lanta and the lesser known island national parks of Mu Ko Surin and Mu Ko Tarutao.

In the far south, beyond the town of Hat Yai, the San Sara Khiri Mountains rising as high as 1 490m divide the region from Malaysia. Until recently, this mountainous terrain was used as a hideout by Muslim separatists but now peace has been restored. The southern provinces of Satun, Yala, Pattani and Narathiwat remain heavily influenced by Islam.

Ko Phi Phi

CLIMATE

From the northern tip at Mae Sai to the southern end of the Malay Peninsula, Thailand's regions have alternating rainy and temperate seasons, although both temperatures and annual rainfall can vary markedly. In the central region, the north and the northeast, the climate is more predictable with a dry season, a hot season and a wet season. In the south, the climate is less changeable throughout the year with rain occurring during most months.

Northern, northeastern and central regions – During the cool season from November to February, temperatures average 26°C (79°F) with cooler temperatures recorded in the more mountainous northern region and around Loei Province in the northeast. In the hot season from March to May, temperatures can reach 40°C (103°F) with some of the highest temperatures recorded in the northeast. In the wet season, from June to October, humidity remains extremely high with an average rainfall of 1 438mm. In the north, the average yearly rainfall is lower with the greatest precipitation likely to occur in August and September, the latter months of the monsoon.

The tropical south – In the southern region, there are considerably fewer fluctuations in climate, although temperatures and rainfall can vary from coast to coast. From May to October, the southeast monsoon comes up from the Andaman Sea bringing heavy rain to Phuket, Krabi, Ko Phi Phi and Phangnga. From November to February, the northeast monsoon sweeps across from Cambodia spreading rains and wind over Ko Samui, Ko Phangan and Ko Tao. Waters can be choppy during these months. The average annual rainfall for Phuket is 2 500mm.

FLORA AND FAUNA

Thailand was once densely wooded and rich in animal and plant life. It still offers an amazing variety of flora and fauna, although the forests have been reduced by illegal logging, land encroachment and slash-and-burn agriculture. Roughly 17% of land is now estimated to be covered in primary forest compared with 52% about three decades ago. Thailand's tropical environment still supports some rare animal species including the Khun Kitti Bat, the world's smallest bat, the Tragulus or mouse deer, and the climbing perch known as Pla Maw. There are also estimated to be more than 5 000 species of plant and tree throughout the kingdom.

Forests – They are usually evergreen, pine and redwood and they are found mainly in the national parks. Although less common, oakwood is also a feature of Thailand's forests. Teak trees, once abundant in the northern region, are now a rarity. Eucalyptus which is used in commercial plantations is widespread, although it drains the soil of valuable nutrients. Since 1989 a nationwide logging ban has been in effect in a bid to halt the deforestation. Only strict implementation of the ban and concerted re-afforestation schemes will save Thailand's once-rich forests.

The tropical **rain forest** which exists in southern Thailand is a complex environment with high humidity where thrive varied types of vegetation and animal and plant species. Under the canopy of tall trees grow evergreen plants mainly of the Dipterocarpaceae family with ferns, bushes and small trees at ground level. There are also extensive **mangrove forests** which provide a suitable habitat for many species of flora and fauna.

Plants – There are more than 1 000 varieties of **orchids**, almost all renowned for their subtle fragrance and elegance. Main orchid-growing areas are in the north around Chiang Mai and the Mae Sa Valley where the exotic blooms are specially cultivated for export.

Azaleas and rhododendrons also thrive in the cool northern climate. Numerous species of bougainvillaea and hibiscus flourish in the countryside along with acacia, lotus, frangipani and jacaranda. Even in Bangkok, there are believed to be more than 500 species of plant and shrub.

Animals – Tigers, elephants and bears inhabited the forests of Thailand in large numbers until the early 20C. These days, they are largely restricted to national parks and wildlife reserves. The number of elephants has fallen from an estimated 20 000 a century ago to fewer than 5 000 today. Wild boar, gibbons, flying squirrels, deer and tropical butterflies are more numerous. They inhabit the thickly wooded hills around Phetchaburi as well as the vast tracts of conservation land near Um Phang and along the border north of Kanchanaburi.

If these wilder forest regions harbour the occasional bear and tiger, the area around Khao Yai is famous for its birds. Orange-breasted and red-headed trogons, moustached barbets and hornbills can all be found here, along with black-throated sunbirds. For the popular swiftlets whose edible nests are used by the Chinese for expensive soup, travellers must visit the southwest coast around Ko Phi Phi and Krabi. A more sought-after bird in the northern National Park of Doi Inthanon is the rare ashy-throated warbler. Other popular varieties are the yellow-bellied flowerpecker, egrets and purple swamp hens.

In the seas angel fish, parrot fish and manta rays abound as well as prized gamefish such as barracuda, marlin and wahoo. In the northern and northeastern stretches of the Mekong River thrives the **pla buk,** a giant catfish which can grow up to three metres long and weigh up to 300kg.

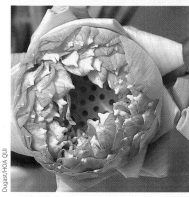

Parks – Thailand's 52 national parks which range from island retreats to dense tracts of rainforest, flower-covered valleys and spectacular waterfalls were set up under royal patronage to protect wildlife and the environment and to prevent deforestation. The oldest and best known National Park, Khao Yai, acts as a magnet for bird watchers and weekenders from Bangkok who spread out along its signposted trails. Other popular parks are the island paradise of Phi Phi Le in the south, the island of Ko Samet in the Gulf of Thailand, and the forests of Kaeng Krachan near the southern town of Phetchaburi. The National Parks Authority is responsible for access to all the parks and will have the latest information on local flora and fauna. The parks generally offer good opportunities for walking. Some provide overnight accommodation or camping facilities. Guides are often available, especially for trekking in remote areas.

AGRICULTURE

Agriculture is the lifeblood of the Thai people. Over one-third of the country's total land area, 171 038sq km, is taken up with agricultural production. Agricultural exports including rice and tapioca represent some 11% of total exports. And while industry and tourism now contribute more to national revenues, it is agriculture that continues to provide a living for the rural majority.

Rice – More than 80% of Thailand's population eat rice, while almost half of the working population is involved in producing it. Rice paddies cover almost all the central plains as well as parts of the north, the northeast and the south. Not surprisingly, Thailand is one of the largest rice producers in the world, harvesting some 20 million tonnes a year. The country also exported 7 million tonnes of rice in 1999-2000 as far afield as the Phillippines, Russia and North Korea. Traditionally rice has been harvested twice a year in irrigated areas in the central valley. Nowadays new strains of rice are being used which offer higher yields, with some parts of the central region producing three crops a year.

Copra – Derived from coconut palms, copra is used to make coconut oil, cosmetics and fats. Thailand is now a major world producer.

Rubber – After Malaysia and Indonesia, Thailand ranks as the third largest producer of raw rubber in the world with an export market worth US$1 525 million. Rubber plantations are located mainly in the southern region, especially in the provinces of Phuket, Surat Thani, Hat Yai and Satun. Exports of dry latex yielded US$556 million.

Other crops – In parts of the north and the northeast, tobacco, sweet corn, maize, sugar cane, tomatoes and cotton are grown. Near Chiang Mai and around the Mae Sa Valley, there are also apples, grapes and strawberries. Thailand produces more than 1.5 million tonnes of vegetables a year. It is also the biggest tapioca exporter in the world ahead of its giant Asian neighbour Indonesia. Tapioca is used mainly as animal feed.

Livestock – Breeding of cattle, water-buffalo, pigs and poultry provides an important source of income for villagers, especially in the northeast where the soil is too poor to support traditional arable crops. In the past, water-buffaloes were mainly used for work in the fields. Nowadays, with tractors on the increase, larger numbers are bred for their meat. There is also a growing dairy industry.

Fisheries – Thailand is the biggest exporter of tinned tuna fish in the world with canned seafood exports reaching US$75 000 million in 2000. It is also a major producer of fresh and frozen shrimp, with exports increasing substantially to over 5% of the world market.

Fishing harbour

Farming Techniques – For thousands of years, water-buffaloes have been as much a feature of life in the fields as the farmers themselves. These rugged beasts of burden have traditionally ploughed the waterlogged soil, and after the golden rice stalks are harvested have prepared the ground for the next crop. Now these ubiquitous animals are being replaced by tractors, by combine harvesters and by other machines designed to increase output and improve productivity. Only in the poorer districts is the water-buffalo likely to have a real future in the paddies.

ECONOMIC DEVELOPMENT

Despite the importance of agriculture as a source of labour and output, it is industry which in recent years has been the driving force of the economy.
Manufacturing along with tourism now account for more than 50% of foreign exchange earnings. Until the mid-1990s, they enabled Thailand to post some of the fastest growth rates in the world (GDP averaged 9% between 1986-96 as opposed to 4% for 1999-2000). But while new factories sprang up all over the country producing everything from textiles to shoes, electronics and car components, the influx of foreign capital also led to over-capacity, inefficiency and in some cases blatant corruption. On 1 July 1997, Thailand devalued its currency signalling the beginning of a major economic re-adjustment that continues to this day. The impact has been felt in every sector. More than 50 finance companies have been closed down while even the major banks have been forced to recapitalize. The collapse of the economy has sent the price of property plummeting and has led to a rapid rise in unemployment forcing migrant workers to return to their villages in search of work – or simply survival.

Financial Support – Under a US$17 billion structural adjustment programme agreed with the International Monetary Fund (IMF), Thailand is committed to reducing government expenditure, strengthening its financial system, boosting exports and selling off state enterprises to the private sector.
To date, Thailand has closely followed the guidelines laid down by the IMF.Structural reforms are helping to lay the foundations of a new era of stable growth. In 1999-2000 there were signs of a fragile recovery as exports improved and as the public and private sectors attempt to upgrade Thailand's competitiveness, an essential factor for its medium and long term economic development.

Industry – Electronics, textiles and car components form the main constituents of Thailand's growing industrial might providing in excess of £10 billion in exports each year. Giant multi-national companies like Mitsubishi, Sony and Toyota have all set up manufacturing plants in Thailand to take advantage of cheaper labour. Some well-known European names like Nestlé, ICI, Unilever and Michelin are also present on the business scene. New efforts are under way to upgrade Thailand's industry from labour-intensive to capital-intensive in order to maintain competitiveness with countries like China, Indonesia and Vietnam.

Mining – Reserves of tin, zinc and fluorite are to be found mainly in the south, with exports reaching £174 million in 1994. Sapphires and rubies are mined in small quantities around Chanthaburi on the east coast. Larger quantities of gems are smuggled over the border from Myanmar and Kampuchea, and brisk trade is carried out at Mae Sot and Chanthaburi.

Textiles – Thailand is one of the world's largest producers of silk as well as of brand labels exported to fashion centres in London and Paris. Textile exports totalled in excess of £3.5 billion in 1997, although fierce regional competition is beginning to take its toll. Traditional silk weavers can be seen in the north and in the northeast around the towns of Chaiyaphum and Khon Kaen.

Tourism – Tourism has proved to be a great boon for Thailand. In 2000, 9.5 million tourists visited the country, spending an estimated US$280 000 million. Bangkok now boasts some of Asia's leading five-star hotels, while Phuket, Ko Samui and Chiang Mai also have an international-class tourist infrastructure. Despite a severe glut of hotels in many areas and growing problems with pollution, the Thai government continues to view tourism as the single most important earner of foreign exchange.

COMMUNICATIONS

Thailand has an excellent road network comprising more than 50 000km of roads and highways serving all major regions. Main highways link Bangkok to Chiang Mai in the north, Nong Khai in the northeast, Pattaya in the Gulf and Hat Yai in the south. Smaller roads offer less traffic and more local colour but a vast programme to upgrade the road network is under way.
Tourists arriving in Thailand generally fly into Dong Muang International Airport in Bangkok. From here, Thai International and Bangkok Airways, the country's two domestic airlines, serve a network of regional airports. A new airport is under construction in Samut Prakan south of Bangkok to handle the increased air traffic (completion of phase 1 scheduled in 2004).
The State Railway of Thailand also operates three major train routes with 3 724km of track linking Bangkok to the south, the north and the northeast, and maintains an efficient service.

Population

Thailand's population numbers 62.3 million (2000). The average density is 121 inhabitants per sq km, although there are major variations from region to region. In Bangkok, the average is 3 580 per sq km, while in the mountainous northern province of Mae Hong Son, the average density is fewer than 20 inhabitants per sq km. According to the latest census, almost half of the population are below the age of 20. The average lifespan of Thai men is put at 70 years and for women it is 74 years.

Outside Bangkok (population of 5.6 million), major urban centres are few. Nakhon Ratchasima (Khorat) now ranks as the country's second largest city with a population of around 420 000. Chiang Mai has a population of around 250 000 while Hat Yai numbers some 300 000 inhabitants. The lack of cities reflects the predominantly agrarian nature of Thai society. Until recently, most people preferred to live in villages tending their fields and supporting extended families. Rapid industrial growth, however, changed that picture. Every year more than a million seasonal migrants left the countryside for the big cities in search of work and every year, fewer of them returned to their traditional homes. Following the recent economic downturn the reverse is now the case as migrant workers have returned in droves to their villages which already face an acute problem as remittances to workers' families have now dried up and where there are few job prospects.

Under a successful family planning programme introduced in the late 1960s and early 1970s, population growth has slowed from 3% to 1.5%, making Thailand one of the most exemplary countries in birth control in the world. Early initiatives included rural programmes like "have a vasectomy, win a pig". Children at school learn birth control songs from an early age. Under a new AIDS awareness initiative, sex education is accessible to all levels of Thai society.

THE THAI NATION

Thailand has the remarkable distinction of being the only country in Southeast Asia never to have been colonised. Neither has it been divided by civil war or troubled by the racial conflicts of neighbouring countries. The country's achievement is reflected in the name Thailand or "Prathet Thai" which literally means "Land of the Free".

Since 1932, when Thailand adopted a constitutional monarchy, the Thai nation has been governed by a prime minister, a cabinet and a national assembly supported by a highly-educated civil service. The country is now divided into 76 provinces *(changwat)*, each with a governor and a provincial capital. The provincial government in turn overlooks the affairs of districts *(amphoe)*, communes *(tambon)* and villages *(mou ban)* which are presided over by the village headman.

Democratic institutions, however, have been overshadowed by military interference. Since 1932, there have been 18 coups or attempted coups as the army has intervened in times of uncertainty. Until recently, the prime minister was almost always a senior military official. Adherence to Buddhism and the continued power of the monarchy have acted as further stabilising factors for the Thai nation, providing a degree of unity rare in most other countries of Southeast Asia.

In 1946, Thailand was granted membership of the United Nations. The country also acted as a founding member of the Association of Southeast Asian Nations (ASEAN), which is a regional economic and political forum.

The Monarchy – Thais revere their monarch and show a degree of respect for the royal family that can be found in few other countries. Photographs of the royal family are found in almost every household and every village. Criticism of the monarchy is viewed as taboo. Constitutionally, the king is the supreme head of state, the head of religion and the head of the armed forces. While the end of the absolute power of the monarchy in 1932 may have reduced the direct power of the king, it has not lessened his influence.

King Bhumibol Adulyadej who came to the throne in 1946 is the longest-reigning monarch. Revered above all as a man of the people, he has travelled to every province in Thailand to meet his subjects. In the palace grounds in Bangkok, he has set up agricultural experiments to find better crops and higher yields for the benefit of the people. In the May 1992 riots, it was the King who called on Prime Minister Suchinda and the protesters to reconcile their differences and who defused a potentially explosive situation. On 5 December every year, a national holiday is declared for the king's birthday, and celebrations and processions are held all over the country.

Migrations – Thailand's long and turbulent history at the crossroads of Southeast Asia has ensured steady migrations of people from neighbouring countries. Over 85% of the people claim to be ethnic Thai, but to these can be added more than five million Chinese, three million Lao, as well as Indians, Burmese, Malays and Mons.

Thailand's mix of races and open assimilation policy have led to greater racial harmony than elsewhere in the region. For the most part, ethnic groups have intermarried and adopted Thai names. The majority regard themselves primarily as Thai citizens.

The Thai – 85% of the country's population claim to be Siamese, a people believed to have originated in Yunnan Province in Southern China. From about the 10C onwards, the Thai started to move downriver into modern Thailand, settling first in Lanna in the north and later in the Central Plain. In the years since, the Thai have assimilated countless ethnic peoples, notably the Mon, Khmer, Lao, Malay, Indian, Persian and Shans as well as the Chinese.

In the 19C and early 20C century, large numbers of **Chinese** settled along the major rivers and in the coastal cities of Thailand to trade in furs, rice, silk and spices. Today they play a disproportionally large role in some of the most important sectors of the economy, notably gold, banking, finance and commerce. Although the Chinese can be found predominantly in the old commercial centre of Bangkok around Thanon Yaowarat, they now form a substantial part of most urban populations.

There are more **Lao-speaking** people in Thailand than in the whole of Laos itself. In all, some four million of them live mainly in the northeast and along the banks of the Mekong River. The majority crossed over into Thailand during the 19C when Siam ruled over parts of Laos. They continue to speak their own language and keep alive the folklore of Vientiane as much as they do the legends of Siam.

The **Khmer** people have been present in Thailand since the 8C, when they occupied parts of the northeast. Major concentrations of them are still to be found around Aranyaprathet and in the northeast of the country, especially in the border provinces of Buriram, Surin and Si Saket. Several refugee camps can be found along the border, although the war between Cambodia and Vietnam ended many years ago. These people are being encouraged to return to their homes in Cambodia.

An ancient Mon culture existed in central Thailand and southeast Burma as far back as the 6C. Nowadays groups of **Mon** people can still be found around Nakhon Pathom and Sangkhlaburi, although many have recently arrived from Myanmar (Burma), forced out by the repressive military regime.

An estimated two million **Muslims** inhabit the southern region, predominantly in the states of Pattani, Yala and Narathiwat which border Malaysia. The majority of these people are of Malay origin and speak Malay as well as Thai. In the 1970s and 1980s, there was a move towards separatism with several incidents sparking unrest along the border. These days the king has a palace in Narathiwat Province, and Islam is widely tolerated.

THE HILL TRIBES

They are found in the northern region, up in the hills and the valleys along the borders with Myanmar (Burma) and Laos. In all there are an estimated 500 000 hill-tribes people or *chao doi* split into six groups: the Akha, the Hmong, the Karen, the Lahu, the Lisu and the Yao. These different tribal groups composed of many sub-groups have their own costumes and sets of belief. They speak different languages and worship the spirits of the winds and the rains.

Originating mainly from Southern China and Tibet, the majority of the hill tribes are relatively recent arrivals having crossed over in the last hundred years. Only the Karen have been here longer. Most tribes prefer to live above 1 000m, practising slash-and-burn agriculture, foraging and breeding livestock such as pigs and chickens. In the past they moved from year to year in search of more fertile land and caused much depredation in the forests and on the mountains.

In recent times, the government has attempted to integrate the tribal people into the fabric of Thai society and to replace opium growing and slash-and-burn cultivation with other forms of agriculture. Potatoes, carrots and cabbages are now grown in addition to rice. Special royal projects promoted by the King and the late Princess Mother have also encouraged the hill tribes to grow temperate fruits and vegetables as cash crops and to sell handicrafts, especially silverware, embroidery and woven goods to shops in the cities. These days, schools are also being built as a means of teaching children about life in Thailand. Health care is also available.

This interaction has been criticised for contributing to the erosion of cultural values and creating a state of dependency. The outside world is encroaching further as more trekkers take to the trails. The **Hill Tribe Research Institute** at the University of Chiang Mai carries out valuable work on tribal culture and aims to help the people preserve their traditions and identity in a fast-changing world.

The Hmong (Meo) – Originating from Southern China, the Hmong (Meo) number around 70 000 and are mainly concentrated around Chiang Mai, Chiang Rai and Mae Hong Son. They generally live at high altitudes between 1 000m and 1 200m growing rice, corn and opium; they worship the spirit of the sky and are fiercely independent. They wear black costumes delicately embroidered with geometric designs, silver necklaces and elaborate headdresses studded with silver ornaments. The women are expert weavers and needlewomen; the men make excellent fighters who have been involved in all major conflicts in the region.

The Lisu – Believed to be from Southern China and Myanmar (Burma), the Lisu number some 24 000 and are spread in nine of the northern provinces. They grow rice, corn and opium and sell domestic animals like pigs and cattle. They can often be identified by their silver ornaments and ornate breastplates made from coins.

Meo

P. De Wilde/HOA QUI

Yao

P. De Wilde/HOA QUI

Akha

P. De Wilde/HOA QUI

Karen

P. De Wilde/HOA QUI

Padong

B. Davies

Lisu

P. De Wilde/HOA QUI

The men sport black costumes and a white turban, while the women wear red and turquoise dresses decorated with stripes, and large headdresses around which are wound multi-coloured tassels.

The Karen – The most numerous of the hill tribes with a population of about 235 000, the Karen are largely concentrated along the western border with Myanmar. They cultivate rice, look after domestic animals and live in houses built on stilts. They worship the winds and the rains; many, however, have embraced Buddhism or Christianity. The women weave a rough cloth in shades of red and orange which is made into tunics often embroidered and decorated with seeds. Karen girls typically wear long white tunics, exchanging them for red ones when they marry. The men are skilled elephant trainers. Many Karen from neighbouring Myanmar have escaped the conflicts waged for an independent Karen state and sought refuge in camps on the Myanmar border.

The Lahu – Originating from the highlands of Tibet, the Lahu number around 55 000 and are concentrated around the districts of Fang and Chiang Rai. Their houses are built on stilts and grouped in villages at high altitude. They practise slash-and-burn cultivation and are famed for their hunting skills. They are strongly animist and hold frequent rituals in order to receive blessings from the gods. They generally dress in black tunics with white piping.

The Akha – Originating from Yunnan in Southern China, the Akha number some 33 000 and are some of the most recent arrivals in Thailand. Large numbers live in villages on the slopes of Doi Mae Salong. They cultivate rice, corn and opium. They are strict animists worshipping the sun and the moon, and erect spirit gates at the village entrance. Their elaborate headdresses are studded with coins and colourful beads. The women wear embroidered black skirts and patchwork leggings.

The Yao – Often known as the Mien, these people originated in China. Some 25 000 live mainly around Chiang Rai, Phayao and Nan. They have traditionally cultivated opium. They worship their ancestors and practise Taoism and are the only tribe which has a written tradition. The women wear ankle-length indigo tunics and baggy pants with small geometric patterns embroidered in cross-stitch, thick purple sashes around the neck and large turbans. Silver ornaments are added for ceremonies and festivals. The children wear close-fitting hats adorned with red pompons.

Other Ethnic Groups – Discovered little more than a decade ago, the elusive **Mrabri** tribe often known as Phi Thong Luang (spirit of the yellow leaves), live around Nan Province and are the only pygmy race in Asia. Traditionally these people have moved with the changing seasons as the leaves from which their huts are built turn yellow, although they too are beginning to settle permanently giving up hunting and gathering as the forests disappear.
The **Sakai**, an aboriginal people, are probably the peninsula's oldest inhabitants. They have flat features, a dark complexion and frizzy reddish hair. They lead a primitive life in the jungle in Yala Province and have their own language, music and dance.
The **Chao Le** meaning Sea Gypsies are nomadic people of obscure origin who inhabit the islands in the Andaman Sea including Phuket. They hold animist beliefs and have their own language and distinctive customs. They are hardy sailors and fishermen.
The **Padong**, an offshoot of the Karen tribe, are a more recent arrival from Myanmar (Burma) in the Mae Hong Son area. The women wear copper spirals round their neck to conform to ritual practices. Young girls from the age of five are selected by the shaman to wear the spirals which are changed every year until they reach 20 years of age. They also wear spirals around their calves.

National characteristics – *Sanuk*, which literally means fun, is the single most important characteristic of the Thais. These resourceful, happy-go-lucky people do not worry about the weather, the pollution or the unruly behaviour of their politicians. They are more interested in finding out where the next laugh will come from or their next snack. Generally hospitable, outgoing and informal, the Thai people have little concept of time. Tomorrow can mean many moons away or never. Their most common refrain is *mai pen rai*, meaning no worries. Thais are, however, hard workers and impeccably mannered. Only when they are pushed into a corner and forced to lose face do tempers fray, and then a darker side comes to the surface.
Respect for elders and figures of authority is taught from an early age and persists throughout adulthood. Older people, especially parents and grandparents are addressed as *Pi* and will be looked up to as a matter of course. So too are teachers, civil servants and those of a higher status. Younger members of society are expected to *wai* to them (a traditional form of greeting) and to obey without question. The level of respect extends especially to Buddhist monks as well as to members of the Royal Family who are addressed in the special Thai court language known as *rachasap*.
Like many facets of Thai behaviour, attitudes to sex remain something of a paradox. Prostitution is widespread, with as many as 700 000 people believed to be involved in the sex industry. The majority of Thai men will have their first sexual encounter in a brothel but, although prostitution is tolerated, sex remains in many ways a taboo subject. Thai women are expected to refrain from sex before marriage. Most live at home with their parents, while live-in relationships are still frowned upon. None the less, growing fears over AIDS (estimates put the number of HIV cases at over 600 000) are reshaping Thai attitudes to sex, leading to better education and a growing awareness of the role of women.

History

Entries in italics represent milestones in world history

Prehistory

BC 10000 to 2000	**Mesolithic era:** domestication of plants, flint and slate tools, pottery. **Bronze Age:** agriculture, animal husbandry, metallurgy.
3000	*Mesopotamian civilisation.*
800	**Iron Age:** ornaments, tools.
early 6C	*The Buddha.*
4C	*Campaigns of Alexander the Great.*

Quaternary Era – Archeological investigation is a fairly recent science in Thailand and large tracts of the country have still to be explored to gain a clearer picture of human occupation in the prehistorical period. Flake and pebble tools dating from 10000 BC to 2000 BC reveal the presence of prehistoric cultures in various parts of the country. The **Spirit Cave,** north of Mae Hong Son, provides startling evidence that early agriculturists and hunter-gatherers probably of Melanesian origin roamed the land in the Mesolithic Era. Finds at Ban Kao (Kanchanaburi), Non Nok Tha (Khon Kaen), Ban Chiang (Udon Thani) indicate the domestication of animals and mastery of metallurgy as early as 3500 BC. The site of **Ban Chiang** provides the most complete picture of human evolution: rice cultivation, copper, tin, bronze and iron smelting, pottery – black and carinated (1000-500 BC) to red-patterned on buff (500-250BC) – and glass ornaments (300BC-2CAD).

First millennium AD

1C-2C	Early migration of Tai-speaking peoples to upland areas.
c **2C**	Mon settlements in the Chao Phraya basin, on the Khorat plateau and in Southeast Burma ruled by the kingdom of **Funan.**
3C	King Ashoka of India sends missionaries to **Suwannaphum** to preach Theravada Buddhism.
3C-4C	*Partition of the Roman Empire.*

Migration – The origin of the **Tai** peoples is shrouded in mystery. There are frequent references in Chinese records to the barbarian peoples south of the Yangtse River who, historians assume, were the forebears of the Tai. Chinese expansion caused the Tai to move south to **Nan Chao** in Yunnan in the upper valley of the Mekong and to the uplands of northern Vietnam and northeastern Laos. The early migrants split into two distinct groups: those to the north of the Red River valley; and a southern group in the valley of the Black River, northeast Laos and south China. The latter were the ancestors of the Lao, Siamese, Shans, and upland Tai. Groups settled in the valleys of northern Thailand.

Nan Chao in southern China which had a large Tai population became a major power from the mid 8C to 9C and established cultural and economic links with India and China. It became a Buddhist state and contributed to the spread of Buddhism and Indian culture.

Traditions and Costumes

Traditions are boundless in number, often trivial in content, but they continue to be embraced in many parts of Thailand. Never have a haircut on a Wednesday or move house on a Saturday. Even in the clamorous streets of Bangkok, tradition/superstition exerts a powerful influence as when drivers hold their palms together as they pass a shrine. Other traditions are religious by nature. Rubbing gold leaf onto a Buddha image and giving food to the monks bring good luck. Some traditions are deepset. Women should never touch monks or pass anything directly to them. Nobody should ever insult the king.

Colourful sarongs known as *pakoma*, jewel-encrusted robes, and bright costumes decked with orchids: these are the images conjured up by Thailand. But to admire these traditional costumes, it is usually necessary to attend a tourist show, a festival or a local celebration. Monks wear robes made of saffron-coloured cotton. Government officials wear suits or military uniforms.

In the countryside, *paisins* or sarongs (a length of cloth wrapped around the waist), woven from homespun cotton or local silk, are commonly worn. Loose cotton shirts called *mohom* and large hats made of palm leaf to keep off the sun are equally common among workers in the rice fields. At such popular festivals as Khao Phansa or Songkran the local women don striking embroidered costumes to perform ritual dances and other religious practices. In the northeast region especially, colourful pieces of cloth known as *sabai* are draped diagonally over the shoulder and fall to the waist. Only occasionally among the hill tribes of the north are traditional costumes worn all year round.

Ban Chiang

Historical records of the period mention other important states which were to shape Tai civilisation: namely the Khmer empire of Angkor, the Mon and Pyu kingdoms of Burma, the kingdom of Champa on the coast of central Vietnam, and another Vietnamese state in northern Vietnam. These rival powers were constantly encroaching on the territory of their neighbours. Champa declined in the 9C-10C while the Khmer Empire expanded to include the southern half of the Khorat plateau, the lower valley of the Chao Phraya, the Mon Kingdom of Haripunchai in the north, the Vientiane Plain in Laos; it had also established a strong presence on the Malay peninsula.

Indian influence – The **Mon** people, of the same stock as the Khmers, occupied a large area comprising the central plain, the eastern part of Lower Burma and the Khorat plateau. They had a well-organised society and were originally animists. As trade relations with India developed they adopted the principle of kingship, Hinduism and Buddhism, and Hindu languages (Sanskrit and Pali), and gradually created principalities on the Indian model. Chinese chronicles refer to an obscure kingdom, **Funan**, which held sway over these territories and about which little is known.

The Dvaravati Kingdom (6C-12C)

571-632	*Mohammed.*
mid-7C	Evidence of a **Dvaravati kingdom** in the central plain.
7C-8C	Foundation of **Haripunchai** *(see LAMPHUN).*
7C-13C	The **Srivijaya Empire** rules the southern peninsula.
9C	*Coronation of Charlemagne.*

Dvaravati Period (6C-11C to 12C) – As the power of Funan waned the Mon principalities grew, and in the mid-7C the accounts of a Chinese monk on a pilgrimage to India mention To-Lo-P'o-Ti which is consonant with Dvaravati found in a Sanskrit inscription on silver coins discovered in Nakhon Pathom. This is the first written evidence of a Dvaravati kingdom which is assumed to be **Suwannaphum** (The Land of Gold) where Theravada Buddhism was introduced in the 3C by missionaries sent by King Ashoka of India. The kingdom probably extended from southern Burma across the central plain to eastern Cambodia. Dvaravati sites have been identified along the trade routes but little light has

---

A land of contrasts

Thailand is filled with the most glaring contradictions. Its urban landscape mixes modern office blocks and BMW cars with spirit houses and the famous three-wheeled *tuk-tuks*. Its temples and archeological sites are surrounded by tinselled lights and giant billboards advertising upmarket whisky brands or the latest fad. Thais see as little contradiction in these opposing elements as they do in their elected prime minister consulting an astrologer. On the one hand, they constantly remind tourists that they were never colonised. On the other, they happily embrace almost anything that is American. Their love of novelty extends to a fascination with technology. Microchips and mobile phones are as much in evidence in Bangkok as tricycles and traffic jams. These days, the country can even boast its own satellite station.

been shed on the culture so far. They are usually on an oval plan and are surrounded by moats. The main centres were at Nakhon Pathom and Ku Bua (Ratchaburi), Phong Tuk (Kanchanaburi), Dong Si Maha Phot (Prachinburi) and Muang Fa Daet Sun Yang (Kalasin). Northern chronicles relate that in the 7C-8C the principality of **Haripunchai** was founded by Queen Chamatewee, the daughter of the Mon ruler of the Buddhist state of **Lavoh** (Lopburi), and flourished until its annexation by King Mengrai of Chiang Mai in the 13C. Except for Wat Chamatewee *(see LAMPHUN)* only the bases of buildings made of brick and stucco decorations survive. Fine pieces of sculpture *(see LAMPHUN, Museum)*, however, are an eloquent legacy of this mysterious people.

The Srivijaya Empire (7C-13C) – The southern peninsula was ruled by a maritime power based in Java and Sumatra which established settlements in Chaiya (Surat Thani) and Sathing Phra (Songkhla). Archaeological finds indicate influences from both Hinduism and Mahayana Buddhism.

The Khmer Empire

9C-10C	Rise of the **Khmer empire** under Jayavarman II and Yasovarman I. Practice of Brahmanism and institution of cult of the *devaraja* (god king).
11C-13C	Migration of the Tai from Nan Chao (Yunnan).
11C	*First Crusade.*
mid-12C	Bas-relief at Angkor Wat depicts Siamese troops – **Syam Kuk** – allied to the Khmer ruler Suriyavarman II against Champa.
12C	Decline of Dvaravati civilisation as the Khmer empire gains control of large territories.
	Jayavarman VII adopts Mahayana Buddhism as the official religion of the Khmer empire. Angkor reaches the peak of its glory.

Khmer rule – From the 9C the Khmer Empire with its capital at **Angkor** expanded west as far as Kanchanaburi and north to Laos and became the dominant power in Southeast Asia. The Dvaravati civilisation declined and the conquered provinces were ruled by governors; the main centres were That Phanom and Sakhon Nakhon (central Mekong valley), Phimai (Khorat region), Lopburi, Nakhon Pathom, and Phetchaburi (Chao Phraya basin) and Sukhothai, Si Satchanalai, Phitsanulok (upper section of the central plain). Institutions and a road network were established to link the provinces with Angkor. Major temples (Prasat Hin Phimai, Phanom Rung, Muang Tham) celebrated the cult of the *devaraja* (god king). The Khmer worship of Hindu gods was superseded by Mahayana Buddhism which was adopted as the official religion in the 12C by **Jayavarman VII** although Brahmanic rituals were retained. Buddha images bore the symbols of kingship. By the mid 12C **Lopburi** which had tried to retain its independence had become the main centre of Khmer power. In the mid 13C Angkor power waned as Tai states began to assert their identity, and by the end of the century the empire had collapsed.

The Rise of Sukhothai (13C-14C)

13C	*Mongol conquests.*
13C	Tai leaders form an alliance and depose the Khmer governor of Sukhothai. **Sri Intradit** declares himself king.
	Glorious reign of King **Ram Kamhaeng**. The Khmers are driven out of the country. Revival of Theravada Buddhism, fostering of national identity and artistic flowering.
	Sukhothai extends its power over several dependencies. Alliance with Chiang Mai and Phayao.
	Death of Ram Kamhaeng in 1289 followed by fragmentation of the kingdom into petty principalities. Lanna rivalry.

The Sukhothai kingdom – A second migration of the Tai from Yunnan occurred from the 11C and the influx grew in the early 13C when the Mongols under Kublai Khan overran the kingdom of Nan Chao. The migrants moved down to the Chao Phraya basin and the Mekong valley as well as to the area now known as the Shan states in northeast Burma. They formed small autonomous entities known as *muang* which later came under the sway of the Khmers. Siamese troops are portrayed on bas-reliefs at Angkor.

In the early 13C Tai leaders who resented the rigid social framework, the arbitrary exactions and impersonal rule of Angkor formed an alliance to challenge the Khmer ruler of Sukhothai. One of the leaders declared himself king and took the title of **Sri Intradit**. This significant event marked the decline of the Khmer world as during the reign of the great King **Ram Kamhaeng** (1279-98) the Khmers had been driven out of Tai territory. As early as 1282 the new kingdom established diplomatic relations with China and paid tribute to the great power. The country thrived and by the late 13C its dominions were extensive. It had freed itself from its Khmer inheritance and developed its own cultural and political identity. It revived **Theravada Buddhism** although Brahmanical rituals were retained at court, and sent missionaries round the country. Alliances were forged with Chiang Mai and Phayao although Lopburi, the former Khmer capital, retained a degree of independence. In the south **Nakhon Si Thammarat** emerged as a regional power which together with its dependencies on the Malay Peninsula came under the aegis of Sukhothai. There arose a benign hierarchical society loosely controlled from the centre and through personal loyalties often fostered by marriage ties between ruling houses. The flowering of a national spirit is evident in Sukhothai's artistic achievements *(see ART)*.

During the reign of Ram Kamhaeng's successor the northern dependencies fragmented into rival petty principalities, the Lanna kingdom encroached on the Sukhothai sphere of influence, and a new threat arose to the south which led to the foundation of Ayutthaya and its later conquest of Sukhothai.

Lanna (13C-18C)

1259	**Mengrai** (d 1317) becomes ruler of **Chiang Saen** and conquers neighbouring principalities.
1262	Foundation of **Chiang Rai**.
1271-95	*Travels of Marco Polo.*
1281-89	Conquest of **Haripunchai** and alliance with **Pegu** against the Mongols.
1292	**Foundation of Chiang Mai.** Alliance with Pagan and defeat of Chinese attack. Chiang Mai pays tribute to China after successful diplomacy. Promotion of Singhalese Buddhism and forging of Lanna identity.

The birth of Lanna – In the north the Dvaravati states conquered by the Khmer faded. Northern chronicles mention rival Tai centres including **Chiang Saen** in the 13C. **Mengrai** (b 1239) came to the throne in 1259 and imposed his authority on his neighbours. He founded a new capital at **Chiang Rai** in 1262 and in 1281 conquered the Mon state of **Haripunchai** (Lamphun). In his youth he had studied at Lopburi and made friends with other princes who became rulers of neighbouring Sukhothai and Phayao. He subsequently forged alliances with them and was called upon to mediate in a dispute between Ram Kamhaeng and King Ngam Müang of Phayao. He expanded his kingdom further by making an alliance with Pegu in Lower Burma which was in rebellion against Pagan in Upper Burma.

In 1292 he chose **Chiang Mai** as his new capital and after consultations with his allies Ram Kamhaeng and Ngam Müang building started in 1296. Mengrai also made an alliance with Pagan to counter the threat of Mongol invasion and successfully repulsed a Chinese attack. After diplomatic moves had resolved the conflict Chiang Mai paid tribute and sent missions to China. Mengrai allowed the Mon culture and Buddhism of Haripunchai to survive but promoted a strict form of Sinhalese Buddhism and built up a strong and prosperous nation known as **Lanna** which wielded power and influence on the Shans to the west, the Lao to the north and northeast and another Tai state to the north. On his death in 1317 his legacy included a just legal tradition. A power struggle broke out among his heirs which weakened the kingdom until 1328, when a degree of stability returned although rivalry over succession remained a great problem over the centuries.

A new city was built in 1328 at Chiang Saen which was governed by several Lanna rulers in succession. In the 14C Chiang Mai under King Ku Na (1355-85) promoted Buddhism which became a major cultural force in the kingdom during the following centuries.

1441-87	Reign of **Tilokaracha**. War with Ayutthaya.
1495-1526	King Muang Kaeo establishes Lanna pre-eminence.
mid 16C	Lanna comes under Burmese supremacy which lasts 200 years.
late 18C-early19C	King **Kavila** restores the Lanna kingdom.

The great King **Tilokaracha** (1441-87) repulsed an attack on Lamphun by Ayutthaya, established suzerainty over Nan and led campaigns against powerful northern states. In the mid 15C a lengthy war broke out after Ayutthaya's conquest of Sukhothai and it remained unresolved as unrest in northern states caused further disruption. The power of Lanna was undimmed at the time of Tilokaracha's death and his successors continued the war with Ayutthaya. King Muang Kaeo (r 1495-1526) patronised Sinhalese Buddhism and founded many temples thus establishing Lanna's intellectual pre-eminence. Civil war raged however in a later succession quarrel between Chiang Saen, Luang Prabang (Laos) and the Shan states, from which a Shan king emerged as victor.

In the mid 16C Lanna was captured by King Bayinnaung of Burma and remained under Burmese sovereignty for the next two hundred years. Lanna proved a strategic position from which the Burmese pursued their war against Ayutthaya.

In 1774 King Taksin *(see Bangkok Period below)* succeeded in driving out the Burmese. Chiang Mai was abandoned and King **Kavila** settled in Lampang (1775-81) where he ruled the north as a tributary state of Bangkok. The Burmese later made further attacks which were successfully repelled. In 1776 Kavila reoccupied Chiang Mai where he ruled until 1813 and revived the Lanna world. His heirs remained on the throne although their powers were curtailed in 1874 as Bangkok took over the responsibilty for granting logging concessions to foreign companies. On the death of the last ruler in 1939 the kingdom became fully integrated in the state of Thailand.

The Ayutthaya Kingdom (late 13C-late 18C)

late 13C	Suphan Buri claims independence from Sukhothai.
1325	*Aztec Empire in Mexico.*
1351-69	**Ramathibodi I** (U-Thong) founds Ayutthaya. Prince **Ramesuan** appointed as ruler of Lopburi. He accedes to the throne in 1369 but abdicates in favour of his uncle.

The rise of Ayutthaya – In the late 13C Suphan Buri, which was dependent on Lopburi and was allied to Nakhon Si Thammarat in the south, dominated the west of the Chao Phraya plain under the suzerainty of Sukhothai. On the death of Ram Kamhaeng, Suphan Buri claimed independence but lacked political leadership until the mid-14C when U-Thong, the Chinese son-in-law of the ruler, was raised to power. An outbreak of smallpox led him to move the population from the area of present-day U-Thong to an island site, where he founded the kingdom of **Ayutthaya** in 1351 and took the name **Ramathibodi I** (1351-69). After he had appointed his wife's brother to govern Suphan Buri and his son **Ramesuan** as the ruler of Lopburi, the kingdom grew rapidly as he used the manpower to develop international trade, although relations were uneasy between the powerful Chinese merchants who dominated trade and Lopburi functionaries trained by the Khmers. He drew up legislation based on Indian law to regulate the new kingdom and built on his political and personal ties with neighbouring principalities and in particular made a pact with Sukhothai.

On his death, Prince Ramesuan came to the throne but following a challenge by his uncle he abdicated after a brief period.

1370-88	**Borommaracha I** wages war with Lanna and Sukhothai.
1388-95	Second reign of **Ramesuan.** Invasion of Cambodia. Rivalry between Ayutthaya and Sukhothai for primacy.

King **Borommaracha I** (1370-88) kept the kingdom unified and challenged the power of Sukhothai; after the death of the ruler, King Mahathammaracha (Lithai), he captured Nakhon Sawan, Phitsanulok and Kamphaeng Phet. He claimed suzerainty over Sukhothai, declared war on Lanna and later with Lanna's support waged further war on Sukhothai.

On his death in 1388 **Ramesuan** reclaimed his throne and in 1390 forced Chiang Mai into submission. Large numbers of captives were resettled in the southern peninsula. Ramesuan invaded Cambodia to counter raids by Angkor on the territory (present-day Chonburi and Chanthaburi) on the east coast. During later reigns Ayutthaya and Sukhothai vied for dominance as Nan, Phrae and other states changed sides according to the fortunes of war.

1409-24	**Intaracha** conquers Sukhothai.
1424-48	**Borommaracha II** launches a campaign and captures Angkor. War with Chiang Mai.
1448-88	**Borommatrailokanat** institutes administrative and social reforms.
1486-98	*Voyages of Bartholomew Diaz and Vasco da Gama.*
1492	*Christopher Columbus discovers America.*

In the early 15C King **Intaracha** (1409-24) reduced Sukhothai to a vassal state. On the death of the vassal ruler Mahathammaracha III he placed his preferred candidate, Mahathammaracha IV, on the throne. The latter ruled from Phitsanulok and his death was followed by the annexation of Sukhothai.

Borommaracha II (1424-48) named his son Ramesuan as viceroy of Phitsanulok and in 1431-32 sent an expedition against the weakened Angkor. After his troops had captured and looted the city, Angkor was reduced to a tributary state. The capital was soon abandoned as the Khmers moved further south to Phnom Penh.

Ayutthaya then declared war on Chiang Mai which lasted over a hundred years. King **Borommatrailokanat** (1448-88) reorganised the legislation and military and civilian administration of the kingdom. He instituted the *sakdi naa* system of land holdings which defined social status in a rigid hierarchy. Trade under royal control increased dramatically during the following centuries and contributed hugely to the economic development of the state.

early-mid 16C	The Portuguese win trading rights. Ayutthaya is in conflict with Chiang Mai, Burma and Cambodia.
1519-21	*Magellan circumnavigates the globe.*
1545-63	*Council of Trent.*
1569-late 16C	Ayutthaya falls to King Bayinnaung of Burma who also captures Vientiane (Laos).
1590-1605	**Naresuan the Great** frees Ayutthaya from Burmese rule. Trading posts established by France, Holland, England and Japan. Ayutthaya is referred to as the Kingdom of **Siam.**

A turbulent time (16C-18C) – In the early 16C the Portuguese established trade relations with Ayutthaya and maritime trade prospered from posts set up in the southern peninsula. **Ramathibodi II** and his successor pursued the war with Chiang Mai and clashed with Burma. In the mid-16C the latter were soon to take advantage of internal dissensions over succession and vast armies marched through the Three Pagodas Pass to the west. King Chakkraphat of Ayutthaya boosted his army and naval forces to withstand further threats from Cambodia to the east. Burmese forces under King **Bayinnaung** captured Lanna and shortly after invaded from the north and took the northern cities of the kingdom. Ayutthaya fell in 1569 after which the Burmese swept north to Laos and captured Vientiane. By the late 16C the Burmese reigned supreme over all the Tai kingdoms.

The next renowned ruler was **Naresuan the Great** (r 1590-1605), the son of the vassal king installed by the Burmese, who was declared king in 1590. He made a determined bid for independence and successfully withstood several Burmese expeditions. In 1593 he won a decisive victory at Nong Sarai *(see SUPHAN BURI)*. Ayutthaya grew in power, prospered from trade and kept the Burmese and other threats at bay. In the reign of his successor, his brother King Ekhatotsarot (1605-11), trade with China, Japan and the Philippines flourished.

17C	Growth of the population. Golden Age of the kingdom.
	Foundation of English East India Company (1600) and of Dutch East India Company (1602).
	Glorious reign of King **Narai the Great** (1656-88). Exchange of ambassadors with the French court of Louis XIV. Missionaries introduce Christianity. **Constantine Phaulkon** gains great influence as royal adviser but is executed by a clique of nationalist courtiers who take power. Expulsion of all foreigners after the demise of Narai. Ayutthaya remains in isolation for a hundred years.
18C	**Borommakot** (1733-58) restores Ayutthaya as a great power. Siamese monks are sent to Ceylon to restore Sinhalese Buddhism.
1760-67	Renewed conflicts with Burma. After the fall of the kingdom in 1767 the capital is razed.

In the 17C, relations with Europe (Holland, France, England), China, Japan and Muslim states grew. Bloody struggles for succession remained a constant factor. Under King **Narai** (1656-88) trade under royal monopoly flourished and treaties were signed. French missionaries were allowed to practise their religion and diplomatic missions were exchanged with the court of the French King Louis XIV. **Constantine Phaulkon,** a royal adviser who acquired great power and wealth, was executed after being implicated in a plot with the French to convert the king to Christianity. This met with strong opposition from the Buddhist royal officials and the king's demise marked a century of isolation as the kingdom closed its doors to Western influences although French missionaries and Dutch traders continued to reside in Ayutthaya in the 18C. Trade with China boomed.

In the reign of King **Borommakot** (1733-58), a devout Buddhist, Ayutthaya sent monks to Ceylon to re-establish the Sinhalese monkhood and again assumed the role of a great kingdom. Later, however, further succession quarrels weakened the state and war with the Burmese became inevitable. In 1760 Ayutthaya came under siege and after years of warfare the city fell in 1767. The Burmese laid the city to waste and took a huge number of captives and vast treasures.

R. Cuzin/ MICHELIN

In sharp contrast to the benign Sukhothai rulers, the Kings of Ayutthaya adopted court rituals based on the Khmer cult of the god-king in order to distance themselves from their subjects. Royal power was absolute, prostration was introduced and no one was allowed to gaze at the ruler. Those who broke the rule had their eyes put out.

The Bangkok Period (late 18C-early 20C)

18C	*The Age of Enlightenment.*
1767-82	**Taksin** raises an army and expels the Burmese. He founds a new capital at Thonburi and declares himself king. Taksin regains Siamese territory and claims sovereignty over Chiang Mai and Lampang. King **Kavila** (1775-1813) of Lanna rules over the north as a tributary state of Thonburi.
1782-1809	**Rama I**, founder of the Chakri dynasty, rebuilds the nation and founds Bangkok.
1776-83	*American War of Independence.*
1789	*The French Revolution.*

The Early Bangkok Period (late 18C-early 20C) – After the Burmese victory **Taksin** a former provincial governor, fled to Chanthaburi in the southeast with a small band of soldiers. He assembled an army and within six months had expelled Burmese forces remaining in the country. He declared himself ruler and after founding a capital at Thonburi, he set about asserting his authority over the territory. He captured Lampang and Chiang Mai and with the help of General Chakri he established suzerainty over the Lao states to the north. Taksin (1767-82) proved a wise leader of men but sadly he became mentally disturbed and was executed because of his erratic behaviour.

Rama I (1782-1809), the next ruler who founded the Chakri dynasty, re-established the Buddhist monkhood, devised a code of law and advocated sound government. He also built a grand new capital using statues and bricks from the old city and recreated court ceremonial to recall the glory of Ayutthaya. He repulsed several Burmese attacks, imposed sovereignty on the states of the Malay Peninsula and created a strong, cosmopolitan nation. His great achievements include the promotion of literature: he was one of the authors of the *Ramakien*, a Thai adaptation of the Hindu epic *The Ramayana*. Among other important works of the period are translations of Chinese historical novels, chronicles and tales from Java, Ceylon and Persia. Trade with China flourished and the new state prospered.

1809-24	Trade with European nations is resumed under **Rama II**.
1824-51	**Rama III** captures Lan Xang (Laos) principalities and resettles the Lao on the Khorat plateau. Treaty signed in 1826 with the British who held Burma and exerted great influence in the Malay Peninsula. Cambodia becomes a tributary state of Siam. American envoys and missionaries arrive in Bangkok and conclude a trade treaty in 1833.

The reign of **Rama II** (1809-24) was characterised by weak leadership as factions of nobles manoeuvred to exert influence. Relations with European trading companies were resumed although the threat posed by them was recognised. Unreasonable concessions demanded by an official British mission led by John Crawfurd were refused. The rivalry between Dutch, Portuguese, British and French interests increased in the aftermath of the Napoleonic wars. Rama II who was a great poet was also famous for his patronage of the arts.

Rama III (1824-51) ascended the throne at the expense of his brother Mongkut who had joined the monkhood on his father's advice to defuse a succession crisis. In 1826 he signed a treaty with the British who had annexed Burma and had strong interests in the Malay Peninsula. Thai influence increased in the northeast as he captured Vientiane and the Lao provinces to the east and resettled large sections of the Lao population on the Khorat plateau. Rebellion of the Muslim states to the south was put down. Clashes with Cambodia and Vietnam also occurred, after which Cambodia paid tribute to the Thai king. Rama III preserved the nation's cultural heritage but also promoted art and science to educate the people and enable them to face the changing world.

1851-68	**Rama IV** (King Mongkut) starts the modernisation of the state and concludes new trade treaties to avert conflicts with Britain, France and the United States.
1868-1910	**Rama V** (King Chulalongkorn) continues the reforms and keeps the country free from foreign interference through diplomacy. Siam becomes a buffer state between British Burma and Malaysia and French Indo-China.
1869	*Opening of the Suez Canal.*

Before Mongkut succeeded his brother, the time he spent as a monk studying the Pali Buddhist scriptures led him to question local Buddhist practices and to found a strict order, Dhammayutika. He was a brilliant scholar and his wide-ranging interests included science, mathematics, astronomy and languages which he studied with Western missionaries. His enlightened reign as King **Rama IV** (1851-68) is marked by pragmatism which preserved the independence of the kingdom in the face of encroachments by the French in Indo-China and by the British on the Malay Peninsula. He modernised the army and navy, built roads, introduced Western medicine and many other reforms. He signed trade treaties with the British envoy Sir John Bowring, as well as with France, the United States and other countries to avert confrontation but this move placed the economy under foreign control.

Modernisation proceeded apace under **Rama V** (Chulalongkorn, 1868-1910) although with some resistance from the traditionalists. He created ministries with foreign advisers, built roads, railways, schools and hospitals to accelerate the process of economic development. The colonial powers were kept at bay by skilful diplomacy but compromises were reached in the face of strong pressure. Laos was ceded to France in 1893; they also occupied provinces (Chanthaburi, Trat) on the Cambodian border. To maintain the balance of power the British laid claim to territory on the Malay Peninsula and were also given logging concessions in the north. In the early 20C the present borders of Thailand were settled as the British and French reached agreement on their spheres of influence. The vision of Rama V, the first Thai ruler to travel abroad, is evident in his efforts to reconcile traditional values with modern influences.

20C-early 21C

1914-18	*First World War.*
1917	*The Russian Revolution.*
1910-35	Rise of nationalism under **Rama VI**. Troops are sent to fight in First World War. End of absolute monarchy in 1932 after the abdication of **Rama VII**. Regency period until the coronation of **Rama VIII** in 1946.
1932-50s	Power oscillates between the socialist **Pridi Panomyong** and the militarist **Phibun Songkhram**.
1939-45	*Second World War.*
1939	The country adopts the official name of **Thailand**. During the Second World War Thailand entered into a military alliance with Japan although war was not officially declared on the Allies.

20C – The period until the end of the absolute monarchy in 1932 was marked by the reign of two of Rama V's sons. **Rama VI** (Vajivarudh, 1910-25) continued the modernisation process with the help of Western advisers but squandered the nation's wealth. He wrote plays, founded newspapers and introduced compulsory education. He also fostered nationalist feelings by advocating the freeing of the economy from foreign control and reducing Chinese economic power. He revised the treaties with Western nations; he also sent troops to fight against Germany during the First World War and participated in the Peace Conference at Versailles in 1919.

The Great Depression of the 1930s had a profound effect on the reign of **Rama VII** (Prajadhipok, 1925-35) as an economic crisis ravaged the country. In 1932 a coup staged by a group of soldiers and civilians brought about the king's abdication in 1935 in favour of his young nephew Ananda Mahidol whose reign was a short one. During the Regency period a civilian government was dominated by two key figures. The socialist programme of Prime Minister **Pridi Panomyong** was rejected and he was forced into exile. Under **Phibun Songkhram** a wave of nationalism and militarism swept the country, which became officially known as **Thailand** – the Land of the Free – in 1939. During the Second World War Thailand, although officially neutral, gave its support to Japan in order to regain its lost territories in Laos and Cambodia. In 1941 they were forced into a military alliance with Japan and to declare war on the Allies. No formal declaration was issued, however, as the Thai ambassador in the United States refused to deliver the letter. Pridi who had returned to act as regent, supported the Free Thai Movement. Phibun went into exile in Japan as the Japanese faced defeat by the Allies.

1946	Accession of **Rama IX** (King Bhumibol). Thailand joins the United Nations.
1949	*Communist victory in China.*
1955	The South East Asian Treaty Organisation (SEATO) comes into force.
1957	*Treaty of Rome: formation of the Common Market.*
1957-92	Thailand is ruled by a succession of military dictatorships with only a short period of civilian government (1973-76). Communist insurrection rages as the Vietnam War escalates. Territory on the Cambodian border placed under martial law (1985-87).
1967	The Association of Southeast Asian Nations (ASEAN) is founded for economic, cultural, industrial and technological co-operation.

The next Prime Minister was Seni Pramoj, the wise former ambassador to the US. He was followed by Pridi who had regained his popularity. In 1945 King Ananda was crowned as **Rama VIII** but a few months later he died in suspicious circumstances. The confusion over the king's death led to the resignation of Pridi and the reinstatement of Phibun whose anti-communist views won the support of America; he remained in power until 1957. In 1946 **Rama IX** was declared king and Thailand joined the United Nations..

From 1957 onwards, coups and counter-coups occurred in succession and the military gained the upper hand. American bases were allowed in the country as the Vietnam War escalated. Martial law was declared as elections were cancelled and students rioted. The Prime Minister resigned in 1973 after violent student demonstrations.

1975	*End of the Vietnam War.*
1982	Bicentenary of Bangkok and of the Chakri dynasty.
1989	Foundation of the Asia-Pacific Economic Cooperation group (APEC) to deal with regional matters including security.
1992	State of emergency declared after student riots and mass demonstrations. Free elections bring a coalition government to power.
1993	Thailand becomes a member of the ASEAN Free Trade Area (AFTA).
1996	King Bhumibol celebrates the Golden Jubilee of his accession to the throne.
1997	Thailand devalues its currency marking the onset of the Asian financial crisis.
1998	A new constitution strengthens Thailand's fledgeling democracy.
2000	A populist government takes office.

Until 1976 civilian governments led by Seni and Kukrit Pramoj were in power and dealt with the student, worker and peasant grievances. To counter the rise of the Communist Party of Thailand, the army again took power and repression and censorship were enforced. In 1977 a more liberal leader was installed and during the next decade he attempted to stem the support given to the Communists and to deal with the influx of refugees from Vietnam and Cambodia as well as the worsening economic situation due to the oil crisis of 1979.

During the 1980s with the collaboration of the army and political parties the economic situation improved as support for the Communists dwindled and a period of stability ensued. Coalition governments followed until a military coup in 1991 which formed a Committee for National Salvation. In 1992 following a state of emergency a decree was passed by Parliament stipulating that the head of government must be an elected member of parliament. The next Prime Minister had a successful term of office and later elections resulted in coalition governments. In 1998 a sharp downturn of the economy and major divisions within the government caused a major crisis. Stringent measures to reform the economic sector have caused hardship but have brought about some improvement. At the start of the third millennium a new government of a different political persuasion is in office and there is cause for cautious optimism.

R. Cuzin/ MICHELIN

King Bhumibol Adulyadej (Rama IX) has presided over these troubled years. As a constitutional monarch he has few powers but his wise counsel and deep concern for the welfare of his people command the immense respect and admiration of the nation. Over the years his prestige has helped to defuse many difficult situations and to smooth over political problems. Royal encouragement and economic prosperity have proved powerful incentives in maintaining democratic institutions. The sovereign celebrated the Golden Jubilee of his accession to the throne in 1996 amid great popular rejoicing.

Art

The rich artistic heritage of Thailand is gaining better recognition both nationally and internationally as recent studies shed more light on the complex religious and cultural influences which have shaped its evolution.

Throughout the ages various artistic trends have been adopted and interpreted in a Thai idiom. An innovative spirit broke through during the Golden Age of the Sukhothai kingdom (13C-16C), and as the power of Ayutthaya (14C-18C) grew, its culture spread to neighbouring territories. The destruction of the old capitals of Sukhothai and Ayutthaya entailed the loss of innumerable works of art. Wooden structures have perished but extant monuments built of stone or brick and statues made of terracotta, stone, crystal, bronze, silver and gold which have escaped destruction give some idea of the artistic flowering of the period.

As Thailand becomes more prosperous, a growing interest among the people in their history and culture has prompted further research and a greater commitment to conservation of important monuments and works of art. Many known archaeological sites have not yet been investigated and significant discoveries are likely which may lead to new interpretations. Until recently the National Museum in Bangkok was the repository of the country's art treasures but under a new policy regional museums – Ayutthaya, Ban Chiang, Chiang Saen, Lamphun, Lopburi, Nan, Nakhon Si Thammarat Sukhothai and Phimai among others – have been created to exhibit the art of particular regions.

Early civilisations – Artefacts – pebble tools, flints, polished adzes, slate knives – from all over the country (Mae Hong Son, Kanchanaburi, Surat Thani) provide precious information about the slow evolution of the lifestyle of prehistoric people: from hunter-gatherers or search-and-kill nomadic groups to permanent settlers able to shape the environmental conditions to suit communal livelihood. The oldest artefacts found are **chipped stone axes** used as choppers dating back to before 5000 C.

Elaborate burial rituals developed as well as farming, animal husbandry and production of earthenware. **Burial sites** reveal that an advanced civilisation flourished at **Ban Chiang** *(see BAN CHIANG)* and No Nok Tha (*c* 5000 BC to 2C AD) in the northeast and produced incised, cord-marked and painted vessels of various types. The red-patterned designs are outstanding. The discovery of the world's oldest socketed tool (WOST *c* 3500 BC, *see Ban Chiang museum*) and fine ornaments provides evidence that bronze technology had also been mastered. A rare terracotta **tripod** dated *c* 2000 BC found at Ban Kao, Kanchanaburi, is probably a local imitation of a bronze original.

Rock paintings of figures, animals and designs abound in caves and rock shelters *(see AO PHANGNGA, UDON THANI, UBON RATCHATHANI)* and are moving testimonies of the activities and rituals of prehistoric man.

Foreign influences – From the beginning of the millennium Indian traders spread the culture of **India,** the birthplace of both Hinduism and Buddhism, throughout Southeast Asia; its influence in southern Thailand can be traced as far back as the 3C AD. Important finds were made at Takuapa *(see RANONG)* and Amphoe Wieng Sa and Chaiya *(see SURAT THANI)*. Early statues (7C-9C) of the three supreme Hindu gods – namely Shiva, Vishnu and Brahma who assume the roles of both creators and destroyers – and the first

Rock paintings, Pha Taem

Wheel of the Law

representations of the Buddha and Bodhisattvas are in the **Gupta** and **post-Gupta** styles. The four-armed Vishnu is portrayed with his attributes – a conch, a disc, a club and a lotus – and wearing a tall mitre and a long robe *(sampot)* with a thick fold at the waist. The artistic styles (Amaravati, Anuradhapura) of southeastern India including Ceylon (Sri Lanka) were also determining influences. Early standing statues show the Buddha in the attitude of dispelling fear *(abhaya mudra)* or preaching *(vitarka mudra)*, dressed in a pleated robe covering the left shoulder with a thick fold draped over the left arm. Shiva lingas representing the Hindu trinity, terracotta images and votive tablets have also been found on various sites.

Among important finds in Kanchanaburi which attest to the influence of other cultures are a bronze **Roman lamp** adorned with the face of the Greek god Silenus (*c* 1C) probably brought to the area by Indian merchants.

Dvaravati art – This refers to artistic forms dating back to the period from the 6C to the 11C and which are comparable to Gupta, post-Gupta and Pala art. Silver **coins** bearing a Sanskrit inscription refer to a Dvaravati kingdom situated in central Thailand and Lower Burma, whose people were probably of Mon origin.

Dvaravati art is associated with the culture of the Theravada Buddhist sect, as can be seen from its main expression in the forms of Buddha statues and in the early aniconic art objects, such as the **Wheel of the Law** (of Dharma) and the crouching deer, which together symbolise the birth of Buddhism, as well as sculptures relating the stories of the Buddha in his previous lives. Standing stone Buddha images present strong indigenous features *(illustration)*: a broad square face, a flat nose, thick lips, prominent eyes, curved eyebrows joined over the bridge of the nose. Other characteristics are large curls, a conical top-knot *(ushnisha)*, a transparent robe covering both shoulders and clinging to the body forming a U-shape at the hem, an undergarment often visible at the waist and at the lower edge. Imposing statues of the Buddha seated in "European" style with feet resting on a lotus base *(illustration)* found at Nakhon Pathom are masterpieces.

Religious sanctuaries (chedis, viharas) were built of laterite or brick. Fine examples of intricately carved boundary stones **(bai semas)**, bas-reliefs, stucco images, terracotta figurines and votive tablets have been found at major Dvaravati sites including the ancient site of Si Thep *(see PHETCHABUN)*.

The regional museums of Nakhon Pathom, Ratchaburi, Prachinburi, Lamphun and Khon Kaen have particularly fine exhibits.

Haripunchai style – According to the northern Lanna chronicles Theravada Buddhism and Dvaravati culture spread north to Lopburi and thence to **Haripunchai** *(see LAMPHUN)* in the 7C-8C. There are particularly fine statues of Buddha with strong features in the Dvaravati idiom exhibited in the museum at Lamphun. But in the 10C-12C when Haripunchai was at the peak of its glory, its sculpture and architecture – square chedi at **Wat Chamatewee★** (Wat Ku Kut) – suggest that its artistic style was more in line with the contemporary artistic form of Pagan (Burma). After Haripunchai fell to King Mengrai of Chiang Rai in 1281, its Buddhist art and culture served to underpin the foundation of Chiang Mai where the invading monarch established a new capital.

Art in the southern peninsula – In the 7C-13C Mahayana Buddhism was well established in the south which was ruled by a maritime power, the Srivijaya empire which probably had its capital at Palambang in Sumatra. **Srivijaya art** was heavily influenced by the Gupta, post-Gupta and Pala-Sena styles. An 8C stone figure of the **Avalokitesvara Bodhisattva★★** and an ornate bronze **Avalokitesvara★★** (8C-9C, *illustration*) found at Chaiya *(in National Museum, BANGKOK)* are admirable. The site of **Sathing Phra** *(see SONGKHLA)* has also yielded many Srivijayan bronzes. Chaiya preserves the best examples of Srivijayan architecture. Wat Kaeo and **Wat Phra Boromathat** are the most important monuments. The original chedi (Phra Boromathat) at Nakhon Si Thammarat was probably in a similar style.

Dvaravati

Dvaravati

Srivijaya

Lopburi

Lopburi

57

The Khmer legacy – Khmer art found in Thailand is usually described as **Lopburi art** as Lopburi became the Khmer administrative and cultural centre. From the 7C to the 13C, Khmer art and architecture had a profound impact on the cultures of both the kingdoms of Dvaravati and Srivijaya.

Khmer **prasats** or ancient sanctuary-towers found in the northeast date back to the 7C-8C and were constructed in accordance with both Hinduist beliefs and the Mahayana Buddhist faith which superseded Hinduism. Religous sanctuaries built of different materials can be traced to different periods: bricks were used in the earlier period, followed by stone and laterite at later dates. The Khmer monuments of Lopburi *(see LOPBURI)* range from different periods. **Prasat Phanom Wan★** (Nakhon Ratchasima), **Prasat Muang Tham★★** (Buriram) and **Prasat Hin Phanom Rung★★★** (10C-13C) rank among the most renowned Khmer monuments, while **Prasat Hin Phimai★★★** deemed to be the most complete example of a Khmer sanctuary pre-dates Angkor Wat. The carved decoration of these sanctuaries is outstanding. Also of interest are the numerous **hospitals** or resthouses built by Jayavarman VII all over the northeast and as far north as Laos.

Outstanding sculptures, some of bronze but mostly made of sandstone, include a remarkable bust of **Uma★★★** (*c* early 7C – *see BANGKOK, Suan Pakkaråd Palace*), a majestic statue of **Jayavarman VII★★★** *(illustration see PHIMAI, National Museum)*, probably a portrait of the monarch. Characteristics of the sandstone Lopburi Buddhas are a flat square face, a band outlining the hairline, eyebrows in a straight line, a protuberance on the crown of the head – sometimes modified into three rows of lotus petals topped by a lotus bud – signifying enlightenment. The robe hangs over the left shoulder and lies in a straight line at the navel. The **crowned Buddha images** *(illustrations)* in regal attire raised on the coils of the Naga king and sheltered by its seven-headed hood were an innovation symbolising the Khmer cult of the god-king *(deva raja)*. Bronze vessels and **glazed ceramics** known as "Khmer jars" usually in human and animal shapes have also been found in large numbers.

A Khmer temple

The plan of the temple is based on Hindu cosmology. A wall representing the earth and moats and ponds symbolising the oceans surround the towers designating the peaks of Mount Meru, the home of the gods. A prasat, a tall central tower on a cruciform plan and crowned by a lotus bud, housed statues of Hindu gods; smaller prasats frame the central tower. The lintels, pediments and antefixes are ornamented with intricate carvings. The temple is built with large blocks of sandstone assembled without mortar. Other features include vaulted roofs, balustered windows, false doors and windows. Only priests had access to the interior for ceremonial rituals. When the Khmer kings instituted the tradition of the devaraja, the god-king, they became the object of worship. After Buddhism was adopted, crowned images of the Buddha were enshrined in the sanctuary.

The Lanna kingdom (11C to early 18C) – The principalities of northern Thailand which made up the Lanna Kingdom under King Mengrai developed distinctive artistic styles.

The early style *(illustration)* is named after the ancient site of **Chiang Saen** (11C-13C) where were discovered Buddha images (12C) of great beauty. Typical features are a strong body, round face, prominent chin, arched eyebrows, large curls crowned by a lotus bud, the fold of the robe terminating in a wavy pattern at the left shoulder. The base of the statues is decorated with lotus petals. The second style, known as late-Chiang Saen or **Chiang Mai**, reveals the influence of Sukhothai – oval face, slender body, the fold of the robe descending to the waist – and later of Ayutthaya, late-Burmese and Lao art. Many statues were made of crystal and semi-precious stones. Some experts surmise that the Emerald Buddha, the most precious statue in Thailand which was found in Chiang Rai, is in the late-Chiang Saen style although others favour the schools of Ceylon or India. A secondary style flourished at Phayao *(see PHAYAO)* in the 15C-16C although this is now disputed.

Masterpieces of Lanna architecture abound besides **Wat Pa Sak★** *(see CHIANG SAEN)*, a unique structure combining Dvaravati, Burmese and Sukhothai influences, the **chedi★★** of Wat Chet Yot *(see CHIANG MAI)* based on the Bodh Gaya shrine in India, and **Wat Chedi Liem★** *(see CHIANG MAI, Excursions)* inspired from **Wat Chamatewee★** (Wat Ku Kut) *(see LAMPHUN)*. The founding of **Chiang Mai** in the 13C and the celebration of the 2000th anniversary of Buddhism in the 15C led to the building of admirable sanctuaries, namely **Wat Phra Sing Luang★★**, **Wat Chedi Luang★**, **Wat Chiang Man★**, and **Wat Suan Dok★★**. The stepped roof structure, elaborate porches with naga balustrades, octagonal chedis, intricate carving and stucco decorations are noteworthy. The site of **Wat Phra That Lampang Luang★★★** *(see LAMPANG)* is the best extant example of a fortified settlement *(wiang)* surrounded by earthen ramparts.

There are also remarkable Burmese-style temples *(see LAMPANG and MAE HONG SON)* with their distinctive plan and roof line and delicate fretwork. They are the legacy of Shan and Burmese merchants engaged in the logging industry and are reminders of the long historical links which existed between Lanna and Burma.

Sukhothai

Lanna – Chiang Saen

Sukhothai

U-Thong

The glory of Sukhothai (late 13C – early 15C) – In the 13C, the emergence of the Sukhothai kingdom, which embraced Theravada Buddhism, gave rise to original forms of artistic expression in order to assert its cultural identity after ending the dominance of the Khmers who practised Mahayana Buddhism.

Sukhothai architecture is celebrated for a unique style of chedis with a **lotus-bud** crown (Wat Phra Si Mahathat, Wat Traphang Ngoen, Sukhothai; Wat Chedi Chet Thaeo, Si Satchanalai) which evolved from the Khmer and Burmese (Pagan) art forms it had inherited. The Khmer prang was also refined as at Wat Si Sawai (Sukhothai). Sinhalese influences are evident in the harmonious **bell-shaped chedi** (Wat Phra Si Mahathat, Wat Sa Sri, Sukhothai) with a square base often highlighted by stucco elephant buttresses (Wat Chang Lom, Sukhothai and Si Satchanalai; Wat Chang Rob, Kamphaeng Phet). A further development derived from the Lanna style consists of a stupa with a square redented base above which rise a square main body pierced with niches housing standing Buddha images and superimposed bell-shapes crowned by a ringed finial. There are examples of these chedis at Wat Phra Si Mahathat (Sukhothai) and at Wat Chedi Chet Thaeo, Si Satchanalai). Large Buddha images and footprints are enshrined in square **mondops** with thick walls (Wat Phra Si Mahathat, Wat Si Chum, Sukhothai; Wat Phra Si Iriyabot, Kamphaeng Phet), derived from the Sanskrit word 'mandapa' although this describes an open hall or pavilion in Indian architecture.

Sukhothai statues of the Buddha in four postures – seated, reclining, standing and walking – are notable for their elegant beauty reflecting religious fervour and quietude in accord with Theravada Buddhism, hence the Sinhalese influence. Characteristics include an oval face, hooked nose, arched eyebrows, small curls, a serene smiling expression, broad shoulders and slim waist. The head is crowned by a tall flame motif, and the flap of the robe is draped over the left shoulder and ends in a wavy pattern at the waist. **Phra Phuttha Sihing** (Phra Thinang Phutthaisawan, Bangkok), **Phra Phuttha Chinasi** and **Phra Phuttha Sassada** – *illustration* – (Wat Bowornivet, Bangkok) are among the most remarkable examples. An original feature is the flame halo framing the venerated **Phra Phuttha Chinarat** (Wat Phra Si Ratana Mahathat, Phitsanulok) which boasts a rounder face, a stouter body and fingers of equal length. The last image has inspired many artists and several versions are enshrined in sanctuaries all over the country.

The sublime **walking Buddha** – *illustration* – *(see SUKHOTHAI, Ram Kamhaeng National Museum; BANGKOK, National Museum)* portrayed in the round and in bronze marks the peak of Sukhothai artistry and is probably based on stucco reliefs (Wat Phra Phai Luang, Wat Traphang Thong Lang – Sukhothai; Wat Si Iriyabot – Kamphaeng Phet). The features and figure conform to the description of the Buddha's appearance in Pali texts. The smooth flowing lines and the flexed posture of the idealised figure are remarkable.

Buddha footprints in stone and bronze which symbolise the presence of the master and reproduce that on Adam's Peak in Sri Lanka gained popularity in the reign of King Lithai (c 1347-68).

Rare **slate engravings** incised with scenes from the Jataka (the early lives of the Buddha) from Wat Si Chum attest to the mastery of Sukhothai craftsmen.

The admirable images of Hindu gods, Shiva and Vishnu *(BANGKOK, National Museum)*, cast in the Sukhothai period must have been inspired by a need for power consolidation and the belief in agricultural fertility associated with Hinduism.

Craftsmen who learned their trade from Chinese masters produced glazed ceramics – plain brown, white, celadon or with a painted design – known as **Sangkalok ware** at large kiln sites in Si Satchanalai and Sukhothai. Vessels and decorative pottery in animal and human shapes were exported far and wide, and artefacts recovered from sunken ships in the Gulf of Thailand and off the coast of Indonesia and The Philippines provide evidence of this important trading activity.

Thai names of Hindu Gods

Indra – **Phra In** – God of Thunder and storms who rides the three-headed elephant **Erawan** and whose emblem is the thunderbolt.

Brahma – **Phra Phrom** – The Creator depicted with four heads and four arms. His mount is a *hamsa* (a goose) and his attributes are a book, a vessel, a spoon and beads. His consort is **Sarawasti**, the goddess of learning and science.

Vishnu – **Phra Narai** – The Preserver portrayed with four arms. His vehicle is **Garuda**, a mythical figure half-man and half-bird and his emblems are a conch, a discus, a club and a lotus flower. His consort is **Lakshmi**, the goddess of prosperity, and his avatars (reincarnations) are Rama, Krishna, the Buddha. He is also represented as a hermit, a dwarf, a lion, a tortoise or a fish.

Shiva – **Phra Isuan** – The Destroyer depicted with a third eye in the middle of his forehead, a snake across his body, a crescent moon on his headdress. His emblems include a trident, a sword and a club and he is mounted on the bull **Nandi**. His consort is **Uma** (Parvati) or **Kali** and his son is **Ganesha** – a mythical being with a fat human body and an elephant head – who is the god of wisdom and the remover of obstacles. The lingam (Shiva linga) represents the creative force of Shiva.

The art of Ayutthaya (1350 to 1767) – Glowing contemporary descriptions by European visitors give only an inkling of the glory of Ayutthaya which boasted numerous glittering temples and magnificent palaces. Ayutthaya identified closely with artistic and cultural traditions inherited from Khmer civilisation and as its power grew its sovereigns promoted the notion of the divine king and became remote figures. The splendour and importance of temple buildings were testimonies of royal power.

The corn-cob multi-faceted **prang** or tower chedi (Wat Ratchaburana) evolved from the prasat or sanctuary-tower in Khmer architecture. The Sukhothai bell-shaped chedi remained a popular structure with pillars added at the base of the ringed finial, although the bell-shape later became smaller in size and rested on a taller base. Redented chedis (Wat Phu Khao Thong) with recessed, indented corners, and with faceted bell-shaped relic chambers marked a new trend. Viharas have typical concave bases, slit windows and pillars topped with lotus capitals.

The **U-Thong style** of sculpture which pre-dates the founding af Ayutthaya and developed in the central plain, was probably named after U-Thong in the province of Suphan Buri. King U-Thong (Ramathibodi I) moved his subjects from there to the site of Ayutthaya. Buddha images which reflect indigenous Buddhist beliefs and patterns reminiscent of Khmer influence belong to the first period (U-Thong A). There was a relatively rapid evolution just prior to the rise of Ayutthaya when the influence of Sukhothai Buddhist sculpture was evident (U-Thong B and C – *illustration*).

The Sukhothai influence prevailed until an idiom distinct to the Ayutthaya period was devised. This, however, lacked verve and fluency and produced images with a severe expression. In the 16C when Cambodia came under Ayutthaya sovereignty, Khmer art provided renewed inspiration to the artists who carved statues from sandstone with lines emphasising the lips and eyes and with the tracing of a delicate moustache.

Ayutthaya's association with Chiang Mai explains the popularity of **crowned Buddha images** which had appeared in the 15C. Initially these images were modestly decorated but later Buddhas in royal apparel *(see Wat Na Phra Men)* came to reflect the grandeur of the Ayutthaya kings. Massive statues *(see Wat Phanom Choeng)* also conveyed the importance of the realm. Figures of disciples were introduced as well as majestic statues of Hindu deities – Shiva *(KAMPHAENG PHET, National Museum)* – in a style similar to the Khmer-Bayon style (13C).

A large treasure including regalia, Buddha images and votive tablets recovered from the crypt of Wat Ratchaburana illustrates the exquisite artistry of the master-craftsmen.

Mural paintings found in the crypt of Wat Ratchaburana are rare survivals from the sack of the town by the Burmese in 1767. The style is reminiscent of Sukhothai art and shows Chinese craftsmanship. Other fine examples may be admired at Wat Yai Suwannaram and Wat Ko Kaeo Sutharam in Phetchaburi. The scenes include floral motifs and mythical animals painted in muted shades – white, yellow, rust, red – against a cream background. Gold leaf came into use at a later stage.

Other art objects typical of the Ayutthaya period include stuccoes, carved door panels, and especially the door panels inlaid with mother-of-pearl, scripture cabinets and boxes holding sacred manuscripts decorated with delicate paintings in gold on black lacquer.

Isan art – The northeast retains a Lao heritage besides its magnificent Khmer temples. The harmonious Lao **that** (stupa) – Wat Phra That Si Song Rak *(see LOEI);* Phra That Phanom, Phra That Tha U-Then, Phra That Renu Nakhon *(see NAKHON PHANOM);* simple **sim** (ubosot) – Phra That Kham Khen *(see KHON KAEN);* Wat Suwannawas *(see MAHASARAKHAM)* – often decorated with a sunburst motif, distinctive Buddha images with oval faces *(UBON RATCHATHANI, National Museum)*, and intricate **wood carving** are worthy of interest.

The Early Rattanakosin (Bangkok) period – After the fall of Ayutthaya (1767) King Taksin founded a new capital of the Siamese kingdom in Thonburi. In 1782 the centre of power moved to Bangkok under King Rama I of the Chakri dynasty. The architectural styles of the new capital city were in large part

B. Davies

Door Panels, Wat Po

61

Mural Painting

inherited from the former kingdom. Religious architectural achievements included the renowned **Wat Phra Kaeo★★★**, **Wat Po★★**, **Wat Suthat★★** and **Wat Arun★★** among others. Buddha images were collected from the ruined former capital and placed in the temples *(see Wat Po)* of the new capital to provide a sense of continuity. The new artistic patterns and designs were even more rigorous than the Ayutthaya models and are considered on the whole to be derivative and less successful.

King Rama III's reign (1824-51) marked the peak of the new kingdom. Crowned Buddha images with elaborate designs remained popular and reflected Bangkok's economic and artistic progress. Traditional Buddha statues, however, were produced in large numbers. Chinese artistic influence was evident during this reign as a result of the large volume of trade with China providing the country with huge benefits. Chinese-style paintings were commonly seen along with Thai traditional paintings.

Mural paintings which illustrate the story of Buddhism follow a set pattern which can be easily read by worshippers. The side walls of the ubosot are divided into two registers. Celestial beings worshipping the principal Buddha image appear on the upper register, and scenes from the life of the Buddha or from his previous lives *(Jataka)* are depicted in the lower section. Buddhist cosmology – The Three Worlds *(Traiphum)*: heaven, earth and hell – is illustrated on the west wall, and the Victory of the Buddha over Mara (the force of evil) on the east wall. Scenes are contained within zigzag lines, and entertaining vignettes of everyday life, animals, plants fill the remaining space. The characters show no expression, and emotions are conveyed by conventional gestures and postures which survive in classical dance. Foreign themes are introduced but are

---

Domestic architecture

Traditional wooden houses ideally suited to the climate are now rare as wood is an expensive commodity. Floating houses are still to be seen on waterways (Thonburi, Phitsanulok) but are usually covered with a corrugated-iron roof. In the central plain, houses with cool verandas, elegant pitched roofs, gables and bargeboards terminating in a curved motif are raised on piles for protection against floods and predators.

Wooden houses are easily dismantled and reerected in a different location, and extended by the addition of modules – **Jim Thompson's House★★**, **Ban Kamthieng★** (Siam Society) *(see BANGKOK)*. Royal houses are on the same plan but are more elaborate. The best examples are the **Tamnak Daeng★★** (Red House – National Museum Bangkok), the **Ho Phra Trai Pidok** (Wat Rakhang Khositaram, Thonburi – *see BANGKOK Environs*), the **Ruan Thap Khwan** (Phra Ratchawang Sanam Chang – *see NAKHON PATHOM*), and the houses in King Rama II Memorial Park *(see SAMUT SONGKHRAM)*.

The northern style presents variations such as walls leaning outwards and the distinctive V-shaped roof decoration known as *kalae*.

treated in traditional style. The artists use simple lines and large expanses of dark colours with no shading or perspective. The best examples are in Wat Phra Kaeo, Phra Thinang Phuttaisawan and the temples of Thonburi. **The Ramakien** (the Thai version of the Hindu epic The Ramayana – The Story of Rama, King of Ayodhaya) is depicted on the walls of the galleried cloister of Wat Phra Kaeo.

The decorative arts flourished: ivory carvings, lacquer ware, mother-of-pearl inlay and niello ware. Multi-coloured porcelain known as **Bencharong** is renowned.

Contemporary art – As the country opened once again to Western civilisation in the late 19C, Thai art was beginning to free itself from the religious frame of reference. The expansion of the capital led to the building of mansions in a composite style combining neo-Classical and neo-Baroque with traditional Thai elements. **Wat Benchamabopit★★** (Marble Temple), with its original plan, use of polychrome marble and stained glass, set new standards and has been reproduced throughout the land. Artists learnt the technique of perspective, and mural paintings became more vivid and included candid scenes and depictions of foreigners which reveal contemporary perceptions, as at **Wat Boworniwet★★**. The artist **Khrua in Khong** is the celebrated master of the period.

In recent years new trends have emerged which augur well for the flowering of the arts in Thailand. A modern architectural idiom featuring pure lines and sobriety draws inspiration from the past (**ubosot★★** of Wat Si Khom Kham, Phayao; Wat Sala Loi, Nakhon Ratchasima; Wat Phra Dhammakaya, Pathum Thani, **ubosot★★** of Wat Phra Kaeo, Chiang Rai). The mural paintings commissioned from modern artists break new ground *(see PHAYAO)*. As the population becomes more prosperous and better educated, interest in the arts and in the country's heritage continues to grow, and art faculties gain new adherents who will pursue their quest with increased enthusiasm.

The Thai Buddhist Tradition

Theravada Buddhism

Theravada Buddhism is the predominant form of Buddhism in South and Southeast Asia. It is the state religion in Thailand, where more than 90% of the population follow this tradition. Theravada, which means "Way of the Elders", spread south and southeastwards from India during the reign of the great emperor Ashoka (3C BC). Sometimes referred to as the Pali School (because of the Pali language of its scriptures), or Hinayana meaning "Little Vehicle" (which has a derogatory connotation), it is widely regarded as the most conservative and orthodox of Buddhist traditions which has managed best historically to preserve the Gautama Buddha's teachings.

This form of Buddhism differs from Mahayana and Tantric Buddhism by placing emphasis on: the historical Gautama Buddha as the single most important source of knowledge (as opposed to multiple Buddhas), the Buddha as a saint (rather than as a saviour), emancipation by self-effort (less by grace), the goal to become an arahant who emphasises attainment of wisdom and the termination of rebirths (instead of a bodhisattva who emphasises compassion and who postpones termination of rebirths).

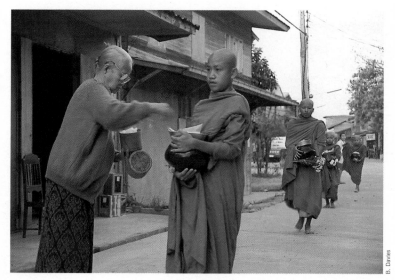

Alms round

The Buddha – Buddha means "awakened" or "enlightened one". The historical Siddhartha Gautama was known as Buddha by his disciples in acknowledgement of his superior spiritual achievement and his release from the cycle of existence. He is one of a range of named Buddhas in this world-system; prior to him there was Kassapa Buddha, and the next Buddha will be Maitreya Buddha. Buddhas mature by attaining perfections *(parami)*. Thus, in a previous life as the hermit Sumedha, Gautama took the vow to become a Buddha in the presence of a previous Buddha, namely Dipankara, and it is through his persistent efforts across lives that he attained the qualities necessary to become a Buddha. The core elements of his teachings are almost entirely practical instructions for living. Apart from his life as the Buddha, no less than 547 lives are attributed to him in the **Jatakas** (stories of his previous lives); the most important of these is his life as **Vessantara**, the penultimate life prior to becoming the Buddha during which, as a prince, he perfects generosity by giving away the kingdom's wealth including the white elephant.

Early life – Born at Kapilavastu (Rummindei in present-day Nepal), Gautama Buddha died at Kusinagara (Kasia in present-day India). Though there are various competing chronologies as to when he lived (ranging from 600 to 400 BC), according to Thai chronology he died (attained **nirvana**) in 543 BC. His life is punctuated by episodes commemorated in Thai literature, calendrical ritual, iconography and art.

His birth into a royal family as Siddhartha was accompanied by a prophecy that he would become either a universal Buddha or a universal king. He married at the age of 16 and, though his father did his utmost to have him grow up to be a universal king by making life pleasurable for him, he could not prevent Siddhartha, during his trips into the pleasure gardens, from seeing four omens – the old, the ill, the dead, and the monk. The first three omens made him question existence, and the last motivated him to accomplish the great renunciation; he left the palace at the age of 29 and became an ascetic in order to understand the nature of existence.

The Middle Way – He visited many teachers and practised various kinds of yoga and asceticism, including starvation. His ability to attain to the highest *jhanas* is represented in the **dhyanamudra**, in which he is seated in meditation with hands folded palm up in his lap.

However, he finally decided that he should practise the Middle Way in which he neither deprived his senses fully, nor indulged himself. After 49 days in contemplation, and subject to attacks and temptations by Mara, the Evil One, he accomplished the great enlightenment under the bodhi tree at Bodh Gaya at the age of 35. Though attained by his own efforts, this episode is often depicted as the Earth Goddess rescuing him from Mara by wringing her hair and causing a flood in witness to the Buddha's great merit (after every merit ceremony a water libation is performed which saturates her hair). This episode is depicted as the Buddha seated in the **bhumisparsa-mudra** position calling the earth to witness with one hand (mostly the right hand) touching the earth.

He preached his First Sermon to his first five disciples in which he characterised the nature of reality **(dhamma)** as a wheel; this sermon is therefore known as "the wheel of the law" **(dharmachakra)**. This is commonly represented by a Buddha with index finger and thumb holding the middle finger of the other hand. He established the monastic order **(sangha)**, and spent the rest of his life teaching his disciples and giving sermons through which he built up a large following.

He entered into **parinirvana** (a state beyond sentient existence) at the age of 80 after which his relics were distributed to various Buddhist kingdoms. This is commonly represented by a **reclining Buddha.** Buddhism spread after it was patronised by powerful rulers who extended its reach beyond India. At the Third Council in the 3C BC the Emperor Ashoka sent missionaries to outlying areas.

Temple offering

The Tripitaka

The Theravada Buddhist canonical texts alone are estimated at about 13 times the size of the Bible. Initially systematised during the third council held during Ashoka's reign (c 272-232 BC), these were orally transmitted until they were written down in Ceylon in the first century AD. The canon comprises the Three Baskets (Tripitaka): the code of discipline of the monastic order (Vinaya), the discourses and sermons of the Buddha (Sutta), and Buddhist philosophy (Abhidhamma). Several councils have been held to ensure the accuracy of the texts transmitted, but not all Buddhists recognise all of these.

The Buddha's teachings

Emphasis is neither on a godly figure nor on doctrine, but on one's own liberation through correct personal practice. The core elements of his teachings are mostly practical, which is why the correct way of treading the Buddhist path is sometimes characterised as orthopraxy (rightness of action) rather than orthodoxy.

The Four Noble Truths – Life is suffering (dukkha), suffering is caused by desire (samudaya), to uproot suffering is to uproot desire (nirodha), suffering may be ended by following the Noble Eightfold Path (magga).

The Noble Eightfold Path – Right view, right thought, right speech, right action, right livelihood, right effort, right mindfulness and right concentration. These are often summed up as comprising charity (dana), morality (sila) and mental culture (bhavana).

Five Precepts – The minimum everyday moral code of conduct for the laity includes prohibitions against killing, stealing, lying, indulging in illicit sexual intercourse and getting drunk. Higher precepts may be adopted on special festive days or by ordaining and following the monastic code of conduct.

The Three Jewels (Triratana) – The Buddha, Dhamma and the Sangha – are the main focus of worship.

Other systems

Buddhist monks do not provide support for the everyday material needs of the laity. There is therefore space in Thai life for other systems more closely geared to taking charge of such needs.

Brahmanism – Historically Brahmins have played a major role in maintaining the ritual purity of the king and in overseeing court and wedding ceremonial. Brahmins are still retained by the king and continue to have a reputation as the best ritual specialists for worldly ends.

Spirits – Buddhism does not deny the existence of either spirits (phi) or more highly placed deities (deva), and Buddhists observe an etiquette of behaviour towards spirits which ranges from acknowledgement to stronger forms of interaction. Their existence is acknowledged as standard by sending loving-kindness (metta) to all life in the world during the water libation ceremony, after offerings have been made to the monastic order. However, stronger forms of interaction include propitiation to prevent malice. Most homes, schools, offices and villages have shrines dedicated to guardian spirits (chao) which look like miniature houses on stilts.

Some practices go beyond propitiation and involve cults of mediums (khon song) and sorcerers (mae mod) which engage spirits with greater intensity. Many Thais regularly propitiate spirits in order to attain mundane goals in this world such as passing an exam or clinching a business deal. One of the most popular shrines in Bangkok is the **Erawan shrine** dedicated to the Hindu god Brahma at the Grand Hyatt-Erawan Hotel. It was erected by the owners after workers had suffered accidents.

Astrology – Astrologers are commonly consulted in Thailand. Though astrological skills are associated with Brahmanism, it is practised by non-Brahmins also. Monks too are known to use astrology.

The Thai Sangha and the King

The first duty of the king is charity, i.e. to be a righteous ruler and, as a buddha-to-be, to protect Buddhism and be a patron to the monastic order. Historians often see the structure of the sangha as responding to the measures of kings. Unlike the other Theravada Buddhist countries, where the link between king and sangha was broken, Thailand has never been colonised and the sangha has continued to be patronised by royalty.

In the past, weak kings had neither the means nor the desire to structure the monastic order. On the other hand, when strong kings appeared the sangha attained a more structured form. This happened under King Mongkut (Rama IV r 1851-1868), who, having been himself a monk for 27 years, founded the reformist **Dhammayutika** branch of the order which put greater emphasis on meditation and learning, and which began to operate alongside the Mahanikay Group, which had a closer involvement with the laity. He centralised the order and institutionalised strong links with the state. After three Sangha Acts, in particular the acts of 1902 and 1962, the sangha was left more centralised than ever before. Today success in the Buddhist order is measured by success in the centrally administered examination system. Also, ordination may not take place and monasteries may not be founded without permission from the ecclesiastical hierarchy, and civil authorities have the power to unfrock monks.

Buddhist cosmology and symbols

Buddhist cosmology posits innumerable world-systems, each with its own characteristics. Each has its own sun and moon, and its own earth with continents and oceans and with a central mountain **(Mount Meru)** which bridges heavens and hells. These are periodically destroyed in long cosmic cycles *(kalpa)*. The point about Buddhist cosmology is not that Buddhists believe that it exists in physical reality. However, it does form the backdrop for understanding Buddhist teachings on the nature of cause and effect and on the ethics of behaviour in an unlimited range of manifestations of life. Such cosmological ideas are implicated in architecture, in particular that of pagodas, and in the organisation of kingship.

Transmigration – Each world-system has 31 planes of existence through which life transmigrates with infinite rebirths. These planes of existence are divided into three. In the world of desire *(kama loka)* rebirths take place of animals, ghosts, humans and some deities, who feel pleasure and pain, and who have form and sensual desire. In the world of form *(rupa loka)* are to be found the 17 Brahman gods who have a subtle form and who, detached from sense-pleasure, experience the joy of four meditative absorptions. The formless world *(arupa loka)* has the higher gods who have no form and exist in pure mental state and contemplate infinity of space, of consciousness, of nothingness and the summit of existence.

The station of one's rebirth depends on the consequences of one's actions *(dharma)*: how one behaved in past lives has contributed to one's current make-up, and how one behaves today will have consequences for one's future state. The realms of the deities are pleasurable, and the lower realms are full of pain. However, only the human realm – which partakes of both pleasure and pain – permits full realisation of *nirvana* and of Buddhahood.

Ordination and monastic life

The monastic order *(sangha)* was founded to realise and preserve the Buddhist teachings. Monks have no particular duty to the laity and do not preside over life-cycle rituals. Nevertheless, the monastery has historically served as more than just a religious centre. Until state schools were set up it served as the educational infrastructure ranging from primary school to university and it was the recruiting ground for the king's ministers and servants. It continues to serve as a community resource in other ways. Monasteries often include pavilions *(sala)* where laity may meet in large assemblies, and monasteries may have motorised water pumps and deep water wells from which villagers benefit. Furthermore, it is through monastic networks that communities are helped in bridging links with provincial and national capitals outside their locality. There are approximately 28 000 monasteries *(wat)* in Thailand inhabited, depending on the period in the year, by as many as 200 000 monks and 100 000 novices and temple boys *(dek wat)* at any one time. Unlike monks in the Christian tradition, entry into the monastic order is not usually permanent but temporary, ranging from a few days to the rainy season *(phansa)* lasting from June to October. Annually during the rainy season as many as 1.5% of the male population will ordain temporarily, swelling the monastic population in the country by as much as 25-40%.

Meditation temples – Buddhist monasteries are often classified according to whether they focus on Buddhist practice *(patipatti)* or scriptural learning *(pariyatti)*, whether their vocation is one of insight contemplation *(vipassana-dhura)* or book learning *(gantha-dhura)*. This is often linked to village monasteries *(gamavasin)* as opposed to forest monasteries *(arannavasin)*. Generally, it is adherents to the latter who capture the imagination of Buddhists and who, renowned for their magical powers, provide the reformist element in the monastic order.

These reformers have historically come from northeast Thailand and include the famous forest monk **Phra Achan Mun** (1870-1949) who became a meditation teacher. His pupils include **Achan Cha**, whose monastery in Ubon Ratchatani attracted many foreign students of meditation. **Buddhadasa** (1906-93) was the most famous contemporary forest monk who had a great following in Thai intellectual circles, and whose students continue to be a reformist influence in Thailand. His monastery **Wat Suan Mokkha Phalaram** still serves as an international meditation centre approximately four kilometres from Chaiya. Adherents to the forest tradition have been major critics of economic and social development and have spoken out against destruction of the forest by developers. Some have even gone as far as ordaining trees with monastic robes to protect them from being cut down.

Monastic rules – In the monastery seniority is measured not by absolute age but by the level of ordination and the number of rainy seasons in the order. Temple boys *(dek wat)* are unordained and learn rudimentary reading and writing while attending to the

Buddhist monks

monks. Novices are most junior ordinands who keep a limited set of 70 Vinaya precepts. Monks are fully ordained from age 20 upwards and their life involves observance of an intricate set of 227 Vinaya rules of conduct, which strongly forbid sexual relations, stealing, homicide and claiming arahantship.

There is no concept such as church or parish in Buddhism, which would bind monks and laity into a single community. Monks have no compulsory duties towards the laity. However, as they are not allowed to make their living from a trade or to prepare their own food, they are dependent on the laity for all their requisites. In return for this support they perform limited ceremonies, such as giving sermons, reciting and chanting at events such as funerals, housewarming ceremonies, national holidays, and other occasions.

Ordination – Ordination into the order is one of the principal mechanisms for the transmission of Buddhist values and is considered highly meritorious for parents and for the ordinand. Few ordain permanently; those who do mostly come from a rural background. However, most men, in the course of their lives, will ordain for short periods of time often for personal reasons, usually when they want to purify themselves or to alleviate some personal suffering, but also to make merit for dead relatives. Leave of absence is normally granted from work for ordination. The ordination ceremony is traditionally elaborate including long festivities; however, it is sometimes also relatively simple with little ceremonial except the required question-answer sessions with monks at the ordination hall and shaving of the head.

A Thai **wat** is the focal point of a community and fulfils many functions: as a place of worship, an education centre, a meeting hall.

The main building within the religious compound is an **ubosot** or ordination hall which enshrines the main Buddha image and where are performed religious ceremonies, especially the ordination of monks. **Bai semas** or boundary stones sometimes in a leaf motif or housed in small pavilions mark the sacred area. A **vihara**, an assembly hall or a chapel, is a place of worship for lay people and monks which houses Buddha images. The rectangular buildings are covered with tiered sloping roofs adorned with **chofas** representing a stylised bird's head, and bargeboards terminating in a naga. The gable is decorated with intricate carving of deities, animals and foliage; lotus capitals crown tall columns.

Other structures commonly found are a **chedi**, generally a bell-shaped reliquary surmounted by a ringed finial which contains relics of the Buddha, holy men or royal personages; a **prang**, a Khmer-inspired reliquary-tower often in the form of a corn-cob; a **sala kanprien** which is an open-sided pavilion where monks assemble and where sermons are delivered to the faithful; and a **belltower**. A **ho trai** is a small building on piles used as a library for the sacred Buddhist texts. In earlier times the library was sited in the middle of a pond to safeguard the scriptures from vermin. Large temples usually have several viharas and salas. A wall separates the religious compound from the **monastic precinct** where are the monks' lodgings or cells **(kuti)**.

Buddhist temples and relics

The earliest Buddhist monuments were **stupas,** funeral mounds which contained the remains of kings and great men, including the Buddha and his disciples. Such stupas today represent the Buddha's death, but also are the image of the dynamic creation of the universe. As they were built mostly by kings, they are supernatural centres of the kingdom and legitimate royalty as an agent in maintaining the universe.

Everyday religious life and popular beliefs

Merit-making – Merit-making through charity *(dana)* is the most pervasive element in everyday life. It is thought to have the most immediate effect on one's future rebirth. This includes offerings of flowers and food early in the mornings to the Buddha and to the monks, and the distribution of merit *(bun)* attained to all sentient beings.

The most highly regarded merit-making activities are ordered approximately as follows: becoming a monk; building an entire monastery; having one's son ordained; visiting Buddhist shrines; contributing to the repair funds of a shrine; providing the *sangha* with sustenance; becoming a novice; attending duty days and observing the eight precepts; observing the five precepts at all times.

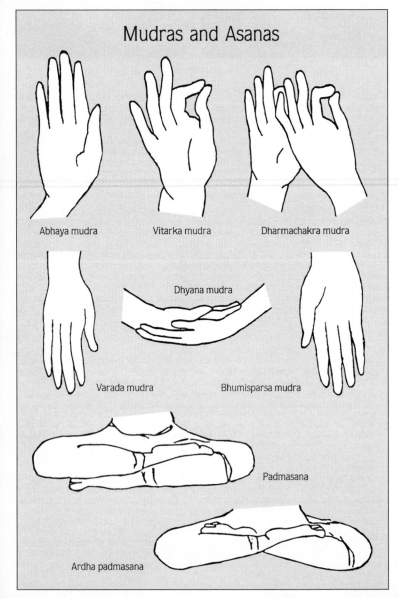

Mudras and Asanas

Abhaya mudra   Vitarka mudra   Dharmachakra mudra

Dhyana mudra

Varada mudra   Bhumisparsa mudra

Padmasana

Ardha padmasana

Meditation – Over the last few decades the popularity of meditation has greatly increased among the Thai Buddhist laity. This may be broadly classified into:
– concentration meditation *(samatha)* which focuses on attaining mastery and control over the body and on the acquisition of power. In the Thammakai movement a variant of this is practised.
– insight contemplation *(vipassana)* which focuses on the impermanence and insubstantiality of existence and the attainment of purity and wisdom. This technique has been influenced by the Burmese traditions, in particular by those of the Mahasi Sayadaw, whose student Achan Thong set up a main centre at Wat Rampung in Chiang Mai which is today the headquarters of several dozen centres spread across the country.

Amulets – It is striking how many people wear amulets in Thailand. Depicting the Buddha, the king or revered monks, and blessed by monks, these are worn to protect against disease and accidents.

Other religions

Mahayana Buddhism – The Chinese have been in Thailand predominantly as traders since at least the 15C. Their population is estimated at 12%. However, they have intermarried to such an extent that most Thai have some Chinese blood, and many have adopted the Theravada way of life. Their presence is strongest in the urban areas where their Mahayana temples are located, and their belief system is a mixture of Mahayana Buddhism, Confucian ethics, veneration of ancestors and Taoist supernaturalism.

Islam – The majority of the two million Thai Muslims living in the southern provinces of Thailand are of Sunni background, though some belong to the Shiite sect.

Animism – The tribal peoples numbering approximately 500 000 are often designated as "animist", meaning that they adhere to no universal religion but practise localised spirit cults.

Christianity – Christians have not been successful in converting Buddhists in Thailand, though they have had some success in the tribal regions. Today there are at most 200 000 Christians in Thailand. However, Christian priests have historically played a major role in making the Thai aware of Western values and in mediating between the Thai and foreigners.

Others – There are also some Hindus and Sikhs.

A Buddha image

After the death of the Buddha, aniconic symbols of significant events in his life were adopted: the lotus flower (birth); the wheel of the law (his teachings) – sometimes with a crouching deer to represent his first sermon at Deer Park in Sarnath; the Bodhi tree (enlightenment); the stupa (entry into *parinirvana*); the throne and footprint (his presence).

With the passage of time it became evident that a more tangible reminder was required by converts from other traditions, and in the 1C AD the first images of the Buddha were fashioned. A Buddha image is primarily an object of worship, and in order to stress the master's physical perfection and spiritual radiance, the Buddhist Sangha laid down strict iconographic rules for artists which were codified in Sanskrit and Pali texts: **mudras** (gestures), **asanas** (postures), **lakshanas** (32 major and 80 minor physical marks).

The most common **mudras** in Thailand are as follows, although variations exist:

Abhaya mudra – one or both hands raised with palm outwards and standing position. This denotes freedom from fear or reassurance.

Vitarka mudra – right arm raised, fingers pointing upwards and the thumb and forefinger forming a circle (wheel), left hand resting on lap (sitting position) or holding the flap of the robe (standing position). This signifies teaching.

Dharmachakra mudra – both hands at breast level, palms facing each other and thumb and forefinger forming a circle. This recalls the preaching of the first sermon and the setting in motion of the wheel of the Buddha's teachings.

Varada mudra – right hand facing downwards, palm out, sitting or standing position. A gesture of charity.

Dhyana mudra – both hands palms upwards and resting on lap. A gesture of meditation.

Bhumisparsa mudra – right hand placed on the knee and touching the ground, left hand on lap palm upward, seated position with legs crossed. This represents the Buddha's enlightenment and is known as calling the earth to witness or Victory over Mara as his resolve is tested by the temptations of Mara, the force of evil.

Buddha images are portrayed in four different postures: seated – **padmasana** (lotus) and **ardha padmasama** (half-lotus); walking; standing; and reclining (the Buddha attaining *parinirvana*).

Language and Literature

Thai, also known as Siamese, belongs to the Sino-Tibetan group of languages. Tonal, mono-syllabic and uninflected, it includes many words from Pali and Sanskrit to which it is closely related. Differentiating high, middle, low, rising and falling tones is crucial to meaning. Thus *mai mai mai mai mai*, pronounced in the correct manner, means "New wood doesn't burn does it?" Vocabulary tends towards the simplistic. Foreign people when angry have *chai ron* (hot heart). By contrast the Thai people tend towards *chai yen* (a cool heart).

The romanisation of Thai words is based on phonetic transcription. This accounts for the many variations in spelling which may be confusing to foreign visitors.

Grammatically Thai is considerably easier than European languages. Tenses are indicated by auxiliaries used before the verb, and there are no prefixes, plurals or verb conjugations. Each of Thailand's major regions has its own dialect, often spoken instead of the national language. Khmer may also be used and in some dialects, seven tones are used to differentiate meaning. Several speech levels are used in spoken Thai depending on age, sex and various social factors. A special language based on Sanskrit, Pali and Khmer is used to address royalty.

Letters

The people had an oral tradition until the 13C when King Ram Kamhaeng of Sukhothai devised a Thai script based on Sanskrit and using Khmer characters. It consists of symbols for 44 consonants and 32 vowels, of which 14 are simple vowels and the rest diphthongs. Words, often freely borrowed from other languages, are written from left to right without spaces.

A **stone inscription** (1283 – *in National Museum, BANGKOK*) by King Ram Kamhaeng is the earliest written evidence. The Suphasit Phra Ruang (Maxims of King Ruang) paints a picture of a prosperous kingdom ruled by a just and benign monarch. The aristocracy and the monks were instructed in the art of writing but original manuscripts inscribed on palm leaves have perished. Buddhist texts in prose or verse that survive are copies of copies. The **Traiphum Phra Ruang** (The Three Worlds of King Ruang), an important work on Buddhist cosmology dealing with the three Buddhist realms – heaven, earth and hell – was probably written by King Li Thai (1347-74).

The Hindu epic, the Ramayana, inspired a seminal work, **The Ramakien,** in which the odyssey of Rama, the King of Ayodhya, is transposed into a Thai context. The influence of this classic tale is evident from the name adopted by the new kingdom which rose to power in the mid-14C. Early Thai versions of the Ramayana were lost when the Burmese ransacked Ayutthaya in 1767. The earliest surviving interpretation is by King Taksin. A very fine later version is deemed to be the work of King Rama I.

The arts flourished during the Ayutthaya period and new verse forms – *chan, kap, khlong, klon, rai* – evolved. Long narrative poems known as **nirat** which were popular in the late 17C sing the pain of absence or separation. Rama II, a talented sovereign versed in the arts, wrote poetry and staged a theatrical presentation of **Inao**, a Javanese tale. The 18C-19C, however, are marked by a versatile poet, **Sunthorn Phu** (1786-1855), who composed romantic poems. **Phra Aphaimani** and *Khun Chang Khun Phaen* rank among his masterpieces; the latter conveys a picture of life in the early 19C.

20C works are characterised by the influence of western literature. Rama VI (1910-25) is the author of translations and adaptations of the dramatic works of Shakespeare. The clash of Thai and Western cultures and the political upheavals of the 1930s and the 1950s to the present day have inspired radical novelists. Love, romance and dreams are, however, the common themes of popular literature. The most successful works are *Si Phaen Din* (The four reigns) and *Phai Daeng* (Red Bamboo) by Mom Kukrit Pramoj. Many Thai novels have been translated into English.

Comics and romantic stories in pictures are in great demand. Several newspapers are published including the English-language *Bangkok Times, Bangkok Post* and *The Nation*.

The Ramakien

In the Thai version of the Ramayana, Ram (Rama), the king of Ayodhaya, renounces his throne after being caught in a web of court intrigue. He goes into exile with his wife Seeda (Sita) and his devoted ally Hanuman (the monkey god) and they embark on a long and difficult journey. In the second part of the epic Seeda is abducted by the evil king Ravana and Ram wages war against and defeats the demons of Langka island with the help of Hanuman and his band of monkeys. In the third part Seeda is reunited with her spouse with the help of the gods. Other storylines are interwoven which bring into play historical events, folk tales, local customs and a multitude of relevant themes in order to fire the imagination of the Thai masses.

Cultural and Leisure Pursuits

The rich culture of Thailand is celebrated with great pride throughout the land. The pomp of traditional ceremonial occasions enhanced by the splendid costumes reflects the glory of the kingdom. Royal patronage ensures the survival of the country's heritage and encourages the active participation of the population. The colourful spectacle and the vibrant atmosphere rank among the most memorable attractions of Thailand.

Classical Dance – Thai classical dance represents one of the most sophisticated forms of artistic expression. The most popular classical dances are the **khon,** traditionally performed by men concealed behind brightly-coloured ornate masks, and the **lakhon** dances, performed by women.

The dances are taken from the **Ramakien,** the epic Thai version of the Hindu Ramayana, which tells of the triumph of King Rama over the forces of evil. In these highly stylised dances, the characters do not speak, each prescribed movement of the hand or foot indicating a subtle change of mood or feeling. Narrative verses accompany the performance. The glorious costumes made of brocade and decorated with jewels complement the artistic achievement.

Dancers

Music – Thai classical music has been heavily influenced by Javanese, Indian, Burmese and Khmer musical traditions. Orchestras, known as **piphat,** consist of between five and 20 woodwind and percussion instruments. These include an oboe-like instrument known as the *peenai,* an assortment of finger cymbals known as *ching,* a series of semicircular gongs called *kong wong yai* and a curved wooden xylophone called a *ranart.* The piphat has few similarities with Western music owing to its complex set of musical scales.

Modern Thai music has less to recommend it. It is generally a mixture of heavy rock'-n'-roll, country music and love songs, with almost nothing of local distinction. Loud pop-music is played everywhere and karaoke clubs are very popular.

Puppets – Puppets *(nang yai)* and marionettes *(hun Krabok)* were important forms of entertainment during the Ayutthayan period, when they were used to enact classical stories like the Ramayana in the theatre and royal courts. There is a fine collection of puppets which were used for court performances during the reigns of Rama V and VI, at the National Museum in Bangkok. The **shadow-play** puppets made from cowhide are still to be found in the southern province of Nakhon Si Thammarat with their finely wrought depictions and intricate design. At rare public performances, they are mounted on wooden sticks and manipulated from behind a backlit white screen.

71

Musicians

Theatre – The most popular form of theatre in Thailand is a mixture of slapstick comedy and sexual innuendo known as the **likay**. Performed by men dressed up as women, it bears a close resemblance to pantomime. The stories are based on legends or events of daily life which concern the people. Typically, troupes of actors travel from town to town entertaining their audiences with a potent combination of bawdy jokes and dances. These days, the number of troupes has fallen although they can still be seen during festivals in several parts of the country, especially the poorer northeast.

Leisure

When they are not working, Thais are normally playing. It may be a game of football, a display of Thai-style boxing or a get-together over a drink. The only requirement is that it is *sanuk* (good fun).

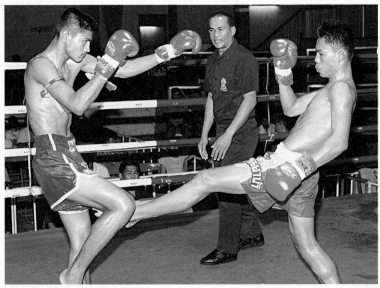

Thai Boxing

Sports – From football to boxing and from snooker to golf, Thais are avid sports followers. At night, they crowd around televisions to watch the latest boxing match, while at weekends they flock to Sanam Luang to fly their kites. **Muay Thai** or Thai boxing attracts the most attention. Like normal boxing, fighters can use their gloves, but they are also allowed to use their feet or any other part of the body except the head.

Takraw, a ball game which probably dates back to the early 17C, is no less popular. Groups of players use their feet, knees, elbows and heads – but never their hands – to knock a rattan ball from one player to the next without it touching the ground.

Kite Flying – Kite flying, introduced in Ayutthayan times to spur the rains, has long since become a competitive sport. Two kites are used in a symbolic battle of the sexes. The giant male kite **chula** tries to snare the more agile diamond-shaped female kite **pakpao** with a bamboo hook and force it down into his territory. The spectacle is held at Sanam Luang, opposite Bangkok's Grand Palace, on most weekends in the dry season.

Fish Fighting – A rare breed of fish known as the **pla kat** provides the Thai with a source of frenzied betting. The fish are about 5cm long and only the males take part in the fights. Although outlawed, fish fighting is favoured among the local people both in Bangkok and in the provinces. Two fish with short sturdy round fins are put into a tank whereupon they change colour and attack one another. The contest is over when one of the fish dies or takes refuge in a corner.

Tourism Authority of Thailand

Kites, Sanam Luang, Bangkok

Festivals

The natural sense of fun of the population is given free rein during the numerous festivals which are celebrated with great zest throughout the year. These joyful occasions provide a unique opportunity to appreciate the age-old traditions which create a powerful bond among the people. The birthdays of the King (5 December) and of the Queen (13 August) are celebrated amid great popular rejoicing.

Festivals are listed in the Practical Information chapter at the end of the guide.

Songkran *(April)*, the Water Festival, marks the beginning of the Buddhist year and is a very festive occasion. The whole population joins in the fun and enjoys dousing passersby with water. In Bangkok the Phra Phuttha Sihing is taken from the Phra Thinang Phutthaisawan to the Sanam Luang where the people make libations to the sacred image and offer food to the monks. In the past, fish and caged birds were set free.

The celebrations are even more animated in Chiang Mai and last up to seven days. A grand offering of food is made to the monks at Pratu Thapae. A procession is headed by the Phra Phuttha Sihing Buddha image and the Venerable Abbot, followed by numerous Buddha images from other local communities.

Each temple sends dancers and folk music groups. A special Warrior Drum Dance *(Klong Sabat Chai)* is performed. Residents and other participants from schools, colleges and organisations wear the traditional blue peasant dress or period costumes inspired from the mural paintings in Phra Wihan Lai Kam. Groups drive round the town in trucks and give everyone a good soaking.

The festive atmosphere can be enjoyed at all the main temples in the north and northeast.

Songkran Festival

Loy Krathong *(November)* which pays homage to the water spirits and marks the end of the rainy season is one of the most romantic festivals, held on the night of the full moon in November. Krathongs are leaf or paper floats beautifully decorated with flowers, lit candles and incense sticks, set adrift on rivers and canals to honour the water spirits and wash away the sins of the previous year. In Bangkok the main venue is the Mae Nam Chao Phraya.

The most romantic setting, however, is Sukhothai where the festival originated in the 13C. A Son et Lumière show relates the story of Nang Nophamas, a royal consort, who created the first krathong for King Ram Kamhaeng as an offering to the "Mother of Waters" *(Mae Nam)* for past lapses. The monuments are lit up by flickering lights and the atmosphere is magical.

The residents of Chiang Mai hold a lively festival with a parade of a Giant Krathong based on various themes. The crowning of Miss Nophamas (Lotus) is the highlight of a beauty contest. A procession of decorated floats with giant krathongs and partici-pants in colourful costumes wends its way across town. Fireworks, fire crackers and hot-air balloons create a lively atmosphere, especially along Thanon Thapae to the Mae Ping which is filled with illuminated krathongs. Theatrical shows and musical performances including lanna folk songs are held along the riverside.

The **Royal Ploughing Ceremony** *(May)* is an ancient Indian ceremony of Brahmanic origin which survives only in Thailand. It marks the beginning of the rains when planting starts in the rice paddies. In the past the king took part in ploughing a field to ensure the fecundity of the soil and an abundant harvest. The ceremony now takes place at Sanam Luang in Bangkok. The soil is watered for several days

Loy Krathong Festival

74

in advance. The King presides over the ceremony which is attended by members of the Royal Family. Participants wearing ornate traditional costumes drive the team of sacred water-buffaloes. The team leader (Phraya Raekna) selects one of three pieces of cloth of different length, and based on his choice Brahmanic astrologers make predictions on whether it will be a time of drought or of plenty. After the soil has been ploughed, the rice is sown. Then the King presents awards to farmers who have achieved the highest yields in the previous year. After the ceremony there is a free-for-all as spectators attempt to retrieve the rice grains from the freshly turned ground and end up covered with mud.

Thot Kathin *(October)*, which takes place towards the end of the lunar calendar (mid-11 to mid-12 lunar month), marks the end of Buddhist Lent when new robes and gifts are presented to the monks. A Kathin is literally a set of saffron robes presented on a beautifully decorated tray.

Kathin Luang or Royal Kathin is performed by the King and the Royal Family at the main royal temples in Bangkok. Government departments and other important collectivities also make large donations and organise prestigious presentations. In special celebration years the King rides to Wat Arun in a spectacular ceremonial procession of royal barges.

As temples are allowed to accept only one kathin a year, prosperous families often reserve the right to make a presentation. Other donors can then make a contribution to the main donation.

Migrant workers usually return home for this festival which is an occasion of great rejoicing. Colourful parades are held and boat racing takes place on the waterways, in particular at Nan, Phitsanulok and Nakhon Phanom.

Shadow puppets

B. Davies

The **Makha Bucha Festival** *(January)* commemorates the first sermon of the Buddha to his disciples who had come together spontaneously. On the night of the full moon of the third lunar month the faithful take part in candle-lit processions around the temple.

The **Flower Festival** *(February)* in Chiang Mai is a riot of colour and rejoicing. The highlights are a procession of splendid floats decked with flowers, beauty contests and the election of the Festival Queen.

Food and Drink

To find a place to eat turn to the blue pages in selected chapters in the Sights section and consult the list of addresses – restaurants, brasseries, cafés – chosen to suit a variety of tastes and budgets.

The culinary excellence of Thailand wins high praise from gastronomes everywhere. The delicious fare, the exquisite presentation of the dishes with finely carved vegetables and fruits, and the harmony of colours and textures are a feast for the senses.

A simple life – King Ram Kamhaeng's stone inscription (13C) celebrates the bountifulness of nature: "In the water there is fish, in the fields there is rice". Early accounts mention the simple, wholesome fare enjoyed by the people – rice with dried or salted fish and vegetables seasoned with spices and the pungent fish sauce. Spices – cloves, nutmeg – were introduced as a result of trade with the East and the large Asian communities which had settled in Ayutthaya. Chillies which originate in South America were probably brought in the 16C by the Portuguese. The latter's influence is still evident today in some Thai desserts based on sugar and egg yolk.

Appetizing Thai meal

Palace cuisine – During the Ayutthaya period a refined type of cuisine prevailed in noble households. Aristocratic ladies and their attendants perfected their skills in floral decoration, in the art of fruit and vegetable carving and in the preparation of elaborate dishes combining subtle flavours and visual appeal. This required much skill and long hours of preparation. The delectable fare was complemented by fine porcelain, in particular Bencharong (five-coloured) ware. This tradition survives in prosperous Thai homes and in the elegant surroundings of high-class establishments.

A blend of flavours – Chinese, Indian and Malayan influences have contributed to the culinary sophistication of Thailand. From spicy green curries to steamed fish with lemon and sizzling barbecued chicken, Thai food offers a subtle blend of flavours. Contrary to popular belief, it is not inevitably hot and there is a host of less piquant or plain dishes served with rice and vegetables. Diners who are wary of chillies should specify *"mai pet"* (not hot) when ordering.

Thai cooking also combines a wealth and breadth of spices that can be found in few other cuisines around the world. Galangal, a spice resonant of ginger, provides a delicious blend of hot and sweet flavours. Tamarind adds fruitiness, and coriander a wonderful sweet aromatic essence. Ginger, sweet basil, garlic, kaffir-lime leaves, lime and lemon grass give extra pungency.

To these spices are added up to 40 different varieties of chilli ranging from the wonderfully-named *prik khi nu* (bird's eye peppers) to the fearsome *prik chi fa.*

All over the country there is a rich base of ingredients brought fresh from the market place: chicken, beef, pork, fish and seafood are merely the basics. There is a great variety of tropical vegetables: morning glory (water convolvulus), yard-long beans, green papaya, purple aubergine, exotic mushrooms and black peppercorns. Common vegetables include cabbages, carrots, spring onions, tomatoes and bamboo shoots.

Even when it comes to rice, Thais are perfectionists. The country produces over 50 different kinds of rice. But while Thailand is the largest exporter of rice in the world, it still keeps the best varieties for itself in the belief that most foreigners cannot appreciate the difference. The delicate flavour of jasmine rice is highly prized.

For visitors who prefer more familiar fare, Bangkok has some of the finest international restaurants in the world serving French, Italian, German, Japanese, Indian and Vietnamese food. Prices are reasonable by comparison with European countries and standards of cleanliness and service extremely high.

A Typical Meal

A typical Thai meal will consist of a curry, a steamed dish, a fried delicacy, a spicy salad, a soup and a plate of vegetables. The dishes will also combine beef, pork, chicken, fish and seafood. All the dishes are generally served together and are accompanied by plain rice *(khao suay)* or occasionally by noodles. A variety of sauces and condiments is added such as *nam pla*, a pungent sauce made from fermented fish, *nam phrik* with chopped chillies as well as pickled or fresh garlic, cucumbers, spring onions and fresh chillies.

Tom yam, a clear spicy soup, is a pungent broth made with ginger root, onions, tomatoes and chillies, to which are added lime juice and lemon grass. It can be cooked with either shrimp or seafood, chicken, beef or pork. Probably the most popular dish to order is *tom yam kung*, which is served with prawns. *Tom ka kai* is a creamy soup with coconut milk and chicken.

Yam, a spicy salad made from either meat or seafood, is generally accompanied by lettuce, garlic, chillies and lemon, and tends to be rather hot.

There are different kinds of curries which are all delicious. *Kaeng khieo wan*, a fragrant creamy curry, is a favourite which combines the pungency of chillies with the blandness of coconut milk and baby aubergines. **Kaeng phet pet yang**, a spicy duck curry, is a great delicacy.

There is an amazing variety of fresh fish: sea bass, tuna fish, catfish, eels, prawns, squid, mussels, clams and the famous Phuket Lobster. Order *pla thot* for fried fish and *pla neung* for steamed fish. Other delicacies include *pla phat king*, which is fish cooked with ginger, and *pla priowan*, a sweet and sour fish.

Vegetarians can also have a field day in Thailand. Tofu pronounced *tao hu* can be found in almost any restaurant, generally served in rich gravy or fried with oyster sauce. *Pak bung fai daeng* which is morning glory stir-fried in a wok is also popular. For a plate of mixed vegetables, simply ask for *phat phak ruam*, which is usually a variety of French beans, cabbage, carrots, tomatoes and mushrooms fried in oyster sauce.

There are plenty of other staple dishes which are served in most Western-style restaurants. Those include *khao phat* (fried rice), *phat thai* (Thai-style fried rice noodles) and *po pra* (spring rolls).

Regional Variations

The remarkable diversity of Thai food is best appreciated by visiting the regions. The spicy Isan food reflects the amazing ingenuity and imagination of the people of the arid northeast and has brought the region culinary fame throughout the kingdom.

Larb is one of the most common dishes. Generally made from a combination of minced beef or pork mixed with shallots, chilli peppers and coriander, it is typically accompanied by sliced cabbage and mint leaves. Another local favourite is **namtok**, which consists

Succulent fruits

Light bite Thai-style

of very spicy beef and is usually served with sticky or glutinous rice known as *khao nieo*. Spicy Isan sausages and grilled chicken with a piquant sauce are delicious.

A speciality is **som tam**, a salad that combines shredded green papaya with dried shrimps, lemon juice, fish sauce, garlic and lashings of chillies. Adventurous diners can also try local delicacies such as fried crickets, chicken claws and snail curry.

Northern Thailand also has its own distinctive cuisine, often influenced by neighbouring Burma. *Kaeng hang le* is a thick pork curry infused with garlic and ginger. *Khao soi* is a popular dish made from noodles and curried sauces.

The traditional way of dining in the north, however, is the **Kantoke** dinner served at a low round table. It comprises a selection of dishes including *kaeng kai*, a chicken curry, *cap moo*, a type of crispy pork skin, and *nam prik ong*, a local speciality made from pork, tomatoes, onions and chillies, and glutinous rice. Several restaurants in Chiang Mai specialise in Kantoke dinners. They are generally geared towards tourists and feature classical dances and hill-tribe shows.

The South, where the cuisine has been influenced by Muslim-style cooking, claims to serve the hottest food. *Kaeng tai pla* or fish-kidney curry is a fiery dish whereas *kaeng Mussaman* is an Indian-style curry made with either beef or chicken. Malay fish curries are often garnished with fresh fruit.

With its vast coastal waters and countless fishing villages, this is also the region to eat freshly cooked lobster, steamed crab and mussels, fried squid as well as the delicious *tom ka kung*, made with prawns cooked in coconut milk with galangal root – sometimes served in a coconut shell.

Sweetmeats

Thai desserts are works of art in their own right. Widely referred to as *khanom*, they are brightly coloured, beautifully presented and almost always sweet. Rice cakes, coconut custards *(sangkaya ma phrao)*, egg-yolk cakes, jellies, sweet palm kernels *(luuk taan cheuam)* and sweet vermicelli in coconut milk are just some of the delicacies. Ornamental fruits made from bean paste may also be used for special occasions. Some are coloured with food dyes and soaked in jasmine or other aromatic flowers to provide a pleasing fragrance. Diners who prefer something less sweet, but equally exotic, should ask for *pon la mai*. This is a selection of fresh fruits ranging from pineapple *(sapparot)*, papaya *(malakaw)*, to rambuttans *(ngaw)*, longans *(lamyai)*, water-melon *(teng moh)*, mangoes *(mamuang)*, bananas *(kluay)*. In season the durian *(thurian)* is also on offer. This fruit arouses strong passions. Some who dislike it describe it as a strong Camembert cheese on account of its strong smell and creamy texture but for *aficionados* it is the king of Thai fruits.

Table Etiquette

A Thai meal is a social occasion. A selection of dishes and condiments is placed around a large bowl of rice and guests serve themselves to a little of everything in any order. It is customary for hosts to serve their guests from dishes placed out of reach rather than pass the plate around, and for hosts or waiters to serve more food to diners unless they indicate clearly that they have finished their meal. Forks and spoons are offered as a rule; knives are not required as Thai food is usually cut into bite-sized pieces. In the north and northeast, it is proper to use one's fingers to form balls of glutinous rice which are then dipped in the sauces.

Markets

Thais enjoy their food with the same compulsive exuberance with which they appreciate life itself. They like it spicy and they like a constant supply of it.

As a result there has sprung up a veritable industry providing them with sustenance, often 24 hours a day. In the street markets, vendors offer pieces of meat or chicken on skewers cooked over red hot coals, great vats of curried chicken, beef or pork as well as the popular barbecued chicken known as *kai yang*. Almost without exception the food is delicious. Visitors newly arrived in the country, however, should go easy to begin with, as market food can cause gastric problems.

Noodle stalls *(ran kuay thieo)*, simple Chinese-style kitchens, offer *kuay thieo*, a soup made from boiling stock and noodles with chicken or fish balls to which are added vinegar with sliced chilli, a small spoonful of sugar, and ground peanuts.

Diners who do not speak enough Thai to order can simply point to the dish that takes their fancy and sit down at a nearby table. It is extremely rare that the vendors will overcharge tourists.

Drink

Local people generally drink whisky or beer to accompany their food. Local whisky, including the potent Mekong, is made from fermented rice or sugar-cane and tastes similar to rum. Scotch whisky, however, is favoured by the fashionable crowd. There are excellent European-style lagers brewed locally as well as Singha, a distinctly Thai beer, which are very popular. All kinds of soft drinks including the familiar brands are sold in Thailand. Wines from Australia and Europe are on offer in most European restaurants at a price. They are also available in almost all the business-class hotels as well as the major supermarkets. A dry white wine made from the Chenin blanc grape is produced in Loei in the northeast. It marks the initial achievement of a fledgeling local wine industry.

Bottled water is available from many shops and restaurants. *Nam yen* means cold water. In view of the heat, it is advisable to drink at least two litres a day. Ice is added to most drinks. Ice cubes made from purified water are fine, but ice chipped from large blocks should be avoided.

Phanaeng Kai Dry Chicken Curry (3-4 people)

Place sliced chicken (3 pieces) in a saucepan over a medium heat. Add 1 cup of coconut cream and bring to the boil, then simmer until the meat is tender. Remove the chicken and leave the coconut cream to simmer stirring the sauce from time to time. Then blend 1/4 cup of curry paste and reduce the sauce by half. Add the cooked chicken, 1/4 cup of roasted peanuts coarsely ground, 2 tablespoons of palm sugar and 2 tablespoons of fish sauce. Mix well until the sauce is thick and creamy. Garnish with fresh basil and serve.

Tom Yam Kung Spicy Prawn Soup with Lemon Grass (2 people)

Bring 2 cups of water or chicken stock to the boil. Add 1 chopped shallot, lemon grass (1 stalk cut and pounded), 2 slices of fresh or dried galangal and 3 kaffir-lime leaves and return to the boil. Add 4-5 medium-sized prawns and 150g of mushrooms, simmer for 3 minutes until the prawns are cooked, then add half a tablespoon of fish sauce, lime juice to taste and 2-3 chopped chillies. Remove from the heat and garnish with fresh coriander and spring onions. Serve hot.

Tom Yam Kung

Glossary

amphoe – district

antarala – passage between the antechamber and sanctuary of a Khmer temple

ao – bay

apsara – celestial dancer, a decorative element of temples

arahant – a person who has attained perfection

Avalokitesvara – a compassionate Bodhisattva *(below)* in Mahayana Buddhism, also known as Amitabha and Lokesvera

bai sema – leaf-shaped stone marking the sacred precinct of the ubosot and also called boundary stone ; often decorated with carvings and raised on pedestals or in pavilions

ban – village, hamlet

baray – pond or reservoir for irrigation near a Khmer temple

bikkhu – Buddhist monk

bodhi – *ficus religiosa* – tree under which the Buddha attained enlightenment

Bodhisattva – a future Buddha, an enlightened being who delays nirvana in order to help mankind in their quest for enlightenment

bot – *see* ubosot

bung – lake, pond

buri – town

changwat – province

chedi – monument enshrining relics; reliquary

chofa – stylised bird decoration on the roof of temple buildings

dhamma – Buddhist teaching

dharmachakra – wheel of the law

doi – mountain

farang – foreigner, derivation of *farangse* – français (French)

garuda – mythical animal with human trunk and arms, head, wings and claws of a bird of prey, the mount of the Hindu deity Vishnu

gopura – doorway often with inner galleries giving access to Khmer temples

hamsa – mythical bird, symbol of the Hindu deity Brahma

hang yao – long-tail boat

hat – beach

heo – waterfall

ho trai – small pavilion housing the sacred scriptures often built on stilts in the middle of a pond to protect the manuscripts from vermin, library

kaeng – rapids

kala – a demon with grinning face and protruding eyes, a door guardian; *see* makara

kamphaeng – wall

khan thuai – ornamental roof brackets in temple buildings

khao – peak, mountain

khlong – canal, waterway

khuan – dam

kinari – a mythical figure half-bird, half human

king-amphoe – sub-district

ko – island

ku – ornate altar with the Buddha image enshrined in a chamber

kuti – monastic cells or temple lodgings

laem – headland, cape

lak muang – foundation stone; guardian spirit

linga – phallic symbol symbolising the Hindu trinity, Brahma, Shiva and Vishnu

mae nam – river

makara – a mythical monster with the body of a dolphin, a crocodile's head and an elephant's head; it is often depicted as a door guardian on lintels together with the kala

mandapa – antechamber of sanctuary of Khmer temple

Mara – the force of evil

Meru – the home of the gods in Hindu and Buddhist cosmology

mohom – loose blue cotton shirt worn by peasants

mondop – square building often crowned by a tiered roof, and housing an object of worship, generally a Buddha footprint

mu ban – *see* ban

mu ko – archipelago

muang – town, city

mudra – hand gesture in Buddhist iconography

naga – mythical 5- or 7-headed snake which is believed to have raised the meditating Buddha from the ground on its coiled body and sheltered the master from the rain under its hood

nakhon – town, city

nam phu ron – hot springs

nam tok – waterfall

nang – shadow play

nirvana – end of the cycle of rebirth

paknam – estuary

Pali – Indian language of sacred texts of Theravada Buddhism

pha – cliff

pha sin – length of cloth wrapped around the waist, a type of sarong

phi – spirit

pho, ton pho – *see* bodhi

phra that – reliquary or temple enshrining relics of the Buddha

phu, phu khao – hill, mountain

pom – fort

prang – tower shaped like a corn-cob decorated with stucco; one or more staircases lead to a shrine or shrines for images of the Buddha

prasat, prasat hin – Khmer stone castle, sanctuary tower

pratu – gate

rat, ratcha (prefix) – royal

richi, russi, reussi – hermit, ascetic

sala – meeting hall, pavilion or shelter

sala kanprien – Buddhist lecture hall, often used as assembly hall where sermons can be held

sanuk – fun

saphan – bridge

sathani – station

sema – *see* bai sema

sim – ordination hall *(ubosot)* of Lao temple

simha – mythical lion

singha – *see* simha

soi – street, alleyway

stupa – *see* chedi

suan – garden

talat – market

tambon – sub-district

tantima – mythical bird

Tavatimsa – heaven, abode of the 33 Hindu gods at the summit of Mount Meru

tha – pier, jetty

thale – sea

thale sap – lagoon

tham – cave

thanon – street, road

that – reliquary, a spire or domed structure for Buddhist relics found in the northeast

thong – flag

thung – banner

thung kradang – wooden banner common in Lanna and Isan art

Traiphum – the three worlds – heaven, hell, earth – of Buddhist cosmology

Trimurti – the Hindu Trinity – Brahma, Vishnu, Shiva

Tripitaka – the Pali canon of Theravada Buddhism

ubosot – sanctuary or main chapel where are held ordination and other ceremonies

urna – a curl on the Buddha's forehead, a distinctive mark

vihara – assembly hall, chapel

wai – traditional Thai greeting

wat – temple, temple compound

wiang – fortified town

wihan – *see* vihara

yaksa – mythical demon

Wat Phra Kaeo, Bangkok

Ph. Benet

Sights

ANG THONG

Ang Thong – Population 53 058
Michelin Atlas p 24 or Map 965 – G 5

Ang Thong is a typical sleepy capital of a small agricultural province on the west bank of the Mae Nam Chao Phraya. Its main attraction lies in the temples dotted in the flat plain where verdant rice paddies stretch to the far horizon. It is also a fruit-growing and fish-breeding area. The region is famous for wickerware, weaving and drums.

EXCURSIONS

Wat Chaiyo Wora Wihan – *16km north by 309, turn left at Km 72.* The original plan of the temple with its communicating ubosot and vihara is enhanced by the single façade, the triple-tiered roof, square pillars and finely carved gables and pediments. A venerated **seated Buddha** in the attitude of meditation is enshrined in the vihara and the ubosot is decorated with charming frescoes.

Wat Pa Mok – *12km south by 309. Access by boat from Wat Phinit Thamsan.* According to a chronicle King Naresuan of Ayutthaya visited the monastery in the late 16C on his way to do battle with the Burmese. In the two viharas are a 15C reclining Buddha (22m long) and remains of wall paintings.

Wat Pho Tong – *30km northwest by 3064, turn left at Km 45-46 opposite Wat Thaklong Wittiyaram into 3454.* In the middle of a field stands an elegant ruined pavilion, **Phra Tamnak Khamyat,** which served as the residence of Prince Uthumphon of Ayutthaya (mid 18C) during his monkhood. The pointed arches, keel-shaped base, stucco decoration, wooden window frames are typical of the late-Ayutthaya style. Also of note are the porch adorned with pilasters capped with lotus capitals, and the niches by the door inside the building.

Wat Khun Inthra Pramun – *7km northwest by 3064. After 5km turn right and proceed for 2km.* The brick pillars of a ruined vihara frame a reclining Buddha (50m long) at this peaceful temple. The revered statue with a serene, smiling face has been restored in recent years following a collapse. On a raised terrace are a small Sukhothai bell-shaped chedi and a ruined sanctuary.

AYUTTHAYA★★★

Phra Nakhon Si Ayutthaya – Population 131 296
Michelin Atlas p 24 or Map 965 – G 5

The modern thriving town which has grown to the northeast of the island at the confluence of the Mae Nam Chao Phraya, the Mae Nam Pasak and the Mae Nam Lopburi preserves the memory of the great capital of the fabulous kingdom of Ayutthaya which held sway from the mid 14C to the late 18C. The town has excellent tourist facilities and a colourful market as well as fine floating restaurants.

The rise of Ayutthaya – The fabled capital city, founded in 1351 by King U-Thong who took the name **Ramathibodi I**, reflected the power and grandeur of the state which in the 15C triumphed over the first Thai kingdom of Sukhothai and its satellite towns of Kamphaeng Phet and Phitsanulok.

Ayutthaya originated as a Khmer outpost in the 11C. U-Thong who ruled over the principality of U-Thong, Sukhothai's vassal state in the province of Suphan Buri, moved his people to the area to escape a disastrous plague. In his bid for power he was probably supported by well-established and powerful townships and principalities such as Suphan Buri, the fief of his wife's family, and Lopburi later ruled by his son.

During the 15C and early 16C Ayutthaya extended its territory by annexation. In 1402 **King Ramathibodi II** invaded the weakened Angkor empire and, after several confrontations, in 1412 Sukhothai became a vassal state. **King Borommatrailokanat** (1448-88) founded the administrative system of the kingdom, granting special powers to civilian and military authorities which were to influence the course of Thailand's history.

In the 16C Ayutthaya also formed a close association with the principality of Chiang Mai after many years of conflict and rivalry, thus laying the foundations for its supremacy.

The legendary pomp and ceremony associated with the rule of the 36 sovereigns of Ayutthaya derive from the notion of divine power claimed by the Khmer kings. Brahmanic rituals were included in the coronation ceremony which pertain to this day. The kings marked their reign by building Buddhist temples and magnificent palaces.

A prosperous era – The town which controlled the crucial trade routes in the region grew into a dynamic cultural and commercial centre and according to accounts by foreign visitors in the 16C and 17C it was one of the most splendid cities in Asia. Fleets of ships sailed up the Chao Phraya, and European and Japanese trading companies established settlements outside the city. The kingdom established diplomatic relations with foreign powers and at the height of its glory **King Narai** (1656-88) welcomed a mission from King Louis XIV of France and Siamese envoys were received at the French court. The cosmopolitan population which comprised Chinese, Indians, Japanese and

Europeans lived both within and outside the town area, foreigners reached influential positions at court and received preferential treatment, and Christian missionaries were allowed to practise their ministry. This trend was strongly opposed by nationalist courtiers and after the death of King Narai, although some foreigners were allowed to remain in the country, Western influence waned until the early 19C when relations with European trading companies were resumed.

The Burmese threat – Over the centuries the Burmese waged war with Ayutthaya to further their ambitions for power and territorial expansion. An invasion by the King of Pegu in 1549 failed but two decades later Ayutthaya fell. King Mahachakrapat was taken captive, a large section of the population was moved by force to Burma, and the city was ransacked. Ayutthaya became a vassal state ruled by King Mahathammaracha. His son **King Naresuan** restored Ayutthaya's sovereignty in 1584 and also gained territory from the Khmers in the east. The Burmese threat remained constant over the next decades until 1767 when Ayutthaya was conquered after a 15-month siege. They left the city in ruins after looting and melting the gold from the statues, and took thousands of captives, including numerous craftsmen, and the booty back to Burma.

A cultural landmark – After the future King Taksin had rallied his troops and finally driven the Burmese out of the country in the late 18C, a new capital was founded at Thonburi *(see BANGKOK Environs)*. The ruins of Ayutthaya were abandoned although King Rama I revived many of the traditions when he ascended the throne. He made use of building materials from the old city when he built his new capital in Bangkok and also removed large numbers of Buddha images to the new temples. Since 1956 under a major archeological programme several temples have been restored and the historic city has been accorded World Heritage status by UNESCO.

Out and about

Tourism Authority of Thailand (TAT) – Thanon Si Sanphet, Amphoe Phra Nakhon Si Ayutthaya. ☎ 035 246 076-7, Fax 035 246 078

Sightseeing – **Elephant ride**: by the TAT office; by long-tail boat from the pier near Chandra Kasem Museum, Thanon U-Thong: **boat hire** 500 Baht (non-stop, 1hr 15min), 600 Baht (stopping at three temples).
It is worth taking an evening drive around the historical park to view the illuminated monuments.

Where to Eat

Ruan Thai Mai Suai – 8/2 Mu 3 Wat Yai–Wat Phanan Choeng Road, Klong Suan Plu. ☎ 035 245 977/9. Typical Thai cuisine.

Ruan Thep Niyoum – 19 Thanon U-Thong, Pratuchai. ☎ 035 322 259. Delicious Thai fare.

Bhan Watcharachai – ☎ 035 321 323. Excellent Thai food in simple surroundings.

Pae Krung Kao – 4 Moo 2, Thanon U-Thong. ☎ 035 241 255. Riverside restaurant with fish specialities.

Where to Stay

Budget

Ayothaya Riverside Inn – 17/2 Moo 7, Baan Pom. ☎ 01 644 5328; US$4-10. Traditional Thai house with splendid views of the river and of the historical park.

River View Place Hotel – 35/5 Thanon U-Thong. 035 241 729/730; 1 500-2 200 Baht. Comfortable hotel overlooking Mae Nam Pasak with restaurant, swimming pool and fitness centre.

Ayothaya Hotel – 12 Moo 4, Thanon Thessaban. 035 232 855, 035 252 250; Fax 035 251 018; 900-3 500 Baht. Well-appointed hotel conveniently located in the historical park.

Moderate

U-Thong Inn – 210 Moo 5, Thanon Rojana. ☎ 035 242 236-9; Fax 035 242 235; uthong@ksc.th.com; www.uthonginn.com; 1 200-15 250 Baht. Fine establishment with excellent facilities and good views at some distance from the town centre.

Krung Si River Hotel – 27/2 Moo 11, Thanon Rojana. ☎ 035 244 333; Fax 035 243 777; 1 250-5 000 Baht. Well-appointed rooms, pleasant atmosphere, restaurants.

HISTORICAL PARK ⓥ

Tour : at least 2 days for a full visit or 1/2 day for a short tour. The inner area may be toured on foot but a car is recommended for the more distant sites.

Inner city

The royal capital occupied a strategic island site in a loop of the Mae Nam Chao Phraya in the fertile central plain. A man-made canal was dug to link the Mae Nam Lopburi to the main waterway, and walls, gates and forts were built – only the ruined Pom Phet is on view. Traces remain of the palatial wooden buildings – **Wang Luang** (Royal Palace) and Wang Lang (Rear Palace) described in vivid accounts by foreign visitors to the royal court. The Grand Palace in Bangkok is modelled on the layout of the Ayutthaya royal compound. The restored Wang Chandra Kasem (or Wang Na – Front Palace) houses a museum *(see below)*. The imposing ruins of over 200 monuments, mainly religious sanctuaries which were formerly faced with gold plates, evoke the splendour of the Ayutthaya era. Only a selection of the most important temples is described below but other ruined sites will also reveal many artistic treasures.

Wat Mahathat – The sacred spiritual centre of the capital city was built in the 14C in the reign of King Borommaracha I after the king received a revelation. The temple housed a holy relic of Buddha and maintained its importance throughout the Ayutthaya period. The imposing ruins within a walled enclosure have yielded many treasures now displayed in the museums in Ayutthaya and Bangkok.

The central **prang**, of which only the laterite and sandstone terraced base and monumental staircases (restored) remain, was remodelled many times especially in the late Ayutthaya period. Small chedis in varying styles were added at different times along the sides within the cloistered area. The chedi in the northwest corner retains traces of mural paintings in its cavity featuring former Buddhas in keeping with a popular belief in the early Ayutthaya period. In the outer courtyard stand rows of ruined chedis and viharas.

★★ **Wat Ratchaburana** – According to historical evidence the temple was established in 1424 during the reign of King Borommaracha II, also known as King Sam Phraya, and was built to house the ashes of his elder brothers, Chao Ai and Chao Yi, who killed each other in armed combat fought on elephants to settle their dispute over the throne. The powerful **prang** with its fine **stucco decoration** of nagas, garudas and standing figures is fairly well preserved. Cloisters formerly lined with statues of the Buddha mark the sacred area.

A treasure trove of valuable objects including regalia, Buddha images and votive tablets was uncovered from three crypts during restoration work in 1957. These invaluable pieces of historical evidence are displayed at the Chao Sam Phraya National Museum.

Mural paintings (15C) in relatively good condition were also discovered in the two upper crypts *(steep steps)*. The interesting paintings on the lower level reveal a Chinese influence, while

those in the first crypt illustrate fables in Buddhism, such as those of the 24 former Buddhas, as well as stories of the present Buddha (Buddha Sakyamuni) including episodes of the Jataka (the story of his former lives).

Also of note are the ruined chedis around the prang and the walls of viharas on either side as well as the minor sanctuaries within the walled compound.

★★ **Wat Phra Ram** – In a beautiful garden setting by a lotus pond the romantic ruins of this important temple founded in 1369 and restored in the 15C form a fine prospect. The galleried layout with **viharas** framing the main **prang**, which is quartered by smaller chedis, conforms to the early period. Small bell-shaped chedis were built in between the corner chedis and are of a later style. The **stuccowork** and the standing statues in the niches of the tall prang are fairly dilapidated and the porticoes are in ruins. Ancillary structures were added in the outer area throughout the Ayutthaya period.

★★ **Wat Phra Si Sanphet** – The temple was built in an original architectural style within the compound of the Royal Palace which dated from the establishment of the capital city. In the reign of King Borommatrailokanat the royal estate was donated in 1448 to the monastery and the Grand Palace was moved further north to a location near the river.

The columns of two viharas flank the three harmonious bell-shaped **chedis** aligned east to west on a long terrace. These served as royal tombs for Kings Borommatrailokanat and his sons, King Ramathibodhi and King Borommaracha III; the royal relics were placed in secret chambers with access from the east portico of each chedi. There are porticoes on four sides and the ringed finials are framed by small chedis. The cloister galleries were adorned with Buddha images.

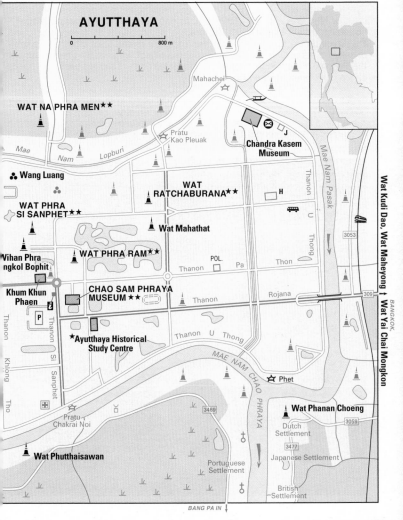

In the outer area bell-shaped chedis and viharas alternate along the temple walls. Other structures were built at regular intervals in between the chedis in order not to disturb the overall plan.

Wihan Phra Mongkol Bophit – A modern temple is dominated by a monumental bronze **statue of Buddha** (*c* 15C) in a seated posture which is greatly venerated. The original building was destroyed in the 18C and until recently the statue remained in the open. Canted pillars with lotus capitals adorn the porch; the pediment and gable are decorated with motifs in low relief on a red ground. Six rows of columns support the graceful low roof; the restricted space emphasises the gigantic size of the Buddha.

To the south stands **Khum Khun Phaen,** a recently-built traditional wooden Thai house on stilts comprising a central sala and four pavilions complete with furnishings.

Wat Thammikarat – The romantic ruins of this imposing royal temple, which pre-dates the Ayutthaya era, rise on a platform. The roof of the wihan was supported by two inner rows of 10 massive brick columns, many of which are still extant, with outer columns rising from the intermediate level of the terrace. Nearby stucco lions punctuate the low wall enclosing a bell-shape chedi which has lost its spire.

Wat Lokayasutharam – A large reclining Buddha in the open is the centrepiece of this temple which included two wihans framing a prang, of which there are few remains. The statue is noteworthy for its gentle, smiling face, long earlobes, head band and pointed top-knot; the headrest is beautifully decorated with a lotus motif.

Outer city : north

★★ Wat Na Phra Men ⊘ – Situated opposite the Royal Palace the temple strategically faces the moat, formerly a river which was a major communication route. The temple was probably built in the early Ayutthaya period and reconstructed in the reign of King Prasat Thong (1629-56), as evidenced by a large **crowned Buddha★★** housed in an imposing ubosot. Two graceful porches flank the large portico, and the carved decoration of the door panels and gable reveals great artistry. Two rows of columns supporting the elaborate coffered **ceiling★** enhance the great beauty of the Buddha image clad in royal attire; the seated posture and the placing of hands on lap conjure up transcendental quietude.

To the east lies a small vihara built in 1838 which enshrines a large **statue of Buddha★★** (7C-8C) – *illustration see INTRODUCTION, Art* – in Dvaravati style originally housed in Wat Mahathat. The powerful seated green-stone sculpture with the feet resting on a lotus stone base evokes nobility and great spirituality and is one of the masterpieces of the period. The original **mural paintings** are also of interest.

Wat Phra Si Sanphet

Wat Phu Khao Thong – *Take 309 north and turn left into 3060.* The focal point of a landscaped **park** with lakes is a majestic equestrian statue of **King Naresuan** in full battle array; he won a decisive victory over the Burmese in the 16C when Thai independence was regained. According to a 17C account the white chedi in the background was probably built to commemorate this crucial event in Thai history. The temple which pre-dates the founding of the city and was restored in the mid-18C dominates the flat landscape. Staircases lead up the four-tiered base of the elegant **chedi** pierced by four projecting chambers with ornate gables and pilasters housing gilded Buddha images. The faceted bell shape is crowned by a slender ringed spire.

Outer city : east

Wat Maheyong – *Take 309 and 3058 east.* The temple built during the reign of King Borommaracha II (1424-48) underwent a major reconstruction in the early 18C. Behind the ruined ubosot stands the plump bell-shaped **chedi** punctuated by niches and with its conical spire lying nearby; elephant-bust **stuccos** ring the base of the terrace. These unusual features in Ayutthaya art reflect the wide influence of the Sukhothai style and imply close relations between the two kingdoms as a result of royal alliances. Rows of similar but smaller chedis frame the main structure and there are also the ruins of a palace.

Wat Kudi Dao – *Opposite.* An arched entrance gives access to the ancient monastery which was also restored in the early 18C. The evocative ruins include a large **ubosot** pierced by arched openings, a bell-shaped chedi on a tall square base and a vihara, all aligned from east to west and framed by rows of smaller chedis. To the north stands a two-storeyed **palace building** similar to the one in Wat Maheyong which attests to royal patronage.

Outer city : south

Wat Phutthaisawan – According to ancient chronicles King Ramathibodi I (King U-Thong 1351-69) built this important monastery in the 14C on the site where he resided prior to founding his capital. On the eastern side of the compound an ancient sanctuary comprises several old chedis, a massive **prang** fronted by a chapel on the east side, a gallery housing Buddha images both old and new, and two small square buildings with elegant tiered roofs. Further west is a two-storeyed building in a composite style combining European and Persian elements and with pointed windows at the lower level. On the upper floor the style of **mural paintings** illustrating Buddhist fables dates from the late Ayutthaya period (17C).

In the monastic precinct to the west, **monuments** of three kings of Ayutthaya stand right on the river bank. The middle statue is believed to be that of King U-Thong, the first king who established this capital city in 1351. The figure on his right commemorates King Naresuan the Great who restored Thai independence from Burmese power in 1592, and on the left is King Ekathotsarot, the latter's able younger brother.

A short distance upstream was the former French settlement. **St Joseph's Cathedral** was built in the reign of King Narai (1656-88) when missionaries made many Christian converts. The 19C building, which includes elements of a former structure, boasts neo-Romanesque additions.

Outer city : west

★★Wat Chai Wattanaram ⊘ – The important monastery was built in 1629 by the riverside probably on his mother's cremation site by King Prasat Tong who toppled the previous king and ascended the throne. Although a common man he had been in charge of the kingdom's military affairs. To assert his legitimacy to rule he founded the monastery which has a principal prang-style **chedi** representing Mount Meru, the abode of the gods, in conformity with the sacred practice of the early Ayutthaya period. At the four corners of the terrace are smaller **prangs,** and the galleries which contain rows of damaged **Buddha images** are punctuated by **chapels** with cone-shaped spires and large crowned Buddha images placed at intervals. Inside the chapels the foliage motifs of the capitals and the coffered wooden ceilings are noteworthy but few traces of the mural paintings remain. On the outer walls of the buildings there are a few remaining high-relief stuccoes illustrating various episodes of the Jataka (the previous lives of the Buddha). The ubosot lies to the east near the river bank and still to be seen on its tall base are two ruined Buddha statues made of sandstone.

Excavations have revealed fragments of a cannon and balls, which indicate that the temple was one of the strongholds facing the Burmese attacks before Ayutthaya fell to the invaders for the second time in 1767.

On the opposite bank stands the Siriyalai Pavilion, a royal residence named after Queen Sirikit.

Wat Phanan Choeng

PICTOR

Additional Sights

Wat Phanan Choeng – *Southeast.* **A colossal Buddha image**★ (19m high) seated on a monumental plinth framed by large columns attracts huge numbers of worshippers. Also of note in the ubosot are other fine Buddha images and attendants at prayer. The rich décor and the restricted space create an overwhelming impression.

Wat Yai Chai Mongkon ⊙ – *East.* The temple is believed to commemorate the victory won over the Burmese in 1592 by King Naresuan. The soaring ringed spires of a large bell-shaped **chedi** on a tall base flanked by smaller monuments are outlined against the blue sky. On either side are the ruined columns of viharas. Modern statues of Buddha are placed at the base of the chedi and in the cloister galleries. A huge **reclining Buddha** in white stucco now lies in the open.

Elephant Kraal – *North by 309, turn right into 3060 and proceed for 6km.*
This is a unique example of an enclosure *(phaniat)* where wild elephants were driven after capture. Once inside, the animals were channelled one by one through a passage and the selected ones were moved into a smaller enclosure while the rest were let loose. The animals were tied to huge timber posts during training. Elephants were greatly prized in war and for other essential tasks such as logging. In the 19C the kings organised spectacular elephant shows here for the entertainment of foreign dignitaries.

Golden Treasure

★CHAO SAM PHRAYA NATIONAL MUSEUM ⊙

The building of this modern museum was financed from the sale of votive tablets found in the ruins of Wat Ratchaburana and it was opened in 1961 by King Bhumibol. The interesting collections reflect the piety and artistic vision of the sovereigns who adorned the monasteries, built to glorify their reigns, with religious artefacts of every period and style. The displays arranged in chronological order trace the evolution of art in Thailand.

Ground floor – A fascinating array of Buddha images includes an early 15C statue of the Buddha showing Mon and Khmer influences, a fine pair of 14C statues of the Buddha subduing Mara in Sukhothai style *(display case right)*, statues found in the left shoulder of a statue in Wihan Mongkol Bophit, a 13C-14C **statue★★** of Buddha in the U-Thong style with a hair band and an enigmatic smile *(3rd case right)*, and a remarkable Dvaravati-style **statue★★** in white crystalline stone of the Buddha preaching.

Further along the hall *(left)* are displayed carved door panels and pediments (17C, Ayutthaya style), two statues of the Buddha seated in meditation under Naga's hood (13C-14C, Lopburi style, *far end*).

The **ceramics** section *(end room)* comprises Bencharong porcelain, terracotta and celadon dolls, brown and celadon ware, Chinese porcelain from the Ming and Ching dynasties as well as a glazed brown jar highlighted in gold.

First floor – Votive tablets and crystal Buddhas and figurines in display cases as well as manuscript cabinets are on view in the main room. In the west room are **precious objects★★** – votive tablets, fish, boxes, seven-tiered stupa with small gold urn, crystal Buddha – found in Wat Mahathat. The glittering **treasure★★★** from Wat Ratchaburana is displayed in the east room: gold regalia, ceremonial vessels, ornaments in precious stones, jewellery, filigree headdress, ornamented elephant with howdah, sword with crystal handle in scabbard inlaid with gold and precious stones with a crystal.

The annexe to the rear contains Buddha heads found in the city and artefacts from the reigns of five dynasties (1350-1767).

★ **Ayutthaya Historical Study Centre** ⊙ – *Thanon Rojana*. The research centre which occupies two sites is devoted to the history of Ayutthaya. In the modern main building a museum presents the social and cultural life of Ayutthaya through displays, artefacts and models relating to its history, activities and communities through the ages. Visitors will gain an invaluable overall view of the Ayutthaya period. The Annexe building *(Tambon Ko Rian)* houses an exhibition on Ayutthaya's foreign relations.

Chandra Kasem Museum ⊙ – *Thanon U Thong*. The palace was built in the 17C during the reign of King Maha Thammaracha for his son, later King Naresuan. It was destroyed by the Burmese and abandoned until restored by Rama IV (King Mongkut) for use as an occasional royal residence. The Phiman Rattaya Hall, the residence of the court women, houses a **museum** which gives an insight into the life of the people. Exhibits include statues of the Buddha, sculpture, domestic and religious articles. West of the Grand Palace is the **observatory** erected in the 17C during the reign of King Narai the Great on the advice of French missionaries, and later reconstructed by King Mongkut to pursue his interest in astronomy.

BAN CHIANG★★
Udon Thani
Michelin Atlas p 9 or Map 965 – D 8

Archeological investigation following a chance discovery of artefacts has revealed traces of early human occupation in the region. The exciting finds which include pottery, glass beads, iron and bronze tools indicate a culture dating back at least 3 000 to 7 000 years, which had developed advanced techniques (bronze working, iron smelting, lost wax process, clay crucibles, bivalve moulds) and challenge the assumption that the Bronze Age originated in Mesopotamia which is generally regarded as the cradle of civilisation.

The Ban Chiang site on a mound surrounded by an alluvial plain suitable for agriculture was inhabited from the prehistoric period to the 2C AD. The peaceful settled community lived in houses built on stilts, raised livestock and cultivated rice; the people were also skilful hunters and craftsmen. Burial practices evolved from infant jar burials to flexed and supine burials with or without grave goods and intact or shattered pottery. Ban Chiang has been designated a World Heritage Site by UNESCO.

Many other similar settlements dating from the same period have been discovered in the northeast (Non Nok Tha, Ban Weng – Amphoe Sawang Daen Din 20km north of 22 – Sakon Nakhon).

Lao migration starting over 200 years ago has led to the repopulation of the region.

Ban Chiang Pottery

The elegance of the designs testifies to the artistry of the potters whose technique evolved through three distinct periods. The early period which is divided into four phases (*c* 3600-1000 BC) is characterised initially by decorative bands on black earthenware (*c* 3600-2500 BC); next came heavy patterns (*c* 2500-2000 BC); followed by decorative bands incised or cord-marked in the clay (*c* 2000-1500 BC); and finally stylised human and animal figures (*c* 1500-1000 BC).

During the middle period (*c* 1000-300 BC) the artists experimented with different shapes with more delicate incised or cord-marked designs but the pottery was also partly painted.

Artistic achievement peaked in the late period (*c* 300 BC-AD 200). The vases and pots had thicker walls coated in red ochre on which the design was painted; unusual forms were developed – round bottom with flared mouth, pedestal-shaped foot, cylindrical, carinated and animal shapes, decorative motifs (human, animal, geometric, spiral, tendril).

At Ban Pulu local craftsmen produce fine reproductions of Ban Chiang pottery which are on sale.

There are splendid displays of Ban Chiang pottery and bronze work in the National Museum and in Suan Pakkard Palace in Bangkok.

Access: 56km east of Udon Thani by 22, at Km 49-50 turn left at Ban Pulu and take 2225, continue for 6km.

National Museum ○ – On the ground floor of the main building the museum presents prehistoric settlement in the northeastern region. On display in Room 1 are iron tools, glass beads, bronze tools (axes) and ornaments. The smelting techniques are explained and a diorama gives a good idea of the dense settlements which were usually located on a mound. Rooms 2 and 3 illustrate the evolution of the different styles of pottery *(see above)*. Most of the items on display were grave goods rather than articles for everyday use and include rollers, spindle whorls, ladles, crucibles. The first floor is devoted to the Ban Chiang discoveries. The excavation work is illustrated and there are displays of ceramics (infant jar burials) and bronze ware. Among the fascinating exhibits are an early-period burial *c* 1500 BC of **Vulcan** with

B. Davies

Pottery, Ban Chiang

a bronze adze at the left shoulder, four bronze bracelets on the left wrist, 30 pellets beside the head and a painted pot at the feet; the world's oldest **socketed axe** (*c* 2700 BC); the burial of a hunter named **Nimrod** with a spearpoint at his left wrist and carved and drilled antler at his left elbow. The last room is devoted to present-day life in Ban Chiang.

In another building *(to the right)* are displayed artefacts from excavations at Ban Prasat *(see NAKHON RATCHASIMA, Excursions)* which reveal a culture comparable to Ban Chiang.

Wat Pho Si Nai – *500m south of museum.* An open-air **museum** ○ in the courtyard of the temple gives an idea of the excavation process and shows the burials in their original state. The skeletons are surrounded by pottery; some wear ornaments.

BANGKOK★★★

Bangkok – Population 5 604 772

Michelin Atlas p 27-28

As the mighty Chao Phraya meanders down to the Gulf of Thailand it describes a graceful curve around the heart of Bangkok, a sprawling conurbation of many facets. The oriental mystery combined with the vibrant modernity of the city weave a spell on visitors who at a first encounter may feel daunted by many conflicting impressions.

The grandiose architecture and dazzling ornamentation of the royal palace and the gleaming spires of secluded temples which evoke the splendours of early Bangkok make a striking contrast to the futuristic skyscrapers of the outlying districts. The narrow khlongs along which wooden barges – now replaced by noisy long-tail boats – plied their trade are a reminder of a traditional water-based way of life. The tranquil courtyards of temples and the verdant tropical gardens which have escaped ambitious development schemes are delightful havens for visitors wanting to escape the bustling main arteries and explore the warren of alleyways. The vivid street scenes reveal the amazing ingenuity and industry of the population as well as their sense of fun as they face the frenetic pace of city life.

Bangkok is famous as an international hub as it offers ample tourist facilities ranging from modest guesthouses to world-renowned luxury hotels, as well as a whole gamut of entertainment catering for the most exotic tastes. The delights of Thai cuisine from the appetising dishes of food stalls on every street to the gastronomic experiences of world-class restaurants deserve high praise.

The City of Angels – Bangkok which derives its name from a small village *(ban)* planted with orchards of olive and wild plums *(kok)* is also known to the Thai people as Krung Thep – City of Angels – an abbreviated form of its cumbersome official title which reflects its pivotal role as the centre of state power in the creation of the Thai nation and as the cultural and financial capital of the modern age.

Following the sack of Ayutthaya in 1767 by the Burmese army, King Taksin established his capital at Thonburi after he had defeated the invaders and claimed the throne. He was succeeded by Rama I, the first king of the Chakri dynasty, who wished to reassert the power of the monarchy and recapture the glory of Ayutthaya. He decided to build a new capital on alluvial land in the bend described by the river which could be easily defended from incursions by foreign powers attracted by the country's abundant natural resources. Bricks from the ruined capital served to build the crenellated city wall, watchtowers and forts. The remaining sections exemplify the defensive policies of the period. Hundreds of statues rescued from Ayutthaya adorn Bangkok's temples. A network of canals dug to serve the new settlement prompted the description "Venice of the East" bestowed by early European travellers whose evocative writings chronicle the period. The colourful dress and lifestyle of the people who lived in traditional floating houses completed the exotic picture. On the land where the new royal palace was built lived a large community of Chinese merchants who at royal request moved eastwards to a location outside the walls. This new settlement marked the beginnings of present-day Chinatown.

A wind of change – Rama IV (King Mongkut), a learned sovereign who had spent many years as a monk, opened the country to modern influences and concluded treaties with foreign powers. Rich trading opportunities aroused renewed European and Asian interest. The new arrivals built their trading-houses, warehouses and diplomatic compounds in a riverside area to the south where the cool breezes brought a respite from the stifling heat and humidity. **Thanon Charoen Krung** (New Road) was the first street to be built in 1862, and as transport needs grew the orchards and canals of early Bangkok were soon a memory of the past.

Inspired by his travels to Europe Rama V (King Chulalongkorn) set the scene for the 20C. To escape from the cramped conditions in the royal palace he built new palaces in neo-Classical style and wide avenues which still give Bangkok an air of formal elegance. He also promoted far-reaching social measures – abolition of slavery and prostration, compulsory primary education, reorganisation of government – to modernise the country.

A reckless gamble – Population growth and economic prosperity have led to uncontrolled expansion at an alarming pace owing to the lack of a coherent town planning policy. Air pollution and other environmental problems are also causes for concern. The skyline is punctuated by dramatic towers – some designs combine innovation and fantasy – as buildings sprouted all over the city to meet increased demand for offices and housing. The economic crisis has brought the building boom to an end and thousands of migrant workers have been thrown out of work. Road schemes have been devised to solve the notorious transport problems. Most of the khlongs have been covered over to allow the building of much-needed roads, and expressways now snake across the city. A mass-transit system provides a fast, reliable and inexpensive link. Although the traffic jams are now less acute, drastic measures are needed to redress the situation and create better living and working conditions for the people.

Ambitious plans for new towns in the suburbs have been curtailed and government policy for decentralisation of ministries and of industry to the provinces has been shelved.

As the metropolis remains the official residence of the royal family and the focal point for political, commercial, financial and cultural activities, it will continue to play a decisive role in determining the future of the country.

Out and about

Tourism Authority of Thailand (TAT) – Le Concorde Building, 202 Thanon Ratchadaphisek. Huai Khwang ☎ 02 694 1222; Fax 02 694 1220/1; center@tat.or.th; www.tat.or.th; www.tourismthailand.org Open Mon-Fri, 8.30am-4.30pm. Town plans and other tourist information are available free from TAT and from most hotel desks. A brochure of accommodation and rates is published by TAT.

Tourist Police – Unicohouse Building, Soi Lang Suan, Thanon Phloenchit. ☎ 1155, 02 281 5051; tourist@police.go.th; www.tourist.police.go.th

Services – Banks: Open Mon-Fri, 9.30am-3.30pm. Most banks operate booths for foreign exchange in tourist and business areas. Hotels usually offer lower exchange rates.

General Post Office – Thanon Charoen Krung (New Road). Open Mondays to Fridays, 08.30am to 4.30pm; Sat, 8.30am to 12midday. The Telecommunications Annex offers a 24-hour service including cables, telex, and international calls. Hotel charges for telephone calls are very high.

For international calls dial 001 followed by the country code and number.

Sightseeing – As traffic is very congested it is best to walk to see the sights. Taxis, the Sky-Train, tuk-tuks and long-tail boats are convenient means of transport for visitors who wish to avoid the heat and air pollution.

By Sky-Train – The Bangkok Mass Transit System offers a fast and convenient way to get around. There are two lines with an interchange at Central Station. Frequent services, clean trains from 6am to 12 midnight. Fares according to distance travelled: 10 Baht plus 5 Baht for each additional terminal. Adult and student passes are available. www.bts.co.th

By taxi – It is advisable to travel by taxis with a TAXI-METER sign (air-conditioned and with meters) which have a minimum charge of 35 Baht plus 4.50 Baht for each additional kilometre. Taxis called through taxi-service centre add a service call charge of 20 Baht. Taxi service centre ☎ 1661, 1681. It is possible to negotiate an amount for the entire distance of travel when making a booking or before starting a journey. It is best to ask a local person to write out the destination in Thai.

By tuk-tuk – A tuk-tuk, a three-wheeled motorbike taxi, is a convenient and cheap means of transport but safety is a concern. It is preferable to travel by tuk-tuk in the early morning or evening. Fares should be negotiated in advance – 30 Baht to 150 Baht.

By bus – A map of bus routes (35 Baht) is available at most hotels, bookshops and at the TAT office. Public buses to most destinations within metropolitan Bangkok: 3.50-5 Baht. Air-conditioned buses: 6-18 Baht. Red and grey microbuses (air-conditioned): 25 Baht for a single journey.

A sightseeing double-decker bus operates a tour of Rattanakosin Island from Sanam Luang by the Grand Palace to Vimanmek Palace and back, with a stop of over an hour to allow a visit of Vimanmek Palace. ☎ 02 645 0710/11. 200 Baht. It is advisable to visit the Grand Palace first as the admission ticket also gives access to Vimanmek Palace.

By boat – Express boats and ferries from the piers at Tha Oriental, Tha Maharat and River City ply the Mae Nam Chao Phraya for visits to the khlongs of Thonburi. Fares 5-15 Baht.

Long-tail boats are available for private hire. Apply at River City pier. The price for a canal tour ranges from 500 to 1 200 Baht depending on the type of boat and the duration.

Shopping – Bargaining is acceptable except in department stores and shops with fixed prices. Most shops are open 12 hours a day all week.

Department Stores: Siam Square, Thanon Phloenchit, Thanon Ratchadamri, Thanon Rama IV. Open 10am-8pm.

Antiques and fine handicrafts: River City.

Duty-free: 7th Floor, World Trade Centre, 4 Thanon Ratchadamri.

Fine Handicrafts: Chitralada Shops – Grand Palace, Oriental Plaza Shopping Centre, Hilton Hotel Shopping Arcade, Vimanmek Palace.

Silk: Jim Thompson, Thanon Surawong and World Trade Centre.

Markets – Talat Pratunam – fabrics, ready-to-wear fashions; Patpong Night Market – clothing and souvenirs; Chatuchak Weekend Market – plants, fruit and vegetables, pets, handicrafts, souvenirs; Talat Thewes – pot plants; Pak Khlong Talat – flowers and vegetables.

Bookshops – Asia Books, Thanon Sukhumwit – Sois 15-17; DK Books, Siam Square.

Entertainment – Dinner cruises: Reservations from River City Pier and major riverside restaurants.

Market, Bangkok

Thai Classical Dance – Show and dinner: Sala Rim Nam, Oriental Hotel; Silom Village, Thanom Silom; Sawasdee Restaurant, Thanon Sathon Nua; Ban Thai Restaurant, Thanon Sukhumwit; Chao Praya River Cultural Centre, Thanon Charoen Nakorn.

Bars, restaurants, nightclubs, jazz clubs – Sois off Thanon Sukhumwit, Thanon Luang Suan, Patpong: Bamboo Bar – Oriental Hotel; Brown Sugar – Soi Sarrasin; Round Midnight Pub – Soi Langsuan; Phoebus – Thanon Ratchadapisek.

Food stalls – Vendors offer an amazing array of fruits and tempting dishes at low cost in the markets and on every street corner. Visitors can just point to the dish that takes their fancy.

Thai Boxing – Ratchadamnoen Stadium (Mon, Wed, Thurs, Sun) and Lumphini Stadium (Tues, Fri, Sat).

Horse Racing – Royal Turf Club and Royal Bangkok Sports Club at weekends.

Amusement and Theme Parks – Dusit Zoo, Mini Siam, Safari World, Siam Water Park, Magic Land.

Golf – There are several golf courses of international standard on the outskirts of Bangkok.

Special interests – **Thai Cooking Schools:** The Oriental Hotel organises weekly cooking courses by the finest chefs; ☎ 02 437 2918 Ext 1044. Also UFM Baking and Cooking School; ☎ 02 259 6020/30.

Traditional Thai Massage – Courses and sessions are held at Wat Po, Wat Mahathat and Wat Parinayok. Thai massage is also available at health centres of good hotels.

Buddhist Meditation – For meditation courses apply to Wat Mahathat, Wat Pak Nam, Wat Chonprathan Rangsarit, Wat Phra Dhammakayaram and Wat Boworniwet.

Excursions – Information on sightseeing tours is available from travel agents and hotels.

1 day – Muang Boran (Ancient City), Crocodile Farm (Bangkok Environs); Damnoen Saduak (Floating Market); Phra Pathom Chedi, Rose Garden, Samphran Elephant Village (Nakhon Pathom); Bang Pa-In; Ayutthaya Historical Park.

2 days – Kanchanaburi, Hua Hin, Phetchaburi, Pattaya; Khao Yai National Park.

Bus Terminals – Talat Mor Chit – North and northeast. ☎ 02 936 3660; Sai Tai Mai – South: ☎ 02 435 1199 – Ekamai Sukhumvit – East: ☎ 02 391 2504.

Railway Terminals – Hua Lamphong: ☎ 02 223 0341/8. Thonburi, Bangkok Noi – South: ☎ 02 411 3102, 02 465 2017.

Where to eat

Seafood Market Restaurant – 24 Thanon Sukhumvit. ☎ 02 601 1255. Buy what you fancy from the wide range of seafood on offer and have it prepared just the way you like it.

Bann Khaitha – 36/1 Soi Prasarnmit. ☎ 02 258 4148. Traditional Thai fare beautifully presented.

Whole Earth – 93/3 Soi Lang Suan, Thanon Ploenchit. ☎ 02 252 5574. Famous vegetarian restaurant, intimate ambience, music.

Bussaracum – 425 Soi 2 Pipat 2, Thanon Silom. ☏ 02 235 8915. Traditional Thai food, splendid décor.

Lemon Grass – 5/1 Thanon Sukhumvit, Soi 24. ☏ 02 258 86 37. Pleasant small restaurant with garden; modern Thai cuisine.

Tum Nak Thai – 131 Thanon Ratchadapisek. ☏ 02 277 3828. Trendy modern restaurant with service by roller-skating waiters, acclaimed as the largest such establishment in the world. Thai and Western dishes.

Sala Rim Nam – Oriental Hotel, see address below. Traditional Thai cuisine, exceptional riverside setting and views. Classical dance evening performances.

Supatra River House – 266 Soi Wat Rakhang, Thanon Arunamarin, Siriraj. ☏ 02 411 0303, 02 411 0874, 02 848 9017. Restaurant ferry from Tha Maharaj. Delicious traditional cuisine in a beautiful Thai house with spectacular river and city views. Dinner theatre on Fri, Sat, daytime cooking demonstrations and small museum.

The Imperial China Restaurant – 199 Thanon Sukhumvit. ☏ 02 261 9000. Wonderful oriental décor, authentic Cantonese cuisine, dim sum at lunch.

Where to stay

Budget

Chaleena Hotel – 453 Soi Lad Phrao 122, Wangthonglang. ☏ 02 539 7101-11; Fax 02 539 7126; chaleena@comnet3.ksc.net.th; www.chaleena.com; 1 700-4 000 Baht. Comfortable, modern accommodation, close to the entertainment centre.

Indra Regent Hotel – 120/126 Thanon Rachaprarop, Phayatai. ☏ 02 208 0022-33; Fax 02 208 0388-9, 656 4246; sales@indrahotel.com, resv@indrahotel.com; www.indrahotel.com; 3 000-9 000 Baht. A good hotel close to Pratunam market and convenient for shops and the sky train.

Manhattan Hotel – 13 Sukhumvit Soi 15, Thanon Sukhumvit. ☏ 02 255 0166/3481; Fax 02 255 3481; hotelmanhattan@bigfoot.com; www.hotelmanhattan.com; 1 400-6 200 Baht. A moderately priced hotel in a good location for restaurants and entertainment.

The Montien Hotel – 54 Thanon Surawong. ☏ 02 233 7060, 234 8060; Fax 02 236 5218/9; bangkok@montien.com; www.montien.com; 4 000-25 000 Baht. A pleasant hotel with spacious accommodation in a central location.

Moderate

The Dusit Thani – 964 Thanon Rama IV. ☏ 02 236 0450-9; Fax 02 236 6400/7238; dusitbkk@dusit.com; www.dusit.com; US$145-400+. A first class hotel with well appointed rooms and fine amenities in the city centre, across from Lumphini park and convenient for business and entertainment.

Le Royal Meridien – 971-973 Thanon Ploenchit. ☏ 02 656 0444; Fax 02 656 0555; information@meridien-bangkok.com; www.lemeridien-bankok.com ; www.forte-hotels.com; 4 000-25 000 Baht. An elegant hotel with attractive rooms in the city centre.

Siam Inter-Continental – 976 Thanon Rama I, Patumwan. ☏ 02 253 0355-7; Fax 02 253 2275; bangkok@interconti.com; www.interconti.com; US$125-202. A charming luxury hotel with magnificent gardens.

Expensive

Oriental Bangkok – 48 Oriental Avenue. ☏ 02 236 0400; Fax 02 236 1937-9; bscorbkk@loxinfo.co.th; www.mandarinoriental.com; US$250-2 000. Prestigious hotel with historic wing dedicated to illustrious writers; spectacular river views, gourmet restaurants.

Grand Hyatt Erawan – 494 Thanon Ratchadamri. ☏ 02 254 1234; Fax 02 254 6308; sales@erawan.co.th, reservation@erawan.co.th; www.bangkok.hyatt.com; US$260-1 660. An elegant hotel with luxurious amenities and a harmonious ambience.

The Westin Banyan Tree – 21/100 Thanon South Sathon. ☏ 02 679 1200; Fax 02 679 1199; westinbangkok@westin-bangkok.com; www.westin-bangkok.com; US$190-731+. Luxury accommodation and lovely gardens in the heart of the city, close to the entertainment and business district.

HISTORIC BANGKOK

★★★ Grand Palace ⊘ (KY)

Entrance: Thanon Na Phra Lan. Formal dress and behaviour are expected.

The splendours of the royal palace which epitomise Thai creative genius and artistry remain a potent symbol of the ethos surrounding the Thai sovereigns which prevailed until the constitutional monarchy was established in 1932. The palace is the official residence of the monarchs and, although Rama III was the last to live there permanently, it is the scene of major royal ceremonies. The theatrical roofline and fabulous ornamentation of the buildings, which were erected in different reigns, inspire a sense of wonder.

In the central area within the precinct stand the official mansions and audience halls; to the south lies the forbidden quarter for the queen and the royal consorts and children; the royal chapel occupies a site in the northeast corner. The administrative offices were located to the north in an outer courtyard.

> The official name of Bangkok wins a place in the Guinness Book of Records as the longest name for a capital city.
> Krungthep Mahanakhon Bovorn Rattanakosin Mahintharayuttha Mahadilokpop Noparatratchathani Burirom Udomratchaniveymahasathan Amornpiman Avatansathit Sakkathattiya-avisnukarmprasit.

Access – Pass through the outer courtyard adorned with topiary. A **museum of coins and decorations** presents a glittering display comprising the royal regalia, crown and jewellery, the seasonal ornaments of the Emerald Buddha, bejewelled decorations and medals, precious betel-nut sets as well as a collection of coins and notes.

★★★ Wat Phra Kaeo (KY)

The dazzling Wat Phra Kaeo, the Royal Chapel, attests to the essential role of Buddhism in the national life and combines deep reverence with sheer fantasy. The wat, which has no monastic quarter, features the major styles of Thai architecture: gilded chedis, powerful prangs, graceful mondops, elegant viharas with tiered roofs, all highlighted by a profusion of typical decorative elements: ornate carved gables and

Dusit Maha Prasat, Bangkok

B. Davies

pediments, delightful mythical animals and creatures, slim finials, colourful glass mosaics, ceramic tiles, floral motifs, and delicate mural paintings. First impressions are overwhelming but visitors should step back and admire the overall plan and the incredible variety of the structures. The enchanting scene will remain one of the most memorable experiences of the splendour of Thailand.

Galleries – The cloister galleries are punctuated by elaborate gabled doorways and angle pavilions. The 178 **mural paintings★** *(start from the east gate)* depict tales of the Ramakien, an Indian epic, in a composite style combining the dramatic action with scenes from daily life. Explanatory poems composed under the patronage of King Rama V are inscribed on marble tablets.

Pavilions – By the west entrance stand two small chapels containing statues of the Buddha. The north vihara is notable for its remarkable mural paintings in faded tints.

Ubosot – *No photography.* Small salas used for ordination ceremonies and ornate *bai sema* frame the marble terrace, on which rises Thailand's most sacred shrine built in the late 18C by Rama I to house the deeply venerated **Emerald Buddha** (Phra Kaeo Morakot). The ornate pillars, gabled porch (Vishnu on Garuda against a floral ground) and inlaid doors give a foretaste of the exuberance of the interior decoration. Mythical lions in bronze guard the entrance and a frieze of garudas and nagas runs along the walls.

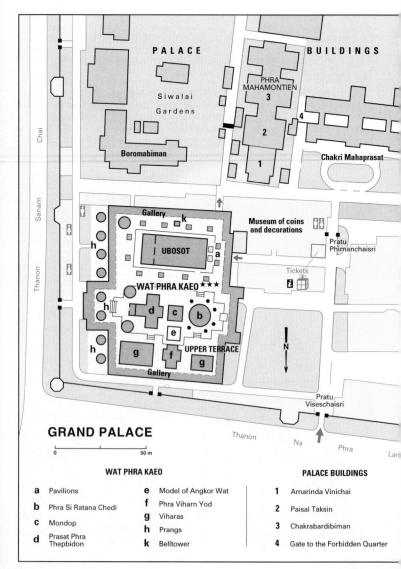

GRAND PALACE

WAT PHRA KAEO		PALACE BUILDINGS	
a Pavilions	**e** Model of Angkor Wat	**1** Amarinda Vinichai	
b Phra Si Ratana Chedi	**f** Phra Viharn Yod	**2** Paisal Taksin	
c Mondop	**g** Viharas	**3** Chakrabardibiman	
d Prasat Phra Thepbidon	**h** Prangs	**4** Gate to the Forbidden Quarter	
	k Belltower		

On a gilded pedestal high up on a glittering **altar** adorned with floral motifs, delicate filigree canopies, standing Buddha images in royal apparel, friezes of nagas, praying disciples and mythological creatures, is enshrined the small Buddha image in green jasper, an object of national reverence. The scent of flowers and incense fills the air as worshippers make their devotions. The outstanding **mural paintings** in traditional style relate the life of the Buddha *(above the windows)*, the temptation and enlightenment *(east wall)*, and the Buddhist conception of the universe *(west wall)*.

Upper terrace – Three important monuments are aligned on a raised platform dotted with fabulous creatures – birds, elephants, demons, nagas, kinnari – in gorgeous array. Small white chedis with slim finials surround the glittering **Phra Si Ratana Chedi** erected by King Rama IV (Mongkut) to recall the glory of Ayutthaya. Four porches surmounted by small gilded chedis and housing Buddha images pierce the tiered base. Above the graceful bell shape, slender columns support the base of the ringed finial.

The exquisite **mondop** crowned by an elaborate tiered roof and a slender spire is modelled on the Phra Phutthabhat in Saraburi and is used as a library to hold the sacred Buddhist scriptures. The splendid doors inlaid with mother-of-pearl and ebony, replicas of 9C statues of the Buddha from Borobudur in Java and the monuments dedicated to the sacred white elephants, symbols of royal power, are noteworthy.

A gorgeous frieze of demons in bright glass mosaic surrounds the slender gilded chedis guarding the entrance to the imposing **Prasat Phra Thepbidon** built on a Greek-cross plan. It served as the Royal Pantheon and now contains life-size statues of the kings of the Chakri dynasty. A green prang crowns the intricate roofline bristling with chofas and the gables are decorated with floral motifs. The harmonious building covered in red and blue tiles is enhanced by crowned nagas flanking the steps, graceful pillars, windows adorned with gold and black lacquer, and other splendid decorative features.

A **model of Angkor Wat** which evokes the divine power of Khmer rulers is a good illustration of Khmer architecture. The model was commissioned by King Rama IV to mark the period in the mid 19C when the area where the monument is situated was under Thai sovereignty.

Phra Viharn Yod *(north)* has a fine ceramic decoration in the Chinese style. Dotted within the enclosure are chapels **(viharas)** with ornate gilded pediments.

Prangs – Along the main east entrance are aligned eight Khmer prangs covered with glazed ceramic tiles in pastel shades which symbolise Buddhist cosmology.

Belltower – The elegant tiered structure crowned by a soaring finial is beautifully decorated with glazed ceramic tiles.

Palace buildings

The Grand Palace, at the heart of the capital, celebrates the glory and power of the monarchy. Beautiful formal gardens highlight the varied architectural styles of the noble mansions built by successive kings of the Chakri dynasty. Some of the buildings are open to visitors.

Phra Mahamontien – The imposing Grand Residence which comprises three buildings in Thai style was erected by Rama I. The **Amarindra Vinichai★★** with its gilded wall and ceiling decoration is a fine setting for court events such as investitures and the reception of ambassadors. The centrepiece is a throne surmounted by a canopy and a splendid boat-shaped altar. Behind the closed door is the **Paisal Taksin** *(not open)*, the scene of the solemn coronation ceremony when the monarch receives the regalia after being invited to take up the reins of power by the people's representatives.

Map labels:
★**Dusit Maha Prasat**
★★**APHON PHIMOK PRASAT**
Maharat
Wat Phra Kaeo Museum
Thanon
Royal Institute
🏠 Shop
ℹ Information
🚻 Toilets

R. Cuzin/ MICHELIN

Walk round to the west side of the building to view the antechamber of the **Chakrabardibiman** *(not open)*, the private residence of Kings Rama I, Rama II and Rama III, where subsequent kings spend at least one night after the coronation according to custom. Among the pavilions dotted around the building is a small sala *(west)* adorned with glass mosaic where the king changed from his court apparel to mount the royal elephant tethered to the red and gold posts outside the walled enclosure.

Further to the south is the **gate to the forbidden quarter** once reserved for the royal wives and children and their attendants. The king was the only man admitted to this private world.

Boromabiman – *Not open*. East of the Mahomontien stands a modern palace crowned by a quadrangular dome built by a German architect for the Crown Prince, the future Rama VI, and now serving as residence for visiting foreign dignitaries. Other royal residences, a chapel and ceremonial pavilions are surrounded by the Siwalai Gardens.

Chakri Mahaprasat – *Not open*. King Rama V commissioned an English architect to design this dignified neo-Classical building culminating in a charming Thai-style roofline. Inside, the Throne Room and state rooms are beautifully ornamented with marble pilasters, coffered ceilings, stuccowork, paintings and precious objects.

★★ **Aphon Phimok Prasat** – The exquisite architecture and decoration of the pavilion mark a high point in Thai artistry and craftsmanship. This is where the king changed from his ceremonial dress before stepping into a palanquin.

★ **Dusit Maha Prasat** – This is one of the original palaces built by Rama I. The stepped roofs are surmounted at the crossing by an ornate tiered spire and slender finial. A grand **throne** encrusted with mother-of-pearl graces the former audience hall where the urns containing the mortal remains of deceased members of the royal family lie in state before the cremation ceremony.

The small **Wat Phra Kaeo Museum** nearby displays a scale model of the Grand Palace and Wat Phra Kaeo, inscriptions and ornamental features from the original buildings as well as a throne and fine statues of Buddha.

★★ Wat Po ⊙ (KY)

Entrance: Thanon Thai Wang.

South of the Grand Palace is Wat Po, the popular name of Wat Phra Chetuphon, established in the 16C during the Ayutthaya period and thus the oldest temple in Bangkok. The vast compound comprises the monumental area and the monastic quarters on either side of Thanon Chetuphon. Monuments are dedicated to the early Chakri kings who bestowed favour and riches on the temple.

Hundreds of statues recovered from Ayutthaya by Rama I were brought to Bangkok and a large collection illustrating various styles is exhibited in the galleries surrounding the ubosot.

The monumental gates and walled enclosure are guarded by fearsome demons, huge top-hatted figures and charming animals. These Chinese stone figures as well as fine pagodas were originally used as ballast for ships engaged in the rice trade.

Rama III boosted the educational role of the temple in order to make knowledge accessible to all. Mural paintings and inscriptions deal with varied subjects such as literature, warfare, archeology and astronomy. Geology is explained by small mounds of stone specimens scattered in the grounds. Statues of hermits illustrating yoga postures for relaxation and meditation, murals showing ancient massage techniques and prescriptions for remedies were used as aids for treatment. The temple remains a centre for traditional medicine; astrologers and palmists also practise their arcane arts.

Wihan of the Reclining Buddha – King Rama III built the great vihara to house the gilded reclining figure which portrays the Buddha reaching nirvana. Although it is impossible to appreciate its vast size (45m long and 15m high), some features are notable: the 108 auspicious signs inlaid on the soles of the feet, the fine modelling of the face, and the long earlobes denoting noble birth. Only the upper sections of the mural paintings remain.

The **belfry** *(east)* is echoed by another such structure in the south courtyard.

Chedis of the Four Kings – The slim redented chedis clad in glazed ceramic with delicate floral motifs are dedicated to the first four kings of the Chakri dynasty. The harmony of colour and form is delightful.

By the entrance to the enclosure is the **pavilion for traditional medicine** *(south)* now used as a lecture hall. Treatment (traditional massage) is dispensed in two small buildings by the east entrance.

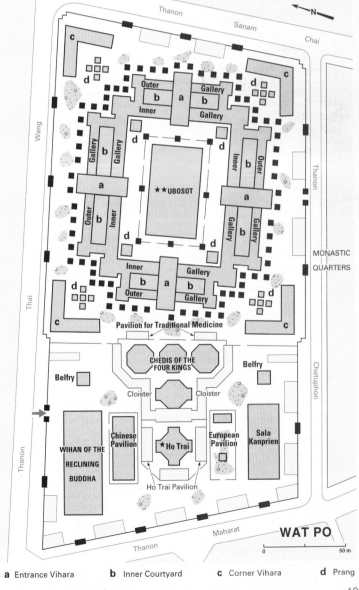

a Entrance Vihara   **b** Inner Courtyard   **c** Corner Vihara   **d** Prang

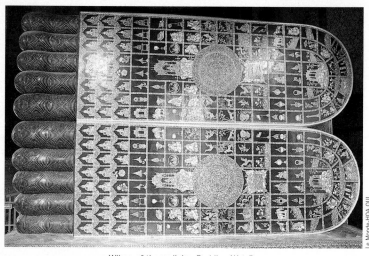

Wihan of the reclining Buddha, Wat Po

West enclosure – The floral decoration of the **ho trai★** which houses the sacred texts complements the four chedis. The ornate double gables and pediments are dominated by a cupola and finial rising above the crossing.

The library is flanked by a **Chinese pavilion** and a **European pavilion**, so-called because of their distinctive decorative styles. Further south is a **sala kanprien** for assemblies. The small buildings along the wall are used as classrooms.

East enclosure – In the outer area which is crowded with **corner viharas**, **prangs** and small white chedis, note the mounds with stone figures of hermits and original door guardians. The cloister is pierced by four **entrance viharas** with peaceful gardens in the **inner courtyards**.

Pass into the central area to view the rare **collection of Buddha images**, many from Ayutthaya, in the double galleries. Four marble **prangs** frame the ubosot raised on a platform guarded by fierce lions in bronze.

★★ **Ubosot** – The vivid scenes on the **marble panels** relating the story of the Ramakien on the boundary wall and on the splendid doors with mother-of-pearl inlay are remarkable.

The interior of the harmonious structure surrounded by a galleried porch is notable for its massive painted pillars, brightly decorated ceiling, lively mural paintings (damaged), and an elaborate gilded altar enshrining a seated Buddha image.

★★★National Museum ⊘ (KX)

The private collection of antiquities of King Rama IV (Mongkut) formed the nucleus of Thailand's first museum founded in 1874 by his son King Rama V (Chulalongkorn). Formerly housed in the Grand Palace, the museum moved in 1887 to Wang Na, the Palace to the Front, built for the Prince Successor (Second King), after the title and position were abolished by Rama V.

Over the years the museum has amassed vast collections from all over the country. Its current policy is to create regional museums which will exhibit works of art characteristic of the various regions. In due course many masterpieces will be transferred.

Palace Buildings

Wang Na, the residence of the Prince Successor, was erected in front of the Royal Palace for the protection of the sovereign in keeping with the tradition of Ayutthaya. The galleried central building (**4-15**) has an interesting plan as the apartments, each with a suite of rooms giving onto a courtyard, were designed for the seasons – the north wing was occupied in summer, the south rooms in the rainy season and the central area in winter. Audiences were given in the **Throne Room** (**4**) – now used for special exhibitions.

The delightful **pavilions** (**18-21**) ornamented with intricate woodwork and gilding are fine examples of traditional architecture which have been transferred from various royal palaces.

Tamnak Daeng★★ (**22**), a former royal residence built of teakwood stained red – hence its name "The Red House" – contains splendid furnishings which give a glimpse of the elegant lifestyle enjoyed in royal circles in the late 18C.

The cool, airy mansion, **Issaretrachanusorn Hall** (**16**), furnished in the European style, was occupied by King Pin Klao, Second King to Rama IV.

NATIONAL MUSEUM

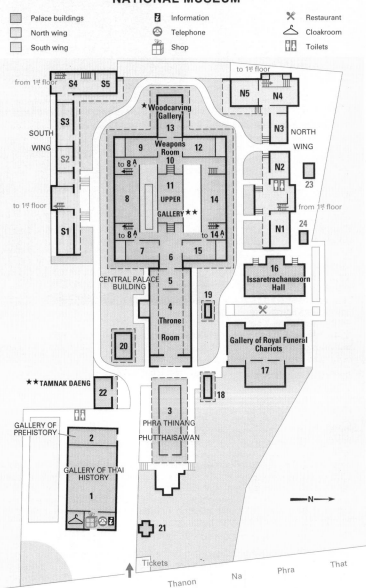

Palace buildings	
North wing	
South wing	

- Information
- Telephone
- Shop
- Restaurant
- Cloakroom
- Toilets

Phra Thinang Phutthaisawan (3)

The palace's private chapel built in the late 18C to enshrine the revered **Phra Phuttha Sihing** *(see CHIANG MAI)*, is characteristic of the early Bangkok period with its chofa finial, barge-board and roof brackets terminating in a naga. The pediment features the Hindu god Brahma in three pavilions, and stucco carvings and glass mosaic highlight the lacquered doors and windows. The gilded Buddha image (mid 15C) which is typical of the Sukhothai style – fingers of equal length, tall flame, slim figure – sits on high under an elegant mondop. The remarkable **murals★★★** – vivid scenes from the life of Buddha between the windows, and bands of divinities and demons above – are among the oldest in Bangkok and repay careful study of the detailed scenes peopled with figures and depicted in a traditional style. Behind the altar are splendid cabinets, laquered and gilded; the backs are decorated with scenes from the Ramakien.

Museum

The collections of precious works of art ranging from the prehistoric era to the Rattanakosin (Bangkok) period illustrate the artistic heritage of Thailand, and the religious and cultural influences which have shaped it.

Gallery of Thai History – Stone inscriptions, manuscripts, dioramas and other artefacts present a fascinating historical survey of the origins of the Thai nation. Pride of place is given to the **stone inscription**★★★ of King Ram Kamhaeng recording the history of Sukhothai. The King is reputed to have invented the Thai alphabet which is derived from the Khmer adaptation of a South Indian script. A copy of a stone **bas-relief** depicting Thai vassal troops from Angkor Wat (Cambodia) marks a significant event in Thai history. Incised **slate panels** from Sukhothai relate episodes of the Jataka, the tales of Buddha's previous lives. Costumed figures on a lacquer cabinet attest to the growing European presence in Southeast Asia. The seat belonging to **King Taksin** is a reminder of his role in freeing the country from the Burmese invaders after the destruction of the Kingdom

R. Cuzin/ MICHELIN

of Ayutthaya. Exhibits from the reigns of the kings of the Chakri dynasty show the modernisation of the country, in particular under Rama IV and Rama V who were enlightened rulers, and under the present king Rama IX.

Gallery of Prehistory – Excavation sites – Ban Kao (Kanchanaburi), Non Nok Tha (Khon Kaen) and Ban Chiang (Udon Thani) – have yielded evidence of prehistoric cultures from the dawn of civilisation: flints, tools, pottery (rare **tripod**★ *c* 2000 BC, cord-marked and painted vessels), bronze ornaments, jewellery, drums, burial site.

South Wing

Room S1 – The art of Asia (China, Ceylon, India, Java, Japan) has shaped the cultural and artistic expression of Thailand. The traditions of Ceylon and India have been particularly strong influences especially through the dissemination of Buddhist doctrine. The Gupta- and Ghandara-style exhibits are of special interest. A stele of the standing Buddha in Gupta style (5C-6C) is from Sarnath in India. A gilded plaque of the life of the Buddha in eight episodes (9C-13C) illustrates Palasena art. A bronze Roman **lamp** (3C) found at Phong Tuk (Kanchanaburi) reveals contacts with the Western world probably through Indian traders.

Proceed up the steps to the first floor to follow the chronological order.

Rooms S6, S7 – The Dvaravati kingdom of the Mons flourished from the 7C to the 11C and finds mostly in stucco, stone and terracotta from the main sites of Nakhon Pathom, Khu Bua (Ratchaburi), Lopburi, U-Thong attest to an advanced civilisation. Among the remarkable exhibits are an 8C terracotta **head of Buddha**★★★ *(display case)* with strong features and an enigmatic expression, stucco heads and reliefs of Hindu deities and large statues of the Buddha with raised arms and long, transparent garment. Wheels of the Law, some with a deer at the base, symbolise Buddhist doctrine. There is also an exquisite **stucco**★★ of five female musicians. Silver **coins** (7C) bearing the words "Dvaravati kingdom" are of great historical importance.

Rooms S8, S9 – The distinctive Hindu culture of a dynamic kingdom established in Central Java was prevalent from the 8C to the 13C in the southern peninsula of Thailand. Dancing apsaras and a powerful statue of **Ganesha**★★ with a band of skulls at the base illustrate Javanese art. Finds from Chaiya comprise an admirable **seated Buddha with a naga canopy**★, richly-attired Bodhisattvas in bronze, and in particular a sandstone **Avalokitesvara**★★ (mid 7C) of great simplicity.

Room S4 – A fine **collection of Hindu deities**★ from Si Thep and south Thailand includes imposing stone statues of the four-armed **Vishnu** with a cylindrical mitre and a sarong twisted at the waist and falling to the ground.

Rooms S3, S5 – Lopburi was the centre of Khmer power which prevailed between the 10C and the mid 13C in the northeast and as far west as Kanchanaburi, and Lopburi art is the term used to describe Khmer-inspired works in Thailand. The intricately carved

lintels from the Khmer stone sanctuaries illustrate the rich symbolism of Khmer culture: Hindu deities, mythological animals, foliage. A 12C **seated Buddha★★** sheltered by the naga king Muchalinda – *illustration see INTRODUCTION, Art* – features a diadem, long earrings and a conical ushnisha (top-knot) and a thin band marking the hairline on the forehead. Also of note are statues of Bodhisattvas and a small statue of a **female deity**, probably Uma, with a pleated dress in the Baphuon style (11C).

North Wing – *Start at west end on ground floor and proceed to first floor.*

Room N5 – Outstanding among Buddha images of different styles and periods are a colossal **Buddha image★★** in white quartzite and a fine Buddha in meditation sheltered by a naga, both from the Dvaravati era (7C-12C); a head of a Bodhisattva in Khmer style (8C); and a large head of a Buddha image (15C-16C) from Ayutthaya.

Room N6 – The gallery of **Lanna art** (11C-18C) features objects from excavations at Hot (Chiang Mai) – small bronzes (16C elephant base for offerings, duck-shaped water vessel), crystal and bronze Buddha images, replica of Lanna regalia, ceramics.

Rooms N7, N8 – The brilliant Sukhothai culture (mid 13C-14C) marked a high point of Thai art. The tall bronze **statues of Hindu gods★★★** honoured in Brahmanic rituals are masterpieces: Shiva in rich apparel and pleated robe, the four-armed Vishnu with conch and disc, and Harihara which combines the attributes of both deities. The idealised **Walking Buddha★★★** is an inspired creation with its perfect figure, elegant stance and serene expression. **Sangkalok ceramics** which were in great demand throughout Southeast Asia denote the skill of the craftsmen. Buddha footprints were a popular expression of piety.

Rooms N9, N10 – The kingdom of Ayutthaya held sway from the 12C to the late 18C. The early U-Thong period combines Dvaravati and Lopburi elements – head of Buddha, Buddha subduing Mara. **Buddha images in royal attire★★★** and on tiered pedestals are typical of the late period. Votive tablets, a stone Bodhi tree, and a large seated Buddha in red sandstone are noteworthy. There are beautiful **cabinets** lacquered and gilded, painted or carved in high relief.

Room N1 – The Rattanakosin (Bangkok) style which developed from the late 18C combines elements from old styles. On display are bronzes, drums, reliquaries and Buddha images. The finest exhibits are a naturalistic Gandhara-style Buddha image and a **bejewelled Buddha image★★** on a tiered base (19C-20C).

Rooms N2, N3, N4 – In the section on decorative arts are exhibited examples of niello, lacquer and silver ware, manuscript covers. Textiles and coins are on display in the next two rooms.

Central Palace Building – *Entrance on the south side.*

Rooms 5, 11 – The craftsmanship of the precious objects discovered in the crypt of Wat Ratchaburana in Ayutthaya is outstanding. The most important items of the treasure are displayed in the Chao Sam Phraya Museum *(see Ayutthaya)*. The **upper gallery★★** displays votive tablets, Buddha images enamelled, with jewels and in glass, gold plaques in high relief, gold plate inscriptions. The royal pavilion **reliquary** embellished with carving, gilding and glass mosaic is noteworthy. At the east end the display cases contain the **regalia** including the body chain belonging to the Phuttha Sihing, and Buddhist offerings and ritual accessories.

Room 6 – The highlights are an exquisite ivory howdah and gilded royal palanquins which are among the finest examples of Thai woodcarving.

Room 7 – Khon masks, shadow-play figures, colourful puppets, ivory chessmen illustrate some of the popular forms of entertainment.

Rooms 8, 8A – Ceramics from Europe and Asia. Lopburi glazed ware, Sangkalok stoneware and celadon, and brightly-coloured Bencharong porcelain are excellent examples of the skill of the Thai artisans. The upper room contains intricately-carved elephant tusks and models of white elephants.

Rooms 9, 10, 12, 13 – On display are exquisite mother-of-pearl inlaid objects and lacquer ware: screens, food containers and vessels. The **Weapons Room** is dominated by an elephant in full battle array. The stone inscriptions (8C-18C) in various Oriental scripts in Room 12 are important historical records.

Among the delicate exhibits in the **woodcarving gallery★** are panels with reliefs of deities, ornamental roof brackets, celestial beings (kinari), elaborate pulpits with canopies, reliquaries and in particular a massive oak door-panel from Wat Suthat carved in high relief by King Rama II and other artists.

Rooms 14, 14A, 15 – A gorgeous array of textiles and costumes includes Chinese silk, Indian cotton, Khmer ikat, Lanna brocades. Upstairs the gallery presents objects relating to Buddhism – cases for prayer books, models of stupas, fans, robes and requisites for monkhood.

The musical tradition of Thailand is exemplified by instruments in ivory, bamboo and carved wood used by orchestras – xylophones, cymbals, gongs, drums, flutes, string instruments. The Javanese gamelan orchestra was a gift to King Rama VII.

Gallery of Royal Funeral Chariots (17) – A splendid collection of chariots and palanquins used for royal cremation ceremonies. The form of the elaborate structures (busabok) is derived from Hindu cosmology. The chariots are drawn by soldiers in traditional dress.

Sanam Luang (KXY) – A place of popular assembly for national celebrations and leisure activities (kite flying, takraw games). Also known as the Phra Men Ground where royal cremation ceremonies are held, it is the scene of the Ploughing Ceremony held in May and of festivities for the King's Birthday and the New Year.

Government ministries housed in modern buildings and Western-style former palaces line the east side. A statue of the Earth Goddess **Thorani** fronts the Ministry of Justice (Thanon Ratchadamnoen Nai).

Lak Muang (KY) – South of Sanam Luang. A pavilion crowned by a prang and with recessed pediments supported on square pillars houses the gilded City Pillar, a phallic symbol of the town's guardian spirit. Local people flock to the shrine with offerings of flowers, incense, food and petitions for good fortune in all spheres of life. Devotees also commission performances of classical Thai dancing. Distances are measured from the City Pillar.

Wat Mahathat (KY) – West of Sanam Luang. The monastery which houses an important school of Buddhism pre-dates the foundation of Bangkok. King Mongkut spent his monkhood at the temple and was one of its abbots. Within the cramped walled compound are two finely-proportioned viharas and a mondop with a gilded pediment and a cruciform plan. The faithful flock to the amulet market which is the largest in Bangkok.

South of the wat stands Silapakorn University (Fine Arts) while to the north are Thammasat University (law, science), the National Museum and the National Theatre with the National Gallery across the road.

Wat Ratchabopit (LY) – Thanon Ratchabopit off Thanon Atsadang by Interior Ministry. Picturesque armed guards decorate the doors leading into the temple compound. Its unusual layout is enhanced by brightly-coloured glazed tiles. Four open salas frame a circular cloister; white pillars forming inner and

outer galleries support the roof. Decorated porches mark the doors *(north and south)* and two viharas *(east and west)* punctuating the cloister. The centrepiece is a tall, gilded chedi enshrining a Lopburi-style seated Buddha image. Royal insignias in black lacquer and gold and mother-of-pearl inlay adorn the doors and windows of the ubosot *(north)*. The neo-Gothic vaulted interior decorated in brown and gold is in sharp contrast to the colourful exterior.

A shady burial ground *(west)* with funerary monuments of members of the royal family in varied styles is a tranquil oasis.

Giant Swing (LY) – *Thanon Bamrung Muang*. Shops selling Buddhist offerings and monastic requisites line the road to the giant swing, Sao Ching Cha. A richly-carved transverse beam highlights the red teak frame (27m high). A Brahmanic ceremony to mark the end of the rice harvest which included a daring contest was banned in 1932 after many fatal accidents. Teams of three youths precariously balanced on a narrow board swung high up in the air, with the leader attempting to snatch a bag filled with silver coins hanging from a post 23m tall.

Nearby is a Brahman temple *(Thanon Dinso northwest)* dedicated to the Hindu Trinity which became assimilated within the Buddhist tradition. The chapels contain interesting statues of Vishnu, Shiva and Brahma; in front are a replica of the swing, a chariot and mythical birds.

★★**Wat Suthat** (LY) – *Thanon Bumrung Muang*. Royal patronage was lavished on this splendid temple built in the classical Thai style between the late 18C and mid-19C during the reigns of the first three kings of the Chakri dynasty.

Within a walled courtyard Chinese pagodas, warriors, bronze horses and ornate salas enshrining Buddha images frame the galleried **vihara**★★ with its richly orna-mented porches. Three-headed elephants and foliage motifs adorn the gables, and the pillars are capped by lotus capitals. The intricate carving on the massive **doors** featuring delightful animals frolicking amid the foliage attests to the artistry of King Rama II and other craftsmen. The imposing aisled interior is dominated by the revered 14C Buddha image, **Phra Buddha Sakyamuni,** brought from Wat Mahathat in Sukhothai. The base contains the ashes of King Rama VIII. The early-19C **paint-ings**★★★ on the walls and pillars, which unusually relate the lives of the 28 incarnations of Buddha in the Theravada Buddhist tradition, are of outstanding nar-rative quality and mark a significant evolution in art history.

A low wall surrounds the **ubosot** (early 19C), which is in a similar but less har-monious style and stands curiously at right angles to the vihara. Statues of Westerners guard the doors and Chinese structures are dotted all around. The spacious interior is also decorated with interesting mural paintings depicting the incarnations of Buddha on the lower register and the life of the master on the upper register. The group of disciples attending the Buddha image on the altar is an original feature.

W. Buss/HOA QUI

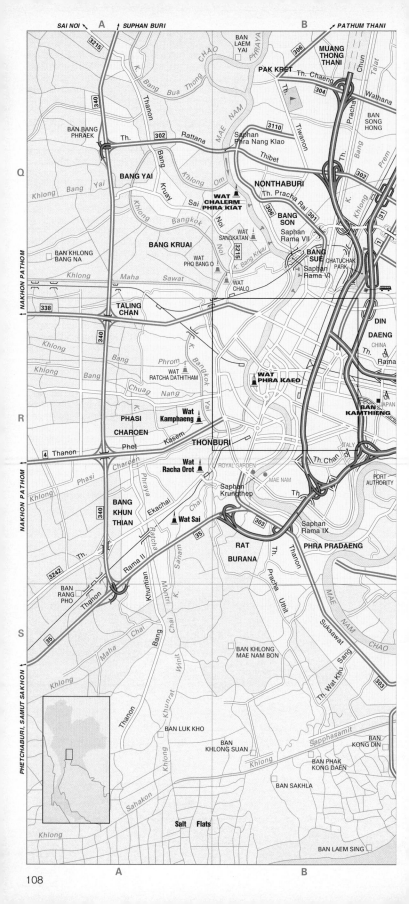

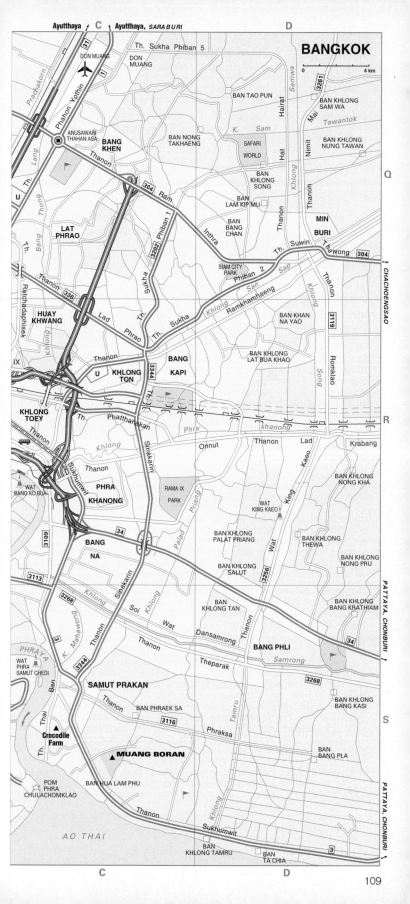

Wat Ratchapradit (LY) – *Thanon Saranrom.* A charming temple in white and grey marble built by King Rama IV (Mongkut). The open salas at the four corners, Khmer-style prangs at the front and back and a stupa at the far end of the sanctuary are typical of the architectural styles favoured by the king. The decorative elements of the gables, pediments, doors and window frames are admirable.

Golden Mount (LY) – *300 steps. Thanon Boriphat.* A gilded bell-shaped stupa containing relics of the Buddha presented in 1897 to King Rama V by Lord Curzon, Viceroy of India, is a famous landmark crowning a man-made hill known as **Phu Khao Thong.** It was created by King Rama III and completed by Rama V to replicate a similar mound in Ayutthaya and is a major engineering achievement in view of the unstable terrain.

From the upper terrace an unforgettable **panorama★★★** unfolds to the far horizon taking in the exotic roofs of the royal palaces and temples, the winding course of the Chao Phraya and the bristling modern towers. The faithful perform their devotions at a small shrine.

Wat Saket (MY) – *Thanon Chakkaphatdi Phong.* It is one of the oldest temples in Bangkok founded by King Rama I. A gallery surrounds the ubosot which is decorated with fine **wall paintings**. The elegant **vihara** enshrines a huge standing Buddha image, **Phra Attharot**, originally from Sukhothai, with paintings of disciples on either side on the wall. Behind the altar a seated Buddha image is framed by statues of disciples in bronze. Figures in 17C costume portrayed on the shutters of the **ho trai** evoke Thailand's past relations with Europe.

Wat Ratchanadda (LY) – *Thanon Mahachai.* An amulet market in the forecourt is popular with devotees searching for the most effective specimen to ward off misfortune. A colourful ceramic decoration enhances the harmonious ubosot and two viharas built at right angles in a tranquil courtyard.

In well-tended gardens overlooking Thanon Ratchadamnoen Klang stands the **Lohaprasad**, a curious three-storeyed building surmounted by a pavilion pierced by four pillared openings and a slim chedi; a row of white chedis highlights each storey. It was started in the early 19C by Rama III – but only recently completed – in accordance with a Buddhist tradition originating in India with a rich convert who built a magnificent mansion to provide shelter for meditation for the master and his disciples. This and another equally splendid structure built in Ceylon are no longer extant.

An open pavilion and a statue of Rama III are also of interest. From the gardens there is a good **view** of a section of the old wall and of the Golden Mount in the distance.

Wat Thep Thidaram (LY) – *Thanon Mahachai.* The canal-side location adds to the charm of this temple also built by Rama III in a similar style to Wat Ratchanadda. The ceramic floral decoration of the gables adds a delightful feature to the elegant ubosot and viharas aligned within walled compounds. Prangs frame the ubosot in the centre which contains a precious white marble Buddha on a gilded boat-shaped pedestal. Extensive restoration is under way to return the buildings which are excellent examples of the Rattanakosin style to their former glory.

Follow the signs through the shady alleys to view the residence of Thailand's celebrated poet, **Sunthorn Phu** *(see INTRODUCTION, Language and Literature; and RAYONG, Excursions)*, who took holy orders at the temple.

Democracy Monument (LX) – A distinctive monument marks the end of the absolute monarchy in 1932 after a bloodless revolution. A new constitution set up a national assembly. Bas-reliefs at the base of the monument are the work of Professor Corrado Feroci.

★★ Wat Boworniwet (LX) – *Thanon Phra Sumen.* Royal associations abound from the time when King Mongkut served as the abbot of the temple and founded the strict Dhammayuttika sect, and over the years with the ordination of several members of the royal family including the present monarch. It is also the seat of the Supreme Patriarch and the Sangha, the sacred college, and a renowned meditation temple attended by many foreign monks.

A stately **ubosot** preceded by a pillared porch enshrines a fine 13C Sukhothai-style Buddha image, **Phra Phuttha Chinasi**, flanked by disciples and overshadowed by another large seated statue in the transverse section. The spacious interior divided into a nave and two narrow aisles is adorned with **mural paintings★★★** by the artist Khrua In Khong which mark a departure from traditional artistic tenets with the introduction of perspective and amazingly-detailed foreign themes in dark colours. The panels between the windows depict Buddhist rituals and, above, scenes of the master, his doctrine and Buddhist leaders while the pillars illustrate spiritual development. There are statues in various styles (Dvaravati, Lopburi, Sukhothai) on both sides of the building as well as a Buddha footprint.

In the centre of the compound rises a tall, gilded chedi; behind are two viharas enhanced by revered Buddha images and mural paintings. At the far end a large reclining Buddha is on view.

In the monastic area stand two elegant buildings where resided King Mongkut and other royal personages.

Along Thanon Phra Sumen may be viewed remnants of the old crenellated wall with two octagonal **forts**, the riverside Pom Phra Athit and Pom Maha Kan near the bridge, built to repel invaders.

NEW ROYAL CITY – *North*

The wide, shady avenues lined with government buildings, private mansions, gardens and parks, prestigious schools, a hospital are a far cry from the orchards which grew in fertile alluvial soil when Bangkok first expanded outside the confines of the inner city on Rattanakosin Island during the reigns of Rama V (King Chulalongkorn) and Rama VI (King Vajivarudh). The area retains a dignified character.

Chitralada Palace (GT) – One of the numerous royal mansions built by Rama V is the official residence of the present sovereign. Within the large grounds the King pursues experimental agricultural research with a view to improving the output of the poorer regions and the life of the farming community.

Among the landmarks surrounding the royal compound are the fashionable **Royal Turf Club** (GU) *(south)*, the shady **Dusit Zoo** (GT) *(entrance Thanon Ratchawithi)* and the Italianate, domed **National Assembly** (GT G) *(east)*. The focal point of the square in front of the building is an equestrian **statue** of King Chulalongkorn. Nearby are a park, Suan Amphon, and a former royal palace, Wang Dusit.

★★★**Phra Thinang Vimanmek** ⊘ (GT) – *Entrance off Thanon Rachawithi*. A marvel of traditional architecture in golden teak, the 31-room Vimanmek Palace built by King Rama V originally stood on Ko Si Chang *(see CHONBURI, Excursions)*; it has been restored to its former glory and furnished in contemporary style by the present queen. The tour of the elegant reception rooms, the stately throne room and the private apartments gives a fascinating insight into the royal lifestyle, which combined the strict observance of traditions with a modern outlook gained from Rama V's travels in Europe. The palace was the first building in Thailand to be lit by electricity and to have a modern bathroom with shower, although water had to be brought up the stairs by an army of retainers. The queen and royal consorts occupied separate quarters delightfully decorated in pastel colours.
An open sala features Thai classical dance in a cool lakeside setting. An elegant building houses the **Support Museum** (precious objects in gold, silver, niello, hide and wood carving, textiles). The stables have been converted into an interesting **Royal Elephant National Museum** devoted to the royal white elephants and related traditions. Near the Carriage Museum, the fine **Suan Hong** Mansion presents an exhibition on the rituals marking significant traditions (ordination ceremony, ploughing ceremony, royal barge procession among others). Several charming pavilions in the grounds have been turned into **museums** (photographs, royal paraphernalia, textiles).

★★**Wat Benchamabopit** (GT) – *Thanon Si Ayutthaya*. The innovative design with strong horizontal lines of the Marble Temple built by Prince Naris, the King's architect brother, has been reproduced throughout the land. Gardens, topiary, a canal and bridges create a harmonious setting. The original style combines Thai, Khmer and European architectural elements.

Phra Thinang Vimanmek, Bangkok

S. Bouquet/ MICHELIN

BANGKOK

BANGKOK

J — K

0   400 m

Wat Dusidaram

ROYAL BARGES MUSEUM

Khlong Bangkok Noi

Th. Arun Amarin

Thanon Somdet Phra Pin Klao

THA SAPHAN PHRA PIN KLAO

POM PHRA ARTHIT

Th.

BANG LAMPHOO

Th. Athit

THA PHRA ATHIT

Saphan Phra Pin Klao

Thanon Phra Athit

Ram

Buttri

Soi

Thanon

Th.

BANGKOK NOI/ THONBURI

WAT CHANA SONGKHRAM

X 46

WAT AMARINTHARAM

CHAO

PHRAYA

Th. Chao Fa

NATIONAL GALLERY

Soi

Thanon

BANGKOK NOI

THA RAILWAY

46

NATIONAL THEATRE

Thanon

MUSEUM OF FORENSIC MEDICINE

MAE

NAM

NATIONAL MUSEUM

ROYAL

WAT WISETKAN

Thanon

THA SIRIRAJ

THAMMASAT UNIVERSITY

That

THORANI

Trok

Th.

WAT BURANASIRI

S. Wat Wisetkan

Phrannok

THA PHRA CHAN

Phra

Thanon Ratchadamnoen Nai

Trok Wang Lang

THA PHRANNOK

Th. Phra Chan

Sanam Luang

Th.

7

Arun

Mahathat

Na

Thanon

S. Sala Tonchai

THA MAHARAJ

Wat Mahathat

J

40

Soi Wat Rakhang Khositaram

Trok Silapakorn

Phra

57

WAT RAKHANG KHOSITARAM

Chang

SILAPAKORN UNIVERSITY

Lan

Lak Muang

Amarin

THA CHANG LUANG

Th. Na Phra

Th. Lak Muang

MINISTRY OF DEFENCE

Y

Ban

Soi

WAT PHRA KAEO

Rachini

Khu

Muang

Soi Matum

Thanon

M

27

Th. Saran Rom

Wat Ratchapradit

NAVAL HARBOUR DEPARTMENT

M

GRAND PALACE

SARANROM PALACE

WAT PHRAYATHAM

Thanon

RATANA KOSIN

Sanam

Thanon

Mon

THA ROYAL

Th. Thai Wang

Th.

Deem

Khlong

Arun

WAT KHRUA WAN

Maharat

WAT PO

Rachini

WAT NAKKLANG

THA TIEN

Th. Chetuphon

Th. Phra Phiphit

42

Thanon

S. Setthakan

Itsaraphap

Maharat

Chai

7

Soi Itsaraphap

Soi Prok Wat Arun 3

WAT ARUN

Thanon

WAT MAI PHIREN

90

Amarin

Doem

Wang

Pom Wichai Prasit

THA RACHINI

Soi Tha Klang

Talat Pak Khlong

Thanon

Z

25

Soi

Wat Hong

WAT MOLILOKAYARAM

WAT KALYANAMIT

Thanon Saphan

Soi 27

Thanon

BANGKOK YAI

WAT KALYANAMIT

Soi 38

Wat Hong Rattanaram

Santa Cruz

S. Kudi Chain

Soi 36

Soi 23

Soi 34

Soi Itsaraphap 28

Khlong Bangkok Yai

Soi

Wat

Kanlaya

Sai 1

Soi 32

Soi 30

Itsaraphap

Wat Ratcha Sittharam

Thanon Thetsaban Sai 2

Thanon

Thetsaban

Wat Prayunwong

Th. Thetsaban Sai 2

J — K

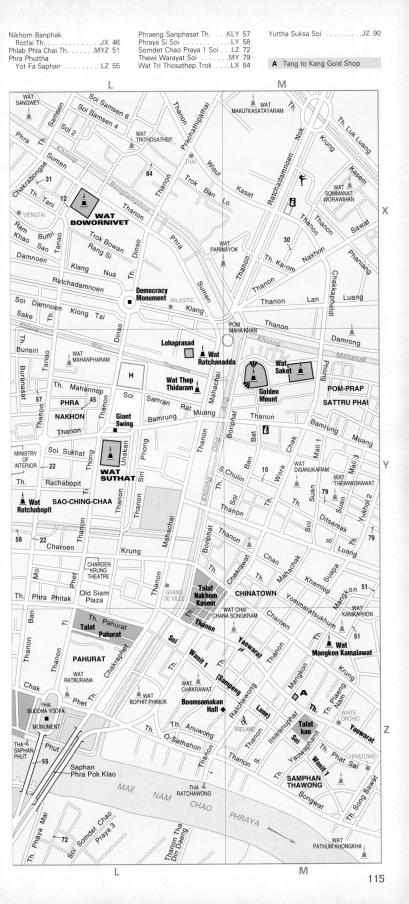

115

Traditional features include the stepped roof with glazed tiles, chofas, roof brackets and ornamented gables. A low balustraded wall surrounds the sanctuary which derives its name from the marble facing. Marble lions guard the pillared porch of the ubosot leading into the spacious interior which boasts an unusual cross-plan, stained glass in vibrant colours, multi-coloured marble flooring, walls painted in Thai motifs, a replica of the Phra Phuttha Chinarat *(see Wat Mahathat, PHITSAN-ULOK)*, and recesses adorned with famous religious monuments from all over the country.

King Rama V assembled in the cloister galleries the best examples (also copies) of the various styles of religious art from Thailand and neighbouring countries. In the centre of the courtyard an open chapel houses a tall **Buddha**★★ in royal apparel which is one of the finest examples of the Lopburi style. Walk round the cloister to admire two remarkable **Dvaravati standing Buddha images** in niches *(south)* and a Sukhothai-style **walking Buddha**★★ *(by west door)*.

Further to the east **Talat Thewes** (**FT K**) *(beside Khlong Krung Kasem)*, the Flower Market, is a riot of colour which will delight enthusiasts of exotic plants and flowers.

The National Library *(Thanon Samsen)* is an imposing building in which are exhibited ancient steles and scripts dating from the Ayutthaya period. The King Rama VI building is dedicated to this literary sovereign who was a fine poet.

Wat Ratcha Thiwat (**FT**) – *Thanon Samsen and left by Thanon Wat Ratcha.* The centrepiece of this shady riverside temple is a white chedi decorated with elaborate stuccowork. Mythical lions stand sentinel at the base, the deep niches contain statues of Buddha in black stone from Java seated on pedestals. At the south end there are two elegant royal houses in traditional style – Rama IV resided in the building with the arched frontage *(back)* and the wife of Rama V lived in the house with shutters *(front)*.

Walk down to the river to admire a harmonious wooden **mansion**★★ also built by Prince Naris.

CHINATOWN

In the late 18C at Rama I's request the Chinese community moved east outside the city walls to free the land on which was built the royal palace. With their entrepreneurial flair they soon created a thriving commercial centre with a teeming life and exotic atmosphere where all kinds of licit and illicit entertainment could be enjoyed – theatres, gambling houses, brothels, opium dens, cockfighting – and which have fascinated travellers to the East. The handsome architecture of the old buildings often obscured by shopfronts is reminiscent of a bygone age.

A sensory experience – The enclave bounded by Thanon Triphet *(west)* and Khlong Krung Kasem *(east)* is best appreciated by exploring on foot the main thoroughfares **Thanon Yaowarat** and Soi Wanit 1 **(Soi Sampeng)** (**LMZ**), and the warren of narrow lanes (Soi Issaranuparp) lined with a bewildering array of specialist shops and street pedlars.

The strange smells, fascinating sights, noisy traffic and seething crowds create an overwhelming spectacle. Goods on sale range from Chinese lanterns, incense sticks, paper funerary offerings in the shape of cars, houses, planes, which are burned to please the deceased, to embroidered wedding pillows. Dazzling jewellery shops are crammed full with rows of gold chains and ingots – the **Tang To Kang Gold Shop** (**MZ A**) on Soi Sampeng is notable. Traditional pharmacies dispense folk remedies for all types of ailments.

In the early morning the locals flock to **Talat Kao** (**MZ**) (Old Market – *Soi Issaranuparp*) and to **Pak Khlong Talat** (**KLZ**) *(by Memorial Bridge)*, the wholesale fruit and vegetable market where barges line up to unload fresh produce from the countryside. The colourful scene and intense activity will amaze and delight visitors. The dubious origin of the articles previously on offer in **Nakhon Kasem** (**LYZ**) (Thieves Market – *Thanon Chakrawat*) prompted the given name. Most of the antique shops have moved to more fashionable locations and there are few discoveries to be made.

Charoen Krung Theatre *(by Thanon Triphet)*, once the most elegant venue for Chinese opera, has been converted into a modern cinema.

A vibrant religious tradition – Amid the intense commercial activity the numerous temples in Chinatown attest to the all-embracing devotion of the people. Fierce dragons guard Taoist temples wreathed with incense, while others are dedicated to Theravada and Mahayana Buddhism. All schools of Buddhism find expression at the venerated **Wat Mangkon Kamalawat** (**MZ**) *(Thanon Charoen Krung)*, where take place the colourful celebrations of the annual **Vegetarian Festival**. Another venue is the elaborate **Boonsamakan Hall** (**LMZ**) *(off Thanon Rajawong)*.

Chinatown

Tourism Authority of Thailand

Wat Pathum Khongkha built in the Ayutthaya period is one of the oldest temples in Bangkok. Wat Kanikapon was founded by a brothel-owner. The pride of **Wat Traimit** ⊙ (**GU**) *(junction of Thanon Yaowarat and Thanon Charoen Krung)* is an imposing golden **Buddha image★★** *(3m tall)* in the Sukhothai style which is of unknown origin. It was hidden under a coating of plaster and was fortuitously rediscovered in the 1950s.

Cultural diversity – A sizeable Indian and Muslim community has settled in Chinatown and their distinctive cultures add to the dynamic atmosphere. In the Indian quarter **"Little India"** *(near Thanon Chakraphet and Thanon Chakrawat by Khlong Ong Ang)* restaurants, food stalls, wedding shops, fabric shops and markets abound. Near **Talat Pahurat** (**LZ**) is a Sikh temple. The Muslims worship at a **mosque** *(off Thanon Songwat)* located in a Western-style mansion.

OLD COMMERCIAL DISTRICT

The riverside area witnessed the early foreign settlements in the 19C, as European trading houses lured by the country's immense natural resources increased their commercial activities. Only one of the original companies, the **East Asiatic Company** (**GV Y**), and the **Old Customs House** (**GV Z**) remain on their original site. A mosque and cemetery and Indian establishments nearby are symbolic of more recent arrivals.

An age of elegance – Overshadowed by high-rise buildings, fine 19C wooden buildings complete with shutters and verandas at the Portuguese and French Embassies recall the flavour of the period, as does the Authors' Wing at the historic **Oriental Hotel** (**GV E**) which is dedicated to famous writers and celebrities bitten by wanderlust and searching for inspiration in the exotic East. The luxurious shops in the adjacent shopping centre and the antique shops at **River City** (**GV**) (Royal Orchid Sheraton Hotel) attract discerning shoppers. Luxury riverside hotels enjoy unique **views★★★** of the fast-flowing Chao Phraya where ferries and barges transport people and goods in a flurry of activity.

Also of interest are the 18C **Holy Rosary Church** (**GV B**) built by the Portuguese and originally sited at Thonburi, and the handsome **Cathedral of the Assumption** (**GV D**) which dates from the early 20C.

Modern expansion – At the heart of a thriving business district run **Thanon Silom** (**GV**) and **Thanon Surawong** (**GV**) lined with modern office towers, banks, luxury hotels and shopping complexes. Night-life is centred around **Thanon Patpong** (**GV 48**) and neighbouring streets where an amazing variety of bars, clubs, discotheques and other exotic venues as well as a night market attract all-night revellers.

A fashionable residential quarter has grown along Thanon Sathorn Nua and Thanon Sathorn Tai.

The picturesque market, **Talat Bang Rak** (**GV K¹**), by the riverside serves the neighbourhood.

Patpong night life, Bangkok

Snake Farm (GV) – *Thanon Rama IV*. The research work of the long-established and well-respected Pasteur Institute which specialises in vaccines against snake bite is dramatically brought to the attention of the public by live demonstrations when poisonous snakes are milked of their venom. There are large numbers of local species in the snake pits and a slide show presents the work of the institute.

EASTERN QUARTER

The city continues to expand eastwards to meet the needs of a growing population. Only a few khlongs remain as a reminder of the garden landscape of early Bangkok. The skyline is constantly changing as new high-rise buildings (offices, department stores, hotels) are constructed.

The bustling market, **Talat Pratunam** (HU), is a popular landmark while the area around **Siam Square** (GHU) is frequented by fashionable crowds. Student life is centred around Chulalongkorn University. The Royal Bangkok Sports Club *(private)* and the open spaces of **Lumphini Park** (HV), which are a welcome retreat from the frenetic pace of city life, attract fitness enthusiasts. In the early morning the locals perform a graceful ballet as they practise the Chinese art of *tai chi*.
Along Thanon Pahonyothin *(north)* and Thanon Sukhumwit *(east)* are fashionable residential and entertainment districts.

Victory Monument (HT) – *Thanon Rachawithi and Thanon Phyathai*. An obelisk surrounded by bronze statues symbolises military valour in Thailand's stand for its independence over the centuries.

★★ **Jim Thompson's House** ☉ (GU F) – *Soi Kasemsan 2 off Thanon Rama I*. The house and its collections reveal the owner's great interest in Southeast Asian art and Thai domestic architecture. He lived here only for seven years and the house is now owned by a charitable trust. It was the setting for elegant social occasions.
Seven beautiful wooden houses from various regions assembled in luxuriant gardens by a khlong evoke a delightful image of the past although modern amenities have been skilfully added. The exquisite **art treasures**★★ – statues, porcelain, paintings – on display are enhanced by the splendid furnishings.

★★ **Suan Pakkard Palace** ☉ (HU) – *Thanon Si Ayutthaya*. The eclectic **collections**★★ of Thai art of the deceased Prince and Princess Chumphot are well presented in five traditional pavilions in landscaped gardens overshadowed by disparate modern buildings. **House I** displays superb examples of Khmer art, in particular a graceful 7C stone **statue of Uma**★★★ and a rare 12C-13C **Ardhanarisvara**★★ showing both Shiva and Uma; fine seated Buddhas in the U-Thong style (13C-14C); a model of a Thai throne, and a painting showing the horoscope of Prince Chumphot. A footbridge leads to **House II,** formerly a bedroom, which exhibits betel nut boxes, a Thai toilet set, inlaid containers and a howdah. In **House III** note a palanquin and umbrella, musical instruments, colourful Bencharong porcelain and fine 17C French drawings. **House IV** which served as a chapel contains several Buddha images; the lower floor is used as a dining area.
In the houses to the west is a brilliant display of minerals and shells in the lower rooms as well as an important **prehistoric collection**★★★ from Ban Chiang, Nakhon Phanom and other districts: unpainted and painted pottery, bronzes and jewellery.

Follow the path to the exquisite **Lacquer Pavilion★★★** over 100 years old, a treasure of Ayutthayan art. It boasts remarkable gold and black lacquer paintings on the inner walls relating events from the life of the Buddha and scenes from the Ramayana. Stroll round the peaceful gardens with ornamental shrubs and flowers, a lily pond which attracts birds, and rock sculpture. A teak barge by the canal running through the gardens recalls an earlier mode of transport. There is a small exhibition on puppet theatre with beautiful masks near the entrance.

Talat Pratunam (HU) – *Junction of Thanon Phetchaburi and Thanon Ratchadamri.* A vast bazaar with bustling stalls and countless pedlars which attracts large crowds. Also of interest are open-air restaurants and a shopping complex *(by Indra Hotel)* and the soaring Bay Yoke II tower.

Erawan Shrine (HU L) – *Thanon Ratchadamri by Grand Hyatt Erawan Hotel.* A colourful scene occurs daily at the shrine (San Thao Maha Phrom) dedicated to the Hindu god Brahma as crowds gather with offerings of incense and flowers to pray for various causes. Performances of Thai dance are sponsored by grateful devotees.

★**Ban Kamthieng** ⏱ (BR) – *Siam Society, Soi 21, Thanon Sukhumwit.* A generous member of the learned society has donated a harmonious teak house which originally stood in Chiang Mai and is now furnished in traditional style to create a picture of daily life. A rice barn nearby, as well as carts, farming implements and other artefacts are also typical.

BANGKOK Environs

Bangkok

Michelin Atlas p 26-27 – Plan of conurbation see Bangkok and Atlas p 26

The phenomenal growth of Bangkok is such that the outlying districts are becoming integrated into a great conurbation although industrial, residential and leisure development have now slowed down. In the last decades the working population has risen to meet the demands of fast industrialisation. Flooding in the rainy season is a major problem for the outskirts of the city but the people face the crisis with great resilience and resourcefulness.

THONBURI (ABR)

Excursions by express boat or long-tail boat-taxi from Tha Tien, River City or pier by Memorial Bridge. Or by road across Saphan Phra Phuttha Yot Fa (Memorial Bridge), Saphan Phra Pin Klao, or Saphan Krung Thon.
Temples near the river can be visited on foot through the narrow lanes off Thanon Prachatipok, Thanon Somdet Chao Phraya and Thanon Issaraphap.

Thonburi is the place where life still unfolds at a slower pace in the traditional floating houses along the canals crisscrossing the alluvial terrain. Khlongs Bangkok Noi, Bangkok Yai, Bang Khun Si and Bang Kruai are the busy main waterways, and as one penetrates deeper into the network the peaceful verdant scenery of orchards and tall trees framing old temples and houses is a delight. Scenes of children splashing in the water, families modestly clad in sarongs bathing, people going about their domestic chores or watching the world go by are features of a traditional way of life which is on the wane as the modern world impinges with television sets and other modern conveniences. Most sights can be reached by road, however, at the cost of missing out on the more picturesque aspects.

A new dawn – **King Taksin** established his capital in Thonburi in the late 18C after driving out the Burmese invaders who had destroyed Ayutthaya *(see AYUT-THAYA).* King Taksin's royal palace, sited at the junction of Khlong Bangkok Yai and the Mae Nam Chao Phraya marked by a ruined fort **Pom Wichai Prasit** (KZ), no longer exists. This time of glory was short-lived as Taksin's successor, Rama I, was concerned that the open site was vulnerable to enemy attack and moved the capital to the east bank of the river. Thonburi, however, boasts many admirable temples built by the kings of the Chakri dynasty which remain among the best examples of Rattanakosin architecture and decoration; some are adorned with admirable mural paintings. Besides the temples described below it is well worth exploring at leisure and discovering hidden treasures in the monastic compounds.

★★**Wat Arun** ⏱ (JZ) – *Access by boat from Tha Tien.* The monumental **Temple of Dawn**, is a spectacular riverside landmark and a cherished symbol of Bangkok. The temple, which dates from the Ayutthaya period and was the royal chapel in the reign of

King Taksin, housed the Emerald Buddha before its installation in Wat Phra Kaeo. The soaring late Ayutthaya-style **prang** (114m high), framed by four smaller prangs encrusted with ceramic and fragments of porcelain shaped into floral motifs glittering in the sunlight and decorated with a profusion of mythical animals and figures, is built on marshy land and is an architectural masterpiece started by King Rama II and completed in the following reign. At the foot of the stepped base, Buddha images in four pavilions depict birth, meditation, preaching and enlightenment and guard the steep staircases leading up to the upper platform, which affords splendid **views★★★** of the river and of the Royal Palace and the sprawling city on the opposite bank. The great prang symbolises Mount Meru, the realm of the gods, while the four outer prangs contain statues of Phra Pai, the god of the wind.

The massive door to the cloistered precinct to the north is guarded by colourful demons *(yaks)* flanked by statues in niches. The porticoed ubosot, vihara and mondop form a harmonious group.

At the end of the rainy season the King makes a traditional visit to Wat Arun to present saffron robes and gifts to the monks in a solemn ceremony *(Kathin)*. In the past the event was accompanied by a glorious procession of royal barges but this now occurs only in special celebration years, such as the Bicentennial of the Chakri dynasty, the King's 60th birthday and the Golden Jubilee of the King's accession to the throne.

★**Museum of Royal Barges** ☉ (JX) – *Khlong Bangkok Noi*. The magnificent collection of royal barges attests to the glorious pageantry attached to the Thai monarchy and recalling the traditions of Ayutthaya which dazzled many foreign observers. A procession of the brightly-coloured, gilded crafts with fantastically-shaped prows, skilfully rowed by a crew arrayed in traditional costumes is an impressive spectacle. Two steersmen set the course, a flagman holds the flag aloft, while an officer strikes the rhythm with a bamboo pole and a singer chants to the cadence of the oars.

The King rides in the finest barge, **Sri Suphanahongsa**, a 45m-long gilded vessel boasting a prow in the shape of a mythical swan and paddled by 50 oarsmen. The King is seated in a gilded wooden pavilion on a raised platform decked with royal umbrellas. Other impressive figureheads include a seven-headed serpent hood, garudas, dragons and figures from the Ramakien. The magnificent barges parade in full panoply only on special occasions such as the King's Jubilee or for visiting foreign royalty or heads of state.

★**Wat Rakhang Khositaram** (JY) – *North of Wat Arun*. The ubosot, prang and chedis of the peaceful temple, which dates from the reign of Rama I, have fine decorative elements. An architectural gem is **Ho Phra Trai Phidok★**, the scripture library housed in three elegant late-18C wooden buildings which served as the residence of Rama I before he came to the throne, and which were a gift to the temple. Of special note are the finely carved gable and door panels and the exquisite **murals** depicting scenes from the Ramakien and of the Buddhist cosmology.

Wat Arun

From Saphan Phra Pin Klao

★ **Wat Suwannaram** (EU) – *Soi Charan Sanit Wong 32.* The temple founded by Rama I and restored in the third reign is notable for the stucco and carved ornamentation of its harmonious ubosot and vihara in front of which stands a slender chedi. The artistry and originality of the 19C **murals**★★ are admirable. The west wall features the three worlds of Buddhist cosmology (heaven, earth and hell); on the entrance wall is the Victory of the Buddha over evil, and the side walls depict deities at prayer and scenes from the previous lives of the Buddha with amusing vignettes of contemporary life.

Wat Dusidaram (JX) – Double bai semas surround the ubosot which features late 18C-early 19C **mural paintings**★★; note in particular the vivid depiction of the Buddha victorious over evil above the entrance.

From Saphan Phra Phuttha Yot Fa (Memorial Bridge) – Tha Saphan Phut

The principal interest of **Wat Prayunwong** (KZ) is a hillock crowned with small chedis and surrounded by a pond teeming with tortoises which are regularly fed by the faithful. A tall chedi, two viharas ornamented with mother-of-pearl encrusted doors and ornate gables are additional features of the temple which dates from the third reign (early 19C). The distinctive cupola of **Santa Cruz Church** (KZ) is visible further to the north. **Wat Kalyanamit**★ (KZ) is described below.

Wat Phichai Yat (FV) boasts imposing chedis, a Chinese-style vihara and three towering prangs on a tiered platform.

The curved base of the ubosot of the delightful **Wat Thong Thammachat** (FV) recalls the Ayutthaya style, and **mural paintings**★★ depicting traditional scenes are noteworthy. The west wall features a contemporary townscape with wooden Thai houses and Chinese shop-houses. Nearby is **Wang Lee House** (FV X), a riverside mansion belonging to a prosperous Chinese family.

The assembly hall of **Wat Thong Nophakhun** (FV W) is decorated with bronze panels recounting scenes of the life of Buddha. The ubosot has original round windows, fine stuccowork and quaint wall paintings.

Along Khlong Bangkok Yai and Khlong Dan

Temples on the banks of Khlong Bangkok Yai can be reached by car and on foot while access to those further west is by boat only. A tour affords charming glimpses of a riverine way of life.

A colossal Buddha image and fine wall paintings adorn the imposing **ubosot** of **Wat Kalyanamit**★ which boasts an attractive riverside setting.

Wat Hong Rattanaram (JZ) founded during the Ayutthaya period comprises a splendid **ho trai**, a restored vihara and a porticoed **ubosot**. The latter has gables highlighted with carvings and glass mosaic, door and window panels adorned with trees and mythical birds. There are also interesting Buddha images.

Wat Sang Krachai (EV), which is of ancient foundation, is worthy of note for the ornamentation of its elegant **ubosot**.

A statue of **King Taksin** (FV) and a stele precede the ubosot of **Wat Inthararam** (EV), a favourite royal retreat marked by two chedis dedicated to the king and his queen. Two viharas frame the sanctuary which enshrines a gilded Buddha image; the walls are unusually decorated in gold and black.

The ancient **Wat Paknam** (EV) is renowned for its monastic school and meditation centre.

The lush vegetation and orchards along Khlong Dan and the smaller khlongs create an attractive setting for a multitude of temples which have interesting ornamental features, in particular fine wall paintings, porcelain decoration and venerated Buddha images, and include **Wat Kamphaeng** (AR) (vihara), **Wat Nang Chi** (EV) (vihara, ubosot) **Wat Ratcha Orot** (AR) (chedis, ubosot, vihara) and **Wat Sai** (AR) (pavilion).

NONTHABURI (BQ)

Access by express boat or north by 301 and 3110.

The small town situated on the banks of the Mae Nam Chao Phraya was formerly part of the kingdom of Ayutthaya and has a mixed population of Mon, Chinese and Muslim origin.

The main sights in the town are the elegant **Old City Hall** *(near the clock tower by the pier)*, the **Natural Historical Museum** and the **Prison Museum.**

Take a tour by boat to enjoy the activity and scenery along the picturesque waterways and khlongs (Bang Yai, Bang Kruai) lined with fine temples – Wat Prang Luang, Wat Prasat, Wat Bang Khanun, Wat Pho Bang O, Wat Chalo. Nonthaburi is famous for its beautiful **flower gardens** and fertile **orchards** which grow a variety of succulent tropical fruits. Local artisans produce fine **pottery.**

★**Wat Chalerm Phra Kiat** (BQ) – *East bank. Tambon Ban Si Muang. Access by boat from town pier.* Rama III built the temple dedicated to his parents on the site of a 17C fortress erected in the reign of King Narai. The walled compound comprises three imposing porticoed buildings and a powerful chedi. Undulating nagas and colourful floral motifs in porcelain adorn the roofs and gables, and stuccowork highlights the doors and windows.

PATHUM THANI

The landscape around Pathum Thani is typical of the delta of the Mae Nam Chao Phraya and boats ply the waterways and khlongs. The fertile rice-growing land brings prosperity to the town which is populated by Mons, who migrated here from Burma during the Ayutthaya era and then in the late 18C in the reign of King Taksin. The Mon language is still spoken in the area.

Wat Pai Lom – *East bank. Amphoe Sam Khok. Access by 307 and 3309 north or by boat.* The main attraction of this ancient monastery founded in the Sukhothai period (13C) is its population of open-billed storks, which migrate from Siberia in November to their wintering ground at the temple and usually depart in June when the young birds are strong enough to fly. The trees are covered with storks which live on snails from the rice fields. The fascinating spectacle attracts bird lovers and ornithologists who study the phenomenon.

SAMUT PRAKAN (CS)

In the past decades the small province sited at the head of the Gulf of Thailand has attracted many industrial enterprises which have changed its character although some seaside resort areas such as Bang Pu remain very popular. The coastal area formerly covered with mangrove forests now supports shrimp farms drained by tidal currents.

Crocodile Farm ⊙ (CS) – *Tambon Thaiban.* One of the largest crocodile farms in the world where the reptiles can be seen at various ages. The skin is processed into leather for export. There are also elephants, tigers and chimpanzees. Demonstrations of crocodile feeding and wrestling.

Summer Palace, Bang Pa-In

★★ **Muang Boran** ⓥ (**CS**) – *Near Tambon Bang Pu Mai.* The site of this remarkable open-air museum which bears the name "Ancient City" and extends over 80 hectares – 197 acres, is designed in the geographical outline of Thailand. The country's most famous monuments and places of worship are recreated in authentic detail, some in actual size and others on a scale of 1 to 3, with the help of expert advisers and craftsmen and are placed in their exact geographical location. This outstanding achievement presents a unique opportunity to gain an appreciation of Thailand's heritage and traditions. The fascinating exhibits which include stupas, mondops, prangs, temples, palaces as well as traditional Thai houses, floating market, fishing village and gardens, recall the splendours of Sukhothai, Ayutthaya, Lampang, Phimai, Chiang Mai, Phetchaburi and Bangkok among other important centres. A **museum** is devoted to folk culture: pottery, rice cultivation, fishing, musical instruments. This inspired venture financed by a rich Thai philanthropist also aims to promote traditional craftsmanship.

> At Phra Pradaeng *(west bank)* the popular **Paklat Songkran Festival** *(Sunday following Songkran Day – 13 April)* is celebrated according to the Mon tradition (games, procession, setting free birds and fishes) and attracts crowds from the capital.

BANG PA-IN★★

Phra Nakhon Si Ayutthaya

Michelin Atlas p 24 or Map 965 – G 5

The royal estate situated on an island in the Mae Nam Chao Phraya is easily accessible from the capital en route to Ayutthaya. The original palace was built in the 17C by King Prasat Thong, who was born in the region, as a summer residence

which was also popular with his successors. After the destruction of Ayutthaya in the 18C the site was abandoned until the late 19C when it found new favour with King Rama IV (Mongkut) who built a new palace. His son King Rama V (Chulalongkorn) added further buildings in a variety of styles which reflect his interest in the outside world. Bang Pa-In which is now used occasionally for state ceremonies is a charming retreat in a setting of ponds and parkland.

TOUR ⓥ

Access to the palace grounds is through the visitor centre.

Entrance – An avenue lined with semas leads past a Khmer-style prang shaded by a bodhi tree and containing a revered statue of King Prasat Thong.

★★ **Phra Thinang Aisawan Tippaya** – The focal point in the middle of a lake is the graceful pavilion, a jewel of Thai architecture, with stepped roofs and slender spire, which houses a life-size statue of Rama V. The pavilion built in 1876 is modelled on the Phra Thinang Aphon Phimok Prasat in the Grand Palace in Bangkok.

On the right the waters lap the steps of a broad terrace on which stands a circular building in Russian style used as a reception hall. Nearby is an elephant-feeding area. A bridge with covered access for female members of the household marks the boundary between the outer and inner court.

PICTOR

123

Phra Thinang Warophat Phiman – The palace adorned with pilasters and a pedimented portico in the Italian Renaissance style is used for state receptions. The Audience Room which contains a canopied throne is decorated with a regal portrait of Rama V and scenes from Thai history and literature.

Beyond are examples of French colonial and Spanish architecture and a miniature bridge from Italy lined with statues and lamps capped with eagles.

Ho Withunthasana – Return to the park to see the fine Royal Observatory, a Portuguese-style tower highlighted with ochre bands where King Mongkut, a keen astronomer, carried out his celestial observations.

Phra Thinang Uthayan Phumisathian – The original teak building in the style of a Swiss chalet was destroyed by fire and only the water-tower remains. Nearby stands a white pavilion.

** **Phra Thinang Wehat Chamrun** – The magnificent Chinese pavilion presented by wealthy merchants is a fine example of classic oriental architecture. The ceiling carvings depicting the history of three kingdoms in Chinese history, the hand-painted mosaics and symbolic animal sculptures were executed by Chinese craftsmen. A throne is the focal point of the entrance hall which is notable for a remarkable carving of a mythical animal (head of a cow, body of a snake, 5 claws of an eagle, antlers of a deer, tail of a fish), a cycle of epic poems inspired from Chinese poetry inscribed in a frieze, and the symbol of a fish inset in the floor (yin/yang symbol). Also of interest are the elaborately carved furnishings, a hand-powered elevator and a bathroom with a dragon spout.

Park – Among the monuments dotted in the pleasant grounds is a tall marble obelisk with medallions in memory of Rama V's consort and her daughters who drowned in 1881 when their boat capsized on the river. The attendants were prevented from giving assistance because by law it was an offence to touch members of the royal family. The law was repealed after the tragic event. Another monument (1887) is dedicated to another royal consort and her three young children.

Further along is the water gate through which passed the royal barge.

ADDITIONAL SIGHTS

Wat Chumphon Nikayaram – *Thanon Phra Chom Khao, northeast of the palace near the railway station.* The foundation of the temple dates from the reign of King Prasat Thong (17C) and it has been restored by later rulers. The gable of the vihara bears the emblem of Rama IV in stucco and the interior is ornamented with mural paintings and decorated pillars. In the grounds there are also two harmonious redented **chedis**★ from the same period which are fine examples of Ayutthaya architecture.

Wat Niwet Tham Prawat ⊙ – *West of the palace.* King Rama V (Chulalongkorn) built the temple (19C) on a neo-Gothic plan in a shady island site. Interesting elements include a stained glass window depicting the king and a large statue of Buddha cast by Prince Pradi Worakan.

Crafts

Visit the **Royal Folk Arts and Crafts Centre** (*Tambon Chang Yai, Amphoe Bang Sai. 18km west by A 347 and local road)* to watch farmers at work as they learn traditional arts and crafts: basketry, flower making, weaving, wood carving, furniture making. An extensive array of high-quality products is on sale in the shop located in a modern Thai-style building.

In landscaped gardens stand buildings in varied architectural styles where demonstrations and shows are held. The Royal Lodge, where the present queen who sponsors the project stays, is built of local materials. A freshwater aquarium, Wang Pla, and a Bird Park are enjoyable features.

BURIRAM

Buriram – Population 199 618

Michelin Atlas p 14 or Map 965 – F 8 – Local map see Nakhon Ratchasima (Khorat)

On the edge of the Khorat plateau, the capital of Buriram province, originally an important part of the Khmer empire, is a good base for visiting Khmer monuments, in particular the impressive **Prasat Hin Phanom Rung**★★★ and **Prasat Muang Tham**★★. There are many ruins of lesser interest (Prang Ku Suan Taeng, Prasat Hin Kuti Russi, Prang Kuti Russi, Kuti Russi, Prasat Nong Hong) dotted all over the countryside which is dominated by **Khao Kradung**, an ancient volcanic hill (265m high). A forest park has been created at the foot of the hill *(6-7km south by 219). Access to hill top by car or by staircase 265m long.*

EXCURSIONS

★★★**Prasat Hin Phanom Rung** – *See Prasat Hin PHANOM RUNG.*

★★**Prasat Muang Tham** – *Ban Khok Muang, Tambon Chora Khe, Amphoe Prakhon Chai. 8km from Phanom Rung.* The ruined "temple of the lower city" dedicated to Shiva and probably built in the 11C-12C as a residence for the Khmer governor forms an evocative picture. Pilasters, lintels and pediments, richly decorated in the Khleang and Baphuon (Angkor) styles with mythical animals (kala and naga), garlands and floral motifs, illustrate the mastery of the Khmer craftsmen.

The outer wall with its heavy moulded coping is pierced by four gopuras framed by elegant windows decorated with balusters. The main entrance with three doorways to the east opens into an enclosure with four L-shaped stepped ponds surmounted by the stone body of a five-headed **naga★★** with their tails framing stone gates. The ponds symbolise the four oceans surrounding the sacred Mount Meru.

An inner galleried wall with four doorways surrounds the sanctuary. A standing Simha and a seated ascetic adorn the door frame of the eastern gopura. The outer gable depicts a seated deity over a Kala face with a five-headed naga in the upper register; the inner gable features a Simha, a monkey and an elephant in a floral motif and the lintel shows Krishna subduing the Naga.

Four of the original five prangs remain in the compound. In the front row the larger middle prang has collapsed; nearby a fine sandstone lintel portrays a seated deity over a Kala face with seated above seven ascetics in a row. On the **lintel★★** of the northern prang Shiva and Uma ride the bull Nandin; above is a row of 10 ascetics sitting on the back of a Naga. The **colonnette★** of the door frame is finely carved in a diamond pattern. The southern prang is decorated with a deity seated on a Kala face spouting garlands above which is a row of 9 seated ascetics.

In the rear the lintel of the northern prang depicts Krishna lifting Mount Kowathana while that of the southern prang shows the god Aruna seated on a throne supported by three swans perched over a Kala disgorging garlands.

A large rectangular pond 200m to the north feeds the network of canals which are part of the irrigation scheme of the plain.

Prasat Muang Tham

B. Davies

Ban Kruat Stone Quarries – *141km south by 219, at Amphoe Prakhon Chai inter-section, 2075 to Tambon Ban Kruat.* Blocks of sandstone scattered over the fascinating site (1sq km) testify to the intense activity which probably reigned during the period when the Khmers were building their temples. Visitors can see all stages of quarrying from incision marks to deep vertical cuts.

Lam Nang Rong Dam – *Ban Non Din Daeng. As for Ban Kruat above, then 2075 west to Amphoe Lahan Sai, turn left and take 3068 past Amphoe Pa Kham inter-section, continue to Ban Non Din Daeng, bear left 500m before a monument.*
The tranquil area around the dam is notable for the multicoloured volcanic stone (Hin-Loi) and is ideal for recreation. Nearby are a smaller dam and Prasat Nong Hong which comprises three prangs.

CHAI NAT
Chai Nat – Population 74 489

Michelin Atlas p 11 or Map 965 – F 5

The tranquil agricultural town on the east bank of the Mae Nam Chao Phraya has a glori-ous past as it was an important base from which Burmese attacks were repelled, hence its name Chai Nat meaning "place of victory". Its location also placed it right at the centre of the territorial conflict as Ayutthaya challenged the power of the Sukhothai kingdom. The scenery around Chai Nat is typical of the central plain – lush rice fields crisscrossed by a network of canals fed by the Chao Phraya dam. The town was an important trading centre in the heyday of fluvial transport but decline set in as roads were built.

Straw Bird Fair

A procession of huge straw birds perched on elaborately decorated floats is the highlight of the fair which celebrates Chai Nat's rice-farming tradition *(Feb, Chai Nat Bird Park).* Local handicrafts and food products are on sale.

SIGHTS

Wat Phra Boromathat – *Mu 2, Tambon Chai Nat. 7km by 3183.* The ancient temple dates back to the late-Sukhothai to early-Ayutthaya period (14C-15C). An important feature is the **chedi** on an indented square base with four twin-gabled niches housing seated Buddhas punctuating the body and a further tier of small niches capped by slim finials. At the base of the finial is a ring of lotus petals. The structure has some elements of the Srivijaya style. The vihara contains a stucco Buddha image discovered at the site and placed on a pedestal in front of the presiding Buddha.

Chai Nat Muni National Museum ⊘ – *Wat Phra Boromathat.* The museum presents artefacts from the Chainat region, religious art ranging from votive tablets to Buddha images in vari-ous styles, and Chinese and Thai pottery.

Chai Nat Bird Park – *Tam-bon Khoa Tha Phra.* Walk through the large enclos-ures to admire brightly hued birds which inhabit the park set in landscaped flower gardens.

EXCURSIONS

Sankhaburi – *25km south by 311 and 3010.* The Mae Nam Noi bisects the peaceful small town where archeological remains attest to its past political

S. Bouquet/ MICHELIN

Wat Phra Boromathat

importance in the rivalry between the Sukhothai and Ayutthaya kingdoms, and as a cultural and artistic centre where Dvaravati and U-Thong art as well as Sukhothai and Ayutthaya influences were at play. The walls and moats of the ancient fortified town still remain.

Wat Mahathat – The site of the temple which dates from the Ayutthaya period (14C) is dotted with ruined chedis and prangs including one in a fluted, bulbous shape, a dilapidated vihara and an ubosot. There are also fragments of statues, a seated Buddha near a bodhi tree.

Wat Phra Kaeo – *South of town.* The temple is renowned for its harmonious **chedi★★** which rests on a powerful square base. The square body is marked by pilasters, stucco panels and niches surmounted by a canted upper section also pierced with niches, mouldings, an elegant bell and a ringed spire. The vihara houses a fine seated Buddha in the U-Thong style.

CHAIYA★

Surat Thani – Population 42 905

Michelin Atlas p 20 or Map 965 – L 4

The present modern town does not do justice to its glorious past. The theory that it was probably a regional capital of the Srivijaya Empire between the 8C and the 10C is hotly disputed although the ancient name is derived from Siwichaiya, the Thai rendering of the Javanese. However, significant archeological finds (bronze and sandstone statues of the **Avalokitesvara Bodhisattva** – *in National Museum, Bangkok*) attest to its historical importance *(see SURAT THANI)*.

SIGHTS

★★ Wat Phra Boromathat – *From Surat Thani north by 41, turn right between Km 66-67 into 4191 and continue 2km.* The temple which dates from the Srivijaya period (8C-13C) was abandoned after the fall of the empire until 1896 when major restoration was carried out. Further work followed in 1901 during the reign of King Rama V.

A door leads into the cloister where Buddha statues are aligned in the gallery. A shallow moat surrounds the **Phra Mahathat Chedi★★** (24m high) which is a fine example of Srivijaya architecture. Four blind porches and horseshoe gables highlight the square structure indented at the corners; the upper tiers are topped by 24 small stupas and the whole is crowned by an elegant gilded spire. At three corners stand ringed chedis.

The renovated **ubosot** *(west of the chedi)* which unusually faces west stands on the original base; in front are the original bai sema. The interior enshrines a red sandstone Buddha statue of the Ayutthaya period. To the east of the chedi is **Wihan Luang** which contains several statues.

The Bangkok-style **Na Phrathat Chedi** near the main entrance dates from the reign of King Rama V and is also noteworthy. Three restored **statues** of the Chaiya school dating from the Ayutthaya period are believed to stand on the site of an ancient vihara.

Chaiya National Museum ⊙– *In the compound of Wat Phra Boromathat Chaiya.* The museum was set up by a former abbot who collected archeological objects found in Chaiya and the surrounding area and displayed them in the ubosot and gallery of the wat in 1931.

The first building to the east of the temple displays stone and bronze statues found in Chaiya. The second presents art and archeological objects from prehistoric times to the Bangkok period, including a beautiful engraved Frog Drum from Ko Samui, a reproduction of the famous bronze sculpture of the **Avalokitesvara Bodhisattva**, clay votive tablets, Southern minor art, folk art and ritual objects.

Wat Long – *Continue by 4191. Turn right before Wat Padung Wiengchai and proceed along Thanon Santimit. The ruin is on the left opposite Chiwittaya school.* A square basement is all that remains of a ruined prasat in Srivijaya style made of brick curiously set with sap, which enshrined an image of worship.

Wat Kaeo – *Past Wat Long continue for 500m beyond a bridge then bear left towards Wat Rattanaram and proceed for a short distance.* This important ruined Srivichai monument comprises a brick building with a cruciform plan and five chambers resting on a square terrace with stairs on the east and west faces. The exterior walls are punctuated by pilasters. The south porch still has the ornamental miniature arch motif (horseshoe) which was probably common to all faces.

EXCURSIONS

Ban Phum Riang – *6km east by 4011.* The picturesque fishing village with its houses built on stilts on Khlong Lung, is famous for silk weaving and wickerware. Proceed to **Laem Pho** *(2km further by 4011)*, a natural sandy cape which affords a fine **view★★** of the bay and where a fishing village nestles amid the mangrove. Excellent seafood restaurants are an added attraction.

Wat Suan Mokka Phalaram – *North by 41, turn left between Km 70-71.* A revered monk, Achan Buddhadasa (1906-93), founded the temple renowned as a meditation centre in a beautiful forest setting. The unorthodox teaching comprises Zen, Taoist and Christian elements and attracts many foreigners seeking the light. Meditation cells dotted on the hillside provide peace and solitude. There are several teaching pavilions; the outer wall and the interior of the Spiritual Theatre are decorated with modern Buddhist paintings and poems illustrating moral precepts.

Road 41 north runs through a fertile landscape of orchards. There are charming villages (Tha Chana, Lang Suan) off the main highway.

CHAIYAPHUM

Chaiyaphum – Population 198 643

Michelin Atlas p 12 or Map 965 – F 7

The small provincial town was formerly a trading post between Ayutthaya and Laos. It is of little interest except as an excursion base to enjoy the fine natural attractions of the area; however, in the past Khmer kings and their officials broke their journey at Chaiyaphum on the long route from Angkor to Si Thep and other northern destinations.

To the north the remote verdant hills (Phu Phra – *see below* – Phu Phaek, Pha Koeng) provide a tranquil atmosphere for hermits and meditation temples.

A loyal subject

Phraya Lae and his followers, fleeing from conflicts at court in Vientiane (Laos), moved to the right bank of the Mekong. In 1819 he founded a town in the Chaiyaphum area and opted for the protection of King Rama II of Bangkok. In 1826 when King Anuwong of Vientiane mounted an expedition to attack Bangkok, he refused to join and alerted the Khorat officials. The invasion was crushed and King Rama II awarded him the high-ranking title of Phraya Phakdi Chumphon; he is also known as Chao Pho Phaya. He was later captured and executed by Laotian troops.

He is revered as the protector of Chaiyaphum and is commemorated by a monument where he is depicted in traditional official costume with a document in his right hand *(in front of the provincial hall, Thanon Banakran)*). His shrine is located on the outskirts *(3km west near Nong Pla Thao swamp by 225)*. Nearby a tamarind tree marks the spot where he is said to have been killed in 1826 by an invading Laotian army.

EXCURSIONS

Prang Ku – *2km east of provincial hall.* Tall trees shade a laterite Khmer temple built by Jayavarman VII (1181-1218) to serve a hospital on the road linking Angkor, Phimai and Si Thep. The entrance gate *(gopura)* is roofless; on the north side is a sandstone lintel depicting the churning of the sea of milk, a scene from Hindu mythology. The shrine oriented to the east has three blind doorways and contains a statue of Buddha; in front of the west door is an Ayutthaya-style standing Buddha with a lotus-decorated base, whereas the seated Buddha by the north door is in the Dvaravati style. Nearby are scattered fragments of lintels. Conservation work in progress. Bathing rites are held each year on the day of the full moon in April.

Tat Ton National Park – *21km north by 2051.* This small forest park (218sq km) with its rich wildlife and beautiful scenery including caves and waterfalls is popular for leisure activities. At the end of a track by the entrance is **Nam Tok Tat Ton**★ which tumbles down majestically from a wide rock platform especially in the rainy season.

Phu Phra – *Tambon Na Sieo 12km north by 201; or by 2051 after 7km turn right into a track and right again into a dirt road. Park by a school.* Hermits live in this hilly site where is located a shrine surrounded by tall trees but unfortunately roofed over. Stone slabs shelter a seated Buddha, known as Phra Chao Ong Toe, in the attitude of subduing Mara (touching the earth) and seven smaller Buddha images in the same position, all carved in the rock. The carvings probably date from the late 13C U-Thong period.

Wat Khon Sawan – *35km east by 202 and 2054.* A small museum in the grounds contains a large standing Dvaravati **Buddha statue** and a collection of ancient **bai sema** (boundary stones) depicting scenes from the Jakata. Nearby is a typical Laotian-style wooden ubosot *(sim)* surrounded by an open gallery and with a radiating motif carved on the gable.

Ban Khon Sawan was an ancient town of the Dvaravati period girt by an oval-shaped moat surrounded by swamps.

Phra That Nong Sam Moeun – *104km north. Take 201 for 90km to Ban Nong Song Hong, turn left into 2055 for 9km to Ban Kaeng, then left and proceed 5km to the wat.* The site was the centre of an old town as evidenced by earthen ramparts and moats still visible in the area. The **Phra That,** a tapering brick structure rising to a height of 24m from a square base and crowned by a lotus bud, probably dates back to the early Ayutthaya period. Standing Buddhas adorn the niches framed by pilasters in the middle section.

A short distance further the **Sala** of a thousand rooms is an unusual structure. In a shady area is aligned a collection of old *bai semas.* Nearby grimacing plaster sculptures illustrating a popular notion of the Buddhist hell strike a warning note to wrongdoers. High up on a rise a large reclining Buddha overlooks the fertile plain below.

★ **Pa Hin Ngam Forest Park** – *Tambon Ban Rai 29km from Amphoe Thep Sathit. From Chaiyaphum 112km south by 201 to Ban Nong Bua, then right into 205 for 65km and at Km 293-294 right again into 2354 to Ban Na Yang Kalak Sap Yai. Visitor Centre.* Rocks eroded by water and rain into fantastic shapes (Dragon Rock, Castle Rock) are scattered over a large area (320sq km). A mass of purple wild flowers (Dok Ka Jeaw) makes a colourful show in the rainy season (July). The viewpoint *(2 640m from the park office)* affords spectacular **views★★★** over the cliffs to the Khao Phang Hoei range, the westernmost of the Khorat plateau, of the valley in which runs the small Lam Sonti river and of the mountain chain on the horizon tapering down to the central plain. There are also several waterfalls in the area.

Wat Mai Ban Kut Ngong – *South by 201, turn left at Km 116, continue for 13km by laterite road, after 9km turn left in the bend and proceed for 5km to the temple (school).* Fine collection of **bai sema** of the Dvaravati period, in particular one depicting the Bodhisattva standing upright on a lotus flower and scenes from the Jataka or the birth of Buddhism.

The area with its low fertile rice fields with a swamp is typically that of an ancient town of the Dvaravati period.

Silk weaving is a profitable activity carried out in surrounding villages *(Ban Khwao, 13km west by 225)* and fabrics are on sale in local shops.

The area is also famous for its **birdlife,** as from November to April thousands of birds migrate and nest at Nong Waeng *(35km east by 202)* and at Nong Laharn *(40km south by 201).*

CHANTHABURI★

Chanthaburi – Population 124 942

Michelin Atlas p 18 or Map 965 – I 7 – Local map see Pattaya

The lively town on the west bank of Mae Nam Chanthaburi lies in a lush plain backed by mountains culminating in Khao Soi Dao (1 670m) to the northwest. There are pleasant beaches and capes along the indented coastline.

It is renowned for its rich deposits of rubies, sapphires and other precious stones but because of the unfavourable economic trend the mines are no longer active. The workings may be viewed near Ban Kacha *(4km west).* Most of the gems traded in town are from other sources (Kamphuchea, Myanmar).

A Christian tradition – Chanthaburi has given refuge to an influx of Vietnamese settlers escaping religious or political persecution throughout the centuries. The imposing **Notre-Dame Cathedral** *(east bank)* and many Christian schools are enduring testimonies of their faith.

A land of plenty

Orchards produce an abundance of succulent fruit (rambutan, mangosteen and durian, pomelo, jack-fruit, mango, pineapple) which is on sale at roadside stalls and in the market and is celebrated by a delightful **Fruit Fair** *(May or June).*

The centre of the **gem trade** is Thanon Si Chan. Lucrative deals are struck in its small jewellers' shops where dealers often rent a stall. Visitors should take great care and deal only with reputable jewellers.

SIGHTS

Town centre – A pleasant park cooled by a lake dominated by an equestrian **statue** of King Taksin is a focal point. Nearby are many restaurants and food stalls.

The bustling Thanon Si Chan with its jewellers' shops and artisans' workshops is well worth a visit. In the side streets *(Thanon Sukha Phiban)* there are examples of fine colonial architecture resplendent with wood carving and stuccowork. From the two bridges visitors can catch a glimpse of the façades and of the activity on the river.

An equestrian **statue** *(Tha Luang Road, near the old governor's office)*, housed in a curious building in the shape of a cavalryman's hat, commemorates **King Taksin** who quashed an attempt by the governor to break away from the new kingdom established at Thonburi in the 18C after the Burmese had razed Ayutthaya. Nearby is the **Lak Muang** (the city shrine).

Khai Noen Wong – *3km south by 3 then turn west into 3146 for a short distance.* The walls of a fort built by Rama III recall the threat of invasion by Vietnamese forces which the country faced in the mid 19C. French and English cannons are reminders of the interest shown in the region by the European powers. In the grounds are **Wat Yothanimit** which has a bell-shaped chedi and is girt by a Chinese-style wall, and the **Underwater Archeological Museum.** Investigation and conservation techniques are explained, and on display are finds (Sangkalok earthenware and ceramics) from the sea-bed of the Gulf of Thailand.

Continue for 10km along 3146 to **Ban Tha Chalaep,** a picturesque fishing village with houses on stilts at the mouth of the Mae Nam Chanthaburi.

EXCURSIONS

Laem Sing – *25km south by 3, turn right at Km 347 for 15km.* A busy fishing pier at Ban Pak Nam presents a colourful spectacle. Nearby are **Teuk Daeng,** a red building which was the headquarters of the Phitak Patchamit Fort where lived French officers and now used as a library, and **Khuk Khi Kai** *(1km further, turn left opposite the beach),* a rectangular brick structure with slit windows which was used as a chicken coop as well as a prison for the locals during the period when the French occupied the town (1893-1904). **Oasis Sea World** ⊘is a breeding and conservation centre for humpbacked and Irrawaddi dolphins.

Khao Khitchakut National Park – *30km west by 3 and at Km 324 right into 3249.* The park adjoins the wildlife sanctuary of Khao Soi Dao. In addition to the beautiful forest scenery and rich flora and fauna the highlights include curious rock formations, a **Buddha footprint** *(3hr on foot)* at the top of Khao Phra Bat, caves (**Tham Russi** contains a well with medicinal waters – *2hr on foot*), and the impressive 13-tiered **Nam Tok Krathing** *(300m from the park office).*

Nam Tok Phliu National Park ⊘ – *15km south; by 3 for 13km then left for 2km.* A popular recreation area at the foot of Khao Sa Bap refreshed by several waterfalls. **Nam Tok Phliu** cascading down the rock face into a pool is particularly fine. Also of interest is a pyramidal monument containing the ashes of Queen Sunantha who drowned on the way to Bang Pa-In *(see Bang Pa-In).* From the chedi built by Rama V there is a fine **view** of the waterfall. Walk up the stairs to the right to reach the upper level for a plunging view.

CHIANG KHAN

Loei – Population 61 936

Michelin Atlas p 8 or Map 965 – D 6

The modest linear riverside town ringed by mountains retains some wooden shophouses *(Thanon Chai Khong),* and temples (Wat Pa Klang, Wat Mahathat) with French-Lao elements (viharas with painted shutters and colonnades), and murals (Wat Si Khun Muang) which are worth a visit. Riverside restaurants offer excellent Isan food in a picturesque setting.

EXCURSIONS

★★**Scenic road to Nong Khai** – *300km east by 211 – 3 hr.* From Chiang Khan the road runs parallel to the Mekong through beautiful lush scenery, passing Pak Chom (hill-tribe settlement), Sang Khom, Si Chiangmai (Lao and Vietnamese settlers) and Tha Bo (busy agricultural market town – bananas, herbs, tomatoes, Huay Mong Dam, public park).

Wat Tha Khaek – *2km.* This old temple is famous for its marble statue of Buddha which is highly revered and for an Isan-style mural decorating the ubosot *(sim).*

Kaeng Khut Khu – *3km.* The rapid in the middle of the Mekong is a spectacular sight as the swift current swirls and tumbles round the rocks (best seen from February to May). Good **views** may be enjoyed from the salas. Kaeng Tha Khaek is another rapid upstream.

Nam Tok Than Thip – *Turn right between Km 97-98 and continue for 2km by laterite road. Easy access from parking.* A fine three-tiered waterfall in a pleasant shady spot.

Turn left at Km 73-74 for a fine **view** of the Mekong from the scenic area. At Km 71-72 on the left is another popular waterfall, Nam Tok Than Thong *(Ban Pha Tang, Amphoe Sang Khom)*.

Wat Hin Mak Peng – *Tambon Phuttha Bat, Amphoe Si Chiangmai. Turn left at Km 64.* In a peaceful forest setting by the Mekong is a meditation temple which has fine modern buildings – a Lao-style mondop with a three-tiered roof crowned by a slender golden finial – and evocative river views from the terrace. There are old Dvaravati sandstone *bai sema* near the assembly hall. A new Isan-style chedi dominates the meditation area. The monks live in cells on a cliff high up above the river *(no access)*. On the opposite bank in Laos stands a forest temple.

Phra Chao Ong Toe – *Wat Nam Mong, Amphoe Tha Bo. Turn right at Km 31 and continue for 2km by dirt road.* Old *bai sema* surround the ubosot which contains a Lao-Lanna style **seated Buddha** in gold, silver and copper with a serene expression believed to date from 1562 (BE 2105) in the reign of King Chaichetta of Lan Xang (Laos); it is sacred to people on both sides of the Mekong. The casting for which was invoked the assistance of all gods is said to have taken seven years and seven months. Two rows of five blue-glazed mosaic columns support the ornate ceiling highlighted in red and gold.

Muang Wiang Khuk – *8km before the road junction turn left to Ban Wiang Khuk.* There are few remains (thats – Wat Thep Phon Pradit Tharam, Wat Sao Suwannaram, Wat Si Mongkhon Thammawat, huge octagonal columns, a colossal head – Wat Yot Kaeo) of a 12C city which attained its greatest prosperity in the 16C like its twin city Muang Sai Fong in Laos.

Wat Phra That Bang Phuan – *Tambon Don Mu. Turn left at Km 10.* According to legend a stupa was built here to house Buddha relics during the same period as was **Phra That Phanom★** *(see Nakhon Phanom)*. The restored tiered white chedi with gilded statues in the niches was probably built in 1562 by King Chaichetta. It contained 16C statues of the Buddha and other relics. Nearby in the peaceful shady grounds are several ruined 16C Lao-style chedis (some with statues), a colossal Buddha, a seated Buddha sheltered by a nine-headed naga in ceramic, and the round brick base of a long-lost structure.

CHIANG MAI★★★

Chiang Mai – Population 225 044

Michelin Atlas p 3 or Map 965 – C 3

Its fortunate setting on the banks of the Mae Nam Ping in a fertile valley dominated by Doi Pui, and the picturesque old town girt by a moat combine with the natural attractions of its environs to make Chiang Mai, also known as the 'Rose of the North', a favourite destination from which to explore the northern region. It benefits from a cool, dry climate, is well served by air, road and rail links and has excellent tourist facilities. Its growing prosperity has led to a building boom and traffic congestion but it retains a certain provincial charm. Its splendid temples and wooden buildings are reminders of its glorious past as the capital of an independent kingdom. It is also a university town with a lively, dynamic atmosphere.

The people are renowned for their warm welcome to visitors and their natural sense of fun which is evident during the colourful **festivals** celebrated all through the year *(see INTRODUCTION, Festivals)*.

An irresistible attraction is the bustling **night market** *(Thanon Chang Khlan)* offering an amazing variety of goods for sale – woodcrafts, antiques, silverware, leather goods, clothes and jewellery.

An independent state – There is evidence of human occupation in the Chiang Mai valley in the Paleolithic era. At a later stage the Lawa tribe inhabited the area prior to the 13C.

King Mengrai

An important figure in northern Thai history, he was first the ruler of Chiang Saen and later the founder of Chiang Rai *(see CHIANG SAEN and CHIANG RAI)*. After his conquest in 1281 of the thriving Mon empire of Haripunchai *(see LAMPHUN)*, he moved his capital to Chiang Mai in 1292. According to legend, the auspicious sighting of rare animals – white mice and sambar deer – led to the choice of the present site. His two allies King Ram Kamhaeng of Sukhothai and King Ngam Muang of Phayao are reputed to have assisted Mengrai in planning his new capital, an event which is commemorated by a **monument** to the three rulers in Thanon Rajwithi *(in front of the Old City Hall and Provincial Court)*. Mengrai ruled for 21 years and founded a dynasty which dominated the northern territories for two centuries. A shrine *(junction of Thanon Ratchadamnoen and Phra Pho Klao – below)* marks the spot where he is said to have been struck down by lightning.

Out and about

Tourism Authority of Thailand (TAT) – 105/1 Thanon Chiang Mai-Lamphun, Tambon Wat Ket or East Bank of the Mae Nam Ping near the Iron Bridge and Rim Ping Supermarket. ☎ 053 248 604, 053 248 607, 053 241 466. Fax 053 248 605.

Tourist Police – As above. ☎ 1155 or 053 248 130. 053 242 966.

Transport – Regular air, rail and bus services operate to and from Chiang Mai.

International Airport – ☎ 053 270 222-34. **Thai Airways International**, City Office, 240 Thanon Phra Pokklao ☎ 053 210 210, Airport Office ☎ 053 277 782. **Bangkok Airways**, Airport Office ☎ 053 922 258

Bus Terminal – To Bangkok: Chiang Mai Arcade. To the south: Pratu Chiang Mai. To the north: Chang Phuak. To Chiang Rai: Chiang Mai Arcade.

Railway Station – 27 Thanon Charoen Muang, east of the town, off Road no 106. ☎ 053 242 094, 245 363/4, 244 795.

Getting around – The best way to see the sights is on foot. Samlors (bicycle rickshaws) are also popular.

By bicycle or motorcycle – For hire from local shops. From 150 Baht. Check the vehicle carefully and take special note of insurance cover.

By bus – Local buses (song tao – converted vans with seats along the sides) – are convenient for sights on the outskirts. It is best to negotiate the price in advance.

Shopping – Night Market, Thanon Chang Khlan: souvenirs, handicrafts, clothes. The road to San Kamphaeng is lined with factories and shops for all the handicrafts for which Chiang Mai is renowned.

Bookshops – DK Books, Thanon Thapae; Suriwongse Book Centre, Thanon Sri Dornchai.

Entertainment – **Kantoke Dinner and Show**: Old Chiang Mai Cultural Centre, 183/5 Thanon Wualai (on road 108 to the airport). ☎ 053 275 097, 053 274 093/540: open-air performances, hilltribe shows.
Phet Ngam Hotel, near the Night Market: an old teak mansion by the river
Imperial Mae Ping Hotel, Thanon Si Don Chai ☎ 053 270 160: beautiful Lanna-style pavilion in a garden setting
Nakorn Lanna 1296, 84 Thanon Chang Khlan. ☎ 053 818 428/9 in a former cinema not far from the Night Market

Bars and Restaurants with music – By the riverside, Huen Suntharee.

Festivals – Flower Festival – colourful parades, beauty contest, fair – in February. Songkran (New Year) – 13-15 April.

Sompet Thai Cookery School – 100/1 Chiang Inn Plaza Basement. ☎ 053 280 901, 01 671 3190 (mobile); sompet@thaimail.com; sompet67@hotmail.com; www.welcome.to/sompet Learn Thai cooking in a lovely riverside house and have a leisurely meal on the terrace.

Excursions – Travel agencies (Thanon Thaphae and Pratu Thaphae) and hotels will give information on tours for sightseeing.

Trekking, Rafting – The TAT publishes a list of reputable trekking agencies and recommendations for visiting hill-tribe villages. Ask for the licence number issued by TAT to registered agencies.

Mae Ping River Cruises – From the pier at Wat Chai Mongkhon (☎ 053 274 822 for transport) enjoy a leisurely trip upriver by long-tail boat to a farm house and garden (8.30am–5pm) or an evening boat ride with dinner (from 7.15pm).

Chiang Mai Sky Adventure – 143 Moo 6, Chiang Doi, Doi Saket. ☎ 053 868 460; flying @cmnet.co.th; www.northernthailand.com/sky Take a microlight flight (15-20min) for splendid views.

Where to eat

Galae – 65 Thanon Suthep. ☎ 053 278 655, 053 811 041. A waterside restaurant serving Thai and Northern food in a beautiful forest garden. Panoramic view of the city.

Ban Suan Sri Chiang Mai – 51/4 Moo 1, Soi Wat Buak Krok, on the San Kamphaeng road (1.5km from Super Highway intersection). ☎ 053 262 569. Northern Thai dining in pleasant gardens.

Le Coq d'Or – 68,1 Thanon Koh Klang, Nong Hoy. ☎ 053 282 024. Well-established restaurant serving fine European cuisine in a country house setting.

Come-Inn House – 79-3 Thanon Sirithorn (off Super Highway northwest). ☎ 053 212 516/683. Authentic Thai and Northern cuisine in a traditional teak-wood house

Sala Mae Rim – Regent Resort Chiang Mai, Mae Rim-Samoeng Road, ☎ 053 298 181-8. Beautiful Lanna décor. Northern cuisine, vegetarian specialities and international menu.

The Riverside – 9-11 Thanon Charoen Rat. ☎ 053 243 239. Popular venue with good food and live music.

River Deli – 233 Thanon Charoen Rat. ☎ 053 260 404. Riverside restaurant serving food from around the world

The Gallery Restaurant and Bar – 25-27 Thanon Charoen Rat. ☎ 053 248 601. Traditional cooking in a teakwood house filled with art treasures in a romantic riverside setting. Music evenings.

Mae Ping Khantoke – 153 Thanon Si Don Chai. ☎ 053 270 181. Royal Thai cuisine served on Benjarong Thai porcelain and cultural show with Thai music

Where to stay

Budget

Once upon a time – 385/2 Thanon Charoen Prathet. ☎ 053 274 932; 1 000-1 500 Baht. Charming accommodation in Lanna-style buildings and traditional furnishings in pleasant gardens beside the Maenam Ping.

Chiang Mai Plaza Hotel – Thanon Si Don Chai. ☎ Thanon Si Don Chai. ☎ 053 270 036-50, 02 276 2622-6; Fax 053 279 547, 02 276 2628-9; 1 600-12 000 Baht. Comfortable rooms in modern hotel west of the town a short distance from the Maenam Ping.

Pet Ngarm Hotel – 33/10 Thanon Charoen Prathet. ☎ 053 270 080-5; 053 271 482. A good modern hotel by the Maenam Ping. Restaurant offering Kantoke dinners.

Moderate

Novotel Chiang Mai – 183 Thanon Chang Phuak. ☎ 053 225 500, 02 237 6064; Fax 053 225 505, 02 233 1000; novotel@chiangmai.a-net.net.th; 2 600-5 000+ Baht. Well-appointed hotel with excellent facilities to the north of the town centre.

Lotus Hotel Pang Sua Kaew – 99/4 Thanon Huay Kaeo. ☎ 053 224 333, 02 669 2900-8; Fax 053 224 493, 02 243 5177; lotus.htl.psk@chiangmai.a-net.net.th; 900-4 500 Baht. Fine accommodation in first class hotel, restaurants, health club to the northeast of the town.

Lanna View Hotel – 558 Near Lanna Hospital, Chiang Mai-Lampang Road. ☎ 053 217 784-6, 210 740-4, 02 267 9993-4; 1 400-6 500 Baht. A comfortable hotel with good amenities to the north of the town.

Expensive

The Imperial Mae Ping – 153 Thanon Si Don Chai. ☎ 053 270 160; Fax 053 270 181, 276 486, 206 720; maeping@loxinfo.co.th; www.maeping-hotels.com, www.imperialhotels.com; 3 000-50 000 Bahts. Excellent accommodation and facilities in modern hotel in town centre.

Westin Chiang Mai – 318/1 Chiang Mai-Lamphun Road. ☎ 053 275 300, 02 254 1713-5, 02 254 1716; Fax 053 275 299, 02 254 1716; westincm@loxinfo.co.th; 5 200-12 500 Baht. A luxury riverside hotel with splendid facilities, restaurants.

Regent Resort Chiang Mai – Mae Rim-Samoeng Old Road, Mae Rim. ☎ 053 298 181-8, 02 251 6127; Fax 053 298 189, 02 254 5391; US$350-2 000. Attractive hotel in Lanna architectural style, splendid amenities, gourmet restaurants, beautiful décor and gardens.

The walled town which was founded in 1292 by **King Mengrai** *(see below)* and boasted a royal palace and important temples became the capital of a powerful Lanna Thai empire and was remodelled by later rulers. The kingdom of Chiang Mai flourished and reached the zenith of its power and glory in the 15C in the reign of **King Tilokaracha**, who built more admirable temples to mark the Eighth Buddhist Conference in 1477 celebrating the 2000th anniversary of Buddhism and conducting a revision of Buddhist doctrine.

War between Ayutthaya and Burma destabilised the kingdom which fell to the Burmese in 1558 and remained under their rule for two centuries until they were defeated by King Taksin, who recaptured Ayutthaya and subsequently laid claim to Chiang Mai (1776) which became a tributary state of the kingdom of Siam. The town fell into decline and was abandoned in favour of Lampang. Twenty years later (1796) King Rama I installed King **Kavila** of Lampang as the new ruler and Chiang Mai remained a separate state until the demise of the last Prince of Chiang Mai in 1939 when it came under the central administration in Bangkok.

Phra Wihan Lai Kham, Wat Phra Sing Luang

SIGHTS

Town centre – Thanon Thaphae starting from Saphan Nawarat, the first bridge to span the Mae Nam Ping, is lined with fine temples and leads to the east gate, Pratu Thaphae, which gives access to the moated town. Although the town walls have been demolished the surviving corner forts and the rebuilt gateways give an idea of the overall effect. Large, tree-shaded avenues run parallel to the moat with a public garden as well as a flower market by the roadside on the southwest corner beyond Pratu Suan Prung, and a bustling market near Pratu Chiang Mai.

The numerous temples in a variety of architectural styles testify to Chiang Mai's role as a major religious centre. The compounds are havens of peace and harmony although few of the buildings have escaped remodelling, sometimes in questionable taste.

The east bank of the Mae Nam Ping is mainly a pleasant residential area with many elegant old wooden houses and shady gardens, where formerly resided foreign employees of companies which had been granted logging concessions. Chiang Mai has a vibrant night-life with cafés, restaurants and nightclubs in particular on the east bank.

Wat Saen Fang (CX) – *East of Thanon Thaphae*. A naga undulating along the wall marks the entrance to the temple. The buildings have fine decorative elements : two Lanna *ho trai* and a vihara with intricate carving in red and gold, a Burmese chedi framed by gilded parasols and mythical lions and decorated with multi-coloured glass mosaic, and Burmese-style monastic buildings.

Wat Buppharam (CX) – *Opposite*. The jewel of this temple is an exquisite Lanna-style **vihara**★ dating from *c* 1500. Pillars with lotus capitals support the roof and on the altar is a gilded Buddha image, Phra Buddha Chailap Prassittichok, framed by two large Buddhas. A Burmese-style **chedi** rises from a redented square base with three chedis at each stepped corner. In the main vihara on the left, the Hoh Monthientham in a mixed Lanna-Burmese style, a Chiang Saen Buddha framed by deities graces the main altar with on the right a Buddha image, one of the largest statues carved in teak. The walls are decorated with vivid relief scenes of King Naresuan's conquest of Lanna.

The carvings on the doors and windows of an art **museum** on the lower floor feature the story of Lord Buddha's most recent life and that of his previous life.

Wat Mahawan (CX) – *Further along Thanon Thaphae*. The main vihara is notable for its stepped roof, intricately carved and gilded porch, and teak pillars. Behind it is a tall Burmese-style **chedi** flanked by mythical lions.

On the north side of the road are three Burmese-style chedis at **Wat Chetawan** (CX).

Wat Chaï Si Phum (BX) – *Thanon Chai Ya Phum to the right of Pratu Taphae*. Located just outside the ramparts the temple boasts a vihara with a gilded, carved pediment, an elegant ubosot, a library and a fine chedi.

★ **Wat Chedi Luang** (BY) – *Thanon Phra Pho Klao*. The main feature of the temple is a ruined great **chedi**★ which was built in 1401. It was raised to a height of 90m by King Tilokaracha in 1454 and housed the Emerald Buddha *(see BANGKOK, Wat Phra Kaeo)* from 1468 to 1552. An earthquake in 1545 reduced it to 60m. Naga staircases lead up to the porticoes decorated with stucco foliage motifs, elephants jutting out along the base *(southwest)* and large Buddha images standing majestically in the niches. An ornate porch with a carved pediment leads into the vihara; the coffered vaulted ceiling rests on tall columns and the huge standing Buddha, Phra Attharot, is flanked by disciples. A small building by the entrance contains the city pillar, the **Lak Muang.**

Wat Phan Tao (BX) – *Thanon Phra Pho Klao*. The panelled walls, the windows with spindle-turned uprights and the portico and its ornate gable with peacock motifs in classical Lanna style add to the harmony of the **vihara**★★ which has a five-tiered roof. The interior is remarkable for its massive wooden red pillars, an old pulpit and a Buddha image in the late Chiang Saen style.

At the road junction beyond the temple stands the **Mengrai shrine** *(see above)* which is revered by the local people.

★★★ **Wat Phra Sing Luang** (AX) – *Thanon Phra Sing*. The focal point of the road is the famous temple founded in 1345 to enshrine the ashes of King Kam Fu. Among its noteworthy elements are: the elaborate wooden façades of the restored main vihara; the graceful wooden **ho trai**★★★ decorated with wood carving and glass mosaic as well as stuccowork (foliage and deities on the base) of great artistry; the admirable carved wood panels and doors and the stucco decoration of the **ubosot**★; the white **chedi**★ with decorative elephant stucco protruding from the square base and framed by four small chedis. The exquisite **Phra Wihan Lai Kham**★★★, built to house the sacred Phra Sing **Buddha image**★, is enhanced by the delicate carved decoration of the **gable**★★, door and windows and the remarkable 16C **mural paintings**★★ portraying stories from Lanna literature and showing fascinating details of costume and daily life. Behind the vihara is a reliquary *(ku)* with five lotus-shaped spires and niches enshrining Buddha images.

Wat Phuak Hong (AY) – *Off Thanon Samlan*. An interesting feature of this temple is the tiered round **chedi** (16C-17C) with meditating Buddhas in niches which reveals an unusual Chinese influence. The carving on the gable of the ubosot is particularly fine.

Wat Mengrai (AY) – *Soi 6, Thanon Ratchamakkha*. A gilded doorway richly orna-mented with deities, mythical animals and floral motifs, and a square chedi pierced by niches containing Buddha images and surmounted by a green-glazed bell and a gilded finial are the most interesting features of this temple dedicated to King Mengrai. The bronze Buddha in the vihara is thought to bear a resemblance to the king.

★ **Wat Chiang Man** (BX) – *Thanon Ratchaphanikai*. It was founded in the 13C by King Mengrai and is probably the oldest temple in Chiang Mai built on the site where once stood the royal stronghold. A brief historical account is given on a stone inscription near the entrance to the main hall. The **chedi**★ was remodelled in the 15C and again in later years. A naga staircase rises from the elephant-decorated base to the next level which has three niches on each side; the upper section comprises an indented base supporting an octagon with a bell shape and a slim finial. The Lanna-style **vihara** houses a crystal figurine of the Buddha revered for its rain-making powers. Another Buddha image, Phra Sila, is a fine example of Indian (Gupta) craftsmanship. The upper part of the **ho trai** shows the skill of Northern Thai wood carvers.

Wat Ku Tao (BV) – *Thanon Sanam Kila (behind the sports stadium). Turn left off Thanon Rattanakosin beyond the white elephant shrine near the bus station.* On the right of the ubosot stands an unusual chedi (*c* 16C-17C) with superimposed spheres adorned with ceramic floral motifs and Buddha images in niches.

★★ **Wat Suan Dok** – *Left off Thanon Suthep* (AX). Pass through the **ceremonial gate** into the compound. The tall **chedi**★ bristling with smaller chedis was built in the 14C in the garden of the ruler of Chiang Mai to house a holy relic discovered by a monk named Sumana from Sukhothai who introduced Theravada Buddhism to the kingdom of Lanna. The bright faience decoration is a recent addition. The reliquaries behind the chedi contain the ashes of the royal family. Tall wooden pillars decor-ated with red and gold lacquer, mural paintings depicting the life of Buddha and a Lanna (Chiang Saen) bronze **Buddha image**★★, Phra Chao Kao Tue, adorn the small vihara. The open sala is of little interest.

Ho Trai, Wat Phra Sing Luang

Wat Umong – *8km west, turn left past a canal off Thanon Suthep* (**AX**). The underground **cells★** of the old forest monastery (1380) were used by monks for meditation. The tall bell-shaped chedi rising on a large platform is decorated with lotus motifs and small statues below the finial. The peaceful forest temple attracts many devotees.

Nearby are the ruins – **chedi★** – of **Wat Pa Daeng** *(turn right and continue for 100m)* which was built in 1447 by King Tilokaracha and is of great historical interest.

★Wat Chet Yot – *Near Chiang Mai Museum off 11. Leave by Thanon Huay Kaeo.* (**AV**) The **chedi★★** with its seven spires, a vaulted chamber with a Buddha image, and stucco figures of deities is a unique monument modelled on the Mahabodi temple in Bodh Gaya (India). On the right is the Lanna-style Phra Chedi containing the ashes of King Tilokaracha who convened the Eighth Buddhist Council (1477) at the temple. A stepped, redented base supports the main body adorned with pilasters and niches and crowned by a bell shape and finial.

★Museum ⓥ– *Super Highway, Muang District. Leave by Thanon Chotana* (**BX**). The gable of the two-storeyed building is decorated with the *kalae* typical of North Thailand. The museum presents rich collections relating to the arts and archeology of Thailand from the prehistoric era to the early-Bangkok period, with special emphasis on the northern region.

Ground floor – Fine **pottery★** from Omkhoi, San Kamphaeng, Wieng Kalong and Sukhothai illustrate the various styles. Among the masterpieces on display are: rare Buddhist temple **banners**, a Lanna Buddha **footprint★★** in wood inlaid with mother-of-pearl with an inscription on the back; a bronze Buddha subduing Mara in Lanna style; a large bronze **head of the Buddha** with a serene expression; a sandstone pedestal for a Buddha image decorated with four elephants; a scripture box in red and gold lacquerware. Other interesting exhibits include terracotta pottery, votive tablets and decorative elements from monuments in the kingdom of Haripunchai, Buddha images and miniatures in crystal, silver and gold discovered in Chiang Mai province, objects found in Hot district before the construction of the Bhumibol Dam.

First floor – The displays relate to the way of life of the northern people: crafts, costumes, farming implements, utensils, musical instruments. A section devoted to the royal family of Chiang Mai features a throne, regalia and guns, an ivory palanquin, an elephant howdah, Chinese and European porcelain, and betel nut sets.

ADDITIONAL SIGHTS

Hill Tribe Research Institute ⊙– *University of Chiang Mai, Thanon Huay Kaeo* **(AV)**. The institute carries out studies of the traditions and way of life of the hill tribes with the aim of easing their integration into the modern world. A **museum**★, library and open-air exhibition are open to visitors.

Chiang Mai Arboretum [pendule]– *Thanon Huay Keo* **(AV)** *6km northwest*. This is the place to see indigenous species of trees planted on the site of the old town of Wieng Chet Rin marked by an earthen wall.

Chiang Mai Zoo ⊙– *Thanon Huay Kaeo* **(AV)**. Situated at the foot of Doi Suthep it was formerly a private zoo started in 1956 and is now the largest in Thailand with a large collection of local and exotic animals. A part is laid out as an open zoo with animals roaming freely in large compounds.

There is a small waterfall nearby (market and food stalls). Some distance further stands a statue dedicated to Kruba Srivichai, a respected monk who built a road to the **Wat Phra That Doi Suthep**★★★ *(see Wat Phra That DOI SUTHEP)*, with the help of volunteers in order to facilitate access for pilgrims who previously had to use steep and difficult paths.

EXCURSIONS

★**Wat Chedi Liem** – *5km southeast by 11* **(DY)**. Mythical animals stand guard around the stepped pyramid built in the 8C in a similar style to Wat Chamatewee *(see LAMPHUN)* and restored in the early 19C. The four niches at the base contain seated Buddha images; the standing Buddhas in the niches of the pyramid are of diminishing size at each level.

Wiang Kum Kam – *4km east of Mae Nam Ping by road to Lamphun.* King Mengrai founded the ancient moated town before he built Chiang Mai. The town was abandoned when the Mae Nam Ping changed its course. Extensive ruins (Wat Kan Thom) until recently hidden in thick groves have been uncovered.

Wat Bua Krok Luang – *East by 1006. 2km after crossing 11 turn right.* Craft shops where local artisans may be seen hard at work line the road to San Kamphaeng.
The wat is famous for the remarkable **mural paintings**★★ adorning the interior of an old Lanna-style vihara. The vivid colours and the naive figures outlined in black are typical of northern art. Massive painted columns support the roof and a Buddha image presides at the altar decorated with glass mosaic.

S. Bouquet/ MICHELIN

Wat Chedi Liem

San Kamphaeng Hot Springs ⊙– *37km east. After 14m by 1006 take the road to Mae On for 12km then turn left and continue for 11km.* A pleasant excursion may be made to the hot springs (100°C) gushing in the middle of a landscaped park. There are facilities for hot baths and camping in the grounds.

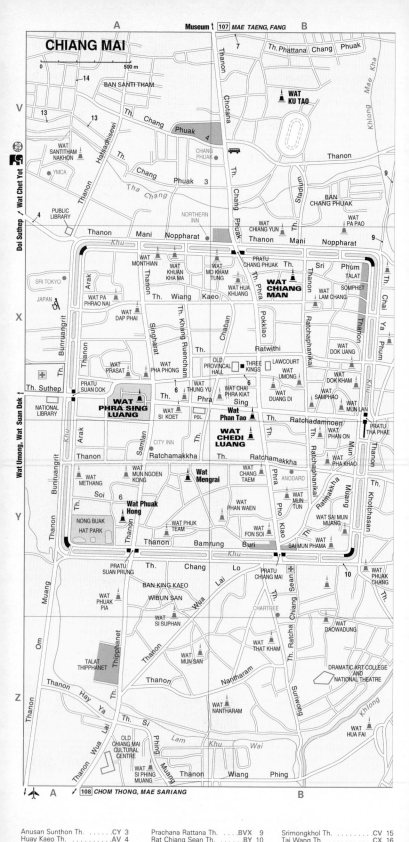

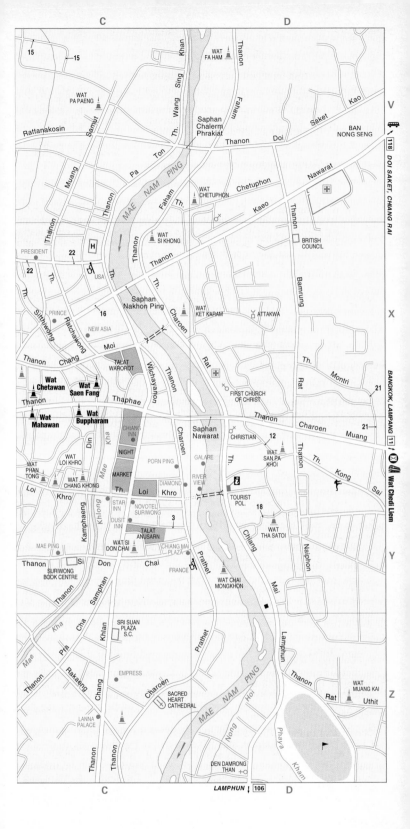

Visitors should behave with great composure. Patience and good humour achieve better results than a display of strong emotions. Saving face is an important consideration in Thailand

---

Crafts

An ancient craft tradition has survived in Chiang Mai and the skill of the artisans may be admired at workshops in town and the craft factories and villages on the outskirts: silverware (Thanon Wualai near Pratu Chiang Mai south), pottery (Mengrai Kilns, road north to San Kamphaeng), umbrellas (Bo Sang), textiles (Pa Sang, San Kamphaeng), woodcarving (Ban Tawai south), lacquerware (road to San Kamphaeng).

In the south pottery is produced in Muang Kung which has houses on stilts. Wickerware is on sale in the shops of Hang Dong and woodwork is the speciality of Ban Tawai and is distributed worldwide.

★★ **Scenic road southwest by 108** – Along the road south, visitors will be lured by villages specialising in various crafts (**Muang Kung, Hang Dong, Ban Tawai** – *see above*). **Chom Thong** *(58km)* is famous for its beautiful temple *(below)* and its cattle market held on Saturday mornings. A turning (1009) leads to **Doi Inthanon★★** *(below)* – after 3km turn left to visit the modern Wat Lanna Yannasawararam – while 108 continues to the new town of Hot – the old town was submerged following the building of the Bhumibol dam – **Ob Luang** gorges and on to Mae Sariang *(see MAE SOT – Excursions)* through wonderful mountain scenery.

Wat Phra That Si Chom Thong – *Left on the main road.* A white Burmese-style chedi by the main entrance precedes the glittering 15C Lanna-style **chedi★★** – note the squat recessed base and ringed bell – and the **vihara★** (16C, rebuilt early 19C) with its elaborate gables. Inside, massive painted columns support the roof, and at the altar in the form of a large gilded reliquary with elephant tusks in front are fine wooden statues of Buddha. There are also Buddha images in silver and gold in display cases.

★★ **Doi Inthanon National Park** – *Bear right into 1009.* The granite massif, part of the Thanon Thongchai range, is the highest peak (alt 2 565m) in Thailand and is often wreathed in mist. The area is a vital watershed feeding the Ping which in turn flows into the Chao Phraya in the plain. Its temperate climate, forested slopes, lush vegetation with rare exotic flora (orchids, ferns) and wildlife (over 300 bird species) and its superb **views★★★** attract visitors from all over the country.

Most of the hill-tribe villages (Hmong, Karen) have been moved out of the park to reduce the danger of deforestation and erosion. A royal project has introduced the tribesmen to the cultivation of temperate crops (strawberries, asparagus) which are on sale at roadside stalls.

Tour – A good road winds up to the summit and there are trails leading to spectacular caves *(Borijinda, 4km from entrance)*, waterfalls and viewpoints *(guides from park office)*. The waterfalls **Nam Tok Mae Klang★** *(near entrance)*, Wachirathan *(by Km 21)* and Siribhum *(Km 31)* are easily accessible; the powerful **Nam Tok Mae Ya★** to the south is reached by a 15km-long track *(1 day)*. Treks to hill-tribe villages can also be arranged.

On the way up, stop at two towering marble **Royal Chedis** *(116 steps)* embellished with terracotta reliefs and dedicated to the Thai sovereigns. The distant mountain **views★★★** are splendid.

A radar station occupies the summit. Park the car on the esplanade to admire the spectacular mountain **views★★★** and savour the cool, clean air. Tall trees shade a chedi wreathed with incense containing the ashes of the last ruler of Chiang Mai, Chao Inthawichayanon. The **shrine** is a pilgrimage centre.

Walk down to an old rhododendron **grove** (Thung Kulap Phan Pi) which is in full bloom in late April-early May. A raised walkway runs past gnarled mossy tree trunks.

★★ **Mae Sa Valley** – *North by 107 and after 13km west by 1096.* A range of attractions including waterfalls, orchid and butterfly farms, elephant training camps and landscaped resorts draws visitors to this picturesque green valley. To enjoy the beauty of Thai flora visit the Queen Sirikit Botanical Garden in a lush mountain setting which specialises in rare and endangered species. For a round tour to Chiang Mai to enjoy the superb scenery, proceed along 1096 past Samoeng to Hang Dong *(above)* and take 108 north.

Chiang Mai to Pai – *150km northwest by 107 and 1095.* Proceed towards Ban Pa Pae *(58km west)* with Doi Mae Ya (alt 2 065m) looming to the south of the road. At Km 42 a track (steep and difficult; four-wheel drive vehicles only) branching off to the right gives access to the Pong Duet National Park over which hovers a cloud of steam from the **Pa Pae hot springs★★**. The geysers spurt to a height of 2m and the temperature reaches 100°; hot baths are available.

Further along, the road passes near the Huai Nam Dang National Park *(turn left at Km 65-66)* in which rises Doi Chang *(alt 1 587m – viewpoints 3km north)*. The site is renowned for the beautiful scenery (waterfalls) and misty views especially at sunrise.

Pai – This small town is a popular destination for trekking and rafting enthusiasts *(guide recommended)* owing to its idyllic location in a broad valley hemmed in by mountains and rivers. The Shan and hill-tribe villages add to the interest of the province.

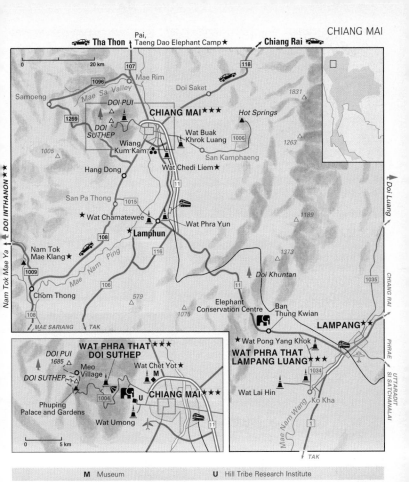

M Museum   **U** Hill Tribe Research Institute

Some of the temples in the centre of town are of interest. The gilded ringed chedi of **Wat Klang** rests on a tiered platform framed by eight chapels and crowned by small chedis. **Wat Nam Hu** which has a spring in the grounds boasts a harmonious chedi and an elegant vihara with a porch, square windows and a tiered roof. At **Wat Luang** the powerful chedi with its fine gilded crown is flanked by 12 smaller chedis and four mythical lions. East of the town are Phra That Mae Yen and Phra That Chom Chaeng (**views** of the valley).

The road west is described in reverse order from Mae Hong Son.

Road east via Doi Saket – *180km by 118.* A direct route to Chiang Rai via Amphoe Wiang Papao which affords spectacular mountain scenery runs past the village of Doi Saket dominated by a temple. On either side of the road extend the wonderful scenery of the forested Khun Chae, Chae Son and Doi Luang National Parks and the Mae Nam Lao flows along part of the way. Detours can be made to waterfalls, hot springs and to the Mae Guang Dam.

★**Scenic road north to Tha Ton and the Golden Triangle** – *190km – 1/2 day.* The drive along this former trade route to the Shan states in Burma and the Lan Xang kingdom (Luang Prabang in Laos) will inspire a sense of wonder as the grandiose scenery unfolds: fertile valleys, lush forested slopes, fast-flowing rivers and craggy gorges with the limestone mass of Doi Luang Chiang Dao (alt 2 190m) looming in the distance to the north. All along the road, detours can be made to spectacular natural attractions – caves (Tham Chiang Dao, Tham Tab Tao), hot springs and waterfalls, but some roads are difficult. The wildlife sanctuaries (Doi Luang Chiang Dao, Doi Ang Khang, Doi Pha Hom Pok) teeming with a variety of montane birds are a veritable paradise for birdwatchers and offer dramatic scenery and exotic vegetation. Tribal villages – Lahu, Lisu and Karen – abound *(guides essential)* in the foothills and at higher altitude, and there are thriving development centres set up as part of a royal initiative, which grow tea and coffee and other temperate crops and provide health and social support for the tribes (Doi Ang Khang project).

★**Taeng Dao Elephant Camp** – *Turn right at Km 56.* The camp on the west bank of the Mae Nam Ping is a popular place to see the huge animals wallowing in the river at bath time followed by a demonstration of their working skills.

Chiang Dao – *77km.* The peaceful small market town at the head of the valley is frequented by hill tribes in their colourful costumes, who bring their goods for sale.

★★ **Tham Chiang Dao** ⊙– *5km west.* A pond at the foot of the covered stairway is filled with sacred carp. The impressive caves which extend deep into the mountainside are held in great veneration by the Shan people and the first chamber contains many Buddha images in Burmese style. Spectacular rock formations may be admired in the maze of underground passages *(guide essential).*

Fang – It was formerly an important trading post which held out against the Burmese invaders until the early 18C and was recaptured in the latter part of that century; it later became part of the Kingdom of Thailand. It is now a bustling town with a mixed population – Shan, Burmese, Karen – often caught up in border conflicts and in the fight against the drug trade. Visitors who wish to explore distant regions should exercise great care and seek advice from the police.

At Ban Muang Chom *(8km northwest of town),* in rocky terrain against a wooded backdrop **hot springs** give out a strong whiff of sulphur. The water is hot enough (*c* 100°) to boil an egg.

Ban Tha Ton – *24km north of Fang.* The little town located on both banks of the Mae Nam Kok which originates in Myanmar is dominated by an imposing white Buddha image at Wat Tha Thon and there are fine **views**★★ of the river and town from the temple. Tha Ton is a popular starting point for **excursions** ⊙ by raft or boat up and down the swift Mae Nam Kok as far as the Myanmar border and Chiang Rai – **views**★★★, rapids, tribal villages.

A good road which runs at low altitude in the early stages and climbs in hairpin bends to **Mae Salong** *(40km further; see CHIANG RAI – Excursions)* affords breathtaking **views**★★★ of mountain peaks and fertile valleys dotted with tribal villages (Yao, Lahu, Lisu, Akha). Reforestation is underway to replace the forest cover stripped by the slash-and-burn cultivation methods of the hill tribes. The sensitive area which was notorious for opium cultivation and smuggling has been the scene of fierce battles as the Thai Army routed the drug barons. Visitors are advised not to wander off the beaten track.

CHIANG RAI★★

Chiang Rai – Population 222 738

Michelin Atlas p 3 or Map 965 – B 4 – Town plan Atlas p 30

The expanding town is strategically situated on the south bank of the Mae Nam Mae Kok which flows north to join the Mekong. Although overshadowed by the more sophisticated town of Chiang Mai it has many attractions and good transport links and tourist infrastructure, which make it a good base for trekking and excursions by road or river to explore the beautiful hilly countryside populated by hill tribes. Handicrafts (textiles, silverware) from the tribespeople are popular souvenirs.

Popular festivals include the **King Mengrai Festival** *(late Jan)* and the Lychee Fair *(late May).*

An eventful history – Tradition alleges that **King Mengrai,** who founded Chiang Rai in 1262, chose the site following a chance escape by an elephant which came to a halt on a small hill overlooking the Mae Nam Mae Kok. However, it has an ancient history although little evidence remains. King Mengrai later moved his capital to Chiang Mai. During the centuries of war between Thailand and Burma, Chiang Rai which was a major trading centre was held by the Burmese until 1786 when the Thai army regained the lost territory. Although it was practically abandoned during the 19C it experienced a slow recovery. In recent times the drab provincial capital has become a major tourist centre as the gateway to the north, and this has brought about unregulated expansion. As the original walls had been pulled down in 1920, a new section of wall has been erected based on an engraving to evoke the ancient past, and an elaborate city pillar crowns Doi Chom Thong. The temples have been spruced up to attract visitors.

SIGHTS

Wat Phra Sing – *Thanon Singhakrai.* The temple housed the revered Phra Phuttha Sihing image before it was transferred to Chiang Mai *(see also BANGKOK and NAKHON SI THAMMARAT).* A copy is on view in the attractive modern Lanna-style vihara which has finely carved decorative elements and a low roofline.

Wat Phra Kaeo – *Thanon Trairat (behind Wat Phra Sing).* The discovery of the **Emerald Buddha** in 1434 after the octagonal chedi was struck by lightning brought great renown to the temple.

According to legend the King ordered the transfer of the statue to Chiang Mai, but the elephant carrying the Buddha image was diverted to Lampang where the statue was enshrined for 22 years at **Wat Phra Kaeo Don Tao**★★ *(see LAMPANG).* It was then taken to Wat Phra Sing in Chiang Mai for 32 years and later removed to Luang Prabang and Vientiane in Laos for 125 years. In 1678 it was reclaimed by the Siamese and is now installed at Wat Phra Kaeo in the capital *(see BANGKOK, Wat Phra Kaeo).*

Out and about

Tourism Authority of Thailand (TAT) – 448/16 Thanon Singakhlai, Amphoe Muang, Chiang Rai 57000. ☎ 053 717 433, 053 744 674/5. Fax 053 717 434.

Tourist Police – As above. ☎ 1155, 053 717 779, 053 717 796.

Transport – Regular air and bus services operate to and from Chiang Rai. **International Airport** ☎ 053 793 048-57; **Thai International Airways** ☎ 053 711 179, 053 715 207.

Bus Terminal, Satani Khonsong, Chiang Rai. ☎ 053 711 244.

Car rental: Avis, Chiang Rai Airport ☎ 053 793 827 and Dusit Island Resort ☎ 053 715 777; avisthai@loxinfo.co.th; www.aviathailand.com; **Budget**, Golden Triangle Tours, 590 Thanon Phaholyothin ☎ 053 711 339, 716 918; central reservation ☎ 02 203 0250; www.budget.co.th

Tricycles and **motorcycles** are popular for getting around. Check vehicles carefully and take note of insurance cover. Take great care on the road.

Boat rental: From piers along the Mae Nam Kok. Long-tail boat from Rim Nam, Tha Chiang Rai.

Shopping – **Night market,** Thanon Ratanaket (between Wiang Inn and Wiang Come hotels). **Market**, Talat Tetsaban (near Wat Muang Muang): fresh produce brought for sale by hill-tribespeople in their colourful costumes, mostly Yao.

Trekking and Rafting – The TAT publishes a list of reputable agencies and recommendations for visits to hill-tribe villages.

Excursions – Chiang Saen, Doi Mae Salong, Doi Tung, Chiang Mai, Chiang Khong, on the Mekong, Lampang.

Entertainment – **Laan Tong Mekong Basin Cultural Park**, 99 Moo 13 (Km 12 on A 1089), Amphoe Mae Chan. ☎ 053 772 127/135. A cultural show featuring 6 ethnic groups in a beautiful natural setting. Elephant and ox-cart riding. Food centre.

Restaurants – Food stalls and popular restaurants around the area of the clock tower (Ho Nalika). Local restaurants near the bridge with views of the Kok offer trips upstream from 900 Baht for 3-4 persons. Fine establishments at fashionable hotels (Dusit Island, Rimkok).

Where to eat

Rattanakosin Antique Thai Restaurant – Night Bazaar, 053 740 012; www.ratanakosin.com . Fine setting with antique furnishings, excellent Thai food.

Cabbages and Condoms – 620/25 Thanon Thanalai, ☎ 053 740 784. A branch of the well-known Bangkok restaurant which combines good food with health awareness.

Krua Arom Dee – Thanon Sanambin. ☎ 053 756 041-3. Typical Thai restaurant, friendly ambience.

Yunan – 211/6 Thanon Kwae Wai. ☎ 053 713 263. Riverside Chinese restaurant.

Where to stay

Budget

The Golden Triangle Inn – 590 Thanon Phaholyothin, ☎ 053 711 339, 716 996, 713 918; gotour@loxinfo.co.th; 600-900 Baht. Spacious rooms with antique furniture, gardens, pleasant restaurant.

Y.M.C.A. International Hotel – 70 Thanon Phaholyothin. ☎ 053 713 785/6; Fax 053 714 336; 300-500 Baht. Comfortable rooms, swimming pool, sauna, restaurant.

Little Duck Hotel – 199 Thanon Phaholyothin, ☎ 053 715 620-38; Fax 053 715 639-40; chitpong@chmai.loxinfo.co.th; www.thaitourist.com/littleduck; 1 200-2 000 Baht. A fine modern hotel with pool and restaurant in town centre

Wang Thong Hotel – 299 Moo 7, Thanon Phaholyothin, Mae Sai ☎ 053 733 388-95; Fax 053 733 399; 800-1 500 Baht. Comfortable rooms, modern building, restaurants.

Wiang Inn Hotel – 893 Thanon Phaholyothin. ☎ 053 711 533; Fax 053 711 877; wianginn@samart.co.th; www.wianginn.com; 1 400-2 000+ Baht. An excellent hotel with a wide range of facilities, restaurants centrally located.

Ban Ton Nam 31 – Doi Tung Royal Villa, Mae Fah Luang. ☎ 053 767 015-7; Fax 053 767 077; tourism@doitung.org; 2 800 Baht. Comfortable accommodation with scenic verendah in mountain setting, restaurant and gym.

Moderate

Chiang Rai Inn – 661 Thanon Uttarakit, ☎ 053 712 673, 711 483, 717 700; Fax 053 716; 1 600-8 000 Baht. Well-appointed rooms, garden restaurant.

Wangcome Hotel – 869/90 Thanon Phamawiphat. ☎ 053 711 800/811; Fax 053 712 973; wangcome@loxinfo.co.th; 1 200-4 000 Baht. Comfortable accommodation, pool, music room, fine ambience, in town centre.

Rimkok Resort Hotel – 6 Moo 4, Chiang Rai-Thaton Road. ☎ 053 716 445-60; Fax 053 715 859; 1 700-8 000 Baht. An attractive riverside hotel with excellent facilities.

Suanthip Vana Resort – 49 Chiang Mai-Chiang Rai Road, Tambon Takok, Amphoe Mae Suay (Km 107 on H 118), ☎ 01 224 6984/5; Fax 01 224 0983; rsvn@suanthipresort.com; www.suanthipresort.com; 1 800-2 000 Baht. Luxurious forest retreat with Thai-style pavilions ideal for relaxation.

Expensive

Chiang Rai Country Resort – 128/25 Moo 16, Ban Pa-Ngao. ☎ 053 716 175; Fax 053 716 175; 5 000-7 000 Baht. Excellent accommodation and facilities, river views.

Le Meridien Baan Boran – 229 Moo 1, The Golden Triangle, Chiang Saen. ☎ 053 784 084, 02 653 2201-7; Fax 053 784 090, 02 653 2208/9; lmbboran@loxinfo.co.th; www.lemeridien.co.th/baanboran; US$110-270. An elegant riverside hotel with luxury facilities, delightful ambience.

The Imperial Golden Triangle Resort – 222 Golden Triangle, Chiang Saen. ☎ 053 784 001-5; Fax 053 784 006; goldentriangle@imperialhotels.com; www.imperialhotels.com; US$85-450. Traditional Lanna architectural style, excellent facilities.

Dusit Island Resort – 1129 Thanon Kaisonrasit. ☎ 053 715 777-9, 053 744 188; Fax 053 715 801; chiangrai@dusit.com; www.dusit.com; 2 800-16 000 Baht. A splendid riverside hotel set in pleasant gardens with superb amenities.

An elegant Lanna-style wooden **vihara★** enshrines an ancient Lanna (Chiang Saen) Buddha image of great size as well as several fine bronze statues. It boasts an intricately carved façade and a sweeping roof, and sets off the rebuilt bell-shaped chedi on a redented base.

Thai artists, including the renowned Thawan Duchanee, have designed a modern **vihara★★**, Ho Phra Kaeo, which aims to combine the rich Lanna heritage with modern techniques in the architecture, the building materials and the exquisite carving. The roof decoration terminating in elephant trunks is an original touch. A new Buddha image carved from jade by a Chinese artist has pride of place at the altar.

A large teakwood building, **Wihan Sangkaw★**, is a recent addition. It is exquisitely decorated with elaborate pediments featuring dragons, scrolls and a figure of the Buddha, signs of the Zodiac repeated on the end brackets and lotus motifs in gold on the wood panels.

Wat Ngam Muang – *West of Wat Phra Kaeo, access Thanon Ngam Muang.* Steps flanked by a naga railing lead up to a platform on which rises a brick chedi (built 1318 and later remodelled) containing the ashes of King Mengrai (d 1317). In front is a statue of the king.

Wat Phra That Doi Chom Thong – *North of Wat Ngam Muang, access by Thanon At Amnuay.* A Lanna-style gilded **chedi★** dominates Doi Chom Thong. It is believed to date from the 10C and was later remodelled.

According to tradition this is the place from which King Mengrai is said to have first surveyed the site and it affords excellent **views★★** of the Mae Nam Mae Kok and the surrounding area.

Lak Muang – The design of the city pillar which stands to the right of the Phra That is based on Thai cosmology. A moat representing the ocean encircles a terrace (the earth) bearing a complex of 108 granite pillars, with a larger pillar in the centre as the navel of the universe.

EXCURSIONS

Rai Mae Fa Luang – *Ban Pa Ngiu, Tambon Robwiang. 6km north by 1.* A hill-tribe foundation, formerly under the patronage of the Princess Mother (1900-95), aims to provide education and agricultural training and to promote handicrafts for the benefit of the tribespeople. In the grounds stand some notable buildings. A covered stairway gives access to the **Ho Kham★★**, literally the golden pavilion, which is built of wood from 32 old houses from villages in the north. The walls of the three-storeyed structure lean outwards in typical Lanna style. Carved floral and leaf motifs adorn the windows, and gold panels depict mythical creatures and Lanna folklore. Canopies crown the tiered hipped roof covered in wooden shingles. Inside there is a large collection of Lanna art.

Also of note are wooden banners *(thung)* by the Sala Kham which is used as a cultural centre and workshop.

Wat Phra Kaeo, Chiang Rai

★★ **Doi Mae Salong** – *80km northwest by 1 and 1234.* Also known as Santi Khiri (Mountain of Peace) the isolated village precariously sited at high altitude has an unusual character as it is inhabited by the descendants of Nationalist Chinese refugees (93rd Regiment of the Kuomintang – KMT) who fled mainland China after the Communist takeover in 1949.

Mandarin is spoken by the older generation and shops stock an amazing assortment of Chinese delicacies. The architecture of the old wooden houses protected by household spirits is typically Chinese. However, tourism and land speculation are rapidly eroding the traditional nature of the remote village. The morning **market** ⊘ *(west of the village)* is a colourful affair as the hill tribes bring their goods to market. An interesting landmark is the white marble mausoleum of the Chinese general who led his regiment and their families into Thailand. The Sakura (cherry blossom) Festival is held in January. Santi Khiri is a good base for excursions to nearby Akha villages.

★★ **Doi Tung** – *48km north from Chiang Rai by 1, then turn left between Km 871-872 into 1149 (viewpoints Km 10, 14).* The peak (alt 1 364m) belongs to the Phi Pan Nam range which borders the Chiang Saen plain to the west and remained inaccessible until recent times. The dense forest cover has been destroyed by the nomadic tribes. The terraced slopes are cultivated as part of a scheme to eradicate opium cultivation and repair the damage to the land as well as encourage the tribes to adopt a settled way of life.

The winding **scenic road** from Ban Huai Krai, which affords panoramic **views**★★★ as far as Laos and Myanmar on the horizon, passes several traditional villages clinging to the slopes and leads to a royal summer residence with typical Lanna *kalae* roof decoration. It is now a **museum** dedicated to the late Princess Mother who led a simple life here tending flowers and was passionately devoted to the welfare of the hilltribes and the reforestation of the mountain slopes. Near the entrance are poles decked with traditional banners *(thung)*. The beautiful landscaped **garden** ⊘ with colourful flower-beds, water features, a rock garden and a sculpture garden is delightful.

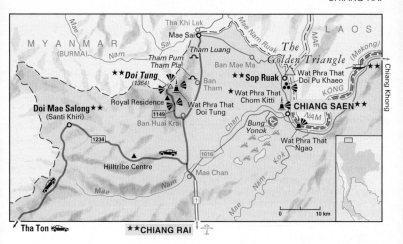

Wat Phra That Doi Tung – *As above*. Pilgrims flock to the 10C temple which is renowned as the earliest reliquary in the Lanna kingdom. According to legend it was built to enshrine a relic of the Buddha brought by one of his disciples. The site was marked by an immensely tall banner *(tung)* from which the name Doi Tung is derived.

Filigree canopies frame the two stupas (restored) covered in gold mosaic which stand on a square base. Standing Buddha images are enshrined in the niches with decorative arches punctuating the redented main body. The bell is surmounted by a ringed spire and a Burmese-style crown. The vihara contains a Lanna-style (Chiang Saen) Buddha image. From the terrace there is a splendid **view** over the countryside.

The road climbs to the ruined Phra That Chang Mup which takes its name from a rock in the form of a crouching elephant (west of stupa) near the summit of Doi Tung once denuded but now tree-clad. Nearby is the **Mae Fah Luang Arboretum** bright with rare species of trees, orchids, azaleas and rhododendrons. There are walkways, picnic spots and a scenic viewpoint.

Mae Sai – *70km north by 1*. Thailand's northernmost town is the gateway to Myanmar – foreigners require a visa. The busy markets of this dusty little town on the south bank of the Mae Nam Mae Sai attract people from both sides of the border and there is an amazing variety of exotic goods for sale: Burmese and Chinese crafts, antiques, precious stones, etc. Perched on top of a hill is **Wat Phra That Doi Wao** *(west of the main street)* – naga staircase *(207 steps)*, chedi, vihara – which offers fine **views** of the town and river and of Myanmar in the distance.

There is evidence of an earlier settlement, Wiang Si Tuang, delimited by the existing moat, part of an earthen wall and a gate to the east and west.

Some **caves** in the vicinity are worth a visit. Tham Luang *(6km southwest)* has several chambers with fantastic rock formations; Tham Pum, and Tham Pla *(13km southwest)* are sited near a lake. Ban Tham is inhabited by Muslim Chinese who emigrated from Hunnan.

A frontier land

The mountains of Thailand's northernmost province which has boundaries with Burma (Myanmar) and Laos are inhabited by tribes with a distinctive way of life unchecked by frontiers. In the Mae Fa Luang district (3-5hr by 4-wheel drive vehicle) Doi Mae Salong *(see above)* is inhabited by Chinese settlers whereas in the more remote areas of Baan Therd Thai and Doi Hua Mae Kum are to be found four main tribal groups: Lisu, Akha, Meo and Lahu *(see INTRODUCTION, Population)* – visit the **Hill Tribe Museum** *(Thanon Tanalai)* for an informative presentation of their unique culture.

In this sensitive area war is still raging in Myanmar while in Thailand efforts are being made to curtail drug cultivation and trade with some success. As the roads improve the tribes benefit from better education and health care and agriculture (tea, coffee, fruit and flower cultivation) brings economic gains. The cool air is invigorating and the scenery in the mountain ranges is spectacular; wild sunflowers bloom from late November to December. An annual hilltribe festival at Baan Hua Mae Khum (18-19 Nov) aims to encourage cultural and environmental awareness among the tribes and to promote the area for tourism.

CHIANG SAEN★★

Chiang Rai – Population 55 096

Michelin Atlas p 3 or Map 965 – A 5 – Local map see Chiang Rai

The dramatic site on the south bank of the Mekong adds to the mystery of the ruins of the fortified city shaded by tall trees. There are 76 temples within the town walls and 63 more in the outer perimeter which mark the site as an important religious centre. Part of the wall has been restored but the present town covers only a small part of the old precinct while many ruined temples have not yet been surveyed. A drive around the walls gives an idea of the layout of the town. A model of the walled town surrounded by ditches is displayed at the visitor centre.

A **Boat Racing Festival** in which long narrow barges from Thailand and Laos compete takes place in April annually.

An ancient settlement – According to legend the Khmers founded a town on an island in the Mekong near the mouth of the Mae Nam Kok which was later destroyed by the current. There is evidence that an earlier settlement existed which was part of a kingdom that wielded great influence and was probably overrun by the Khmers. **Mengrai** became ruler of Chiang Saen in the mid 13C and later founded Chiang Rai *(see INTRO-DUCTION, History)*.

A new town was founded in the 14C by King Saen Phu of the Mengrai dynasty. It came under the rule of Chiang Mai with the rise of the Lanna kingdom and was invaded in the mid 16C by the Burmese who ruled for more than two centuries. After its recapture in 1804 by Rama I it was razed to the ground to prevent it from falling again into the hands of the Burmese. Seventy years later a prince of Lamphun rebuilt the town to resettle the descendants of the original population.

SIGHTS

★ **Wat Pa Sak** ⊘ – *200m west outside the walled precinct; leave by Pratu Nong Mud.* The pyramidal **chedi**★★ built by King Saen Phu is deemed to be the earliest in Chiang Saen and is the only extant example of early Lanna architecture which reveals Haripunchai, Burmese and Sukhothai influences. In the niches around the base, fine standing or walking Buddha images and celestial beings alternate. Decorative stucco frames and motifs – garudas, makaras, Kala faces, stylised lotus petals – highlight the relic chamber which is surmounted by a ringed spire. In front of the chedi is the ruined vihara. The temple derives its name "Temple of the Forest of Teak" from the teak trees *(sak)* which were planted along the walls.

Golden Triangle

Take 1016 west to see the dilapidated Wat Ku Tao just beyond the Mae Nam Chan. Then turn back and go north to view the two temples on a hilltop to the northwest of the ancient town.

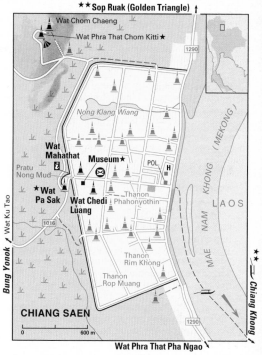

* **Wat Phra That Chom Kitti** – *3km north of Wat Pa Sak*. A stairway *(350 steps)* lined with stately teak trees was the ancient approach to the 10C temple. A rectangular plinth supports the redented relic chamber pierced by four niches housing Buddha images and surmounted by tiered mouldings, bell, ringed spire and slim canopy covered with copper plaques. Fine **views**★ of the town, the river and Lao territory in the distance.

Opposite is **Wat Chom Chaeng**, which boasts a small ruined brick chedi and a charming modern **vihara** decorated with delicate carving of foliage, a tiered roof with naga bargeboards and slim windows with shutters; it is a fine example of Lanna architecture. A traditional ceremonial gateway is a recent addition.

★ **National Museum [pendule]**– Chiang Saen is the origin of one of the major styles of Thai art. The art and archeology of the ancient town are illustrated by finds from excavation sites: stucco heads and motifs, stone inscriptions, garudas and deities. The most prized exhibits are four bronze seated **statues★★** of Buddha in Lanna style which repay careful study. Also on display are arms, drums, gongs, wicker and laquerware.

Wat Chedi Luang – *Next to the museum.* Tall trees surround the large compound with several ruins indicating the importance of the temple. The 13C octagonal chedi built of brick soars to an imposing height of 58m; heavy mouldings mark the central part. The vihara retains a highly venerated seated Buddha and a massive pillar.

Wat Mahathat – *Near the visitor centre.* All that remains is the squat redented base of a chedi with an east-facing niche.

EXCURSIONS

Bung Yonok – *5km southwest by 1016, turn left at Km 27 and continue for 2km.* The tranquil lake which attracts wintering wildfowl – mandarin ducks *(aix galericulata)* and other rare species – is an ideal spot for birdwatching.

Wat Phra That Pha Ngao – *Ban Doi Chan 4km southeast by 1290.* At the base of the temple precinct is a vihara, with a revered **statue★** of Buddha with tight curls and a serene expression in the Phayao style which dates between the 8C and the 14C. The statue which is half buried in the ground was discovered during renovation of the large stucco bust. Murals in high relief tell the story of the Buddha. To the left a chedi rises on a huge boulder with a Buddha in a niche.
Proceed to the hilltop crowned by a modern white **chedi** with a silver canopy atop the spire. The heavy mouldings detract from the overall effect. Inside two rows of columns with lotus capitals support a balustraded gallery; 4 Buddha images frame a ruined stupa; fine mural paintings in delicate colours depict scenes of daily life and of the Buddha preaching, and a Lanna-style Buddha sits on the altar. From the platform there are wonderful **views★★** of the surrounding area and of the majestic course of the Mekong.

Pla buk is a giant type of catfish *(Pangasianodon gigas)* from the Mekong which can reach 3m in length and 300kg in weight. Every year in April celebrations are held when the giant fish are caught. Overfishing has sadly depleted the fish stock and the Chiang Khong Fishery Station at Ban Hat Khrai has launched an ambitious breeding programme in an attempt to stem the decline.

★★ **Sop Ruak (Golden Triangle)** – *North by 1290.* At the confluence of the Mae Nam Ruak and the Mekong which serve as boundaries to Thailand, Myanmar and Laos is a picturesque area designated as the centre of the notorious Golden Triangle. The opium-producing region comprises, however, the area north of Chiang Mai and large adjacent tracts of land in Myanmar and Laos. Nowadays the atmosphere of Sop Ruak is quite tame with souvenir stalls, shops, restaurants and resorts along the riverside; there is even a casino on an island in the Mekong. Boats from China bring produce for sale. Fine **views★★** may be enjoyed from the ruined Wat Phra That Doi Pu Khao situated on a hill *(between Km 29-30; access by staircase or by small vehicle)* and boats can be hired for a tour on the river.
A small **Opium Museum** ◷ *(between Km 30-31)* has an excellent presentation on the story of opium cultivation and traffic as well as the social costs of addiction.

★★ **Excursion to Chiang Khong** – A boat trip downriver *(1hr 30min)* is an exciting way to enjoy the exotic scenery with rapids and the mountainous landscape of Laos adding to the interest. Chiang Khong can also be reached by a good road which for the most part runs parallel to the river.
The busy border town has **ferry** ◷ links with Laos (it is now an official crossing point and visas are required) and watching the activity on the river from a restaurant terrace is a pleasant pastime. **Fort Carnot** (now obscured by trees and buildings) built on a hillside in Laos by the French is a reminder of the strategic importance of the region in colonial times. A short river crossing gives a unique opportunity to visit Lao villages on the north bank of the river where the people earn a living through fishing, weaving and farming.

Visit the unspoilt Meo and Yao villages in Amphoe Chiang Khong to experience traditional life in the hills. A round tour can be made to Chiang Rai by taking 1020 through unspoilt mountain scenery, and from Thoeng, a fertile rice-growing valley.

CHONBURI

Chonburi – Population 242 292

Michelin Atlas p 24 or Map 965 – H 5 – Local map see Pattaya

The prosperity of this coastal town is derived from its fertile agricultural hinterland (tapioca, coconut, sugar-cane) and its growing industrial activity as well as from coastal and deep-sea fishing. The opening of the deep-sea port at Laem Chabang has attracted large international companies which have set up factories in the area (Michelin).

Chonburi has a colourful fishing port and its temples – Wat Yai Intharam, Wat Thep Puttharam and Wat Tham Nimit – are noteworthy. The **Chonburi Buffalo Races** held in October each year provide robust amusement to the local population.

EXCURSIONS

Bang Saen – *10km south.* The coast road passes **Ang Sila** *(5km south)* famous for stone mortars and weaving. Sam Muk Hill crowned by a shrine affords an extensive view of the coast.

The relaxed atmosphere of Bang Saen which has a long sandy beach and a leisure park Ocean World (slides, swimming pool) attracts local people. There is a well-presented **aquarium** ⓥ at the Scientific Marine Centre.

Continue to **Si Racha** *(14km south by 3)* renowned for its hot chilli sauce *(nam phrik si racha)*, fruits (pineapples) and oysters. A jetty giving access to Ko Loi, a rocky outcrop crowned by a temple, affords fine views of the open sea.

Khao Khieo Open Zoo ⓥ – *40km southeast by 3 and 32. Turn left at Km11 or 14 and proceed for 7km.* The road runs past Bang Phra reservoir which is a haven for birds, and several golf courses. The hilly contours

Squid and shrimps drying in the sun

J.-P. Garcin/ PHOTONONSTOP

of a wildlife sanctuary are a perfect setting for the **zoo** where some 50 animal species (rhinos, lions, leopards, gibbons, etc) roam freely in large enclosures. A vast **aviary**★ is alive with birdsong from a variety of rare species.

Ko Si Chang ⓥ – Visitors can tour the pleasant island with its small fishing village by hiring one of the amazing motorised tricycles which ply the ring road. In a pleasant setting shaded by tall trees by the sea are elegant buildings, foundations and a reservoir, all that remains of the summer **palace** built in the late 19C by Rama V who resided here to benefit from the sea air and dry climate. The palace was abandoned in 1893 when the French briefly occupied the island following a territorial dispute. One of the splendid teak-wood structures was dismantled and re-erected in Bangkok *(see BANGKOK, Phra Thinang Vimanmek)*. Nearby high up on the hill is **Wat Asadang Nimit** which has a vihara and a circular chedi in European style; the latter served as a landmark for ships. The Chakrapong cave gives access to the top of the hill for a bird's-eye **view**★★.

Near the pier a Chinese temple *(steep climb 500 steps)* with richly ornamented buildings is also notable. Ko Si Chang has few beaches: a small one to the north; and Hin Klom with round stones smoothed by the wind on the west coast; but the clear waters are ideal for swimming and snorkelling. There is still much activity in the harbour, although fewer ships unload their cargoes onto barges following the opening of the deep sea port at Laem Chabang. The development of the island proceeds apace with the building of roads and new harbour facilities.

Chachoengsao – *43km north by 3 and 314.* The thriving town nestling on the banks of Mae Nam Bang Pakong in a fertile basin has a chequered history. Its foundation dates from the 16C. After the sack of Ayutthaya in the 18C a Khmer ruler abducted large numbers of people from the town and its neighbours to work in Cambodia.

A tour of the canals is the best way to admire the lush rice paddies and vegetation. Near the imposing town hall is the shady **Sri Nakharin Park** laid out around a large pond. At the riverside **Wat Sothon Woraram Wora Wihan** traditonal dances are performed daily in honour of a sacred Buddha image, Luang Pho Sothon, which is said to be one of three Buddha images found floating in the water.

Further upstream the picturesque **Khao Hin Son** *(Km 51-52 by 304)* bristles with white rock formations. The Development Study Centre – botanical garden, tree and crop experimental plots, fishery and livestock – is under royal patronage. At **Wat Pho Bang Khla** *(17km further by 304, turn left into 3121 for 6km)* visitors will be amazed at the sight of vast numbers of fruit bats hanging from the fronds of large trees.

CHUMPHON

Chumphon – Population 141 001

Michelin Atlas p 19 or Map 965 – K 4

This busy and prosperous town is located at an important crossroads at the eastern end of the Isthmus of Kra. The development of the tourist potential of the area is in its early stages. The attraction of its beautiful coastline (220km) of deserted sandy beaches fringed with idyllic islands and reefs is complemented by a sense of discovery. The varied landscape ranges from open grasslands to the north to a densely forested hinterland against a backdrop of mountains.

EXCURSIONS

Paknam Chumphon – *13km southeast by 4119 and 4001.* An important fishing harbour at the mouth of Khlong Tha Taphao. Visitors can make various excursions to islands along the coast. A chedi and lighthouse on **Ko Mat Phon** *(15min trip; also accessible on foot at low tide)* serve as landmarks for seafarers.

Chumphon provides an alternative departure point for boats to **Ko Tao** ⓥ *(see Ko SAMUI)* from a pier at Tha Yang *(by 4001).*

Ao Thung Wua Laen – *Tambon Saplee, Amphoe Pathiu. 16km north by Apakorn road.* A peaceful bay with one of the finest sandy beaches. Diving excursions to several small islands are popular with enthusiasts. South of the bay Ko Ngam Yai and Ngam Noi *(17km from shore)* with beautiful coral reefs and underwater caves are famous for birds' nests which are highly prized as a delicacy.

Further up is Hat Laem Taen on Ao Bo Mao. A sala on a hill gives a good view of the bay.

★**Tham Rab Ro and Tham Phra** ⓥ– *Tambon Tha Kham north by 4. At Km 490 turn left and continue for 4km by an asphalt road; turn right to Wat Thep Charoen.* The hillside is riddled with caves. Steps lead up to the entrance of **Tham Phra** which contains several Buddha statues in the Srivijaya and Ayutthaya styles and an ancient statue called Luang Pu Lak Muang. Nearby is the spectacular **Tham Rab Ro**★ (path from Tham Phra or staircase from temple) bristling with stalactites and stalagmites. According to legend there are mysterious treasure maps in Tham Ai Teh *(front).*

Nam Tok Kapo Forest Park – *Tambon Salui, Amphoe Tha Sae. 41km north by 4, turn right at signpost and continue for 1km by a laterite road.* The shady recesses of this pleasant park are ideal for relaxation. A small waterfall, a stream and its varied flora add to the interest.

★**Scenic road to Surat Thani** – *193km south by 41.* It is well worth taking the time to explore the beaches off the beaten track to enjoy the splendid seascapes and a wonderful feeling of solitude.

The road runs parallel to **Hat Pharadornphap** *(12km southeast by 4119, turn left at Km 19 at signpost),* a wide sandy beach lined with palm trees (bungalows, restaurants). North of **Hat Sairee** *(15.5km by 4119, bear left at Km 13 and continue for 7km),* a fine beach with white powdery sand is a shrine facing the sea in honour of Prince Chumphon, the patron of the modern Thai Navy. An unusual sight nearby is the torpedo boat *The Royal Chumphon* decommissioned in 1975 and given to the province in 1979.

Make for the **Khao Chao Muang viewpoint** *(from Hat Sairee turn right, then left at the sign, proceed for 1km uphill to the parking area, then take a short walk up)* which over-looks the beautiful scenery of Chumphon bay and various islands (Ko Maphrao, Matra, Tha Lu –birds' nests, Raet, Lak Raet) as well as Ko Tao in good weather.

Ao Thung Makham *(Inner Thung Makham Bay 27km south by 4119, at Km 13 turn right into 4098 and continue for 6km along a surfaced road, turn left at Sala Chalerm Phra Kiat Ror. 9 into a laterite road and continue for 1km)* is fringed by a beautiful sandy beach with an unspoilt fishing village. *(Outer Thung Makham Bay, continue for 3km along a surfaced road and turn left at sign to Wat Pong Pang, proceed for 1km).*

Phra That Sawi – *47km south by 41, turn right at Km 34 and continue for 1km.* The temple is situated in a lush area surrounded by orchards and mangrove near the Mae Nam Sawee which was an important waterway in ancient times. According to legend, in 1260 during the war with Ayutthaya, Phraya Sri Thamma Sokkarat, ruler of Nakhon Si Thammarat, made an expedition to the area and discovered an ancient ruined chedi. Excavations revealed a small box made of gold containing a Buddha relic, now enshrined in the Srivijaya-style **chedi** which rests on a terrace with niches decorated with elephants. At the base are niches with sandstone statues of the seated Buddha. The San Phra Sua Muang *(east)* houses a human-size old statue of the god protector of the temple and Sawee town.

Hat Arunothai – *Amphoe Tako. South by 41, turn left between Km 44-45 into 4096 and proceed for a short distance.* From this pleasant tropical beach *(6km long)* lined with palm trees, boat trips can be taken to nearby islands. Other activities are hiking and rock climbing in the area.

Tham Khao Ngoen – *Tambon Tha Ma Pla (12km from Lang Suan Amphoe office) 70km south by 41, turn right between Km 67-68 and continue for 3km past a temple; proceed for 500m to Suan Somdet.* Hordes of monkeys frolic on the cliff face which is pierced by three caves in a picturesque setting near the river. In front of one is a chedi commemorating Rama V's visit in 1889 with a stone inscription by the king.

Khao Kriab – *80km south by 41 (10km from Amphoe Lang Suan); turn right into laterite road at Km 76-77 and continue for 6km.* Take a path near an isolated temple *(ask for the electricity to be switched on)* to a staircase *(364 steps, steep and slippery)* leading up to a large cave with fascinating concretions. A statue of Buddha stands at the entrance. The cave served as refuge for the locals in times of conflict.

★★ **Scenic road to Isthmus of Kra and Ranong** – *130km west by 4.* The luxuriant landscape is ample reward for the longer journey along this route to Ranong and down the west coast to Phuket, an opportunity to explore this isolated and less-populated region where a traditional way of life is still the rule. In recent times a plan has been mooted to dig a canal linking the Bay of Bengal to the Gulf of Thailand.

The road climbs through narrow valleys to the summit of the pass. A monument marks the narrowest point *(at Km 545)* adjoining Myanmar territory. It then descends along the Mae Nam Kra Buri *(10km)* which forms the natural border with Myanmar to Amphoe Kra Buri, then climbs to the bank of the estuary. Further along cross the wide Khlong Chang to Mae Nam La-Un *(ruined Japanese warship visible at low tide left of the bridge, houses on stilts)*. After Km 597 **Nam Tok Punyaban** *(parking)* cascading from a high cliff is visible from the road *(left)*. Beyond in a bend an extensive **view** unfolds of the estuary, islands and mountains in Myanmar. The road then descends to Ranong *(18km – see RANONG)*.

DAMNOEN SADUAK (Floating Market)★

Samut Songkhram

Michelin Atlas p 24 or Map 965 – H 4 – Local map see Kanchanaburi

Floating markets on the canals crisscrossing the central plain have played a significant part in the social life of the people from time immemorial but are increasingly under threat of modern development. There are several markets (Lak Ha, Khlong Ton Khem, Charoen Sukho, etc) in the area which take place only on certain days, but the colourful early morning scene at Damnoen Saduak which occurs daily is the most authentic experience. Traders bring fresh produce, the fruits of their labour, from far afield.

R. Mattes/ MICHELIN

Floating market

DAMNOEN SADUAK (Floating Market)

> This popular excursion from Bangkok is usually combined with a tour of Nakhon Pathom and a visit to the Rose Garden and to the Samphran Elephant Village. Independent travellers should aim to arrive around 08.00 to savour the spectacle before countless tour buses ferrying hundreds of tourists arrive about 09.00.
>
> **Buses** ⊙ from Bangkok terminate in the town of Damnoen Saduak. Access to the market is on foot, by minibus or by boat.
>
> This excursion is also possible from Kanchanaburi, Ratchaburi and Phetchaburi.

The flat-bottomed boats paddled skilfully by women wearing the typical broad straw hat are piled high with an amazing array of vegetables, fruit, meat, fish and flowers. Cooked dishes are also on offer for those in need of sustenance. Crowds of visitors watch the brisk trading with fascination. The mosaic of colours is a visual feast. Souvenir stalls along both banks of the narrow canal are a less attractive facet of commercial enterprise. The best spot for photographs is from the bridge spanning the canal.

Wat Phra That DOI SUTHEP★★★

Chiang Mai

Michelin Atlas p 3 or Map 965 – C 3 – Local map see Chiang Mai

The majestic scenery of **Doi Pui** (alt 1 685m) forms a splendid backdrop to the monastic buildings of this famous temple where Buddhist festivals are celebrated with great pomp. The temple stands high up at 1 000m on Doi Suthep.

TOUR *1 hour*

Access by cable-car ⊙ *or by a steep stairway (306 steps).*

A statue of the earth-goddess **Thorani** stands at the foot of the stairway, flanked by a splendid naga balustrade symbolising man's quest for enlightenment, and leading up to the terrace where hang four bronze bells. A fine vihara built of teak wood is a recent addition. Walk round to enjoy magnificent **views★★★** of Chiang Mai and of the surrounding countryside. Statues of demons guard the entrance to the temple precinct.

★★ **Chedi** – The glittering five-tier chedi (20m high) framed by four gilded filigree canopies added in the 18C by King Kavila is a majestic sight against the luminous sky.
The original chedi was restored and remodelled in Lanna style to its present appearance in 1478. Further remodelling was later carried out when the slim finial was crowned in the Burmese style. The faceted structure on a redented base is sheathed in gilded copper stamped with delicate motifs.

Viharas – The richly carved and gilded **doorways** and **gables** of the two viharas are fine examples of Lanna craftsmanship. In the main shrine decorated with delicate murals, a seated Buddha in the Lanna style is framed by four attendant Buddhas, two with a flame halo and two with the Wheel of the Law.

Cloisters – Among the bronze Buddha images dating from different periods are fine examples of the Sukhothai and Lanna (Chiang Saen) styles. The mural paintings by local craftsmen are of lesser interest. There is also a small **museum**.

> ### An auspicious foundation
> An angel revealed to the monk Sumana in a dream the place where a casket containing a holy relic of Buddha was buried. As the king of Sukhothai was unwilling to believe in the power of the relic without proof, the monk kept it in his possession and later accepted King Ku Na's invitation to reside at **Wat Suan Dok★★** *(see CHIANG MAI).* At a ceremony held to enshrine the relic in a chedi, the relic multiplied into two by supernatural power. One was buried in the chedi, the other was placed on the back of a white elephant, which was then allowed to roam freely with the king and his retinue following behind. It came to rest finally on a mound below the summit of Doi Pui where resided a hermit. The noble animal trumpeted three times and promptly died on the spot. King Ku Na then built a chedi to enshrine the sacred relic, which ever since that time has been held in great veneration by the faithful.

ADDITIONAL SIGHTS

Doi Suthep – Doi Pui National Park – In spite of extensive encroachment on the park which encompasses two peaks, it abounds in many species of butterflies and birds as well as flowering plants and ferns. The lower slopes are covered with deciduous tree species with evergreen forest at altitude. Scenic trails crisscross the park, some leading to waterfalls. A track leads to the summit affording splendid **views**.

Golden Chedi, Wat Phra That Doi Suthep

Phuping Palace and Gardens ⊘ – *5km further.* The royal summer residence *(not open)* is surrounded by beautiful landscaped gardens ablaze with colour.

It is also possible to visit **a Meo (Hmong) village** located three kilometres beyond the palace *(access by truck from parking along a dirt road)* with its thatched huts, which although modernised will give a glimpse of the traditional way of life of the hill-tribe. Their colourful traditional costume and silver jewellery are highly decorative.

HAT YAI

Songkhla – Population 305 260

Michelin Atlas p 22 or Map 965 – N 5

The booming town of Hat Yai which is served by an excellent road and rail network and an airport is the commercial hub of the south and the gateway to Malaysia with border posts at Sadao (cars, buses and foot passengers) and Padang Besar (rail transport). There is a large Chinese population and a sizeable Muslim community.
The town offers good shopping facilities, a lively nightlife and fine hotels and restaurants which appeal greatly to visitors from neighbouring Malaysia and Singapore. Wat Hat Yai Nai *(4km west from Saphan Hat Yai in Thanon Phetkasem)* which boasts a large reclining Buddha image is of some interest. Hat Yai is a good base for excursions, especially to Songkhla and Phatthalung which are within easy reach *(see SONGKHLA and PHATTHALUNG).*

Hat Yai has an unusual bullfighting tradition. Fights which can last for hours take place at the bull ring (near the airport) twice monthly at weekends. Two bulls are pitted against each other and lock horns until one is pushed to the edge of the arena or takes flight. The events are occasions for heavy betting.

EXCURSIONS

Nam Tok Ton Nga Chang – *13.5km west by 4. Turn left into surfaced road and continue for 13km.* The road leads to the foot of the mountain and then climbs along a verdant river valley to a car park. A bridge and a path lead to the majestic first fall which divides into two, hence the name meaning "elephant's tusks". Access to the six upper tiers is difficult.

★**Scenic road to Satun** – *120km southwest by 4 and 406. Allow two days, not including a two-day trip to Mu Ko Tarutao.* The road climbs gently through a fine landscape dotted with limestone outcrops and rounded hills planted with rubber trees at the foot of the Tenasserim range. The long excursion is well worthwhile for the unspoilt scenery. *See SATUN.*

HUA HIN★★

Prachuap Khiri Khan – Population 71 585

Michelin Atlas p 17 or Map 965 – I 4

This charming seaside resort with its long **beach★★** *(3km)* of sparkling white sand bounded by a rocky headland to the south now rivals the better-known resorts of the east coast, as it is situated on the fast road to the southern peninsula and is equipped with an excellent tourist infrastructure. Its colourful fishing pier, bustling fish market, seafood restaurants and night market *(Thanon Dechanuchit)* complement its fine beach attractions.

It also boasts a renowned **golf course** which is one of the oldest in Southeast Asia, and a quaint **railway station** built in teak-wood on the route of the Eastern and Oriental Express on its journey from Singapore to Bangkok, a revival of the great tradition of rail travel.

Hua Hin is a good base for exploring **Phetchaburi★★** *(north – see PHETCHABURI)* and **Prachuap Khiri Khan** and **Chumphon** *(south – see PRACHUAP KHIRI KHAN and CHUMPHON)* along the coast.

"Queen of Tranquillity" – This was a well-deserved designation as it was the first beach resort which was easily accessible by train from Bangkok. The area was discovered in 1910 by one of the royal princes on a hunting trip and the patronage of the royal family which a summer palace here soon gave it great prestige.

Railway Hotel – *Now Sofitel Hotel.* A wonderful colonial-style **building★** in teak-wood which is associated with the opening of the railway to the west in the 1920s has been refurbished to its full glory. Its beautiful beach and gardens including delightful animal topiary complement its elegance. The hotel is open to visitors for tea or for a meal, an opportunity to savour the delightful setting.

Relaxing on the beach, Hua Hin

EXCURSIONS

★**Phra Ratcha Niwet Marukatayawan** ⊘ – *15km north by the coast road.* An idyllic royal retreat – "Palace of Love and Hope" – built in 1924 by Rama VI in the grounds of a police compound comprises harmonious teak buildings (renovated) linked by elevated corridors with access to pavilions right on the beach. The architectural style reflects a Victorian influence. The feet of the columns are immersed in water for insect control. In the centre were the living quarters of the royal family. There were also throne halls and a theatre. The balcony affords delightful **views** of the sea and gardens.

Ao Takiap – *4km south.* A pleasant excursion offers deserted beaches (Hat Khao Takiap – *Km 238,* Suan Son – *Km 240,* Khao Tao – *Km 242-243)* lined with sea pines and beautiful scenery. Fine **views** of the sea, the mountains and environs may be enjoyed from two hill-top temples (Wat Khao Thairalat – *stairway,* Wat Khao Takiap – *car access)* in traditional fishing communities.

Pran Buri Forest Park – *6km south by 4. Turn left at Km 246.* A road leads to a busy fishing port and to fine beaches where visitors can enjoy a sense of seclusion. The area is undergoing development and there are several resorts.

★**Khao Sam Roi Yot National Park** – *65km south, branch off at Pran Buri. Park office at Ban Khao Daeng (turn left off 4 at Km 286 and continue for 20km).* The rugged outline of the "Mountain of Three Hundred Peaks" (highest peak – alt 605m) with its densely forested slopes and valleys forms a picturesque backdrop to the park which is crossed by several hiking trails. This area was one of the most extensive **wetlands** in Southeast Asia and is now a conservation site. Shrimp farming which has degraded the marsh area has now been banned and it is hoped that the fragile ecological balance can be restored. The wintering season attracts large numbers of birdwatchers as the bird population includes herons, egrets, storks as well as rare spotted and imperial eagles.
Limestone **caves** (Tham Sai past Ban Bang Phu, Ban Khao Daeng and Ban Khung Thanot; Tham Kaeo; **Tham Phraya Nakhon**★★ – *below*) are well worth a visit *(guide advisable for some caves)* for their geological formations – draperies, domes, petrified waterfalls.

★★**Tham Phraya Nakhon** – *Access by boat from Ban Bang Pu – 430m by steep trail from Hat Laem and proceed down 30m to the first chamber – 1 hr 15min rtn.* A steep climb is well rewarded by the sight of two large sinkholes and several chambers and arches. An elegant Thai-style pavilion built for King Rama V adds a touch of fantasy.

★★**Kaeng Krachan National Park** – *See PHETCHABURI – Excursions.*

KALASIN

Kalasin – Population 145 361

Michelin Atlas p 9 or Map 965 – E 8

The bronze **Phraya Chai Sunthorn Monument** *(opposite the post office)* of a man in Thai dress with a sword in his left hand and a water pot in his right hand is dedicated to the founder of Kalasin. It is the modest capital of a small agricultural province. There are ancient settlements in the area which has a rich history.

Wat Klang – *Thanon Phakao, Amphoe Muang.* The wat is renowned for a beautiful black Buddha image in bronze with an ancient inscription at the base, and a Buddha footprint in sandstone probably of the Dvaravati period. The latter was removed from the bank of the Lam Pao owing to erosion.

Wat Si Bun Ruang – *Thanon Somphamitr (behind Wat Klang).* The oldest temple in Kalasin boasts ancient **bai sema** from Muang Fa Daet Sung Yang *(see below)* placed around the ubosot. An admirable example at the entrance depicts a deity flying over a two-storeyed prasat with the royal family portrayed on the lower section.

EXCURSIONS

Lam Pao Dam – *35km north. Leave Kalasin by 213 west, after 9km turn right at Km 33-34 and continue for 26km.* There is a pleasant scenic area (Hat Dokket) along the bank of the reservoir built across the Lam Pao and Huay Yang rivers.
An open **zoo** *(Uttayan Satpa Lam Pao 4km east)* in an unspoilt forest setting contains various species of birds, monkeys, etc. A major project started in 1980 concerns the breeding of the rare Indonesian Banteng bull.

Phra Phuttha Saiyat Phu Khao – *Ban Na Si Nuan, Tambon Non Sila. North by 227, at Km 38 (6km from Sahat Sakhan market) turn left and continue for 1km on a laterite road.* Park near a modern sala, walk to the small vihara and down some steps to a rock shelter with a reclining Buddha, Phra Mokalana (1692). A distinctive feature is that the figure reclines to the left. To the left of the vihara is a Buddha footprint embedded in the rock.

Wat Pho Chai Sema Ram – *South by 214. Turn right at a sign in the village between Km 13-14 and proceed for 6km.* Ancient Dvaravati **bai sema** from Muang Fa Daet Sung Yang are aligned in the garden. The finest (under cover) shows the king and queen paying homage to the Buddha.

Phra That Ya Ku – *As above and turn right opposite the wat and continue for 400m.* The star-shaped stupa is the only significant reminder of the ancient Dvaravati city (7C-9C AD) of **Muang Fa Daet Sung Yang** also known as Muang Sema, although its plan has been identified. The **brick base**★ is original, to which was later added the octagonal stupa. The top section is a restoration.

KAMPHAENG PHET★★

Kamphaeng Phet – Population 233 674

Michelin Atlas p 7 or Map 965 – E 4 – Local map see Phitsanulok

Kamphaeng Phet nestles along a graceful curve of the Mae Nam Ping bounded to the north by a great tract of teak forest. Sirikit Park and a landscaped esplanade on the east bank attract local people out for a stroll and there are open-air restaurants on the west bank. Places of interest in the new town which serves as the provincial capital include **Wat Sadet** (finely incised Buddha footprint – *Thanon Ratchadamnoen*) and **Wat Ku Yang** (early Bangkok-style *ho trai* – *Thanon Lang Wat Ku Yang*).

A strategic site – Extensive ruins attest to the importance of the fortified town which was a major outpost of the Sukhothai kingdom. The name Kamphaeng Phet literally means diamond walls, suggesting great strength. **Nakhon Chum,** a prosperous ancient town on the west bank before the founding of Kamphaeng Phet, was later outgrown by the latter. A Sukhothai inscription gives an account of King Li Thai (1347-68) coming to Nakhon Chum and ordering the construction of a chedi to enshrine relics of the Buddha. Ayutthaya's forces made several attempts to capture the town but it was not until the 15C in the reign of King Borommatrailokanat that it fell, together with Sukhothai. It then became a front-line town on the route to the northern Lanna kingdom which had Chiang Mai as capital.

Its strategic location was recognised by the Burmese army which had to pass through or rested in the town on its way to attack Ayutthaya. When the capital was captured by the Burmese for the second time in 1767, Kamphaeng Phet was deserted by its population fleeing the war. It was not until peace had returned permanently during the Rattanakosin period that people moved back to settle in the town.

★**National Museum** ⊙ – Two stucco elephants from Wat Chang Rob *(see below)* restored to their full glory stand guard by the museum entrance. The collection traces the development of art in Thailand from the prehistoric era.

Ground floor – Pride of place is given to a majestic bronze of **Shiva**★★ dating from the Ayutthaya period (1510) which reveals the influence of the Khmer Bayon style. An inscription on the base proclaims the deity's rule over animals and men. The prehistoric exhibits date back 2 000 to 4 000 years: terracotta, stone and iron artefacts, and grinding tools. Pottery was produced by an active settled community. Coins from the Dvaravati civilisation (8C-9C) feature traditional images – moon, water, naga and fertility symbols whereas the depiction of deer indicates the early influence of Buddhism. An interesting bronze of **Buddha subduing Mara**★ in the early Ayutthaya (U-Thong) style (15C) contrasts with a bronze head of the Buddha in the Sukhothai style.

First floor – Among important finds from digs in the area are remarkable 16C bronze statues of the Hindu deities, **Vishnu**★★ (bust) and **Lakshmi**★★ (body). A stucco head of the Buddha is notable for its large forehead and pointed chin. Also on display are terracotta and ceramic ware (14C-18C) including Sangkalok jars (15C), as well as Sukhothai bronzes.

Annexe – Folk art and crafts are presented in a group of traditional wooden houses.

Festival

The glorious reign of King Li Thai of Sukhothai (1347-68) is celebrated by an annual parade with the participants in traditional Thai attire at the full moon in February (Makha Bucha day). Folk events, local entertainment and sale of local products add to this happy occasion.

HISTORICAL PARK

Site – Entrance gates *(pratu)* and citadels *(pom)* guard the moated, walled town built on a rectangular plan within which are aligned two monumental groups characteristic of the Sukhothai period. Outside the walls is a group of forest-sect temples **(Aranyik)** in a tranquil leafy setting conducive to meditation. Ruins of religious sanctuaries in Nakhon Chum and Kamphaeng Phet number about 81 sites. Their artistic styles reflect historical associations with the Sukhothai, Ayutthaya and Lanna kingdoms.

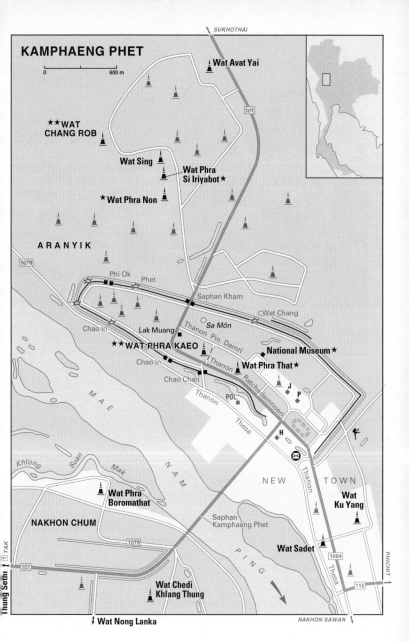

Inner city

★ Wat Phra That – *Opposite the museum.* Two small chedis frame a vihara of which only the foundations remain. The main **chedi★** surrounded by pillars is noteworthy as it exemplifies a unique local style although Sukhothai, Ayutthaya and Lanna influences are apparent. Above the square laterite base rises an octagonal tier and a bell-shaped body crowned by an elegant ringed spire.

★★ Wat Phra Kaeo – According to tradition the principal sanctuary situated in the town centre enshrined the Emerald Buddha *(see BANGKOK, Wat Phra Kaeo)*, hence its name. Within the compound there are several ruined structures and statues – the laterite core of some has weathered into stylised forms. Near the entrance only the base of a statue remains amid the columns of a vihara which precedes a mondop. A second vihara fronts the main **chedi** which retains traces of stucco decoration and statues in the upper niches. The square base features fragments of 32 stucco lions. Next a large seated Buddha and three **colossal statues★** form a remarkable group; note in particular the expressive features of the **reclining Buddha.** Further west stucco elephants highlight the base of another round chedi surrounded by smaller such structures. Near the gate are the **Lak Muang** and ponds (**Sa Môn** – *north*).

R. Strange/ SUPERSTOCK HOA QUI

Wat Phra Kaeo

Outer area

★**Wat Phra Non** – In front of the 15C-16C temple girt by low walls are a square pond, a bathroom and a pavilion where was performed ritual purification prior to entry into the sanctuary.

In the temple area only the ruined base and great pillars of the ubosot remain. A large **vihara**★ for a reclining Buddha now eroded into a rough profile retains walls with narrow window openings and four rows of massive pillars with holes at the upper end into which were inserted beams supporting the roof. These are among the biggest laterite pillars ever found in Thailand. Only the plinths of three seated Buddhas remain in the rear chamber.

The craftsmanship of the large **chedi** at the rear is outstanding: the base is similar to that of a Lanna chedi with, above, two lotus-leaf tiers crowned by a bell typical of the Sukhothai period.

★**Wat Phra Si Iriyabot** – Its name is derived from the four stucco **Buddha images**★ in high relief placed in the curved sides of a tall mondop, which was probably covered by a roof in the form of a terraced pyramid. The statues shown in the four traditional stances, namely standing, walking, seated and reclining, reflect the influence of Sukhothai's artistic style. On a vast balustraded platform are the ruins of a vihara. The line of the ancient moat is now visible as well as a well and bathroom. Also of interest is a laterite quarry on the other side of the road.

Wat Sing – The leafy setting frames a tall seated Buddha image amid the ruins of a vihara and a large chedi flanked by smaller monuments.

★★**Wat Chang Rob** – This is one of the finest monuments of the Sukhothai period as regards the artistic inspiration and execution. A large pond was previously a quarry for the building material. To the north was a small ubosot. Beyond a large vihara the **chedi** featuring **stuccos**★ of elephants previously richly ornamented *(see museum above)* as well as delicate bodhi trees is a memorable sight. Singhas guard the base of the narrow stairs climbing to the terrace on which was built a large chedi; there is space for a clockwise worship march around it. Stucco and terracotta figures of celestial beings and mythical animals adorned the lower part; the bell-shaped upper section crowned in turn by a slender spire has fallen down with age.

Wat Avat Yai – Extensive ruins lie in a densely forested site where excavations have yielded Buddha images, votive offerings and ceramics. Beyond a quarry converted into a pond, pass through the gate flanked by low L-shaped walls supporting the bases of 16 chedis into the temple compound. In the centre stand a large **vihara** on a massive plinth, and the principal chedi. There are salas, wells and bathrooms in the rear area.

Nakhon Chum

Along the southern approach to the town *(101 leading to the bridge and the town)* the extensive ruins of Nakhon Chum on the west bank of the Mae Nan Ping testify to its past importance.

Wat Phra Boromathat – The temple boasts a chedi built to enshrine relics of the Buddha as recorded in a Sukhothai inscription dating from the reign of King Li Thai. Some decades ago the original chedi probably in the form of a lotus bud characteristic of the Sukhothai era was replaced by a Burmese-style chedi built by a rich Burmese log merchant. The harmonious round structure with its delicate gilded crown is noteworthy.

Other sites – A fort, **Pom Thung Sethi**, was built to counter the Burmese threat. The moated **Wat Nong Lanka** (14C-15C) is graced by a bell-shaped chedi capped by a slender crown and adorned with niches and a ruined standing Buddha. **Wat Chedi Khlang Thung** (14C) comprises a vihara and an elegant lotus-bud stupa on a square base in the Sukhothai style.

Excursion

Khlong Lan National Park – *62km southwest by 1 south for 10km, turn right into 1117 then at Km 46 bear right to the park office. Accommodation and camping facilities.*
At Km 25 a minor road branches off 1117 to Ban Pong Nam Ron from which excursions *(guide recommended)* may be made to waterfalls, rapids and gorges up the valley of Khlong Suan Mak.
The steep hills (highest peak Khao Khun Khlong Lan, alt 1 439m) which are part of the Thanon Thong Chai range, are covered with dense forest which had been eroded by hill tribes. The latter are now settled outside the park boundaries. Among the rare animals are gaurs (wild cattle), tigers, hog deer and serows (Asiatic antelope) as well as 68 bird species (crested serpent eagle, thick-billed pigeon). The park highlights include trails, rapids, and waterfalls, in particular **Nam Tok Khlong Lan** *(easy access by a surfaced road from the park office)* which crashes impressively from a sheer cliff, and Nam Tok Khlong Nam Lai.

KANCHANABURI★★

Kanchanaburi – Population 156 228

Michelin Atlas p 11 or Map 965 – G 4

Fast-flowing rivers, dramatic mountain scenery and luxuriant vegetation combined with its long, eventful history make Kanchanaburi a rather special destination. The pleasant modern town has a lively atmosphere and fine tourist facilities (guesthouses, hotels, resorts) and is an excellent base from which to explore the attractive countryside and historical sights. Trekking and river cruises to explore the distant reaches are very popular.
The riverside is lined with raft houses popular with those wishing to experience the simple life and with floating restaurants serving delicious Thai cuisine especially the local delicacy, *pla yisok*, a succulent river carp, in pleasant surroundings. The fish is the symbol of the town. The City Pillar (Lak Muang) shrine and the old part of town are of some interest.
Gem mining (sapphires, spinels, rubies, onyx – *see Bo Phloi below*), has contributed to the prosperity of the town. Tin and wolfram have also been mined in the mountain range on the border.

A potent symbol

A week-long **festival** is held every year *(late Nov or early Dec)* to commemorate the heroic deeds and the enduring spirit of the prisoners of war in the building of the railway to Burma. The bridge is the focal point of the celebrations. Events include historical and archeological displays, cultural shows, vintage train rides and a light and sound spectacular of the history of the "bridge over the River Kwai".

From the dawn of time – Evidence of prehistoric civilisation was first uncovered by a Dutch prisoner of war engaged in the building of the Death Railway *(see below)*. After the end of the Second World War he took part in the archaeological investigation of the area which revealed Neolithic settlements (3 000 BC) near Sai Yok, Bo Phloi and Ban Kao. Artefacts and mural paintings found at other sites probably dating back to the Paleolithic era are still being studied. The museum at Ban Kao *(see below)* presents a fascinating survey of the area. Further investigation is under way and new discoveries will no doubt shed more light on the early occupation of the district.

The Death Railway

In 1942, 61 000 British, Australian, American, New Zealand, Danish and Dutch prisoners of war as well as an estimated 250 000 impressed labourers from Thailand, Burma and Malaysia were put to work by the Japanese Army to construct a railway track 415km long to link Kanchanaburi to Thanbyuzayat in Burma, thus ensuring a direct line from Singapore through Malaysia and Thailand to link up with the rail network in Burma. Apart from supplying their bases in Burma, the railway would also serve in preparing for the invasion of India. The route chosen through the valley of the Mae Nam Khwae Noi to the Three Pagodas Pass ran through difficult terrain but the river was a useful means of transport for building materials. Trees were felled in the jungle and elephants used to ferry the timber. In the rainy season the ground was turned into a quagmire through which the prisoners toiled without respite with inadequate tools. The Japanese High Command ordered the completion of the line within 12 months. The hard labour, harsh discipline, poor diet, exhaustion and lack of medical care exacted a heavy toll among the prisoners. The work was completed in record time in October 1943 at the cost of 16 000 Allied and countless Asian lives. The cruel treatment meted out to the prisoners is a shameful indictment of the Japanese military. After the war the rail track from Nam Tok to the Three Pagodas Pass was dismantled for strategic reasons.

A trading centre – Significant finds at Phong Tuk *(east by 323)* suggest that trade links existed between Southeast Asia and Western culture *(see Ban Kao Museum below)* and that the Mon-Dvaravati civilisation (7C-11C) flourished in the region.

A far-flung empire – Imposing monuments attest that in the 13C Khmer rule extended to the Burmese border. There were well-established communities at this distant outpost.

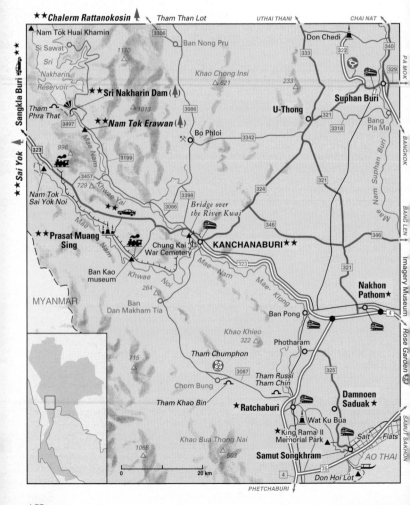

A strategic site – The Ayutthaya period (14C-18C) was marked by the struggle for power between Burmese and Ayutthaya kings. Burmese armies marched through the Three Pagodas Pass to launch repeated attacks on Thai territory, and finally destroyed Ayutthaya. Kanchanaburi was founded by Rama I as a frontier post to counter the threat posed by Burma.

During the Second World War the strategic importance of the region was again to the fore. As the sea routes were under constant threat from the air the Japanese planned to build a railway to provide a secure supply route to their army fighting in Burma and for the invasion of India. Allied prisoners of war as well as Asian slave labourers were put to forced labour in inhuman conditions in the jungle, with appalling loss of life through malnutrition and disease. Kanchanaburi has many potent reminders of this infamous enterprise and visitors from all over the world come to join in remembrance of the fallen. A novel by Pierre Boulle and a hugely popular film have stirred public interest in the heroic achievements of these unfortunate men although both novel and film are entirely fictional accounts.

Out and about

Tourism Authority of Thailand (TAT) – Thanon Saeng Chuto, Amphoe Muang, Kanchanaburi. ☎ 034 511 200, 512 500; Fax 034 511 200

Tourist Police – As above. ☎ 1155, 034 512 668/795

Transport – Timetables for daily bus and rail services to Bangkok and neighbouring provinces available from TAT. Kanchanaburi Railway Station, Thanon Saeng Chuto; Bus station next turning east of TAT.
Tricycles, motorcycles and jeeps for hire (daily or weekly) in Thanon Saeng Chuto.

Sightseeing – **Rail trip** from the railway station to Nam Tok Railway Station.
Rafting and **canoeing trips** (7-10hr return journey or including overnight stay) from the bridge or from the waterfront. Contact TAT for current information and prices.
Trekking (on foot or by elephant) and camping and bungalow facilities are available at Sai Yok, Chaloem Rattanakosin, Erawan National Parks, at Khao Laem Dam and Sangkhla Buri
At **Kanchanaburi Safari Park** near Bo Phloi wild animals roam in landscaped grounds.

Sport – There are golf courses and resorts with excellent facilities.

Shopping – Visit the Jewellery Handicraft Centre at Bo Phloi for splendid items made up of the locally mined stones. Factories specialising in gem cutting and polishing have visitor centres and gift shops.

Hotels and Restaurants – There is a wide choice of establishments in all price ranges from floating restaurants and hotels to simple guest-houses and luxury resorts.

Where to eat

There are excellent restaurants offering Thai and Chinese cuisine and featuring river fish along the waterfront at Thanon Song Kway and also by the River Kwai bridge. Live music is often featured.

Where to stay

Budget

River Kwai Hotel – 284/3-16 Thanon Saeng Chuto. ☎ 034 511 565; Fax 034 511 269; rkhk@riverkwai.co.th; www.riverkwai.co.th; 900-1 600 Baht. Comfortable rooms; restaurants and entertainment.

River Kwai Village Hotel – 74/12 Moo ,Thasao, Saiyok. ☎ 034 634 454-6, 034 251 7828/7552; Fax 034 634 454, 034 255 2350; rkvh@bkk2000.com; www.bkk2000.com/rkvh; 1 200-2 000 Baht. Riverside establishment with some raft-houses 70km northwest from town centre. Restaurants.

Moderate

Suan Srikanokporn Hotel – 149/4 Moo 1, Lumsum, Saiyok. ☎ 034 591 062, 02 880 7350-2, 02 880 8591-7; Fax 034 591 062,02 434 2563; 1 600-5 000 Baht. Well appointed hotel with restaurants, outdoor pool.

Pavilion Rim Kwai Thani – 79/2 Moo 2, Kanchanaburi-Si Sawat Road. ☎ 034 513 800; Fax 034 515 774; 2 500-5 700 Baht. Resort hotel with excellent facilities.

Ratchsuppamit Hotel – Thanon Saeng Chuto, Tambon Tha Makham. ☎ 034 625 128; Fax 034 625 127; 850-5 000 Baht. Fine accommodation near the town.

The Legacy River Kwai – 129 Moo 2 Tambon Klondor, Dan Makham Tia. ☎ 034 515 995, 034 516 788, 02 860 7602-9; Fax 034 515 995, 02 860 7610; 2 500-6 500 Baht. Fine resort with low-rise buildings and landscaped gardens. Restaurants.

Bridge over the River Kwai

"Bridge over the River Kwai" – *4km northwest from the town centre.* The sturdy iron bridge spanning the Mae Nam Khwae Yai, which replaced an earlier wooden structure upstream and was a crucial part of the Death Railway, was built in some 16 months by prisoners and Asian conscripts. The bridge was destroyed in Allied bombing raids towards the end of the war and was later rebuilt by the Japanese as war reparations; only the curved girders are original. After the war the Allies sold the structure to the Thai government. Nearby a small rail museum – rail tracks, vintage locomotives and a curious lorry which ran on rails – adds to the interest of this engineering feat which evokes immense human suffering.

EXCURSIONS

★★ **By rail to Nam Tok** ⊙ – A nostalgic train ride from the little station in the town centre to the end of the line at Nam Tok (77km) affords impressive **views** of the bridge and, further along the line, of a perilous stretch with a wooden viaduct on stout piles hugging a sheer cliff face by the river. The beautiful scenery has been tamed from the jungle which the prisoners had to clear by hand before the sleepers could be laid. The historic journey is a moving experience. The train stops for a few hours and visitors can take in the nearby waterfall, **Nam Tok Sai Yok Noi**, tumbling down limestone cliffs or explore further upriver. There are food stalls and refreshments near the station.

Kanchanaburi War Cemetery ⊙ – *Thanon Saengchuto.* The serried rows of graves with their moving dedications to the memory of the 6 982 men from the Allied armies who died in captivity are a poignant sight. The immaculate grounds are tended by the Commonwealth War Graves Commission. A plaque at the entrance is also dedicated to the estimated 50 000 Asian workers who lost their lives.
Next to the burial ground is a Chinese cemetery with exotic monuments.

JEATH War Museum ⊙ – *Wat Chai Chumphon. Thanon Visuthararangsi.* In the temple grounds is a moving reconstruction of a POW camp with bamboo huts which give an inkling of the grim living conditions and the atrocities endured. On display are tools, bombs, photographs, original sketches and testimonies and memorabilia donated by survivors.

North of the town

On the border with Myanmar a vast forested, mountainous area comprising national parks (Sai Yok, Erawan, Sri Nakarin, Chalerm Rattanakosin) and wildlife sanctuaries (Thung Yai) is devoted to conservation and is of great ecological value. The parks are easily accessible by road.

★★ **Erawan National Park** – *65km north by 323 and 3199. Visitor Centre.* The well-frequented forested park set in the foothills of the Tenasserim Range is a favoured destination of nature lovers. The abundant wildlife including elephants, tigers, deer, monkeys and numerous bird species thrives in the shady recesses. A steep trail runs along the impressive seven-tiered waterfall which tumbles into inviting deep pools at each level. **Nam Tok Erawan** draws its name from the seventh level *(precarious climb)* where the rock formation is shaped like the three-headed elephant Airavata (Erawan), a powerful symbol in Hindu mythology. Picnic areas and accommodation are available.

★★**Sri Nakharin Dam and National Park** – *5km further, turn into 3497.* This park is an extension of Erawan National Park and includes a massive hydro-electric dam which has created an immense lake hemmed in by forested hillsides. Fine **views**★★ of the scenery may be enjoyed from the dam. There are also splendid limestone caves, Tham Phra That *(10km northwest of the dam by trail)* and Tham Wang Badan *(west of the park)* with wonderful concretions in the large chambers. The spectacular **Nam Tok Huai Khamin** *(25km trail northwest by four-wheel drive vehicle or 2hr boat trip)* cascades in several tiers down the ochre limestone rock face. The remote jungle scenery where deer, elephants and tigers roam makes this the highlight of the park. The bamboo groves and deciduous forest cover resound with the trills and squawks of exotic birds (hornbills, parrots, kingfishers among others).

★★**Chaloem Rattanakosin National Park** – *97km north by 323, 3086, 3306 and proceed for 22km by a local road. 4hr not including visit. Visitor Centre and accommodation.* The fast road passes **Bo Phloi**, a gem mining area – sapphires, rubies, garnets, onyx – which in its heyday fuelled wild dreams of riches as speculators flocked to the district. Few mines are still in operation but the district bears the marks of these activities. The workings now fenced off are visible along the road. Marked trails wind through the thick jungle cover of the small **national park** (59sq km) dominated by Khao Kamphaeng (alt 1 257m) to swift-flowing rivers, picturesque waterfalls – Nam Tok Than Ngun and Than Thong *1km from park office* – and dramatic caves.

A stream cuts through the vast **Tham Than Lot Noi** (300m long) beyond which a trail *(2km)* follows the river to the three-tiered Nam Tok Trai Trung. The final precipitous section climbs to **Tham Than Lot Yai**, a spectacular sinkhole, and passes under a soaring natural arch to a forest temple. There is a striking snake-shaped rock formation along the way. The towering trees shelter abundant wildlife including gibbons, deer, gaurs, black bears and elephants as well as many bird species (woodpeckers, fly-catchers, hornbills).

West of the town

Chung-Kai War Cemetery – *Access by ferry from the pier at the west end of Thanon Lak Muang and a trail through fields. Or by road by 323 west and 3228.* The peaceful graveyard in a landscaped riverside setting is the final resting-place of 1 750 Allied prisoners of war.

Two kilometres further south is Wat Tham Khao Pun. Climb up to the limestone caves bristling with stalagmites and housing Buddha images.

Ban Kao Museum ⊘ – *35km west by 323 and 3455.* A fascinating display of Neolithic tools, utensils, jewellery and dioramas is evocative of the distant era when prehistoric man roamed the forest and mountains. Outstanding exhibits are a unique **vessel**★ shaped like a tripod, and wooden coffins.

Nam Tok Sai Yok Yai

N. Wheeler/ PHOTONONSTOP

★★ **Prasat Muang Sing** ⊙ – *7km further by 3455.* The extensive ruins of the temple beside the fast-flowing Mae Nam Khwae Noi are a potent reminder of the Khmer empire. The border town of Muang Sing, "City of the Lions", was probably established as a trading post.

Ramparts enclose the walled compound punctuated by four entrances *(gopuras)* with the principal shrine at the centre. An antechamber *(mandapa)* opens into the sanctuary which enshrines an image of the Bodhisattva Avalokitesvara. Nearby stands another imposing laterite structure.

A Neolithic **burial site** has been uncovered on the river bank to the south. Within the shady grounds an interesting open-air **museum** displays statues of divinities and stuccowork from the shrine.

★★ **Scenic road to Sangkhla Buri** – *240km west by 323. Allow 2 days.* The admirable rugged scenery of the river valley set against rolling hills on the distant horizon is ample reward for the long journey. A massive dam harnesses the resources of this important watershed. The thick jungle through which the railway line cut a swathe in recent times has been tamed and the fertile land now supports agricultural crops – sugar-cane, tapioca, tobacco, maize and cotton.

Death Railway – *Turn left at Km 18-19 and proceed for 11km.* A detour enables visitors to see at close range the **trestle bridge** which carries the rail track. This tremendous achievement claimed many lives. The area was a labour camp, and mementoes (stoves, equipment) are on display near the entrance to the resort. The prisoners lived in caves in the area.

Nam Tok Sai Yok Noi – *77km (Km 46 – 2km from Nam Tok).* The picturesque falls tumble down the limestone cliffs into large pools in a fine setting of tall trees and lush vegetation.

Tham Kaeng Lawa – *Boat hire from Pak Saen Pier, Tam-Bin Tha Sao. 4 hours.* Take a pleasant boat ride upriver to enjoy the wonderful scenery along the Mae Nam Khwae Noi. From the landing a short trail leads to the cave which boasts admirable draperies and concretions in large chambers. It is possible to prolong the tour as far as the delightful Nam Tok Sai Yok Yai *(see below).*

Hin Lek Fai (Hellfire Pass Memorial) – *80km (18km from Nam Tok). Turn left at the sign and continue for 500m past the Royal Thai Army farm.* Trails lead to Hin Tok bridge and Konyu Cutting where a plaque commemorates the ordeal of Australian and British POWs who undertook the hazardous work in precarious conditions at the aptly-named pass.

★★ **Sai Yok National Park** ⊙ – *104km (38km from Nam Tok). Turn left at Km 82 and proceed for 3km to the park office.* The forested expanses of the park on the banks of the Mae Nam Khwae Noi are ideal for recreation. **Nam Tok Sai Yok Yai,** which unusually cascades down limestone bluffs directly into the waterway and is best viewed from a picturesque suspension bridge, has inspired a classic Thai song. Tham Kaeng Lawa *(see above)* and Tham Daowadung *(west bank – 2.5km uphill trail)* which contain fantastically-shaped concretions are easily accessible by boat from the waterfall. Wildlife (barking deer, bats, gibbons and other mammals) shelters mainly in the distant recesses to the west.

★★ **Khao Laem Dam and Reservoir** – *147km. Turn left at Km 139 into 3272 and proceed for 6km.* An immense lake created from the waters of three rivers harnessed by the hydro-electric dam stretches to the far horizon. This tranquil oasis will delight those in search of peace and beautiful scenery. The road north follows the contours of the sparkling lake all the way to secluded Sangkhla Buri. Accommodation and boating facilities are available.

Sangkhla Buri – *220km.* The attraction of this modest outpost inhabited mainly by Mon and Karen tribes and Burmese migrants lies in its very remoteness. A visit to the Mon villages clustering on the banks of the lake affords an intriguing glimpse of traditional life and a boat trip is a pleasant way to enjoy the wonderful scenery. The early morning market is a colourful spectacle.

Wat Wang Wiwekaram *(3km southwest),* a Mon temple of ancient foundation, enjoys an incomparable setting by the lake. The distinctive pagoda is modelled after that of the Indian temple of Bodh Gaya.

Three Pagodas Pass – *4km from Sangkhla Buri.* Three white **chedis** (Phra Chedi Sam Ong) mark the historic border crossing which has witnessed the invasions of Burmese armies during centuries of conflict in the Burmese quest for supremacy. A memorial recalls the lives sacrificed in the building of the strategic railway line by the Japanese during the Second World War. In recent times Mon and Karen liberation armies have found refuge in the thick jungle. The present peaceful scene is indicative of improved relations between Myanmar and Thailand.

KHAO YAI National Park★★★

Saraburi, Prachinburi, Nakhon Nayok, Nakhon Ratchasima

Michelin Atlas p 12 or Map 965 – G 6

Access: 200km east of Bangkok by 2. North entrance on 2090. 5km before Pak Chong turn right into Thanon Thanarat and continue for 40km to TAT office. The south entrance is reached by 1 and 305 to Nakhon Nayok, 33 towards Kabinburi, then at Noen Yay Hom intersection turn left into 3077 north to the park headquarters at Km 41. Visitor Centre.

> Visitors should report to the park office before setting off on a hike and give details of their programme. There are some easy trails but it is advisable to be accompanied by a ranger on the more difficult ones (fee). Insect repellents are essential. Evening trips to view the animals are organised by the park office.

The rich wildlife and the wonderful forest and mountain scenery of Thailand's first national park which opened in 1962 are precious assets.

Khao Yai extends across the boundaries of four provinces *(see above)* and covers an area of 2 168sq km, ranging in altitude from 60m in the valleys to the east and south-west to 600m-1 000m on the gently sloping plateau. The highest peaks are **Khao Laem** (alt 1 328m) and **Khao Khieo** (Green Mountain, alt 1 351m). Khao Yai is an important watershed that feeds six major waterways irrigating the lower part of the northeast region, central Thailand and the Mekong Basin.

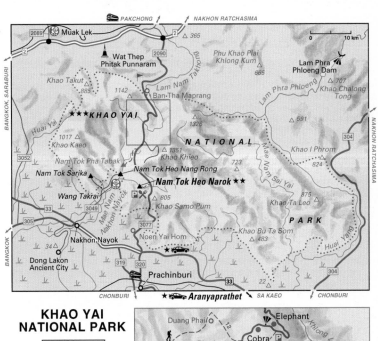

KHAO YAI NATIONAL PARK

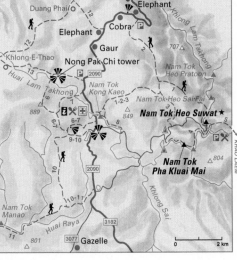

🛈	Tourist Information Centre
✕	Restaurant
⚠	Camping site
⛳	Golf
🚶 12	Hiking trail and number
●	Animal crossing
✚	First Aid

Tourism Authority of Thailand

Khao Yai National Park

Average temperatures range from 17° in the cool season *(Nov-Feb)* to 28° in the hot season *(Mar-May)*. The waterfalls are spectacular during the rainy season *(Jun-Oct)*. The park is very popular with Bangkok residents who come to enjoy a respite from the searing heat of the town.

The immense popularity of the park entails a grave threat to the delicate ecological balance. Illegal logging, poaching and encroachments for development are also serious problems which must be addressed by the authorities to ensure the viability of this wonderful natural attraction.

TOUR *1 day*

This cool and tranquil haven is criss-crossed by 12 marked trails *(1-6hr)* through a varied landscape of grassland and forest offering splendid **views**★★★ and leading to shimmering rivers and lakes, and idyllic waterfalls **(Heo Narok★★, Heo Suwat★, Pha Kluai Mai)** on the Mae Nam Nakhon Nayok and on the Lam Takhong, which describes a loop through the park and is spanned by rope bridges at Kong Kaeo.

Large mammal species include bears, gaurs, leopards and other large cats. Elephants and more rarely tigers may be glimpsed at salt-licks. Dawn and dusk are the best times to view animals (gibbons, deer, serow, slow loris) in the wild at the **Nong Pak Chi tower**. The acrobatic displays of the white-handed and pileated gibbons and of the pig-tailed macaques in the forest canopy are noteworthy. Graceful sambar and barking deer are a common sight. Birdwatchers will delight in the park's 318 migrant and resident bird species: hornbills, pheasants (silver, Siamese fireback), hawk cuckoos, bay owls, scimitar babbler, trogons and eagle owls.

KHON KAEN

Khon Kaen – Population 356 218

Michelin Atlas p 8 or Map 965 – E 7 – Town plan Atlas p 32

Khon Kaen is situated at a major crossroads and is the second largest town in Isan. It is also an important financial and educational centre with the Bank of Thailand and a university as its major institutions. Two lakes (Bung Thung Sang, Bung Kaen Nakhon) are popular recreation spots with picnic areas and restaurants. The town has good facilities and is convenient for exploring the region where the typical landscape of the limestone Khorat plateau gives way to the greener swathes of the Mekong basin.

★ **Museum** ⊘ – The museum presents a comprehensive survey of the art of the northeastern region from prehistory to the 19C.

Ground floor: on the right the discoveries from the prehistoric sites (Bang Sang Du, Non Nok Ta, Non Chai) include tools, pottery, bronze bells, bracelets and drum. A recreated burial site *(far right)* shows pottery placed at the head of the deceased. The Ban Chiang settlement (3600 BC to AD 200) is characterised by pottery with geometric, flower and animal designs as well as bronze objects. On the left the Dvaravati period (7C-11C) is illustrated by **boundary stones**★★ from Muang Fa Daet Sung Yang *(see KALASIN)*, inscriptions, stucco sculptures and reliefs (Life of the Buddha).

Out and about

Tourism Authority of Thailand (TAT) – 15/5 Thanon Prachasamosorn. ☎ 043 244 498/9; Fax 043 513 492; tat.ne@npu.msu.ac.th

Tourist Police – ☎ 1155.

Transport – **Thai Airways** operate 2 daily flights *(45min)* to and from Khon Kaen. Frequent services are run by regular **buses** and air-conditioned coaches *(6hr)* from the Northern Bus Terminal, Bangkok and there are fast trains and an express service from Hualamphong Railway Station, Bangkok.
Tricycles and motorised **three-wheeled taxis** are convenient means of transport. **Minibuses** operate with the city and serve outlying villages.

Shopping – There are souvenir shops in Thanon Na Muang and Thanon Klang Muang.
The province is famous for its **handicrafts** which are on sale in local shops *(Northeastern Handicraft Promotion Centre 12km north by 2)*. Traditional activities include basketry, silverware, cotton and silk *(matmee)* fabrics – *Amphoe Chonna Bot (55km south by 2 to Ban Phai and 10km west by 229)*.
A **Silk Fair** is held in late November or early December *(7 days and 7 nights)*.

Where to eat

In the town centre restaurants to suit all tastes and budgets abound along Thanon Srichan, Na Muang, Klang Muang. Establishments near the fine setting of Bung Kaen Nakhon have a pleasant ambience.

Where to stay

Budget

Kaen Inn – 56 Thanon Klang Muang. ☎ 043 237 744; Fax 043 239 457; 800-1 800 Baht. Reasonably priced accommodation in town centre.

Rosesukon Hotel – 1/10 Thanon Klang Muang. ☎ 043 238 576; Fax 043 239 579; 700-2 000 Baht. Good accommodation near the tourist office.

Khon Kaen Hotel – 43/2 Thanon Phimphasit. ☎ 043 238 711; Fax 043 243 458; 700-2 000 Baht. Hotel with moderate prices and conveniently situated in the town.

Moderate

Kosa Hotel – 250 Thanon Si Chan. ☎ 043 320 320, 043 225 014-8; Fax 043 225 013; 1 100-4 000 Baht. Comfortable hotel in town centre and close to airport and rail station. Beer garden, café with music, Chinese restaurant, karaoke and snooker club, souvenir shop.

Charoen Thani Princess – 260 Thanon Si Chan. ☎ 043 220 400-14; Fax 043 220 438; princess@icon.co.th; 2 160+ Baht. Elegant hotel with luxury facilities.

Hotel Sofitel Raja Orchid – 9/9 Thanon Pracha Samoson. ☎ 043 322 155, 02 237 6064; Fax 043 322 1150, 02 233 1000; sofitel@kkaen.loxinfo.co.th; www.sofitel.com; 3 000-12 000 Baht. Luxury accommodation with restaurants, bakery near a lake.

First floor: Exhibits include silver plaques, votive tablets, bronze statuettes (7C-11C). The Lopburi style (12C-13C) features heads from Buddha images, a large standing statue of a guardian spirit, a small headless statue of Vishnu. Of special interest are a stone lintel depicting Indra on a three-headed elephant (11C), two Lopburi ceramics of Buddha protected by Naga and late Chiang Saen style (15C-19C) statues of Buddha in the subduing Mara and meditation stances.

Courtyard: Folk art relating to rituals and traditional activities *(left)*. Also on view *(right)* are a typical Isan house, costumes and musical instruments. Boundary stones are dotted all around.

Garden: The **collection of bai sema**★★★ in pink or grey sandstone and mostly from Ban Sema (Kalasin) is a remarkable testimony to the artistry of the Dvaravati people.

EXCURSIONS

*★**Ku Puai Noi (That Ku Thong)*** – *79km southeast – 44km by 2, at Ban Phai take 23 (direction Borabu) for 11km, turn right into 2301 for 8km then take 2297 for 16km. On the right before the hospital.*
The shady site of this ruined Khmer temple built in red sandstone, laterite and brick in the late 11C by Jayavarman V is surrounded by a laterite wall. Four ponds represent the four seas. The gopuras and library are beautifully decorated with scrolls

on doorways and windows, sculptured lintels and pediments with scenes from Hindu mythology (Shiva and Uma riding the bull Nandin on the library gable). The sanctuary which comprises three prangs built of brick without mortar stands on a large indented base and has a stone doorframe. In the front is a **lintel** depicting Vishnu in a reclining pose. Dotted around are 13 other lintels with finely sculptured designs.

Wat Udom Khong Kha Khiri Khet – *Southwest by 12 for 14km, 2062 to Amphoe Mancha Kiri, then 229 and 2284 for 10km.* The forest temple is situated in a tranquil, shady site near a hill. The chedi built to enshrine the ashes of the Venerable Abbot Luang Pu Phang is surmounted by a large indented balustraded square platform above which rises a series of heavy mouldings. The golden relic chamber is crowned by a seven-tiered golden spire.

★**Phra That Kham Kaen** – *30km north. Wat Chetiyaphum, Tambon Ban Kham, Amphoe Nam Phong. Take 209 east, turn left between Km 12-13 into 2183 and continue for 15km.* The Phra That, which has given its name to the province, was built on a site where nine enlightened monks and King Lang Kieo, ruler of Nakhon Phanom, are believed to have stopped on their way with a Buddha relic to **Phra That Phanom**★ *(see NAKHON PHANOM).* However, the shrine had been completed by the time they reached their destination. According to legend, on their return journey a dead tamarind tree on the hilly spot was found to have miraculously come to life, and it was decided to construct a chedi to enshrine the relics together with a treasure.

The simple Isan architectural style is similar to that of **Phra That Si Song Rak**★★ *(see LOEI – Excursions):* a graceful lotus-shaped relic chamber soaring to the fine gilded spire on a low square base topped with thick mouldings. Next to it is a Laotian-style **sim** (ubosot) with a radiating motif decorating the gable. Nearby is the smaller That Kruba Tang Kao (That of the Nine enlightened Monks).

Khuan Ubonrat Dam ⊘ – *50km north. 26km by 2, turn left between Km 470-471 into 2109 and continue for 24km.* The multi-purpose dam (electricity, irrigation) on the Pong River is the largest in the northeast (reservoir 410sq km, capacity 2 550 million cu m). **Viewpoints** from the top of the dam and at the clubhouse. It is a pleasant recreation spot.

Phu Kao-Phu Phan Kham National Park – *56km north. As above; from the dam continue for 6km to the visitor centre.* The park area (320sq km) is covered with Dipterocarps forest with mixed deciduous and evergreen forest. Attractions include waterfalls, caves, trails for trekking, and boat trips to islands and fishing villages.

Phu Wiang National Park – *West by 12. At Km 37 at Ban Kut Chim take 2038 to the right for 30km to Amphoe Phu Wiang, then continue for 15km to the park headquarters.* The park area (300sq km) is enclosed by two mountain ranges

Phra That Kham Kaen

forming a crater (the outer rim culminating at 726m and the inner at 470m above sea-level) and has a rich fauna and flora, as well as several waterfalls (Nam Tok Tat Fa 15m high – *18km from Amphoe Phu Wiang ; from the parking 1.5km uphill by trail*). Investigation of **dinosaur fossils**★ unearthed in 1976 has revealed that 200 million years ago the now-arid northeast region was a lush plain with rivers, swamps and lakes, and enjoyed a tropical climate suitable for many kinds of prehistoric animals. Exploration is under way and several sites have been identified: at Site no 3 *(at Huai Pratu Tee Ma near headquarters)* a large bone from a Sauropod (vegetarian dinosaur) is embedded in the soil; at Site no 9 *(at Hin Lat Yao Phu Wiang)* was found a Carnosor bone, the first in Southeast Asia; at Lan Hin Lat Pha Chat *(Amphoe Phu Wiang)* a large stone block features some 60 dinosaur footprints.

Chulaphon Dam – *155km west by 12, turn left at Km 96 and continue for 36km. Cafeteria, accommodation.* Also known as Khuan Nam Phrom, it has a capacity of 188 million cubic metres and is used mainly for irrigation and generating purposes. Fine views of the lake in a beautiful forest setting framed by mountains may be enjoyed from the top of the dam *(70m high)* and from the club-house. An experimental royal project for growing cool-weather plants is being carried out.

The road passes the **Phu Khieo Wildlife Sanctuary** *(only for specialists)*, which covers Amphoe Khon San, Amphoe Kaset Som Boon, Amphoe Nong Bua Deang, and is an animal reserve for the study of rare species (birds and large mammals – two-horned rhinoceros). From the viewpoint *(Km 34-35)* and from the cliff top near the headquarters wonderful **views**★★★ unfold of the fertile valleys and tree-clad mountain range, including the top of Phu Kradung in good weather.

Pha Nok Khao – *125km west by 12 and 201.* The road descends to a distinctive owl-shaped limestone outcrop, with a cool shady park, Wang Phai at its foot. This is the departure point for Phu Kradung *(see PHU KRADUNG National Park)*. Hikers can buy supplies at Ban Pha Nok Khao (restaurants).

KRABI★★

Krabi – Population 80 410

Michelin Atlas p 20 or Map 965 – M 3 – Local map see Phuket

The pleasant town nestles on the banks of the Mae Nam Krabi in a region which combines a spectacular coastline of palm-fringed white beaches and dramatic mountain scenery with karst outcrops rising out of the tropical forest. The hinterland supports vast rubber and palm-oil plantations which contribute to the prosperity of the region. The beauty of the Krabi area explains its growing popularity.

A lively night market operates near Saphan Ja Fa Pier. A cave in the cliff wall of Khao Kanap Nam at the mouth of the river can be reached by boat from the landing-stage. Nearby are Bird, Cat and Mouse Islands.

Krabi is the departure point for boats to Ko Phi Phi *(see Mu Ko PHI PHI)* and Mu Ko Lanta *(see below)*.

EXCURSIONS

★★**Scenic road north** – *Allow 1 day.* This pleasant excursion will enable visitors to enjoy the wonderful scenery dominated by limestone outcrops as well as sparkling sandy beaches.

Su San Hoi (Shell Cemetery) – *19km west by 4034 and 4204.* A path leads down to **rock slabs**★ composed of fossilised sea shells 75 million years old which are visible at low tide. There are only three sites in the world where this geological phenomenon occurs: the other two are in Japan and in the USA.

★★**Ao Phra Nang** – *17km west by 4034, 4204 and 4203.* Take a leisurely tour by boat in the sheltered bay studded with 83 small islands. The limpid waters are ideal for snorkelling, especially around Ko Poda and Ko Hua Khwan. Bungalows and hotels proliferate amid the sea pines and coconut groves along the shoreline.

The dramatic limestone cliffs of **Laem Phra Nang** jut out into the sea to the east. The popular Hat Raileh and Hat Tham Phra Nang are beautiful beaches *(east – accessible by boat)* of pristine white sand.

To the south is **Tham Phra Nang Nok** (Outer Princess Cave). A treacherous trail leads to a spectacular hidden lagoon *(40min)*. **Tham Phra Nang Nai** (Inner Princess Cave) comprises three large chambers with dramatic limestone formations, including a golden stone waterfall.

Hat Nopharat Thara – *16km west by 4304 and 4202.* This beautiful shady beach *(2km)* faces three offshore islands which can be reached on foot at low tide. Tall cliffs clad in lush vegetation frame the river estuary to the north.

Ao Phra Nang

Than Bokkhorani Arboretum – *46km northwest; take 4 north, turn left into 4039 and continue for 1km.* Craggy cliffs overshadow the tall trees in this fine national park. From the parking area a path leads past two salas to a verdant setting at the foot of a cliff where an underground stream surges between two huge boulders into a large pool and flows into a wide stream. This in turn divides into smaller channels through the forest.

Ban Thong Agricultural Station – *22km northwest by 4200 and 4.* A pilot farm for developing new varieties of rubber, tea and coffee plants. Dense stands of rubber trees and sheets of latex hung out to dry are a common sight.

Khao Phanom Bencha National Park – *10km north by 4 and turn right into a side road.* This remote conservation area which includes waterfalls, caves, rare species of birds and mammals is of great scenic beauty and inspires a wonderful sense of isolation. Lush rain forest covers the steep slopes of the Phanom Bencha mountain range which culminates at 1 350m.

Wat Tham Seua – *14km northeast by 4200 and 4 and turn left into a side road.* Tiger Cave Temple, a forest temple, attracts many disciples. A shallow cave serves as the ubosot; and monastic cells *(kutis)* are built into cliffs and caves. Behind the ubosot a path leads through the nuns' village to steep staircases *(left)*. One climbs to the top of a hill which affords a wonderful **view**; the other (by statue) leads to a valley and a labyrinth of caves.

Mu Ko Lanta ⊙ – *50km south by 4, 4206 and car ferry. Rough crossing in the rainy season.* This remote group of 52 islands, of which 12 are inhabited by Muslim and Chao Le (Sea Gypsies) fishermen, remains off the beaten track. The National Park comprises 15 limestone islands with fine coral, deserted beaches and wild landscapes. There is a long stretch of palm-fringed beaches, isolated coves and fine coral reefs on the west side of Lanta Yai, and Laem Kho Kwang (Deer Neck Cape – *northwest*) affords fine views. Ban Sangka-U to the south is a traditional Muslim fishing village. The islands which offer simple accommodation will appeal to those who seek a relaxing holiday.

LAMPANG★★

Lampang – Population 245 945

Michelin Atlas p 3 or Map 965 – C 4 – Local map see Chiang Mai

The cosmopolitan modern town which has expanded on both banks of the Mae Nam Wang and has good transport links and tourist facilities – excellent riverside restaurants – offers many attractions and is a good base from which to explore the fertile plain where agriculture is the mainstay (rice, maize, cotton). Lignite mines at Amphoe Mae Mo to the east contribute to the economic prosperity of the area. The beautiful scenery of the national parks make this an attractive area to explore.

The old shop-houses decorated with fretwork in the bustling market quarter *(talat kao)* near the bridge, Saphan Ratchada Phisek, and the wooden houses in the old town and many temples in the Burmese style are reminders of bygone days.

A chequered history – The foundation of the town, originally known as Kelang Nakhon, by a son of Queen Chamatewee *(see LAMPHUN)* probably dates back to the 7C. Excavations have revealed that the town was the capital of a large Mon kingdom. The walled town on the west bank of the Mae Nam Wang was linked to four secondary fortified settlements, of which the only survival is Wat Phra That Lampang Luang *(see below)*. After its annexation to the Lanna kingdom by King Mengrai it retained a degree of autonomy. It shared the fate of Lanna under Burmese occupation, which lasted 200 years and is recalled in the religious architectural legacy. At the beginning of the 19C after the razing of Chiang Saen *(see CHIANG SAEN)*, its inhabitants were resettled in Lampang by King Kavila of Chiang Mai in an attempt to increase the population decimated by war. The many Lanna temples were built after this migration. In the early 20C Lampang was also an important hub on the trading route with China and Burma. A strong Burmese influence is evident in the town as in the 19C many Burmese settled here and worked in the wood industry which has brought prosperity to the town. There is a strong craft tradition: pottery, paper making, weaving and wood carving.

SIGHTS

★★ **Wat Phra Kaeo Don Tao** – *Thanon Phra Kaeo across Saphan Ratchada Phisek.* The best view of Lampang's principal temple located on a rise and attributed to its first ruler is from the river entrance. The imposing **chedi** on a rectangular base with a gilded bell and finial is the only original structure. In front stands a Burmese-style **mondop★★** with a graceful tiered roof, porches with slender pillars enhanced with fine scrollwork, and coffered ceilings with a profusion of decorative features intricately carved and highlighted in mother-of-pearl and glass mosaic. The harmonious proportions and rich orna-

Horse-drawn carriages

mentation make this one of the finest examples of classical Burmese architecture. It enshrines a very fine Mandalay-style bronze Buddha image.

West of the chedi is the old Wihan Phra Non housing a revered reclining Buddha. The vast main vihara is also beautifully decorated. A bronze statue celebrates the hero of Lampang who in 1732 liberated the Lanna kingdom from Burmese domination; he is shown in traditional costume and with gun in hand.

Wat Suchadaram – Within the Wat Phra Kaeo compound to the south is an ancient temple built on a terrace. Mythical animals mark the entrance to the main vihara which boasts an ornate wooden pediment and roof supports, windows with wooden bars and a seated Buddha presiding at the altar. A low wall, punctuated by

---

Colourful **horse-drawn carriages** decked with pompons and flowers offer a pleasant way to explore the town at a leisurely pace. They were introduced from Bangkok in 1929 by the last ruler of Lampang.

doorways crowned alternately by tiered pagodas and moulded chedis, encloses the great chedi which is flanked by smaller chedis. It has a distinctive redented square base and a ringed main body and finial and is decorated with lotus motifs. To the right stands an elegant small ubosot with a pedimented porch.

Wat Pong Sanuk Tai – *Thanon Pong Sanuk*. Within a shady compound is a modern temple from which a covered stairway gives access to a delightful ancient monastery in Lanna style. From the north side the stuccoed gateway is reached by steps flanked by a naga balustrade. A low wall surrounds the tall ringed **chedi**★★ faced in copper and surmounted by a slim gilded finial. Filigree canopies with posts decorated in blue glass mosaic stand at the four corners. The main vihara contains a reclining Buddha.

Interesting features of the admirable open **mondop**★★ include porches, a tiered roof adorned with fretwork, and a central altar with four Buddha images under a filigree bodhi tree.

Wat Saeng Muang Ma – *Thanon Thamma Oo*. The temple is notable for its harmonious small chedi culminating in a gilded bell shape and finial; it stands on a stepped platform with mythical animals at the angles. A covered pedimented porch guarded by nagas precedes the vihara which enshrines a large Buddha image. Delightful **paintings**★ adorn the wood panels at roof level.

Wat Hua Kuang – *Thanon Wang Kong*. One of the temples erected by Chiang Saen settlers comprises an old vihara with a finely carved pediment and a stepped roof. It contains Chiang Saen statues and precious manuscripts.

Wat Phra Fang – *Thanon Sanam Bin*. This temple offers excellent examples of Burmese architecture. Mythical animals stand sentinel on the platform girt by a low wall on which rises the **chedi**. The octagonal base is unusually punctuated by seven chapels *(for the seven days of the week)* housing alabaster Buddha images and with open porches and tiered roofs. Angle pillars support small chedis. The octagonal drum is surmounted by mouldings, lotus motifs and a slender finial and canopy. Elaborate stucco arches frame the windows of the **ubosot** which has a complex roofline. Inside the large vihara, lacquered and gilded pillars crowned with lotus capitals support the coffered ceiling embellished with floral motifs. An alabaster Buddha image flanked by disciples and a bronze seated Buddha grace the richly decorated altars.

Wat Si Chum – *Thanon Tha Khao Noi*. The temple is worth a visit to admire the elegant **mondop** on a cruciform plan and with elaborate tiered roofing. The wall is marked by gates surmounted by chedis and guarded by mythical animals as well as corner chedis, all with rich stucco ornamentation. The main sanctuary in Burmese style which burned down in 1992 has been replaced by a fine new vihara featuring 2 tiered pagodas and porches with delicate wood carving. Pillars decorated in laquer and gold and a mural grace the interior. The chedi contains a relic of the Buddha.

Wat Chai Mongkhon – *Thanon Sanam Bin*. The principal **vihara** has a fine coffered ceiling and Burmese-style seated Buddha images at the altar. The massive white **chedi** quartered by small gilded chedis is decorated with stucco motifs and a gilded canopy.

Wat Pratu Pong – *Thanon Pha Mai*. The main feature of this modern temple built by the ancient town wall is a beautifully restored Lanna **vihara**. The rich decoration of the façade and of the three doors is noteworthy. A chedi is crowned by a ringed spire and a nine-tiered canopy.

Ban Sao Nak – *Thanon Pha Mai, Tambon Wiang Neua*. A fine example of a Lanna-style mansion built of teak wood and supported by 116 massive pillars.

★★★WAT PHRA THAT LAMPANG LUANG

541 Ban Lampang Luang, Mu 2, Amphoe Kokha. 18km south. 16km by 1 then right by a minor road to Amphoe Kokha.

The splendid temple founded in the 5C is one of the few surviving examples of a stronghold *(wiang)*, surrounded by three parallel earthen ramparts and two moats of which traces remain in the village. The quality of the Lanna architecture and ornamentation is outstanding. The temple is an important Buddhist centre where the faithful flock to great religious ceremonies.

Entrance – Mythical animals flank the stairway to the ceremonial east gate (Pratu Khong) of the walled compound; the admirable stuccowork includes the Wheel of the Law on the round inner lintel.

Wihan Luang – The principal open-sided vihara which dates from 1496 is remarkable for its intricate woodwork, the 19C paintings on the panels below the eaves, the banners framing the ornate redented **ku**★★ (pagoda-like structure) housing a revered Buddha image (1476).

Chedi – The fine Sukhothai-style structure with a recessed base, ringed body sheathed in copper and slim gilded finial, which is believed to contain relics of the historical Buddha, marks the transfer of power from the Lanna bases of Chiang Mai, Chiang Saen and Chiang Rai to the Sukhothai kingdom in central Thailand. A bullet hole in the railing *(east)* recalls the massacre of the Burmese enemy in 1736 by Thai forces who had crept into the compound through a drain. There are filigree canopies at the angles.

Viharas – To the north of the main chapel stands a rebuilt vihara. Behind is the restored early-16C **Wihan Nam Tam**★★ *(north of chedi)*, probably the oldest remaining Lanna structure. The 16C wall paintings depict vivid scenes with wonderful details on contemporary fashion and customs. The **Wihan Phra Phut**★★ *(south of chedi)* is noteworthy for its richly carved woodwork, exquisite decoration and Lanna (Chiang Saen) Buddha images. Behind the chedi stands another modern vihara, which contains a Buddha footprint in wood and a 12C-13C Khmer Bayon-style sandstone Buddha seated on a naga. To the south are a raised mondop and an ubosot.

Outer courtyard – Majestic bodhi trees provide shady areas within the enclosure where are located the monks' lodgings, a museum displaying religious objects and an elegant **library** with a fine wooden upper structure. At the far end is a small treasury where presides the venerated **Phra Kaeo Morakot Don Tao**★★, a jasper statue decked in a filigree gold robe and believed to possess magical powers. Also on view are precious offerings in gold and silver.

EXCURSIONS

Wat Chedi Sao – *268 Soi Sinkanthawong, Tambon Ton Tong Chai. 5km northeast; take 1035 and after 2km turn left.* The whitewashed Burmese bell-shaped spires from which is derived the name of this famous country temple – the temple of the 20 chedis – stand out in the middle of rice fields. Four corner chedi-like towers mark the low surrounding wall pierced by three gates. Niches along the wall house Buddha images and there is also an unusual collection of statuary including figures from Buddhist legends.

Wat Lai Hin – *Amphoe Kokha. As for Wat Lampang Luang but 1.5km before reaching that temple turn left and continue for 6km.* An ornate gateway probably dating from the 16C gives access to the temple. The gable of the old Lanna-style vihara has an elaborate stucco decoration, whereas the fine interior lacquer ornamentation is unfortunately damaged.

★ **Wat Pong Yang Khok** – *As for Wat Phra That Lampang Luang. Proceed for 7.7km and turn right.* The foundation of the temple dates from the 8C. The beautifully articulated 13C wooden **vihara**★ is a rare survival of a Lanna-style open-sided structure *(see Wihan Luang above)*; however, walls have been added around the small **ku** bristling with nagas. Friezes of seated Buddhas and vases of flowers adorn the panels on either side of the ku. The lacquer **decoration**★ featuring a bodhi tree motif is outstanding and the ceiling is highlighted in red and gold. Massive pillars support the three-tiered roof covered in wooden tiles, and the gable is carved with floral motifs.

Elephant Conservation Centre ⓥ – *Ban Thung Kwian, Amphoe Hang Chat. 32km northwest by 11, turn right between Km 25-26.* A stream runs through a beautiful wooded site where young animals are put through their paces at the first official centre to train wild elephants for forest work. The shows which include activities such as bathing and log pushing aim to raise funds for the upkeep of the centre. There is an elephant riding trail.

Wat Chong Kham – *Between Km 673-674 by 1. 12km south of Ngao.* Also known as Wat Chaiyaphum, the temple is a good example of Shan architecture. The dilapidated original wooden buildings were sold by the abbot and have been restored and re-erected at Muang Boran *(see BANGKOK Environs – Samut Prakan)*. In an attempt to make up for this erroneous decision, the monks have commissioned faithful copies of the buildings to be built. The irregular roofline and intricate wood carving of the viharas is typical of the Shan-Burmese style.

The remote **Doi Khuntan** – *northwest halfway between Lampang and Lamphun* – which merges with **Chae Son** – *32km north by 1157 or 1035 and then 1252 through the park* – **National Park** offers the opportunity to appreciate the beauties of nature – caves, dams, waterfalls, forest trails, fauna and flora.

Tham Pha Thai Forest Park – *66km northeast by 1, turn left between Km 665-666* – is notable for a vast network of caves which boast colourful stalagmites and a Buddha. Local guide recommended.

LAMPHUN★★

Lamphun – Population 139 158

Michelin Atlas p 3 or Map 965 – C 4 – Local map see Chiang Mai

The present town was built in the early 19C on the west bank of the Mae Nam Kuang in the fertile plain of the Mae Nam Ping. Agriculture is the mainstay of the province and is complemented by handicrafts – silk weaving and silverware. The scenic road 106 which is lined by majestic age-old trees is the best approach to the charming moated town.

A proud history – According to legend Haripunchai, a town founded in the 7C by a hermit, became the capital of a Mon principality ruled by Chamatewee, a Mon princess from Lavoh *(see LOPBURI)*. During her 52-year long reign Haripunchai was at the peak of its glory; her successors ruled for another six centuries until its capture in 1281 by King Mengrai. The king then set about the unification of the northern territories which became known as the **Lanna Kingdom**. He established his capital at Wiang Kum Kam *(see CHIANG MAI, Excursions)* prior to the foundation of Chiang Mai (1297). The King of Pegu (Burma) invaded Lanna in the mid-16C and exercised supremacy over the region for nearly 200 years.

Haripunchai retained its importance as a religious centre as pilgrims flocked to worship at Wat Phra That. Lanna kings restored the shrine and built religious monuments (chedi at Wat Phra Yun), and the Burmese occupation left many artistic traces. After the defeat of the Burmese in 1775 by King Taksin the town was abandoned until 1796 when people deported from Sipsong Panna (South China) were resettled there. The latter retained their traditions and language which is similar to that of Chiang Mai. Rama V integrated the Kingdom of Lanna into Siam in the late 19C when Haripunchai was renamed Lamphun and became the capital of a prosperous province.

SIGHTS

★**Museum** ⊙ – *Thanon Inthayongyot*. The small museum has a well-presented collection of artefacts found in the region, which traces the evolution of art in Lamphun.

First floor – Dvaravati influence is evident in many exhibits: a sandstone head (late 10C-11C); an enigmatic 12C Buddha **head**★★ in terracotta with curving eyebrows, bulging eyes, curling moustache; a head of Garuda also dating from late 12C. The bronze Buddha images include a **head**★ of Buddha in Lanna style (15C-16C) inspired by Sukhothai art; a serene statue of Buddha subduing Mara. Other interesting items are votive tablets, a 15C bronze stupa and lantern with Chinese motifs, silver objects including an elephant with howdah from Wat Phra That, a **roof decoration**★ with naga and divinity (17C), wood carving and pottery from kilns in Northern Thailand (red funerary jars, water vases).

Ground floor – *Down steps on the right*. Stone inscriptions (*c* 12C) in ancient Mon and Pali script illustrate Haripunchai art which flourished between the 7C and the 13C. Also on display are architectural decorative elements, Lanna crafts and folk art.

Walk round the building to look at a collection of boundary stones *(bai sema)* dating from the early 15C-late 16C including a lotus-shaped stone.

★★**Wat Phra That Haripunchai** – Two fierce Burmese-style lions guard the main east-facing entrance to this ancient monastery founded in the 9C on the riverside site of a former royal palace. Although the temple buildings have been rebuilt in the 20C, there are many interesting features. The great vihara (early 20C), which is noteworthy for its wood carving, pulpit and a large Lanna (Chiang Saen) Buddha image, is harmoniously flanked by an enormous bronze **gong** in a Burmese-style tower *(right)* and by a delightful Lanna **ho trai** (library) highlighted with carved and inlaid motifs and a stepped roof *(left)*.

A bronze railing encloses a splendid Lanna **chedi**★★ with a stepped base and ringed bell-shaped upper part with a gilded copper facing and a slim finial crowned by a gold canopy. This is the most sacred monument in the compound. The original 9C chedi has been enlarged and remodelled over the centuries. In the northwest corner is the Suwanan **chedi**★ in Dvaravati style, a stepped pyramid which once contained 60 Buddha images. There are three serene Lanna (Chiang Saen) Buddha statues at the base. Nearby, a huge seated Buddha clad in a red robe dominates Wihan Phra Jaeo Daeng. At the rear of the precinct west of the main chedi stands Wihan Phra Than Chai which houses a large standing Lanna (Chiang Saen) Buddha image in copper with attendant Buddhas; laquered columns support a red and gold coffered ceiling. In a nearby hall, Sala Phra Bat Si Roi, may be seen four Buddha footprints one inside the other. A small museum displays religious objects. There is another interesting old chedi, Chiang Yan chedi, in an outside courtyard north of the temple complex.

Other temples of minor interest within the moated town precinct include Wat Chang Rong and Wat Si Song Muang to the north, and Wat Suphan Rangsi to the south.

★**Wat Chamatewee (Wat Ku Kut)** – *1km west by 1015*. The two monuments at this temple built in the 8C by the son of Queen Chamatewee are probably the last remaining stupas in the Dvaravati style. The pyramidal chedi which holds the

Wat Phra That Haripunchai

queen's ashes is decorated with standing Buddhas in the niches but it has lost its spire. Its plan, which was probably based on a monument in Sri Lanka, inspired many similar reliquaries in the region (Wat Chedi Liem in Chiang Mai, Suwanan Chedi above). To the left of the modern vihara the smaller octagonal chedi on a high brick base is decorated with standing Buddhas in the niches and a rounded crown.

Wat Phra Yun – *Take 114 east, then turn left into 1029, after 600m turn right.* This important moated temple is renowned for its Burmese-style **chedi** built on the site of a 14C mondop, erected by King Ku Na on the east bank of the Mae Nam Kwang. Steps lead up to the platform framed by four smaller chedis on which rises the squat recessed body punctuated by four niches housing standing Buddha images. The tiered upper section is surmounted by a ringed finial and a canopy. The open wooden sala is also of interest.

LOEI

Loei – Population 114 465

Michelin Atlas p 8 or Map 965 – D 6

The prosperity of this little regional capital, which derives from timber, mining (copper, manganese, etc) and agriculture (cotton and maize), is likely to grow owing to its favourable location near the border with Laos and the bridge over the Mekong at Nong Khai which fosters better contacts with Laos in the fields of trade and tourism.

It is a good base for excursions to enjoy the beautiful, unspoilt countryside and wonderful mountain scenery.

San Chao Pho Kut Pong *(1km east of the Provincial Hall)* is an ancient shrine.

Buddha images and reliefs found in the area have revealed the existence of ancient sites (Muang Tum, Muang Champa: at Ban Pong, Tambon Kok Du, Amphoe Muang) dating back a 1 000 years in the province. Ancient *bai sema* have been discovered at the old villages of Ban Pak Peng and Ban Na Lak in Amphoe Wang Saphung.

EXCURSIONS

★★★ Phu Kradung National Park – *See PHU KRADUNG National Park.*

Phu Luang Wildlife Sanctuary ⊙ – *50km southwest. Take 201 for 30km and 2250 left for 20km. (Or 201 via Amphoe Wang Saphung; at Chumchon Wang Sapung school turn left into a rural road 1027 for 26km to park office).* Although less frequented than other national parks in the area, the sanctuary (849sq km covering Phu Rua, Dan Sai, Wang Saphung, Phu Luang districts, elevation 400-1550m above sea-level) offers wonderful scenery and abundant botanical (sub-tropical flora – rhododendrons, orchids, lichens) and geological features; wildlife (elephants, tigers) abounds in the upper reaches. Scenic points (Lon Mon, Lan Sao Yang Khing, Lon Hin Aoe Kan, Pha Lon Tae) highlight the 14km trek to the top *(time: 6 hours).*

★ Phu Rua National Park – *50km west by 203. Turn right between Km 49-50 and continue for 4km to park office.* The park (area 121sq km, elevation 600-1 000m) comprises sandstone peaks often shrouded in mist, with a pine-covered plateau and an overhanging cliff in the shape of a Chinese junk. The cool temperature can turn very cold in December and January. Excursions may be made *(by car with four-wheel drive vehicle – good road, or treks – 2 1/2 hours)* through a forested landscape (evergreen forest and high-level sub-montane and pine forests) cut by streams, past a rock garden with formations shaped as animals (**Hin Tao** – Turtle Rock to which a legend is attached) or utensils (bowl) to the summit. A seated Buddha image surveys the scene, and a sala affords wonderful panoramic **views★★** of the majestic countryside and on sunny days of the Mekong river and the mountain ranges of Laos on the horizon. The Pha Lon Noi *(3km)* and Pha Sap Thong *(2km)* cliffs and the Nam Tok Huai Phai *(2km, 30m high)* are also popular scenic points. Wild flowers including orchids abound and the fauna, although depleted by poaching, boasts many rare bird species (crested serpent-eagle, Asian fairy bluebird).

From Phu Rua the road runs up- and downhill through rugged countryside.

Dan Sai – *80km west by 203, 2013 and 2113.* This old town is famous for its colourful **Phi Thakon Festival** *(3 days in June)* which includes a masked procession of ghost figures and rocket firing.
At **Wat Phon Chai** a Laotian-style *sim* (ubosot) on a mound contains an interesting Buddha statue. There is also a wooden sala with pierced woodwork.

★★ Wat Phra That Si Song Rak – *83km west by 203 or 1km from Dan Sai.* The Phra That was built between 1560 and 1563 during the reigns of King Chakraphat of Ayutthaya and King Chai Chetta of Lan Xang (Laos) to mark the friendship between the two kingdoms (stele to the right of the that). Steps lead up to the top of the mound crowned by a chapel containing a gilded **statue of Buddha** protected by a naga and a tall Laotian-style lotus-bud **chedi** with a gold motif at the four corners and soaring from a tiered base to a slender spire.

★★ Scenic road to Chiang Khan – Road 2113 continues to Na Haeo. Then take 2195 which runs along the course of the Mae Heuang, the border between Thailand and Laos. The border villages reputedly engage in illegal trade. Model villages have been set up by the government to deter insurgency. Ban Muang Phrae is deemed to be "the end of Siam". The road then dips and climbs affording fine mountain **views★★★** (Khao Noi, Laem, Ngu on the Thai side; Phu Lane, Hat Sone, Nam Kieng on the Lao side) from Pak Man to Ban Nong Pheu, and Chiang Khan.

Wat Pho Chai Na Phung – *Amphoe Na Haeo. From Dansai by 2113, turn right between Km 23-24 and continue for a short distance.* The temple is famous for a bronze Buddha, Phra Chao Ong Saen, which is said to bring fertility and rain. The buildings are grouped in a tranquil setting: an unusually tall wooden belfry, a small tiered chedi, a fine Lao-style galleried **sim★** (ubosot) roofed with wooden tiles. The inner and outer walls of the latter are decorated with murals in blue, yellow and green with black contours depicting folk tales and with amusing features: figures in modern military uniform, court attendants, a train and bicycles.

Phra That Satcha – *50km northwest by 201 and 2115. 2km from Amphoe Tha Li (8km from the border).* The Phra That was built in recent times to celebrate the Thai national spirit in the fight against communist insurgency. The elaborate design is inspired from **Phra That Phanom★** *(see Nakhon Phanom):* the structure (33m) is crowned by three tiers decorated with lotus buds and a delicate gilded parasol.

★★ Tham Erawan – *Tambon Erawan, Amphoe Wang Saphung. Southeast by 201 and 210, turn left near Pha Wang school at Km 31 and continue for 2km. Time: 1 hour.* From afar a large Buddha at the cave entrance can be seen high up the face of a limestone outcrop; access from the temple grounds is by a naga staircase *(about 500 steps, easy climb).* Near the cave mouth are beautiful concretions; sunlight shines at midday through an opening in the vault of the middle chamber; proceed further down in the dark chamber to admire a white stalactite shaped like a triple-headed elephant, hence the cave's name. At the far end is a cool chamber with natural ventilation. The path and steps lead up to a cliff opening which affords fine distant **views** of the landscape.

LOPBURI★★

Lopburi – Population 252 457

Michelin Atlas p 24 or Map 965 – G 5

Lopburi enjoys a pleasant location on the east bank of the Mae Nam Lopburi dominated by the craggy peaks of Khao Wong on the eastern edge of the fertile central plain. To the east in Amphoe Phattana Nikhon *(45km by 3017)* sunflower fields in full bloom from November to January are a glorious sight.

A monument to King Narai **(Sa Kaeo)** marks the east entrance to the town. At the heart of the modern urban sprawl is an old town which has many historical associations. Lopburi has good transport facilities and is also a military centre with an army school and camps adding to the bustle of the town.

Historical notes – Evidence of human settlement in prehistoric times has been unearthed in the province (Ban Khok Charoen, Ban Tha Khae). In the Dvaravati period (7C-11C) the Lawa, a branch of the Mon people, established a town named Lavoh, later altered to Lavapura in the Khmer period, from which is derived the present name. The influence of the Mon spread to the northern territories with the founding of the kingdom of Haripunchai *(see LAMPHUN)*.

Khmer rule – After the fall of Lopburi to the Khmers in the 10C it became their capital, ruling the extensive territory captured in Siam until the rise of Sukhothai in the late 13C. Lopburi evolved a distinctive cultural and artistic tradition combining Mon and Khmer elements, which is exemplified by several monuments such as Prang Khaek, San Phra Kan, Prang Sam Yot and Wat Mahathat. Its reputation as a religious centre drew northern princes and religious leaders who came to study Theravada Buddhism.

A strategic role – In the 14C King Ramathibodi I (U-Thong) installed his son **Prince Ramesuan** as governor and Lopburi became a strategic town fortified by walls and moats during the wars with the Sukhothai rulers. Its importance declined and it became a vassal state when Ramesuan ascended the throne of Ayutthaya in 1388. In the 16C the walls were dismantled to prevent the Burmese from establishing an outpost against Ayutthaya.

A glorious era – In the 17C **King Narai** made Lopburi his second capital as Ayutthaya seemed vulnerable to the fleets of European powers attracted by the wealth of Siam. In 1685 the **Chevalier de Chaumont** accompanied by Jesuit missionaries arrived in Lopburi as envoy from the court of the French King Louis XIV and was dazzled by the display of pomp and splendour at the Siamese court. The city was filled with dignitaries and merchants from neighbouring countries. French architects set about building palaces, forts and reservoirs, of which traces remain. Traditionalists opposed foreign influences symbolised by **Constantine Phaulkon** also known as Chao Phraya Vichayen, a Greek adventurer who had gained immense power and wealth as adviser to King Narai. On the king's death Phaulkon was executed and relations with Europe came to an abrupt end as the new ruler retreated to Ayutthaya and Lopburi was abandoned for over 150 years.

Revival – In the mid 19C Lopburi regained a degree of glory under King Rama III who restored it as an alternative capital to Bangkok, and King Rama IV (Mongkut) who built a new residence within the palace compound.

SIGHTS

★★**Phra Narai Ratcha Niwet** ⊙ – *Thanon Sorasak. Access by the east gate.* High crenellated walls pierced by imposing gates enclose three walled courtyards protected by guardhouses. Oil lamps in the wall niches created a magical scene at night. In former times the sovereigns arrived by river at the ceremonial west gate.

Outer courtyard – A beautiful old house stands to the right near the gate. A water tank fed by water pumped by a hydraulic system built by French engineers, and 12 large warehouses which were filled with gorgeous

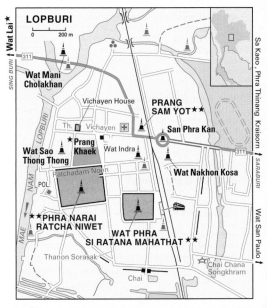

fabrics and exotic goods for trade are visible to the left. Beyond to the south are a private audience hall and a **banqueting hall** with traces of ponds and fountains, and a platform probably used for theatrical entertainment. The elephant and horse **stables** are sited near the wall of the middle section.

Middle courtyard – A serene Buddha image sheltered by a naga guards the Thai-style **Chanthara Phisan Hall**★★ (1665), originally built as a royal residence and later used as an audience hall. The king appeared at a balcony. The displays illustrate the enlightened times when Siam opened its doors to European powers, notably France, and include gifts, letters and other mementoes. A painting shows the solemn reception of the French delegation; there are also two thrones, and bookcases.

The buildings (Phiman Mongkut and Wisutthi Winitchai Pavilions) erected by King Mongkut house a **museum**★ *(see below)*. Behind are the women's quarters.

The ruins of **Dusit Sawan Thanya Maha Prasat**★ built in European style are evocative of the pomp of King Narai's court. Inside the hall which was sumptuously hung with mirrors the ruler appeared at an opening high up in the dividing wall.

Inner courtyard – Little remains of the Suttha Sawan Pavilion set in beautiful gardens, which was King Narai's private residence and where he lay dying as a plot to seize power was being hatched by his opponents. There are traces of fountains.

★**Museum** – The exhibits relating to customs, religion and technology trace the history and art of the central region of Thailand from prehistory to the Bangkok period. On display are sculpture, ornaments, arms, coins and porcelain. On the top floor of the west wing are King Mongkut's quarters complete with furnishings. A section of the ground floor is devoted to agriculture.

> The glory of King Narai's reign in the 17C is celebrated by a colourful **festival** *(Feb)*: a procession of local people dressed in sumptuous contemporary costumes including those worn by the envoys from the French court, a light and sound show and folk entertainment

---

San Phra Kan – *East of the railway line.* A horde of monkeys roams freely at the revered Kala shrine, which comprises a high mound dating back to the Khmer period crowned by a spirit house from King Narai's reign and a new temple housing a four-armed deity, probably Vishnu; the head has been replaced by a Buddha image.

★★**Prang Sam Yot** ⊙ – *Near the railway station.* The 13C Khmer monument founded by Jayavarman VII, which is the symbol of Lopburi, represents the Hindu trinity of Brahma, Vishnu and Siva and was later converted to a Buddhist shrine. The three prangs made of laterite and sandstone and adorned with stuccowork are linked by a central passageway. At the base of the door columns are seated hermits. In the central prang a wooden ceiling with red flower motifs and a seated Buddha protected by a naga are notable features. A 17C wihan to the east houses a large statue of the Buddha in meditation in the Ayutthaya style.

★**Prang Khaek** – *Thanon Vichayen.* The oldest Khmer prang in Central Thailand dates from the 10C. Only the middle tower remains, in a pleasant garden.

Wat Nakhon Kosa – *Near the San Phra Kan.* A small prang pierced by niches housing Buddha images and with traces of stuccowork is the only survival of the 11C-12C sanctuary; it is a fine example of Lopburi craftsmanship. The ruined chedi with its deep foundations is in the Dvaravati style (8C-10C), while the vihara and ubosot date from the Ayutthaya period (17C). Sculpture and votive tablets (8C-9C) have been found on the site.

Opposite stand the fine remains of Wat Indra, also dating back to the Ayutthaya period.

★★**Wat Phra Si Ratana Mahathat** ⊙ – *Thanon Nakala. West of the railway station.* A gallery encloses a slender 12C Khmer **prang** which bears a fine stucco decoration on the gables and lintels, and marks an evolution to a Siamese style. European influence is evident in the arched openings of a large brick **vihara** *(east)* with nine dividing pillars built in the 17C. Remains of numerous chedis and viharas in Sukhothai and Ayutthaya styles are dotted all over the site. A small corn-shaped fluted **prang** *(northwest)* is noteworthy for the seated angels at the base.

Wat Sao Thong Thong – *Northwest of the royal palace.* In the reign of King Narai distinctive buildings (Tuk Pichu, Tuk Kholosan) at the rear of the temple served as residences for foreign guests. The main **vihara**, which boasts pilasters capped by leaf capitals, arched openings and a tiered roof, was a Christian chapel later converted to a Buddhist sanctuary. Inside there are fine Lopburi-style Buddha images in the niches and a seated Buddha incorporating a crucifix at the altar. The octagonal chedi marked by eight niches containing standing Buddhas was renovated in the Bangkok period.

Vichayen House ⊙ – *Thanon Vichayen.* This was the residence of the Chevalier de Chaumont, the first French ambassador from the court of Louis XIV, and his attendants. Within the walled enclosure stand a three-storey building in a composite European-Thai style, a church with a house for the clergy and a belfry, an audience hall and other functional structures. Chao Phraya Vichayen (Constantine Phaulkon) later occupied the residence until his death.

Wat Mani Cholakhan – *Along 311 west near Tha Po market.* A tall redented chedi pierced by niches stands isolated on a small island.

A curious feature in town is the monkey population which roams freely near the shrines. According to legend the Hindu god Rama shot an arrow up in the sky and founded a town on the site where the arrow fell to reward his loyal soldier, the monkey Hanuman. The latter used his tail to construct the city walls, and the ground where the arrow fell turned white. The local clay is rich in alumina used in the production of face powder.

Wat San Paulo – *Thanon Tesaban 2. East. Soi Chang Koi near the moat.* The site was ceded to the French Jesuit missionaries by King Narai. The ground plan of the church is clearly discernible and a brick wall is all that remains of a three-storey octagonal tower.

EXCURSIONS

★ **Wat Lai** – *Ban Tha Khlong, Amphoe Tha Wung. 24km west by 311 and 3028; after 18km turn right, proceed for 6km and turn left.* The temple founded in the Ayutthaya period (17C) is situated near a waterway linked with the Mae Nam Chao Phraya. The exquisite **stuccowork**★★ of the east and west façades of an old vihara, unfortunately very dilapidated, is one of the earliest examples of Ayutthaya craftsmanship. The composition depicts the Buddhist Jataka. Inside, the dividing wall is also adorned with stucco. The seated Buddha image dates from the early 17C. There are also two chedis and another vihara with an ornamented façade. A revered Buddha image, Phra Si Ari, is housed in a modern vihara. A small museum *(if closed ask to visit)* displays a fine collection of porcelain, Buddha images and manuscript cabinets.

Phra Thinang Kraisorn Siharat – *From the Sa Kaeo roundabout take 1 north for a short distance, turn left into Thanon Na Wat Kai, at Ban Pak Chan turn right and proceed for a short distance.* Only the watergates, walls and terraces remain of **Talay Chupsorn**, the reservoir built by King Narai to supply water to Lopburi, as the lake itself has dried up.

A track leads to the romantic ruins of a **summer palace** formerly on an island, where King Narai retired to enjoy beautiful mountain scenery and to view solar eclipses.

★ **Folk Boat Museum** – *Wat Yang Na Rang Si. Tambon Talung. 9km southeast, from Sa Kaeo monument take 3016 east and then 3196 left along irrigation canal. Turn right at Km 81-82.* The temple enjoys a beautiful site by the Mae Nam Lopburi. A large open hall (sala kanprien) built of wood has been turned into a **boat museum.** The collection comprises various types of local boats including a rare one-seat barge, which plied the waterways before the roads were constructed. There is also a collection of oars.

MAE HONG SON★★

Mae Hong Son – Population 45 050

Michelin Atlas p 2 or Map 965 – B 2

This remote town in a valley girt by forested mountains on the Myanmar border was part of the kingdom of Chiang Mai in the 19C. It owed its past prosperity to teak logging and the trapping of wild elephants which were highly prized in war. It was also a place of exile for functionaries who had fallen out of favour. Its isolation ended in 1965 with the opening of the first metalled road from Chiang Mai. Air links have given a new impetus to tourism, as Mae Hong Son with its cool climate and exotic scenery often shrouded in mist is an ideal base for trekking and rafting. However, in view of the sensitive political situation at the border visitors should exercise due care and follow the recommendations of the local authorities.

In the town centre is Nong Chong Kham, a natural swamp surrounded by a park and lush gardens which form a perfect setting for the temples in the background. The site is the gathering point for various festivals. Nearby stand a few traditional wooden houses roofed with leaves.

Prehistory – The early inhabitants in the area left traces of their way of life which have been uncovered by the American archaeologist Chester Gorman. Digs in the **Spirit Cave** in the mountains to the north have revealed tools and seeds (betel nut, almonds, peppercorns, cucumber, pumpkin), which indicate farming expertise and a settled existence in the Mesolithic Age. The exciting finds challenge the accepted theories regarding the evolution of man.

Population – The **Shans**, who belong to the same ethnic group as the Thais, settled in the area in the 19C and make up a large percentage of the population.

Hill-tribesmen and -women (Meo, Karen, Lawa, Lahu and Lisu) in their bright costumes, who come and go across borders, may be seen in town when they bring their produce and crafts to market. The Mae Hong Son province benefits from many projects under royal patronage to encourage the hill tribes to adopt an ecological approach to farming and to change over from cultivation of the opium poppy to temperate crops.

SIGHTS

★**Wat Phra That Doi Kong Mu** – *West. By car from Thanon Padung Muay.* Two white chedis with gilded crowns (1874; the smaller was rebuilt in 1966) lit up at night dominate the summit of Doi Kong Mu, a small hill which affords panoramic **views**★★ of the valley and the circle of mountains. Mythical animals and porches highlighted by stucco motifs and containing Buddha images frame the chedis. Nearby is a Burmese-style vihara with a tiered roof. A stairway leads down to the lower terrace guarded by two huge stone lions (in the grounds of Wat Phra Non). At the Loy Krathong festival the lotus offerings *(krathong)* are attached to paper lanterns and released in the air from the hilltop instead of being set adrift on water.

Wat Phra Non – *Thanon Padung Muay near the stadium.* The temple is notable for its Burmese-style ubosot and a wooden vihara decorated with Shan-style paintings and containing a large **reclining Buddha** *(12m long)* with a realistic expression commissioned in 1875 by the ruler's wife. In a small museum to the left is

Wat Chong Klang

The colourful **Buat Luk Kaeo Festival** *(early April, 3 days)* marks the ordination of young boys as novices with an elaborate ritual. The participants are borne by elephants in a solemn procession to the temple. The young boys smartly dressed in their finery and wearing headdresses decked with bright flowers represent Prince Siddhartha before he gave up his princely attributes to become an ascetic in his quest for enlightenment. They spend the night at the temple and are pampered by their relatives. The following day the novices shave their hair and don monastic dress

Ordination Ceremony

for their simple life at the temple. The ordination ceremony is an occasion of great rejoicing and merit-making for the population.

displayed a collection of porcelain, statues and religious books. The Buddha image and two massive stone lions *(see above)* are remarkable examples of Shan craftsmanship. A shrine *(right of the entrance)* houses the ashes of the provincial rulers.

Wat Kam Ko – *Thanon Padung Muay opposite Wat Phra Non.* An unusual Shan architectural feature is the covered path decorated with fretwork leading to the sala. Huge pillars support the grooved ceiling with gilded highlights. On either side of the Buddha image stand graceful attendants in elegant draped robes.

Wat Chong Klang – *Thanon Chamnansathit, south of Chong Kham public park.* Four chapels pierce the square base supporting the round chedi with its graceful gilded crown. Inside the sanctuary which is covered by a tiered roof a Phra Puttha Sihing Buddha image *(see CHIANG MAI)* graces the altar; the walls to the left are enhanced by rare Burmese **paintings★** on glass (180 in number) depicting scenes from the Buddhist Jataka (the previous lives of the Buddha) by Mandalay craftsmen. In a room to the right is exhibited a collection of 37 wooden figures brought from Burma in 1869, which illustrate the Vessantara Jataka and are fine examples of Burmese craftsmanship.

Wat Chong Kham – *Thanon Chamnansathit, east of Wat Chong Klang.* A large monastery with tiered roof and intricate woodwork replaces the old Shan temple destroyed by fire in 1970. In a modern building with round-arched openings is the Luang Pho Tho Buddha image cast by Burmese craftsmen in 1934.

Wat Hua Wiang – *Thanon Sihanat Bamrung.* In the temple compound there are several old wooden buildings of some interest. In the Shan-style vihara, which was built recently and has traditional slim openings, a bronze replica of a famous Burmese Buddha image is enshrined on a ceramic altar decorated with floral and peacock motifs.

EXCURSIONS

Along the scenic route *(four-wheel drive recommended)* to the north are **Tham Pla** *(by 1095, turn left at Km 17)*, a cave with a limpid pool in which swim exotic fish (carp) in the middle of a teak forest; the Pha Sua National Park *(by 1095, turn left at Km 18 and continue for 11km)* which boasts a seven-tier waterfall, **Nam Tok Pha Sua**; the **Royal Pavilion** at Pang Tong (Tambon Mok Cham Pae); and hill-top villages (Ban Na Pa Pek, Mae-O – *guide recommended*).
The road south takes in the Royal Pavilion at Pang Daeng *(5km by 108)* and more hill-tribe villages.

Boat trips – *From Ban Huai Dai*. The Nam Mae Pai, which rises in the massif to the east and runs through the Mae Hong Son valley before coursing through the mountains to the west to join the Salween, offers many opportunities for excursions by boat or raft to enjoy the invigorating air and the unspoilt forested landscape. A popular though controversial destination *(30min)* is the border village ☉ of the **Padong** or long-necked Karens, a tribe from Myanmar which recently settled in Thai territory; allegations of exploitation and of human rights abuses are rife. From an early age the girls wear copper rings round their necks according to a long tradition *(see INTRODUCTION, Population)*. The remote Ban Nam Phiang Din *(45min)* has a tiny police station where visitors stop to sign their name in the register.

★★ **Scenic road from Mae Hong Son via Pai to Chiang Mai** – *300km east by 1095 and 107. Allow 1 day*. The winding road provides breathtaking **views**★★★ of the jagged, forest-clad peaks – viewpoint at Km 158 – on the way to Pang Mapha. Road 1226 branches north through mountainous terrain to the hill-tribe villages of Ban Mae La Na and Ban Sam Kham Lue on the Myanmar border. The luxuriant landscape abounds in cool streams, roaring waterfalls, and vast limestone caves.

★★ **Tham Lot** ☉ – *8km north from Pang Mapha. Turn left at Km 138-139*. The deep cave formed by the Nam Mae Lang is the highlight of a visit to the Tham Nam Lot Forest Park. A labyrinth of chambers is filled with splendid concretions. The smaller Tham Tuk Ta contains a small doll-like stalactite and prehistoric wall paintings. The floor of the last cave – reached by raft downriver – inhabited by bats is covered by a thick layer of guano. It is famous for the wooden coffins which are evidence of prehistoric occupation.

Beyond Pang Mapha there are several hill-tribe villages (Ban Nam Rin, Ban Pang Paek) along the road to Pai. *The sights from Pai to Chiang Mai are described in reverse order under CHIANG MAI – Excursions*.

The sights along the scenic road (108) south to Mae Sariang are described in reverse order under MAE SOT – Excursions; and from Mae Sariang to Chiang Mai under CHIANG MAI – Excursions.

MAE SOT

Tak – Population 103 546

Michelin Atlas p 6 or Map 965 – E 3

Trade links with Myanmar (Burma) account for the distinctive nature of the small border town where Thais, Burmese and hill-tribesmen conduct business. There are notable temples in the town centre *(Thanon Intharakhiri)*: the gilded Burmese-style **Wat Chumphon Khiri** topped by a lotus bud and crown rests on a square platform bristling with small chedis; **Wat Mani Phraison** boasts Sukhothai and Burmese chedis and a Lanna-style vihara; and **Wat Aran Yakhet** has a Lanna-style chedi quartered with small chedis, and enhanced by statues in niches and stucco motifs.

Colourful **markets** (near the bus station and at the border – *6km west*) offer a wide variety of goods for sale: gems, jade, handicrafts, foodstuffs, etc. A new bridge over the Mae Nam Moei will encourage tourism and improve communications with Myanmar. As part of the Asian Highway project, the A1 links Rangoon with Kampuchea.

EXCURSIONS

★★ **Scenic road from Mae Sot to Um Phang** – *135km south by 1090, allow 2 days Rtn*. A rewarding excursion may be made to Um Phang; wonderful **views**★★★ unfold as the road winds up and down tree-clad mountains, ravines, and valleys dotted with hill-tribe villages. It is fine trekking country. Visitors also have the option to make an additional journey to Phop Phra and Ban Wa Le by branching off south onto 1206. Caves, waterfalls and wildlife add to the attraction of the unspoilt landscape but this is a politically sensitive area and visitors should not take risks.

The war waged by the Burmese against the Karens has led to many refugee camps in Thai territory. The remote forested border area has been the scene of guerrilla activity until recently and nowadays there is much illegal logging and smuggling activity.

★★ **Nam Tok Tilosoo** – *By raft or 47km by a rough road (four-wheel drive vehicle only) from Um Phang. Check road condition especially after rainfall with TIC*. A trip to the falls along the river affords breathtaking scenery with limestone crags, moss-covered and streaming with water. Bird song and dappled light add to the enchantment. The spectacular falls tumble down from a great height into tiered pools amid lush vegetation.

★ **Scenic road from Mae Sot to Mae Sariang and Mae Hong Son** – *Allow 2 days. 492km north by 105 and 108. Road under repair, some stages are difficult*. The first stage of the road runs parallel to the Mae Nam Moei which unusually flows south to north before merging with the Salween, which in turn wends its way south to the Andaman Sea. The cool air and verdant mountain scenery make for an enjoyable trip.

★ **Tham Mae Usu** – *Ban Hin Nua Kho, Mu 5, Tambon Mae Tan. At Km 82-83 beyond Tha Song Yang, branch off left and at the end of the road turn left and continue for 14km. Allow 1 hour. For active people only, guide recommended.* After fording the stream near the entrance to the vast, airy cave, visitors will marvel at the fantastic shapes of the concretions in the large chambers.

Return to 105. All along the way the forest is inhabited by hill tribes and treks may be made to villages. At Km 133 it is possible to visit a 200-year old **Karen village** located on Doi Mae Ramoeng. Unlike the other groups who keep to their nomadic ways the Karens have adopted a settled lifestyle.

Mae Sariang – The pleasant town at the junction of Roads 108 and 105 near the Myanmar border is a good base from which to explore the surrounding area.
In the centre of the town are two attractive Burmese-style temples: **Wat Chong Sung** with its three chedis framed by numerous small chedis, all topped with gilded crowns; and **Wat Si Bunruang** which has a square vihara with a tiered roof and seated Buddhas.

A pleasant excursion may be enjoyed to **Ban Mae Sam Laep** *(52km southwest by 1194, allow 1 day)* on the picturesque bank of the Salween on the border with Myanmar. High limestone peaks covered with luxuriant vegetation form a harmonious backdrop to the white sandy beach.
Trips by boat or raft south on the Mae Nam Yuam to Sop Moei or north up the Salween past Thai villages are possible if the political situation allows *(enquire from the local and regional authorities).*
Several mountain resorts off 108 offer simple accommodation popular with visitors who enjoy peace and quiet, crisp air and wonderful scenery. The misty dawns and glorious sunsets are particularly memorable.

The scenic road to Khun Yuam *(96km)* crosses fertile valleys and verdant gorges with typical villages dotted along the way. In the town are **Wat Muai To** *(north)* which has three graceful Lanna-style chedis with gilded crowns and a bronze seated Buddha, and overlooking the river the old **Wat To Phae** *(7km west from the market)* which boasts an octagonal chedi framed by small chedis and mythical animals and a vihara covered by a tiered roof.
Other attractions along the way include caves (Tham Mae Hu at Km 108 and Tham Mae La Ka nearby), hot springs and waterfalls. **Nam Tok Mae Surin National Park** *(turn right at Km 220 and continue 30km past hill-tribe villages, four-wheel drive vehicle recommended)* features the highest **waterfall**★★ in Thailand plunging for 80m in a single tier down the cliffside into a foaming pool, and spectacular **views**★★★ as the road winds up and down valleys and mountain peaks. In November and December the hillsides *(at Doi Mae U-Kho)* are a riot of colour as the wild sunflowers burst into bloom.
At Km 234 a road to the right climbs steeply for 10km to a radio-telephone relay station on Khao Huai Nang Pu from which enchanting **views**★★★ of the forested landscape may be enjoyed. Road 108 then descends into a green valley and at Km 254 a road to the right leads to Pha Bong Dam built in a narrow gorge on the Mae Ramat to generate electricity. Near the pleasant recreational area (salas) runs a natural spring, Huai Nam Hu Hai Chai.

MAHA SARAKAM

Mahasarakam – Population 143 642

Michelin Atlas p 14 or Map 965 – E 8

Wide avenues give a spacious feel to the town which is reputed for its numerous educational establishments.
A **museum** at Wat Mahachai presents a collection of Buddhist scripts and Northeastern literature written on palm leaves, art objects and a 200 year-old wood carving of the Buddha and ancient *bai sema.*
Kaeng Loeng Chan Reservoir *(4km southwest by 23)* is a pleasant recreation area.

EXCURSIONS

Phra Phuttha Ming Muang – *Wat Suwannawas. Tambon Kok Phra, Amphoe Kantharawichai. 14km north by 213. Turn left opposite the post office at the town entrance.* The highlight of the temple is the red sandstone **standing Buddha image** in the Dvaravati style, also known as Phra Phuttharup Suphan Mali. The tall, slender figure with a serene expression is striking. Also of interest is the fine Lao-style **sim**★★ (ubosot) with its beautiful Isan-style woodcarving: remarkable elongated **brackets**★★ *(Khan Tuai)* with naga head motifs, decorative leaf forms and finials. The simple carving on the door panel depicts a celestial being holding a fly whisk, with a mythical monster Rahu swallowing the moon on the lower part. The doorway and wall are decorated with ornate stuccowork.

Phra Phuttha Mongkhon – *Wat Phuttha Mongkhon. Tambon Kantharat, Amphoe Kantharawichai. North by 213. Turn right between Km 14-15.* The red sandstone Buddha image in the Dvaravati style stands on a mound under a large bodhi tree encircled by *bai semas*. According to legend this important Buddha image was cast by women at the same time as the Phra Phuttha Ming Muang was cast by men at a time of drought; both ensure plentiful and regular rainfall.

Ko Sam Pi Forest Park – *Amphoe Kosum Phisai. 28km west by 208.* Schools of monkeys frolic in a cool shady park by the Mae Nam Chi, which also offers aviaries and picnic sites.

Prang Ku Ban Khwao – *13km southeast by 23. Turn left at Km 93 and continue 1.5km.* A reclining Buddha graces the ruined laterite Khmer prang (8m high) surrounded by a wall. To the east is the ruined gopura.

Ku Santarat – *Tambon Ku Santarat, Amphoe Na Dun. 65km south by 2040 past Amphoe Wapi Phathum, then take 2045 south, after 800m turn right at sign and continue for 200m in dirt road.* A wall encloses the ruined eastern gopura and Bayon-style Khmer temple (13C) with its carved lintel. In the southeast corner are the remains of a smaller building. This site is one of the few standing vestiges of the ancient city of **Muang Nakhon Champasi** (also **Ku Noi** *in a field to the left near the junction*) which have yielded statues and other artefacts now on display in Khon Kaen Museum *(see KHON KAEN).*

Phra That Na Dun – *Ban Na Dun, Amphoe Na Dun. As above by 2040 and 2045, then turn right at Km 56-55 into 2381 for 5km.* At the centre of a modern Buddhism park rises an impressive white stupa in modern style. The tiered base is quartered by small chedis and decorated with terracotta panels. The bell-shaped relic chamber is crowned by a ringed spire with a golden parasol at the apex. Artefacts of several periods have been uncovered in the area.

Crafts

The villages of Ban Po Mo *(5km east by 208)* and Ban Nong Khuan Chang *(11km by 2202 then 2km by 1027 to Ban Non Tran)* specialise in traditional crafts: pottery and silk weaving, and Isan-style cotton goods (triangular pillows, colourful blankets) respectively.

MUKDAHAN

Mukdahan – Population 124 627

Michelin Atlas p 9 or Map 965 – E 9

In an attractive riverside location by the Mekong the town has trading links with Savannakhet directly opposite in Laos and has a dynamic atmosphere. There are good riverside restaurants.

San Chao Pho Chao Fa Mung Muang *(Thanon Song Nang Satit, by the pier)*, a spirit shrine dedicated to a Laotian prince which now serves as the city pillar, probably dates from the town's foundation.

Wat Si Mongkhon Tai – *Thanon Samran Chaikong.* Phra Chao Ong Luang, a seated gilded Buddha in the Laotian style dating from the town's foundation, is said to have been discovered together with an iron Buddha image near a miraculous palm tree. The latter disappeared and the seated Buddha was transferred to the ubosot.

There are several markets including the busy **Indochina Market** *(Thanon Samran Chaikong)* near the pier which is the place to buy a wide range of goods from Laos (herbal products) and Vietnam (furniture inlaid with mother-of-pearl, ceramics) as well as from Russia, Poland and other former socialist countries (binoculars, telescopes).

EXCURSIONS

Kaeng Kabao – *31km north by 212, turn right between Km 184-185 and proceed for 9km to Amphoe Wan Yai office, turn left and continue for 8km.* A rapid only visible at low tide *(March-April)* comprising a large rock platform and a sandy beach. Curious pot-holes also appear at low tide in the area. It is a popular recreation spot.

Phu Manorom – *5km south by 2034 for 2km then turn right and continue for 3km by a laterite road to the parking area.* Steps lead to the hilltop *(500m)* from which may be enjoyed scenic **views★** of Mukdahan, the Mekong and Savannakhet. There is a sala and a Buddha footprint in the area.

Mukdahan National Park – *South by 2034 in the direction of Don Tan, turn right between Km 14-15.* The park (52sq km) which is covered by dry diptero-carp and mixed deciduous forest contains a wide variety of plants and wildlife, and boasts unusual **rock formations** (Phu Nang Hong in the form of a swan, Phu Pha Thoeb – *see below*, Phu Lang Se – view), cliffs, rock shelters (Phu Tham Phra – rock paintings), springs and waterfalls as well as religious sites (Buddha footprint, statues).

Phu Pha Thoep Forest Park – *Tambon Na Sinuan, Amphoe Muang. 17km south by 2034, turn right between Km 15-16 and continue for 2km.* A geological survey (1992) has revealed that until 130 million years ago the area was covered by water. The striking **rock formations★** have been shaped by rain erosion. Walk up to see the camel-shaped Pha Oud, the large stone platform Lan Kujalin (1 200m west) cut by small streams, and the rock shelters which have yielded evidence of prehistoric occupation (rock paintings). There is also an abundant flora.

Wat Klang Don Tan – *33km south by 2034, turn left near the Don Tan public school or 700m east of Amphoe Don Tan office; ask at the temple to view the drum.* An arcaded gallery surrounds the elegant ubosot with a sala nearby. The highlight of the temple is an ancient **frog drum** probably over 3 000 years old dis-covered in Ban Na Time, Laos in 1938 and now housed high up in a wooden belfry. The find is significant in relation to the evolution of bronze casting. The drum is ornamented with a sunburst and 14 frogs (each 86cm long) perched at the corners.

Hat Hin Wœn Chai – *South by 2034; turn left between Km 31-32 and continue for 1km by a laterite road.* A rocky beach on the Mekong which can be enjoyed only at low tide. Nearby are a graceful Lao-style chedi and some old Bai Sema.

Phu Sa Dok Bua National Park – *Amphoe Don Tan. 60km south by 2034 and right into 2277.* In the park located high up a mountain (423m above sea-level) rise several streams which flow down the slopes at an average of 350-450m above sea-level. A beautiful water-lily pond with the flowers growing in 13 holes two to three metres across and filled with water to a depth of 1 metre gives its name to the park (literally the mountain of the lotus pond). The area was occupied by ter-rorist forces in the 1966-84 communist insurgency.

In **Phu Pha Taem**, a vast rock shelter (72m long, 6m deep), have been discovered numerous (92) prehistoric **rock paintings** in red ochre featuring geometric designs and human figures similar to those found at Pha Taem in Amphoe Kong Chiam *(see UBON RATCHATHANI – Excursions)*.

The mighty River Mekong

B. Davies

187

Phu Mu Forest Park – *Amphoe Nikhom Kham Soi southwest by 212, turn left between Km 128-129 and continue for 11km uphill.* An asphalted track takes cars right up to the large plateau on a hilltop (350m above sea-level) which was once teeming with wild boar hence the name meaning literally "wild boar hill". The scenic area near the parking area affords panoramic **views**★★ and from the visitor centre trails lead to viewpoints on both sides of the hill.

Wat Phu Dan Tae – *33km southwest by 212 via Amphoe Nikhom Kham Soi, turn right between Km 132-133.* A colossal Buddha image, **Luang Pho Yai,** in a preaching posture and seated in front of a large Wheel of the Law on a rock platform, dominates this modern temple founded in 1987 and dedicated to King Rama IX.

Nam Tok Tat Ton – *West by 2042 to Kham Cha-I, then continue for 18km towards Kuchinarai, turn right between Km 67-68.* The road passes picturesque villages and rice fields in the plain. At Ban Nong Sung a trail leads up to a waterfall in a pleasant forested area.

NAKHON PATHOM★

Nakhon Pathom – Population 256 868

Michelin Atlas p 24 or Map 965 – H 5 – Local map see Kanchanaburi

The thriving commercial town surrounded by lush orchards and rice fields originated as a coastal trading centre, but the sea receded as a result of alluvial silt deposits from the main waterways of the central plain.

Its main attraction is the imposing Phra Pathom Chedi, renowned as the earliest and holiest Buddhist monument in the country. The town has also many royal associations and is now an administrative centre and the seat of Silapakorn University. Nakhon Pathom is a popular day-excursion from Bangkok.

A popular **Fruit Festival** *(Sept)* and a **Temple Festival** held during the pilgrimage period *(Nov)* celebrate Nakhon Pathom's twin claims to fame.

An ancient site – According to tradition the area was Nakhon Chaisi, the capital of the mythical land of **Suwannaphum,** "Land of Gold", where Buddhism was first introduced by missionaries sent in the 3C BC by King Ashoka, a great Indian ruler, when a sanctuary was erected for relics of the Buddha. Scholars assume that Suwannaphum is the Dvaravati kingdom of the Mons (6C-11C) recorded in 7C Chinese chronicles. Archaeological evidence (Buddha images, votive tablets, rare coins, Wheels of the Law) confirm the theory of the site as the capital. The Mons were probably conquered in the 11C by King Anuratha of Pagan, who was inspired by the distinctive Dvaravati stupas on which he modelled temples later built in Burma. The Khmers may also have occupied the land and rebuilt the shrine.

The population migrated to U-Thong and the area was deserted until the 16C when a new settlement also known as Nakhon Chaisi was established on the bank of the Mae Nam Tachin to counter a Burmese invasion.

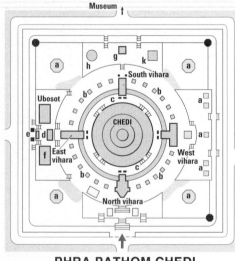

PHRA PATHOM CHEDI

0 — 100 m

a Sacred trees	**e** Sala	**h** Replica of the original chedi
b Belfries	**f** Temple museum	
c Inner gallery	**g** Buddha Image	**k** Replica of the chedi of Nakhon Si Thammarat
d Chinese temple		

A symbol of piety – In the mid-19C during his time as a monk Rama IV (King Mongkut) recognised the importance of the ruined structure and made pilgrimages to the shrine. As the stupa which was restored on his accession to the throne had collapsed during a storm, he planned to build a new chedi enclosing the old stupa but died before the work was completed. His son Rama V (King Chulalongkorn) executed the project, cleared the land, built roads and moved the riverside settlement to the town's present location. The town name was changed to Nakhon Pathom in the early 20C by Rama VI (King Vajivarudh). Both Rama V and Rama VI built palaces and resided in the town.

★★PHRA PATHOM CHEDI ⊘

The golden dome covered in glazed tiles of the great chedi (120m high), which is deemed to be Thailand's oldest place of worship and the tallest Buddhist monument in the world, is a majestic landmark visible from afar.

Precinct – The chedi stands on raised terraces linked by steps within a walled enclosure planted with sacred trees and dotted with mounds and small religious buildings. A monumental staircase flanked by seven-headed nagas and two ceremonial halls at the base lead up to the north entrance. Four viharas housing Buddha images pierce the cloister surrounding the massive chedi.

Start from the north and walk round the monument in a clockwise direction. Bells in small belfries spaced at intervals are rung by pilgrims. Buddha images in various stances are placed in the outer gallery. The doors leading into the inner gallery guarded by stone figures are notable for their Chinese-style moon windows. Also of interest are stone animals and Wheels of the Law. Parts of the inner gallery are used as classrooms for novice monks.

North vihara – The colossal gilded **standing Buddha★** in the Sukhothai style is known as Phra Ruang Rochanarit and is highly revered. The plinth contains the ashes of King Rama VI. In the inner chapel the scene depicts animals bearing food to the Buddha after his fast in the forest.

Nearby are the temple offices, and a public hall which presents the history of the restoration.

East vihara – The Buddha in the posture of enlightenment is placed in an ornate altar against a delicate mural of a spreading bodhi tree. The inner chamber used as a Royal Chapel is adorned with celestial beings, kingly figures and hermits at prayer.

Ubosot – *East terrace – steps*. A majestic **Buddha★★★** preaching is seated in European fashion. The powerful Dvaravati image carved in white quartzite has typical round features, long earlobes, tight curls with rounded topknot, and flowing robe. This is one of four large Buddha statues found in Nakhon Pathom; another is on the terrace by the south entrance. The other two are in the museums of Bangkok and Ayutthaya.

In the vicinity are a Chinese temple, a sala and the **temple museum** – temple offerings, Dvaravati statues and Wheels of the Law.

Phra Pathom Chedi

South vihara – Disciples surround the Buddha image while in the inner room a hooded naga shelters the meditating master.
Walk down to the terrace to admire the large Dvaravati **Buddha image,** and the replicas of the original chedi surmounted by a Khmer-style prang and of the famous chedi of Nakhon Si Thammarat *(see NAKHON SI THAMMARAT).*

West vihara – A colossal Buddha reclines in a relaxed pose with bent knee, while in the inner chapel pilgrims pray beside a smaller image of the Buddha attaining nirvana.

Chedi – The view from the base of the massive cupola is breathtaking. A tapering ringed spire crowned by a triple trident and a tiered canopy soars from a square platform. The chedi is built over a Khmer-style monument, which in turn encloses the original shrine believed to house the Buddha relic brought by the missionaries of King Ashoka.

ADDITIONAL SIGHTS

Museum – *South.* The exhibits displayed in the garden and inside the museum afford an insight into the artistic traditions of the Dvaravati kingdom (6C-11C): stone bells, enigmatic heads of divinities, admirable stucco reliefs from Chedi Chula Pathon, large Wheels of the Law, curious stucco dwarfs, fine stone carvings showing Buddha seated in European fashion and Buddha descending from Tavatimsa Heaven. There are also 13C-14C stone inscriptions from the Sukhothai period as well as stucco heads from the U-Thong period (13C-14C).

★ **Phra Ratchawang Sanam Chan** – *Thanon Rajamakhanai. 550m northwest.* The summer palace built at the turn of the century by Rama VI (King Vajivarudh) comprises fine wooden buildings surrounded by trim gardens, which now serve as offices for the provincial administration. The elegant **Ruan Thap Khwan,** grouping eight structures used as reception areas and sleeping quarters around a central veranda, is a splendid example of traditional domestic architecture. The white building to the left houses a **museum** of contemporary photographs. In front of the compound is a moving monument to the king's beloved pet-dog Ya-Le. Nearby are the premises of Silapakorn University.

Wat Phra Prathon – *3km east of Phra Pathom Chedi by 4.* A tall prang (20m high) dominates the monument which is one of the most ancient Buddhist sites in Thailand.

Legend

A chronicle relates that the sanctuary was built in atonement for heinous crimes in the tradition of Oedipus. A prediction having warned King Phya Kong of Nakhon Chaisi that he would be killed by his son, he ordered the demise of the infant, but the desolate queen spirited the baby away to a forest where he was found and raised by an old woman Yai Hom. The youth Phya Pan was adopted by the King of Ratchaburi, a vassal of King Phya Kong. He waged war against the feudal lord and killed his natural father, and after his victory claimed the queen as his wife. When he learned the truth about his birth, he blamed Yai Hom for his troubles and put her to death. Overcome by remorse, he was advised by the monks to build a stupa of a height equal to that of a turtle dove's flight.

EXCURSIONS

Rose Garden ⊙ – *25km east by 4.* Shimmering pools and tinkling fountains add to the charm of the lush, shady grounds ablaze with flowers, in particular roses and orchids, and ornamental plants. The highlight of a visit is the **Thai Village Culture Show,** an attractive presentation of folk dancing, a wedding ceremony, boxing, cock fighting, sword fighting and other typical entertainment. Accommodation is available in traditional Thai houses or hotels.

Samphran Elephant Village ⊙ – *26km east by 4 (1km beyond the Rose Garden).* The lumbering animals are put through their paces and demonstrate a round-up, training of baby elephants and a war parade. The handling of tropical crocodiles bred in large pens is also presented.

Thai Human Imagery Museum ⊙ – *30km east by 4 and 338 (Km 31 on Pinklao-Nakhon Chaisi Road).* A fine presentation of waxworks devoted to illustrious Buddhist monks, the Kings of the Chakri Dynasty, Thai literature and typical popular scenes of Thai life.

Phra Phutthamonthon – *30km east by 4 and 338.* Within the landscaped Buddhist park are recreations of symbolic sites marking important events in the life of the Buddha: birth, enlightenment, first sermon and nirvana. The centrepiece is a colossal walking Buddha image. The park is the venue for mass gatherings of the faithful.

NAKHON PHANOM

Nakhon Phanom – Population 162 405

Michelin Atlas p 9 or Map 965 – D 9

This ancient town's close association with Indo-China (Laos and Vietnam) is evident from its mixed population and European-influenced architecture. During the various conflicts waves of refugees have crossed into Thailand and settled in Isan. Since the beginning of the century there has been an active Catholic community in the province (schools, seminaries, churches, Ban Tha Rae).

The popular annual **Ngan Khaeng Rua Festival** *(October or November)* celebrated in honour of the Buddha's ascent to heaven features various entertainments including boat races in all the provinces bordering the Mekong and in Laos. The highlight is the spectacular **illuminated boat procession:** originally a bamboo or banana-tree boat (10-12m long), decorated with lit candles or tiny lamps in various designs (Naga serpent, mondop) and loaded with offerings was floated on the Mekong in the full moon; nowadays the boats are of wood or other materials.

Town – A pleasant road along the river, Thanon Sunthon Wichit, affords panoramic views of the mighty Mekong, and of Muang Tha Khaek and the jagged mountains on the Laos side, and passes several interesting buildings: the St Anna Catholic Church, official buildings, the Clock Tower, the Immigration Office, the Custom House and various temples (Wat Okat Si Bua Ban of 1638 – mural painting, stone Buddha image, stuccowork). The renovated former provincial hall (now the National Library) in Thanon Apiban Bancha is a fine example of French Renaissance architecture.

EXCURSIONS

Phra That Tha U-Then – *Amphoe Tha U-Then. 26km north by 212.* In a peaceful setting on the west bank of the Mekong stands this elegant stupa, built in 1912 in the That Phanom style to enshrine relics brought from Burma. Blue mosaic motifs highlight the square tiered base supporting a lotus-bud relic chamber topped by a soaring spire.

Wat Trai Phum – *Mu3 Tambon Tha U-Then, north by 212.* The temple boasts an ancient Lao-style standing statue of Buddha cast in 1465 and highly revered by local people.

★**Phra That Phanom** – *Wat Phrathat Phanom. 50km south by 212.* This is one of the most important Buddhist pilgrimage centres, especially for the people of Isan and Laos. According to tradition the stupa was built by five state rulers to enshrine Buddha relics brought here by a monk in 535 BC (8 BE).

The original shrine was a square brick base decorated with 10C reliefs featuring scenes of princes and local people in the Cham and Khmer styles. The monument was raised to a great height during a

Phra That Phanom

M. Troncy/ HOA QUI

191

17C restoration when a Lao-style chamber was built. Further restoration in the 1940s added 10m more as well as floral motifs. Disaster struck in 1975 when the top-heavy stupa collapsed to the great distress of the faithful.

The slender white chedi (53.4m high) with golden stucco floral motifs, tiered lotus pedestal and gold spire is a reconstruction (1979) and stands in a cloistered court-yard.

An exhibition in the museum behind the cloister describes the evolution of the monument. Also on display are objects including a gilded reliquary, precious stones and metal, and statues of the Buddha found during the restoration.

Old town – A Lao Victory Arch (similar to the one in Vientiane, Laos) spans the road from the pier to the shrine. The architecture of the old houses combines Chinese and French elements. The bustling markets (near the wat and north of the pier) attract traders from both sides of the Mekong who offer a wide range of goods and exotic products.

Renu Nakhon – *Amphoe Renu Nakhon. 61km south by 212, turn right at Km 44 into 2031 for 7km. Or 15km from Phra That Phanom.* The chedi (35m high) founded in 1918 is similar in style to That Phanom pre-1940. Stucco reliefs highlight the solid square base (8.39m); the bulbous relic chamber with gold mosaic motifs is crowned by a golden spire on a pedestal.

The ordination hall nearby contains a fine bronze seated Buddha named Phra Chao Ong Saen.

The local handicrafts especially cotton and silk are renowned and there are stalls in the temple grounds with goods for sale.

The style of Phra That Phanom (pre- and post- rebuilding) has been adopted with variations for several chedis built throughout Isan: Phra That Tha U-Then and Phra That Renu Nakhon – Nakhon Phanom; Wat Phra That Bang Puan – Nong Khai; Wat Phra Phuttabhat Bua Bok – Udon Thani.

NAKHON RATCHASIMA (KHORAT)★★

Nakhon Ratchasima – Population 421 639

Michelin Atlas p 12 or Map 965 – G 7 – Town plan Atlas p 33

The busy administrative and industrial town, also known as Khorat, is the gateway to the Isan region and the capital of a rapidly developing province with a rich Khmer heritage. The improvement of the infrastructure has brought the region out of its isolation and has boosted trading activities. The population is mostly of Laotian origin owing to large-scale migration in the 19C. Khorat served as a military base during the Vietnam war.

Statue of Thao Suranaree

Tourism Authority of Thailand

Town – The earlier settlements of Muang Sema and Muang Khorakhapura *(see below)* were abandoned in the 17C, when King Narai founded the moated town with strong fortifications to counter the threat of attacks by the Khmers. The gateway **Pratu Chumphon** *(west)*, whitewashed and topped with a wooden structure, was renovated after an old photo taken at the beginning of the century. In front is a bronze monument containing the ashes of the revered 19C heroine **Thao Suranaree**, the wife of an official, who together with a band of women defeated a Lao invasion led by Prince Anuwongsa of Vientiane, after plying the soldiers with drink. A colourful annual **festival** *(23 Mar-3 Apr)* commemorates the heroic deed with parades, pageants, displays and fireworks.

Maha Werawong National Museum ⊘ – *Wat Suthi Chinda (opposite the*

Out and about

Tourism Authority of Thailand (TAT) – 2102-2104 Thanon Mittraphap, Amphoe Muang, Nakhon Ratchasima 30000. ☎ 044 213 666, 044 213 030. Fax 044 213 667.

Tourist Police – As above. ☎ 1155.

Transport – Flights to and from Bangkok by Thai Airways. **Domestic Airport** ☎ 044 257 216.
Frequent **buses** to and from Bangkok from Terminal I (by 2) and services to surrounding provinces from Terminal 2 (by 2).
Tricycles and **tuk-tuks** are popular to get around the town.

Shopping – **Night market,** Thanon Manat, 6-11pm. For **Handicrafts** visit the area around Thao Suranaree Monument.

Entertainment – Isan Cultural Show: Sima Thani Hotel. Discos, bars, nightclubs: Thanon Somsurang Yat.

Excursions: Prasat Hin Phimai. Prasat Hin Phanom Rung, Khao Yai National Park.

Where to eat

Good restaurants serving various types of cuisine are to be found along Thanon Somsurang Yat and there are food stalls at the night market. There are also fine open-air establishments on the outskirts.

Where to stay

Budget

Chomsurang Hotel – 270/1-2, Thanon Mahat Thai. ☎ 044 257 081-9; Fax 044 252 897; 950-5 000 Baht. Good hotel with restaurants and outdoor pool near the night market.

Sripattana Hotel – 346 Thanon Suranaree. ☎ 044 251 652; Fax 043 251 655; 500-1 200 Baht. Located near the hospital west of town centre; reasonable prices.

R.C.N. Plaza – 62 Thanon Mukkhamontri. ☎ 044 245 777; Fax 044 254 312; 800-1 200 Baht. Budget hotel conveniently located near the railway station.

Moderate

Sima Thani Hotel– 2112/2 Thanon Mittraphap. ☎ 044 213 100, 02 253 4885/6; Fax 044 213 131, 02 253 4886; sales@simathani.co.th; www.simathani.co.th; 900-7 500 Baht. Well-appointed hotel with restaurants, health club and gardens at the entrance to the town.

Rachphuk Grand Hotel – 311 Thanon Mittraphap. ☎ 044 261 277; Fax 261 278; rgh@korat.lox.info.co.th; 1 000-5 000 Baht. Fine, modern hotel on the main road. Restaurants and health club.

Royal Princess Korat – 1137 Thanon Suranaree. ☎ 044 256 629-35, 02 636 3600 Ext 3800; Fax 044 256 601, 02 636 3543; pkk@dusit.com; www.royalprincess.com; 1 400-7 000 Baht. Luxury accommodation, restaurants, gardens.

Provincial Hall). On display are art objects donated by a former abbot or by the public, and artefacts excavated in the Isan region. Examples of Khmer artistry include carved stone **lintels** from Prasat Muang Khaek *(see Muang Khorat below),* a remarkable 8C statue of **Ganesha★**, a fine 10C sandstone Brahma as well as other Hindu deities (11C-13C). The collection also comprises bronzes (12C-13C), pottery and steles.

EXCURSIONS

★★★ Prasat Hin Phimai – *See Prasat Hin PHIMAI.*

★ Prasat Phanom Wan ⊘ – *Ban Makha, Tambon Na Pho. 14km northeast by 2, then turn right at the sign and continue for 6km.* The small 11C Khmer temple girt by a galleried wall pierced by gates stands on a tranquil secluded site. A ruined prang and door lintels from an earlier shrine are visible in the compound.

A covered gallery *(mandapa)* lit by windows with turned balusters leads into the sanctuary, which is crowned by a sandstone prang and has porticoes on all sides. Above the north entrance is a fine lintel in Baphuon style which dates the foundation of the temple to the early 10C. There are Buddha images of different periods enshrined in the temple.

NAKHON RATCHASIMA (KHORAT)

★★ **Ban Prasat** – *Tambon Than Prasat, Amphoe Non Sung. 45km northeast by 2, turn left at Km 44 and continue for 1.5km by asphalt road. Site 1 is located in the middle of the village, Site 2 400m to the northwest, and Site 3 100m further to the southwest.* The favourable topography of the Khorat plateau with its major waterways (Mae Nam Chi, Mae Nam Mun and Mekong) attracted settlement at different times, from the prehistoric era to the Dvaravati and Khmer periods. Artefacts (pottery – red-slipped, black Phimai vessels, globular pots, ornaments in shell, marble and bronze, and tools) from three burial sites provide evidence of the advanced culture and elaborate rituals of the people who migrated to the fertile region.

Wat Sala Loi – *1km northeast, turn at signpost and continue for 400m.* A low wall topped by red terracotta motifs surrounds the modern ubosot which breaks new ground architecturally, both as regards design – the junk shape recalls the importance of Khorat as a strong outpost of Ayutthaya – and the use of local materials (terracotta reliefs of scenes from the life of Buddha made by Dan Kwian craftsmen). The bronze doors relate the legend of Prince Wessanthon, and whitewashed *bai semas* of an unusual design frame the ubosot.

Dan Kwian – *15km southeast by 224.* The village, on an important trading route to Isan and Cambodia, traditionally produces distinctive dark brown or black earthenware from clay from the banks of the Mun. The kilns are located off the main road and pottery is on sale along the roadside.
There is also a **museum** *(at Din Dam shop)* of beautifully carved ancient bull-carts from all over Thailand.

Muang Khorat – *Tambon Khorat 32km west by 2, turn right between Km 221-222 into 2061 to Amphoe Sung Noen, then turn right at Wat Yanasopitawanaram (Wat Pa Sung Noen).* The road leads to the ancient Khmer settlement of Muang Khorat (Khorakhapura in Sanskrit), a fertile site of strategic importance on the western edge of the Khorat plateau.

The 10C **Prasat Hin Non Ku** *(3km north)* dedicated to Shiva with its elevated sandstone base and door-frames outlined against the sky is an evocative sight. Two libraries frame the prang. **Prasat Hin Muang Kaek** ⓥ *(4km north)*, also 10C, has an unusual north-facing plan with a high base extending east and west and massive door-frames. A lintel on the north side depicts the reclining Vishnu. Other lintels from the site are on display in **Phimai Museum★★** *(see Prasat Hin PHIMAI)*.
Further east is **Prasat Hin Muang Kao** *(6km)*. A wall surrounds a ruined prang pierced with four doors which houses a Buddha footprint. Its lotus-bud crown lies on the ground nearby. Only the east and north porches of the east gopura remain standing.

Muang Sema – *Tambon Sema. As for Muang Khorat, then past Ban Hin Tang 4km from Sung Noen market.* The walls and moats enclosing the oval site of this ancient town, which probably dates from the 9C and may be part of the Dvaravati Sri Chinasi kingdom, are still visible. Sandstone boundary stones are scattered in the open to the east of the surrounding wall and in Ban Hin Tang.

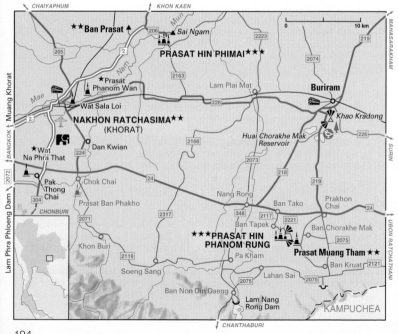

Near the modern ubosot at **Wat Thammachak Semaram** there is a monumental reclining Buddha (mid 7C) made of red sandstone. Artefacts from the ancient site include bronzes, beads and a Wheel of the Law in pale sandstone *(on display in a building to the right of the ubosot).*

★ **Stone Quarry** – *Amphoe Si Khiu. 44km west by 2, turn left at Km 206.* Grooves and chisel marks in the rock face indicate where blocks have been gouged from a sandstone hill. The quarry probably supplied stone used in the building of nearby Khmer religious sites such as Phimai, Phanom Wan, Nong Ku and Muang Khaek.

Wat Khao Chan Ngam – *Amphoe Si Khiu. 52km west by 2, turn left at Km 198 and continue for 4km by laterite road.* High up on the cliff face, prehistoric **murals**★★ in red ochre are a vivid testimony of the lifestyle of the early occupiers of the region some 3 000 years ago. The figures include a man with a bow accompanied by a dog.

Pak Thong Chai – *32km south by 304.* The village is reputed for its silk weaving tradition. The fabric produced locally is on sale in the shops at the entrance to the village *(Silk and Cultural Centre between Km 107-108)* and in Khorat.

★ **Wat Na Phra That** – *Tambon Takhu. As for Pak Thong Chai by 304, turn right between Km 106-105 into 2238 and continue for 5km.* Slender Lao-style reliquaries (thats) frame the old ubosot, which is notable for its carved pediment and mural paintings (early-19C Ayutthaya-Bangkok style – above doorway and on inner walls) of scenes from the Jataka and from daily life (fishing, working in rice fields). The doors of the library (ho trai), built on stilts in the middle of a pond, are adorned with lacquerware motifs (bird, garuda with a lady).

Lam Phra Phloeng Dam – *South by 304, 4km beyond Pak Thong Chai turn right into 2072 and continue for 28km.* The dam on one of the tributaries of the Mun has created a picturesque lake hemmed in by wooded cliffs. Fine views may be enjoyed from the irrigation station. Take a boat trip on the lake to view spectacular waterfalls.

Lam Thakong Reservoir – *Tambon Lad Bua Kao. 62km west by 2.* The road affords lovely **views**★★ of the vast lake against a hilly backdrop. It is a pleasant spot for relaxation, with picnic areas.

Pak Chong – *80km west by 2. Turn at Km 150 and continue for 1km.* The small town lies at the foot of a range of mountains on the edge of the Khorat plateau. At Wat Thep Phitak Punnaram a large white Buddha statue dominates the scenery from a mountain top.

NAKHON SAWAN

Nakhon Sawan – Population 239 396

Michelin Atlas p 11 or Map 965 – F 5

The importance of Nakhon Sawan as a result of its strategic location at the confluence of the Mae Nam Ping and Mae Nam Nan forming the majestic Mae Nam Chao Phraya, diminished as river transport was superseded by railways. Agriculture is now the mainstay of the province. The modern town has a modest claim to fame as the standard price for rice is based on the local market rate.

The past history of Nakhon Sawan is still to be investigated. Traces of an ancient town of the Dvaravati period, **Muang Bon** *(33km south by 1, at Ban Khok Mai Den turn right and proceed for 3km),* have been uncovered.

Traditional crafts include ivory carving at Phayuha Khiri, a village situated 6km south of Nakhon Sawan.

The Chinese New Year *(late Jan or early Feb)* is celebrated in style with a colourful and noisy **Dragon and Lion Procession** attended by Thai and Chinese people from provinces far and near.

SIGHTS

Source of Mae Nam Chao Phraya – *Boat trip from Pak Nam Pho.* A pleasant excursion may be made to the source of the Chao Phraya where the clear waters of the Mae Nam Nan merge with the reddish Mae Nam Ping. The **Chao Phraya** which irrigates the central plain and flows into the Gulf of Thailand is vital to the economic prosperity of the country. The tour allows visitors to catch a glimpse of life on the water and to view some sights along the way: a Chinese shrine and Wat Klieng Krai Klang *(see below).*

Khao Woranat Banphot – *Thanon Tham Withet.* According to tradition the hilltop temple was built over 700 years ago by King Lithai of Sukhothai. A chedi and a vihara housing a Buddha footprint dating from the Sukhothai period are surrounded by beautiful gardens. There is a fine **view**★ of the lush mountain ranges to the west, the bustling Paknam Pho City in the middle ground, and the shimmering Bung Boraphet to the northeast.

EXCURSIONS

Wat Chom Khiri Nak Phrot – *Take 1 south and turn right before the bridge Saphan Dejativong.* Notable features are several Buddha footprints, an ubosot surrounded by a double row of boundary stones, Buddha figures in the Ayutthaya style, and a bell in chased bronze hanging between stone pillars in the courtyard. The hill-top site affords excellent views of the surrounding countryside.

Wat Kriang Krai Klang – *Tambon Kriang Krai. 22km east by 225.* The temple located in a bend of the Mae Nam Nan has interesting buildings. Near an old **ubosot** adorned with mural paintings towers a late-Ayutthaya chedi. A ruined mondop houses a Buddha footprint, and a **sala** is enhanced with wood carving. Monkeys frolic under a tree in the temple compound.

★ **Bung Boraphet** – The lake and its environs which have been designated as a nature reserve teem with wild animals and rare species of waterfowl. The water level is at its highest after the rainy season and the lake expands to 20km in length. At the Fisheries Development Centre *(turn left off 1 into 225, continue for 8km then turn right and proceed for 1km)* which is responsible for large-scale fish farming, there are reed beds, crocodile ponds and facilities for birdwatchers as well as a museum and an aquarium. On the south side of the lake *(30min by boat from landing behind market or 16km by 3004 and a minor road left)* is a pleasant recreation area.

NAKHON SI THAMMARAT★★

Nakhon Si Thammarat – Population 265 524

Michelin Atlas p 21 or Map 965 – M 4

Nakhon Si Thammarat, the capital of a prosperous province, lies at the centre of a rich agricultural region in the fertile coastal plain, backed to the north by mountains covered with lush vegetation and culminating in the chalk massif of Khao Luang.

The centre of the linear town which was originally by the sea (it is now 26km away) has moved north of the fortifications; the historical buildings are in the southern section.

The highlight of the **Hae Pha Khun That Homage Paying Ceremony** *(Feb)* is a traditional procession with a cloth painting depicting the Buddha's life story, which is placed around the stupa of Wat Mahathat.

A rich craft tradition flourishes in the town and includes niello ware, basket ware and shadow theatre puppets and masks.

An ancient settlement – The early history of Nakhon Si Thammarat is rather obscure and it is mentioned under different names in ancient chronicles. Travellers refer to a thriving trading centre known as **Ligor**, which probably had links with the Srivijaya empire (8C-13C). There is also evidence of Khmer supremacy in the 11C over the ancient state of **Tambralinga**, from which a Khmer prince launched a bid for the control of Angkor.

In 1292 King Ram Kamhaeng of Sukhothai conquered the independent principality and in the late 14C it became a vassal state and later part of the kingdom of Ayutthaya. Under King Ramathibodi II (1491-1529) the Portuguese founded a trading post in 1516. After the destruction of Ayutthaya by the Burmese in 1767 the principality became independent again but joined the Thai kingdom under King Taksin.

A tradition which has currency in Nakhon Si Thammarat suggests that King Taksin escaped execution in Thonburi *(see BANGKOK Environs – Thonburi)* and lived as a hermit at a temple in the province.

Religious tradition – Mahayana Buddhism prevailed during the period when the Srivijaya empire held sway over the southern states. In the 13C, however, Nakhon Si Thammarat became a major centre for the diffusion to the four corners of the country of Theravada Buddhism, which originated in Ceylon.

SIGHTS

Old town

City wall and gate – *Thanom Moom Pom near the provincial prison.* Only part of the north section remains of the 13C moated wall; stone from the wall has been used to build the nearby prison.

Proceed south along Thanon Ratchadamnoen.

Wat Sema Muang – On the site was found a Srivijaya inscription telling the story of the traditional greeting "Sawasdee". It is now in the National Museum in Bangkok.

Ho Phra Narai, Ho Phra I Suan – Two red-roofed Brahman temples from the Srivijaya period. Ho Phra I Suan on the right contains several lingams and in the courtyard a swing *(sao ching cha)* used in ceremonies.

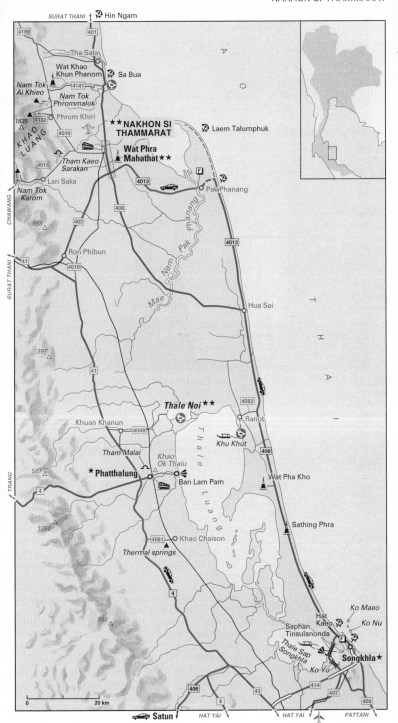

Ho Phra Phuttha Sihing ⓥ – *Near Sala Klang (Provincial Hall)*. An ornate Thai-style shrine houses a fine bronze **Buddha image★** (*c* early 12C-mid 13C) of the Nakhon Si Thammarat school, one of three *(see Wat Phra Sing, Chiang Mai; Phra Thinang Phutthaisawan, Bangkok)* said to have been sent from Ceylon in ancient times – all three differ in size and style. Two standing Buddhas in gold and silver frame the altar. At the back of the building which is located on the site of the former palace of the local ruler stands a prang containing the ashes of the Na Nakhon family.

Wat Phra Mahathat

★★ Wat Phra Mahathat – The most important temple in southern Thailand was probably founded in 757 during the Srivijaya period for the practice of Mahayana Buddhism. An open gallery surrounds the large compound dominated by the bulbous Sinhalese great stupa (**Phra Boromathat** – 75m high) which is believed to cover the original chedi and is surrounded by 158 small chedis. The soaring annular spire is surmounted by a slender finial covered in gold leaf and studded with precious gems, which was added in the reign of Rama V. At the base the gallery of **Wihan Khot,** roofed with glazed tiles and supported by elephant heads in niches, contains 172 Buddha images of various periods.

Access to the terrace (for ceremonies) is from **Wihan Phra Ma** to the north. Inside, a monumental staircase guarded by mythical lions and other animals and surmounted by a red painted ceiling with Corinthian capitals, is framed by two chapels. In the east chapel a standing Buddha in the Sukhothai style and stucco reliefs of scenes from the life of Buddha are of interest. The west chapel contains an altar and Buddha image in the Ayutthaya style.

Wihan Khien ⏱ *(north of Wihan Phra Ma)* houses the treasury which comprises donations (silverware, Chinese porcelain, Sangkalok ceramics) and in particular a Dvaravati **standing Buddha** and a Srivijaya **Buddha with naga** *(in last room).*

Wihan Pho Lanka *(north of Wihan Khien)* presents an exhibition of artefacts found in the vicinity of the temple, including a sandstone statue of Buddha of the Dvaravati period.

Wihan Sam Jom *(north of the compound)* contains a fine image of Phra Chao Si Thamma made of brick and stucco.

Phra Wihan Luang – *South of the compound.* The vihara (used as an ubosot) founded in 1628 has three doors like the Wat Phra Kaeo (Temple of the Emerald Buddha) in Bangkok. The roof rests on inclined pillars. An ornate coffered ceiling also supported by inclined pillars graces the nave. On the altar is a large statue of a **seated Buddha** rejecting Mara, from the early-Ayutthaya (U-Thong) period.

East of the road is Wat Na Phra Boromathat, the monks' residence.

Wat Thao Khot – The old ubosot surrounded by fine Ayutthaya-style semas has a porch with two doors. The wooden wall is decorated with a mural. To the north is a ruined chedi.

★ National Museum ⏱ – *Tambon Salamichai.* The two-storey building displays artefacts from upper southern Thailand from prehistory to the Bangkok period. On the ground floor the prehistory gallery contains rare bronze **kettle drums,** pottery, tools and ornaments. The **Art of Southern Thailand** gallery presents important objects from various schools: three Indian **Pallava sculptures** (8C-9C Vishnu – copy, dancing Shiva, and head of Uma), bronzes of Brahmanic origin, votive tablets, Buddha statues of the Nakhon Si Thammarat school (similar to the Chiang Saen school – *see INTRO-DUCTION, Art* – but on a smaller scale).

On the upper floor the **ethnology section** includes pottery, agricultural and fishing implements, textiles. The ornate walking-sticks (to ward off snakes) are noteworthy. The **ceramics room** displays ware from China, Thailand and Vietnam. A beautifully decorated seat for a royal barge is a fine example of traditional **niello ware**. The last gallery features wood carving, mother-of-pearl inlay and Chinese blue-and-white porcelain.

> Nakhon Si Thammarat is renowned for **niello ware** which is an ancient decorative craft. A delicate outline in dark metal is added to intricate designs etched on a gold or silver base. Skilled craftsmen produced precious boxes, bowls and other objects which were highly prized by rulers and nobles alike.

North of the town

Sanam Na Muang – *Near the Tourist Office.* Prapheni Duan Sip, the 'Tenth-Month Festival', is a ten-day celebration at the city pillar, which includes a procession along Thanon Ratchadamnoen to Wat Phra Mahathat.

Wat Maheyong – A modern temple houses a fine bronze Buddha image exemplifying the Nakhon Si Thammarat school, which developed in the Ayutthaya period. The round face and plump body is reminiscent of the Lanna (Chaeng Saen) style.

Wat Wang Tawan Tok – Within the compound is a remarkable Southern Thai-style **house** (built 1888-1901) comprising three buildings (one floor and three roofs) constructed without nails. The door panels, gables and window frames are ornately carved.

Wat Chaeng – In the compound of the late-18C temple stands a small Chinese-style shrine "Keng Jeen" decorated with wood imported from China, which contains the ashes of one of the Na Nakhon rulers and his wife.

Wat Pradu – According to local tradition the ashes of King Taksin (ruled 1767-82) are enshrined in a boat-shaped chapel – the gable is decorated with a lotus flower. Opposite, a small Chinese shrine is adorned with lattice-work doors.

> Shadow play – **nang talung** – is a popular form of entertainment in Southern Thailand. Brightly-painted masks and articulated puppets made of leather are manipulated by skillful handlers, who sing and act the different parts to the accompaniment of drums, cymbals and gongs. Transparent versions through which light shines are used for night shows.
> Leather which is softened by soaking in water and hammered until it is paper-thin is then fashioned and painted.
> Performances of shadow theatre usually take place during festivals. Suchart workshop *(110/18 Si Thammasok Soi 3)* and Mesa Chotiphan workshop *(558/4 Soi Rong Jeh, Thanon Ratchadamnoen)* welcome visitors.

EXCURSIONS

Khao Luang National Park – *30km west by 401 and 4140 or 4016.* On the slopes of Khao Luang (alt 1 835m, the highest point in southern Thailand), the park covers 571sq km and is thickly forested including rain forest on the lower slopes. It is a reserve for montane bird species (200) and for various types of mammals (90) and reptiles (31).

There are several spectacular waterfalls: **Nam Tok Karom**, Amphoe Lan Saka *(4016 for 9km, turn left to 4015 and continue for 20km to Ban Ron. Bear left at a sign for 3km and walk 500m from parking area)* – A trail passes 19 waterfalls as the water cascades from the mountain top (1 300-1 400m). Nearby is the park office which offers accommodation (bungalows). Along the way is **Tham Kaeo Sarakan** *(4015 and left at Km 12).*

Nam Tok Phrommalok *(Amphoe Phrom Khiri-Lan Saka, 15km northwest by 4016, at Km 21 turn left into 4132 for 5km and then follow a trail for 3km)* is a powerful three-tiered waterfall. **Wat Khao Khun Phanom** *(21km northwest by 4016, turn right into 4141 and continue for 3km; a trail to the left leads to the temple),* at the foot of the mountain in a wooded setting, contains many small Buddha statues in gold,

---

Beaches

Laem Talumphuk *(4km from Pak Phanang)* and **Hat Pak Phanang** *(east by 4013 30km to Pak Phanang and continue for 28km by laterite road):* long, white-sand beaches exposed to the wind. Laem Talumphuk is the place where Buddhism was introduced during the period of the Srivijaya Empire.

Hat Sa Bua, Amphoe Tha Sala *(16km north by 401, turn right and continue for 2km by a good surfaced road):* long, white sandy beach, open bays with strong waves. **Hat Pak Phaying**, Amphoe Tha Sala *(20km north by 401):* beautiful beach near fishing village.

Hat Hin Ngam, Amphoe Sichon *(37km north by 401, take 4161 on the right to Ban Pak Nam and continue 1.5km past fishing village):* "beach of beautiful rock", excellent sandy beach with some rocks framing a splendid bay, restaurants, bungalows. **Hat Sichon** further north is yet another beautiful beach.

Ao Khanom *(80km north by 401 or 25km from Sichon, take 4114 right and continue for 17km and turn right for a short distance):* there are several long beaches (Hat Khanom, Hat Nai Praek, Hat Nat Phlao, Hat Pak Nam) with some rocks; clear water but strong waves and wind as the bay is open to the sea.

---

silver and bronze found in a grotto and in the vicinity. A stairway *(250 steps)* climbs up to a grotto with two chambers where lived a hermit. According to legend King Taksin escaped execution and fled to Nakhon Si Thammarat where he ended his days as a hermit.

Other splendid waterfalls include **Nam Tok Ai Khio**, *(Tambon Thon Hong, 29km northwest by 4016; 3km further from Phrommalok and bear left for a 3km trail)* and the multi-tiered **Nam Tok Krung Ching** *(70km northwest by 4016; 15km further then left; from the parking area 4km by trail).*

The west side of Khao Luang is accessible by 4015 to Amphoe Chawang. A secondary road 4194 to the right leads to Amphoe Phipun.

NAN★★

Nan – Population 81 287

Michelin Atlas p 4 or Map 965 – C 5

The remote town on the west bank of the Mae Nam Nan, which cuts through fertile valleys and dramatic mountain landscape, has a rich heritage illustrated by its elegant old temples.

Colourful **boat races** on the Mae Nam Nan held in October every year to mark the end of the Buddhist Lent elicit great excitement and spirited competition among the local people.

Historical notes – Artefacts made of quartzite and sandstone from the Mesolithic period have been discovered far and wide in the Nan valley. In the 12C the fertile soil suitable for rice growing and the rich salt deposits attracted settlers from Lan Xang (Laos) and Lanna to the Pua region. The population grew and the settlement moved to the city of Nan, founded in 1368 and part of an independent kingdom which practised Buddhism and was closely allied to the Sukhothai kingdom. The salt trade brought prosperity to Nan, which remained autonomous until the mid-15C when it passed under Lanna rule. Although Nan fell to the Burmese in 1558 its culture remained relatively unaffected by Burmese influences, although some temples were renovated in Burmese style by merchants engaged in the logging industry. In 1786 the Burmese were driven out of the country and although Nan then paid allegiance to the Kings of Siam it enjoyed certain privileges, and it was only in 1931 that full integration occurred under the central government in Bangkok.

Nan has a strong artistic tradition which has successfully absorbed trends from the various ruling forces. The fine architecture and mural decoration of the temples merit careful study.

SIGHTS

National Museum ⊙ – *Thanon Suriyapong.* An elegant wooden building, the former palace of the ruler of Nan, houses the museum, which is devoted to the history of Nan province.

On the first floor pride of place is given to the ruling family of Nan and to the foundation of the town. Notable exhibits include a black elephant **tusk**★ supported by a garuda carved in wood, Buddha images, a betel nut set and other personal royal objects. There are interesting displays on the art and archeology of the province and the evolution of the Nan school of art. Artefacts rescued from the area flooded for the construction of the Sirikit dam are also on view.

The ground floor presents the ethnology of the province including the hill-tribes (The Thins, Hmong (Meo), Mien) as well as local crafts (silverware, textiles, costumes). Of particular interest is an exhibition on the lifestyle and beliefs of the **Mrabri** tribe known as the Phi Thong Luang, meaning the "Spirits of the Yellow Leaves" from the colour of their leaf huts.

Wat Hua Kwong – *East of the museum*. Among the features of interest are the fine carving of the wooden **pediment** of the main vihara, an elegant library *(left)* with ornate walls, and a Lanna-style **chedi**★. Its high square base supports the square body punctuated by niches housing Buddha images and celestial beings at the corners and surmounted by lotus mouldings, above which rise a small bell-shaped chedi and a slim canopy.

Wat Phra That Chang Kham – *Thanon Suriyapong or 13 Ban Chang Kham*. The monastery was founded in the 15C, remodelled in the 16C and renovated several times.

Fine statues of Buddha, one walking and another standing with outstretched arms, dated 1426 grace the vihara nearest the street. The other vihara contains an outstanding gold **Buddha image** which was hidden beneath a plaster casing for centuries. These statues were commissioned in the 15C by King Ngua Pha Sun for the temple. Two others are in Wat Phaya Phu *(see below)*.

Elephant sculptures highlight the base of the Sukhothai-style **chedi**. At the far end of the courtyard are a smaller chedi and three shrines containing the ashes of the Nan ruling family. Nearby stands a small reliquary with stucco decoration.

Wat Ming Muang – *Thanon Suriyapong*. The heavy stucco decoration and profusion of details of the vihara are rather overpowering. Inside are mural paintings and Buddhas in niches at ceiling level.

In front of the vihara in a modern shrine which is also very ornate stands the Lak Muang.

★★ **Wat Phumin** – *Thanon Pha Kong*. The celebrated temple founded in 1596 and renovated in 1867 is a fine example of local architecture. Steps lead up to the **ubosot** which has an unusual cruciform plan and doors intricately carved with guardians and floral motifs. Four large Buddhas at the centre dominate the interior which has a rich coffered ceiling. The admirable mural paintings in the folk Thai Lue style depict the Nimi *(west wall)* and Khatta Kamura *(north and east walls)* Jatakas and are of historical interest. Although in poor condition they give fascinating details on fashion in the 19C – costumes, hairstyles, tattoos – and feature delightful vignettes on local life such as the whispering scene *(west wall)* and a portrait of the Nan governor *(east wall)*.

Wat Suan Tan – *Thanon Suan Tan northeast of Thanon Pha Kong*. The temple is dominated by a massive tiered **chedi** with redented corners and terminating in a prang framed by four smaller ones. The restored vihara is notable for the imposing 15C Lanna-style seated Buddha, which is believed to have been cast for King Tilokaracha.

Wat Phaya Phu – *Thanon Suriyapong*. The temple is famous for the two 15C **walking Buddhas**★★ flanking a large seated Buddha in the vihara. They are the only two from the original five *(see Wat Prathat Chang Kham)* still on view. The very fine 19C **door panels**★ depict the Yoma Tutara, the angel of death.

EXCURSIONS

Wat Phaya Wat – *Ban Phaya Wat, Mu 6, Tambon Du Tai. Take 101 south and turn right into 1025 between Km 249-250*. A pyramidal chedi with niches containing standing Buddhas in the Sinhalese style similar to **Wat Chamatewee**★ *(see LAMPHUN)* probably dates from the 17C. The modern vihara houses an ornate altar and a revered Buddha image.

Wat Phra That Khao Noi – *As above. Continue for 2km uphill along 1025 past Wat Phaya Wat*. The stucco motif along the wall surrounding the white chedi quartered by smaller chedis denotes a Burmese influence. The vihara has an unusual plan with a transept. Excellent **views**★ of the town and the Nan plain from the hilltop.

Wat Phra That Chae Haeng – *2km southeast by 1168*. The foundation of the temple to enshrine Buddha relics and votive tablets dates back to 1359. Two huge nagas guard the staircase leading to the hilltop. The gilded Lanna-style **chedi**★ framed by filigree canopies was remodelled twice in the 15C notably by King Tilokaracha, and again early this century. A square recessed base decorated with small chedis supports the ringed body highlighted by a leaf motif. A slender finial crowns the small drum. The elegant vihara features a Lao-style tiered roof with carved wooden eaves and naga roof motifs, and a delicate relief of entwined nagas above the door guarded by mythical animals. An imposing Buddha flanked by attendants sits on the altar which bears stucco decorative motifs. Distant **views**★ of the town and the Nan valley may be enjoyed from the walled enclosure.

★ **Wat Nong Bua** – *Ban Nong Bua. 43km north. Take 1080 north; turn left between Km 39-40 opposite a hospital and proceed for 3km.* Mythical animals stand sentinel by the covered porch of the vihara. The pediments are adorned with delicate carving of foliage and geometric motifs. A north doorway gives access to the interior where tall decorated pillars soar to the coffered ceiling. The **mural paintings★★** in a similar idiom to those at Wat Phumin *(see above)* repay careful study of the delightful scenes of contemporary life. The Candagadha Jataka is illustrated on the east and south walls, and behind the Buddha presiding at the altar are four past Buddhas.

★★ **Round scenic tour** – *210km by 1080, 1256, 1081, 1257 and 1169 by four-wheel drive vehicle; allow 1 day.* The **Doi Phu Kha National Park** dominated by Doi Phu Kha (alt 1 980m) offers grandiose mountain **scenery★★★** as well as numerous caves, waterfalls and rare botanical specimens. A tour of the area which is inhabited by hill tribes – Thai Lue village at Ban Nong Bua where the villagers weave a distinctive fabric and make garments for their own use or for sale – including the elusive Mrabri is a very rewarding experience, as its very remoteness has preserved its bucolic charms. The **salt deposits** at Bo Klua add to the interest.

A longer tour may be made by taking 1080 and 1081 right up to the border area, which gives an awesome sense of isolation.

★ **Sao Din** – *Na Noi. 60km south by 101 and 1026. Difficult track at the site, by four-wheel drive vehicle only.* A dramatic landscape of earth pillars formed by erosion. The weird shapes change constantly under the force of the wind.

NARATHIWAT

Narathiwat – Population 102 915

Michelin Atlas p 23 or Map 965 – O 6

The sleepy little town with its old wooden buildings at the mouth of Khlong Bang Nara is the capital of Thailand's most southerly province, and is a pleasant stopover on the road to Malaysia. Mosques are more common than Buddhist temples as the majority of the population is Muslim, although there is a Chinese presence. The ethnic flavour is evident in the lively markets and fishing harbour.

Narathiwat benefits from royal patronage as the royal family maintains a residence in the province as a sign of their enduring interest, and to allay feelings of alienation on the part of the population of the peninsula who feel greater kinship with their neighbours over the border. Projects to promote local handicrafts (batik is made in Ban Yakang, *4km west by 4055*) and agriculture are under royal patronage.

Narathiwat Fair *(3rd week in Sep)* celebrates the special character of southern Thailand with **korlae** boat racing, dove singing contest, dance *(ram sam pen, ram ngeng)* performances, martial arts exhibition and handicraft displays.

EXCURSIONS

Coast – **Hat Narathat** *(2km north near fishing village)*, a long beach lined with sea pines which is good for windsurfing, is popular with the local people. Stop at the fishing village at the mouth of the river to admire the *korlae* fishing boats with their beautiful designs. There are fine sandy beaches along the coast from Narathiwat to Malaysia 40km south.

Nam Tok Bacho – *27km north by 42. Turn left at Km 73-74 for 2km.* Situated in Khao Nam Kang (dewdrop mountain) which is part of the Budo range, the powerful waterfall tumbles from a high cliff in a beautiful forested area.

Vadi Al Husen Mosque – *15km northwest by 42. Past a bridge between Km 74-75 turn left and continue for 1.3km along a small concrete road. In Ban Talamano, Tambon Lubosawo, Amphoe Bacho, 4km from Amphoe Bacho office.*
The village was settled by people who escaped from Pattani *(see PATTANI)* during the war with Ayutthaya in 17C. The mosque founded in 1624, a wooden building combining Thai, Chinese and Malay architectural styles, is a historical landmark. The roof which was originally thatched was later rebuilt in Thai style, with Chinese elements added by a skilled wood carver. In 1975 the temple was extended north to its present size in keeping with the old style.

Wat Khao Kong – *8km southwest by 4055. Turn right between Km 109-110. Tambon Lamphu, Amphoe Muang.* The hilly landscape is dominated by the **Phra Phuttha Taksin Ming Mongkhon,** a huge seated Buddha statue (15m wide, 25m high) decorated with gilded mosaic tiles. Four large staircases lead up to the statue, which is a place of pilgrimage for southern Thais.

The wat is set in extensive grounds. The **Siri Maha Maya pagoda** dedicated to the Queen has a bell-shaped chedi with a Buddha relic enshrined at the top.

Wat Chontara Singhe

Phra Tamnak Taksin Ratcha Niwet – *8km south by 4084. Turn left between Km 6-7. Open when the royal family is not in residence.* At the foot of Khao Tanyong is the residence where the royal family stays during its annual visit to the south. The rare Bangsuriya palm flourishes in the gardens.

The palace is situated on **Ao Manao** *(8km south by 4084, turn left between Km 1-2 and continue for 3km)*, a beautiful curved bay with a long beach of white sand.

★★ **Wat Chontara Singhe** – *34km southeast by 4084. Turn left between Km 32-33 and continue for 500m to temple entrance. On the bank of the Mae Nam Tak Bai, Amphoe Tak Bai.* The temple was founded in 1860 during the reign of King Rama IV on land donated by the governor of Kelantan. During British occupation of Malaya (1908), the British agreed to set the border at Sungai Golok *(5km south)* because of the cultural and religious value of this temple.

The attractive riverside site enhances the remarkable wooden **vihara** in Sumatra style. The ubosot guarded by mythical demons contains mural paintings depicting traditional and religious life, while a smaller vihara (1873) houses a reclining Buddha decorated with stucco and ceramics. **Sala Tha Nam** overlooking the river has a traditional Thai-style crown roof. There are other interesting wooden buildings in the compound.

Sungai Golok ⊘ – *60km south by 4056.* A modest border town which is the departure point for the east coast of Malaysia. Thais cross over for shopping at Rantau Panjang; Malaysians come shopping for consumer goods and to enjoy the easy life. There is a local batik industry.

From Ban Taba *(5km south of Tak Bai)* there is a ferry crossing to Malaysia and then buses to Kota Baru.

★★ **Peat Swamp Forest Study Centre** – *Toh Deang, 10km from Sungai Golok by 4057. After 5km take Thanon Chavanan and proceed for 3km past a village, then turn right at sign and continue for 2km.* An elevated wooden trail gives access to the peat swamp which is of great ecological importance. Its unique environment supports a lush vegetation of trees and bushes with aerial roots and buttresses. New and rare species of flora and fauna which thrive in the moist atmosphere have been identified. The best time to visit is from February to April.

Caged birds hanging from poles or in front of houses, or on sale in bird shops, are a typical feature of Southern Thailand. The small, greyish and sometimes speckled doves which are renowned for their rolling and trilling are found mostly in the south and in Malaysia. Dove cooing contests are held throughout the peninsula and attract enthusiasts from far afield. The cages are raised on poles three to six metres tall. The birds are judged for pitch ,melody and volume. The ASEAN Barred Ground Dove Festival is held in March in the town of Yala *(see PATTANI, Excursions).*

NONG KHAI

Nong Khai – Population 139 069

Michelin Atlas p 8 or Map 965 – D 7

The border town which is also an important railhead on the bank of the Mekong has a certain charm with its French-Chinese style wooden houses *(Thanon Meechai)*, busy market *(Thanon Rim Khong)* and romantic river views. There are good riverside restaurants.

The **Prap Ho Memorial** *(in front of the Provincial Hall)*, a square structure with niches, each containing an inscription in a different language – Chinese, English, Lao, Thai, honours the fallen who took part in 1877 in the defence of the town against a Chinese bandit army, which attacked several towns in Thailand and Laos. A festival takes place on 5 March every year.

The **Friendship Bridge** ⊙ – Saphan Mittaphap *(Ban Chom Manee, Amphoe Muang link to Tha Nalang, Thanon Tha Duea 20km from Vientiane)*, which opened in 1994 and will also provide rail links at a later stage, reinforces the cultural and economic links between Thailand and Laos. A ferry service also operates from Nong Khai to Laos.

EXCURSIONS

Wat Pho Chai – *Amphoe Muang. East by 212, turn left at Km 2.* The temple is famous for the **Luang Pho Phra Sai** Buddha image, which is believed to be one of three commissioned by the three daughters of the King of Lan Xang (Laos). In 1778 the statues were transferred to Vientiane and in the 19C during the reign of King Rama III they were sent to Thailand. The raft carrying the statues capsized in a storm (1850). One was lost in the river and the remaining two were subsequently salvaged and placed in Wat Pho Chai and Wat Ho Klong. The large statue in a meditative pose is made of pure gold and is deemed to be in the Laotian style. The murals recount these events and depict contemporary scenes of everyday life. In front of the ordination hall stands a slender white *that* which is of interest.

San Kaeo Ku – *East by 212. Turn right into a track.* This temple presents a curious collection of Hindu and Buddhist statues inspired by the teachings of the founder, who has a large following in Thailand and Laos.

★**Scenic road from Nong Khai to Nakhon Phanom** – *300km east by 212. Allow 1 day.* The scenic road east follows the river for nearly 320km. Take 212 for 137km to Amphoe Bung Kan and a further 175km to Nakhon Phanom. In the modest town of Bung Kan the riverside walk gives good **views** of the verdant landscape and mountains in Laos.

Phu Tok – *Amphoe Bung Kan. 185km east by 212, at Bung Kan intersection turn right into 222 for 27km to Amphoe Sri Wilai, then turn left and take 2534 for Ban Kham Kan for 20km. Steep climb. Time: 2 hours.* Phu Tok, which means

Phu Tok

B. Davies

lonely mountain, is a red sandstone massif in a plain, formerly a densely forested area, and is part of a meditation temple. The meditation master, Phra Achan Chuan, and his disciples built a stairway divided into seven levels representing the seven levels of enlightenment, which winds all the way to the top; there are monastic cells dotted all over the mountain. The climb to the summit affords splendid **views**★★ of the striking red rock formations and of the surrounding countryside.

At the foot of the mount in a garden setting stand a modern sala and a chedi housing a museum dedicated to Phra Achan Chuan. The tiered, faceted chedi in the form of an abstract lotus is crowned by a lotus bud enhanced by golden mosaic decoration. Terracotta reliefs on the outer walls depict the monk's life. Inside, the display, which includes a life-size statue and relics of Phra Achan Chuan as well as his personal belongings, illustrates the simple life of a meditation monk.

Phu Lanka – *From Ban Phaeng continue west for 6km.* A lush, shady park with interesting flora and several streams and waterfalls.

Nam Tok Tat Kham Forest Park – *Turn right at Km 220 and proceed for 6km by a metalled road to the parking area.* A small four-tiered waterfall in a shady area is easily accessible.

Nam Tok Tat Pho *(5km from Nam Tok Tat Kham or 11km from Ban Phaeng and about 1 hour by a trail)* situated high up is visible from the highway during the rainy season.

Nakhon Phanom – *See NAKHON PHANOM.*

PATTANI

Pattani – Population 106 893

Michelin Atlas p 23 or Map 965 – O 6

The distinctive character of Pattani reflects the varied history of southern Thailand. The population is predominantly of Malay origin and embraces the tenets of Islam. Their cultural tradition is reflected in the political ideology as well as in the local dress, cuisine and architecture. The Chinese community were later arrivals.

The ethnic diversity is an interesting feature of Pattani, which is a provincial capital and a university town on the Pattani estuary. The attractive coastline and the mountainous hinterland covered in dense jungle complete the charming picture.

A twist of history – There is archaeological evidence of an ancient city (Ban Palawi, Amphoe Yarang) known as Landgasuka which was probably abandoned when the river changed its course. In the 8C Pattani was a trading centre, and in the 15C it became a Muslim principality which was part of the Srivijaya empire. It later came under the overlordship of the Ayutthaya and Bangkok rulers. Trade with Europe and China flourished in the 16C, and Dutch and Portuguese trading posts were established. In the late 19C under an agreement between Rama V (King Chulalongkorn) and the British in Malaya, the present border was drawn, and Pattani and the neighbouring territory (Narathiwat, Yala, Satun) became part of Thailand.

The descendants of the ruling family of Pattani still live in **Jabantigore Palace** *(Thanon Nawang, Soi 2)*, a large dilapidated mansion in a composite Muslim – Chinese style.

A crisis of identity – In the recent past, discontent among the local people, as cultural and economic aspirations remained unfulfilled, have led to serious disturbances. Some political changes have been made by the central government in response to the grievances, and the situation is now more settled.

SIGHTS

Town – A stroll around the town will give a glimpse of the simple way of life. Colourful fishing boats *(korlae)* are tied up along the river as well as in Pak Nam Pattani *(3km north)*. In the Chinese quarter *(Thanon Rudee)* there are galleried shop-houses with typical sloped and tiled roofs, scroll-work roof decoration, arched fanlights and slatted windows.

Pattani Central Mosque ⊘ – *Thanon Yarang.* This fine building flanked by twin minarets is set in a garden. The main hall is adorned with an orange-tiled façade, arched windows with stained glass, and green domes.

Leng Chu Kieng Shrine – *Thanon Anorru.* A gaudy Chinese temple dedicated to a goddess with magical powers revered by Thai Chinese contains a shrine to a spirited heroine named **Lim Ko Nieo** and a sculpture of the tree from which she hanged herself *(see below)*. An annual fair *(Feb-Mar)* includes a lively procession.

Korlae Boats

EXCURSIONS

Kru Se Mosque – *7km southeast by 42.* This is one of Pattani's oldest mosques, although it was never completed as the dome was struck by lightning. The building with its triple pointed arches and massive pillars is highly controversial.

According to legend a Chinese merchant, who had converted to Islam and had begun the construction of the mosque, refused to recant on the entreaties of his sister, Lim Ko Nieo. She vowed that the completion of the mosque was doomed and hanged herself from a tree.

Nearby is Lim Ko Nieo's mausoleum, a source of much displeasure to Muslims.

A short distance further on the right is the barren site of an **iron foundry** in the 16C where the Queen of Pattani had cannons cast, including the *Queen of Tani*, now on display at the Ministry of Defense in Bangkok.

Wat Chang Hai – *Amphoe Kok Pho. 30km west by 42 and 409. Park near the railway line.* The modern temple comprises a tall chedi crowned by a gilded finial and an ornate vihara. Near the temple entrance is the mausoleum of the venerated Phra Luang Pho Thuat, a tiered rotunda supported on columns and topped by a gilded spire.

East coast

From Laem Tachi (Yaring) on the northern tip of Ao Pattani there are long stretches of fine sand all along the coast, although the water is not suitable for swimming near the town. **Korlae boats** decorated with fantastic designs and painted in gaudy colours are berthed at **Hat Talo Kapo** *(14km east)*, and at **Hat Panare** *(3km north of Panare)* which has a big fishing community. Further south the water is clear and there are fine sandy beaches: **Hat Chalalai** *(43km southeast)* shaded by pine trees, **Hat Khae Khae** *(3km from Panare, 51km from Pattani)* with its rocky headland, and the beautiful **Hat Patatimo** (Hat Wasukri) *(53km, near Saiburi – bungalows)* and **Hat Talo Laweng** *(42, 4155, 4136, near the Narathiwat border)*.

Yala – *35km south by 410.* This modern commercial town, with wide avenues, parks and lakes, mosques and Chinese temples, has become prosperous from the rubber and rice industries. The Muslim population lives mostly in the countryside while the Chinese community is active in commerce. Yala plays host to the ASEAN singing bird contest *(Mar)* and to the Southern Thai Culture Week *(early Aug)*. The limestone mountains around Yala are pockmarked with caves, many of which have been turned into temples and are of interest.

The beauty and peace of the Betong countryside are in stark contrast to the turbulent atmosphere which prevailed until some years ago. The mountainous area was a stronghold of Communist forces in the armed struggle to overthrow the government of Malaysia. The Malaysian and Thai armies hunted the guerrillas in the jungle where trails were mined. The rebels laid down their arms in 1990. At the end of the war the Thai government gave Thai nationality and land to the guerrillas.

Wat Khuha Phimuk – *6km west of Yala by 409. Turn right into 4065 and continue for 1km.* A steep staircase *(104 steps)* leads to a vast cave shrine near a modern temple also known locally as Wat Na Tham. Large chambers bristling with splendid limestone concretions are dramatically lit by shafts of light, and contain several statues and a 24m-long **reclining Buddha** over which rise two large seven-headed nagas. It is believed to be a former statue of the reclining Vishnu, which probably dates from AD 757 and was commissioned by a Srivijaya ruler.

Tham Silpa – *2km west of Wat Khuha Phimuk. Ask for the key at nearby school.* An overgrown path climbs up the hillside to the cave which has two chambers decorated with 14C-15C **mural paintings** (deteriorated), depicting the Buddha surrounded by disciples. These are significant in art history as they are perhaps the oldest examples of Srivijaya art in Thailand.

** **Scenic road from Yala to Betong** – Road 410 runs south through the fertile plain of the Mae Nam Pattani, dense rain forest and undulating hills. The splendid scenery is very rewarding.

Nam Tok Than To Forest Park – *55km from Yala. At Km 57 turn left and continue for 1km along a track. Park office, accommodation.* The forest park, which covers 1.6sq km and extends across the border into Malaysia, is the last remnant of the rain forest with rare fauna and flora. There are several waterfalls including a nine-tiered one, trails, hides and a lake with salas.

Bang Lang Dam and Than To Lake – *80km from Yala by 410 in Ban Bang Lang, Tambon Bacho, Amphoe Ban Nang Seta. At Km 46-47 turn left into good road and continue for 12km.* The picturesque lake formed by the dam across the Mae Nam Pattani is framed by beautiful mountain scenery. The winding road affords wonderful **views**★★★. Boat hire, accommodation.

Sakai Village – *70km from Yala, Mu 3, Tambon Ban Rae, Than To. Turn right and continue for 4.5km along a dirt road (difficult).* The Sakai *(see INTRODUCTION – Population)*, a Negrito people, still enjoy a traditional life in primitive huts in the jungle (20-30 households tending small vegetable patches and searching for medicinal roots and trees). Under a development project to help them adjust to the modern world, some work as tappers on rubber plantations.

Betong – This prosperous border town located on a mountain ridge has a cool climate and is often wreathed in mist. It has a large and dynamic Chinese population and attracts many visitors from Malaysia and Singapore. Of interest in the town are the Clock Tower, a large pillar box and a municipal park on the hill which boasts an aviary, zoo and stadium. Climb a stairway decorated with mythical sculptures (kinari, khotchasi, naga, hamsa) to Phiromthat Pavilion for views of the town. A mosque serves a sizeable Muslim community. A curious sight at certain times of the year is the large number of migrating swallows from Siberia which descend on Betong.

Wat Phutthatiwat – *Thanon Ratanakit – east.* A stupa in modified Srivijaya style was built to mark Queen Sirikit's 60th birthday. Note the two-tiered balustraded base, niches containing statues surmounted by four small chedis, and the tall annular bell shape topped by a delicate spire. Fine viharas and an elegant ubosot stand in the temple compound.

Piya Mit Underground Shelter – *19km north, 3km from Nam Tok Inthanason.* Take a short break at Nam Tok Inthanason in a lush forest setting.

A path *(stiff climb)* leads to an underground bunker on a hillside in the jungle built by Communist guerrillas. The network of tunnels and spartan conditions are evidence of amazing ingenuity and endurance.

PATTAYA★

Chonburi – Population 75 178

Michelin Atlas p 17 or Map 965 – I 5 – Town plan Atlas p 34

A spectacular curving **bay★★★** fringed with a long sandy beach sheltered by a rocky headland and steep cliffs forms a perfect setting for this hugely popular resort, which is a far cry from the sleepy fishing village of bygone days. Pattaya which is now easily accessible from Bangkok by the fast Sukhumvit Highway (H3) offers ample accommodation and facilities to suit all tastes and pockets, and boasts amusement and theme parks and golf courses of international standard. All types of water-sports are on offer, as well as boat trips to offshore islands (Ko Lam, Ko Lin, Ko Krok) with their beautiful beaches and coral reefs.

A new image – A determined attempt is being made by the local authorities to change the licentious image of Pattaya gained during the Vietnam War when servicemen from US bases at nearby U-Taphao flocked to the area for entertainment, and to repair the environmental damage caused by uncontrolled expansion in the past decades. Although Pattaya is still famous for its exotic night-life (go-go bars, transvestite shows, nightclubs and discotheques), the resort is being promoted for its beach attractions, sunny climate and tropical vegetation. High-rise condominiums springing up past Hat Jomtien herald a new development trend, in stark contrast to the quaint fishing village of **Bang Sare** (*Km 165-166 south* – seafood restaurants) further along the coast.

Summer Festival

The resort celebrates summer with gusto. Holidaymakers participate in a festival which is held in April and includes a colourful procession of fruit and floral floats, pleasing beauty pageants, inviting food stalls and a spectacular fireworks display on the beach.

Town – The heart of the resort is served by two main roads linked by alleyways and lined with countless shops, hotels and restaurants catering for an international clientele. There is a lively night-life with non-stop entertainment especially in the northern part of town. The shady beach esplanade affords a fine view of the popular beach and of the bay. The best **view★★★** of the marvellous setting, however, is from the Royal Cliff hotel *(south)* which backs onto Pattaya Hill.

EXCURSIONS

★**Hat Jomtien** – *2km south by the beach road.* The long sandy beach is ideal for holidaymakers who enjoy sun, sea and sand, and peace and relaxation.

Mini Siam ○ – *3km north by 3. Turn right at Km 143.* The wonders of Thailand in miniature (over 100 models) illustrating its rich cultural heritage and ranging from ancient times to the present are displayed in a fine landscaped park. A section is devoted to European architectural masterpieces.

Million-Year Stone Park ○ – *9km north by 3. Turn right into 3420.* Amazing rock formations are the highlight of this garden planted with bonsai specimens. There is a also a crocodile farm (over 1 000 reptiles). Shows.

Wat Yansangwararam – *12km southeast by 3, then turn left and proceed for 9.8km.* The meditation temple

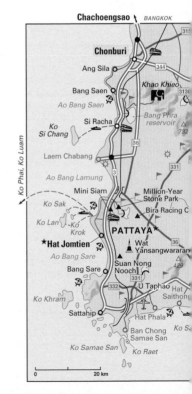

Pattaya by night

which features buildings in various styles in beautiful grounds is famous for its promotion of modern Thai architecture. The main sanctuary is high up on a hill, while on the far side of the lake rises **Wihan Sian** ⊙, a Taoist temple richly decorated in red and gold, which displays precious antiques and art objects from China.

Suan Nong Nooch ⊙ – *15km southeast by 3. Turn left at Km 163.* The beautiful garden offers entertainment for all ages: orchids, ferns, cacti, waterfalls, lake, Thai houses *(accommodation available)*, tropical birds, elephant shows and rides, and traditional dance.

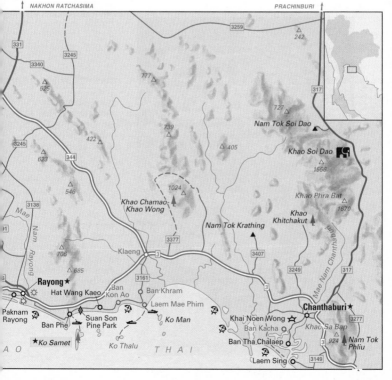

Out and about

Tourism Authority of Thailand (TAT) – 382/1 Mu 10, Thanon Chai Hat (Beach Road), Tambon Nong Prue, Amphoe Bang Lamung, Chonburi 20260. ☎ 038 467 667, 038 428 750. Fax 038 429 113.

Tourist Police – As above. ☎ 1155, 038 425 937, 038 429 371.

Transport – Regular services by air, rail and bus operate to and from Pattaya. **Thai International Airways** – ☎ 038 603 185. U-Taphao Airport, Sattahip – ☎ 038 603 185.
Bangkok Airways, Domestic Representative, Royal Garden Hotel – ☎ 038 411 965.
Bus Terminal – Pattaya North Road. Departures for Bangkok (Ekamai Terminal, Thanon Sukhumwit; Mor Chit, Thanon Phahonyothin) daily, every 20-30min from 5.30am to 9pm.
Buses to Bangkok airport, every 2 hours from 7am to 5pm.
Railway Station – Off the road to Siam Country Club, turn left just before the railway. ☎ 038 429 285. Si Racha Railway Station, east side of Si Racha off 3241 next to Worrarit Village.

Sightseeing – It is easy to get around Pattaya and environs.
By bus – **Minibuses** ply the bay area for a set fare of 5 Baht. Jump on, call out the destination, and pay the fare when you leave the bus. Beyond the bay area, fares range from 10 Baht to Naklua, 30 Baht to Hat Jomtien, to 40 Baht to Royal Cliff Hotel.
By motorcycle and bicycle – A licence is required to ride a motorcycle. Check the vehicle carefully and take special note of insurance cover. Take great care on the road. Bicycles are fun and cheap. Both for hire from vendors on the beach road: motorcycle 500 Baht per day, bicycle 100 Baht per day or 20 Baht per hour.
By car – There are several reputable car rental agencies: **Avis** at Dusit Resort; VIA Rent a Car, opposite Royal Garden Hotel, Pattaya Road II, ☎ 038 426 242.

Entertainment – **Seafood restaurants** – Thanon Pattaya Tai, South Pattaya. Also at Bang Sare to the south.
Bars, nightclubs, discos – Pattaya Nua and Pattaya Klang.

Sports – Enthusiasts will delight in the facilities available in Pattaya.
Golf – There are several golf courses around Pattaya and the east coast.
Bowling – Three bowling alleys open from 10am to midnight.
Bungee Jumping – The Bungee Jump is 52m high. Kiwi Thai Bungee Jump, 191 Thanon Thepphaya. Open 1pm- 9pm. ☎ 038 427 849.
Go-karts – 400m-track open daily, 10am-6pm. 1080m-track at Bira International Circuit.

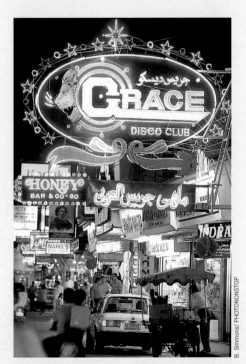

Night-life, Pattaya

B. Simmons/ PHOTONONSTOP

Motor Racing – Bira International Circuit (Km 14 on 36). Racing at weekends – admission charge; surcharge for international events (Formula 3). The track is also open to amateurs.
Horse riding – The Horse Sport Centre (Km 11 on 36 opposite the Bira International Circuit).
Water-sports – Sailing, scuba diving, boat hire, windsurfing, water-skiing from sports centres along the beach road and at Hat Jomtien.
Deep Sea Fishing – Fishing clubs organise trips for anglers. Boat charters are also available.
Parasailing – For hire on the beach.

Excursions – Nong Nooch Tropical Garden, Mini Siam, boat trips to the islands in the bay. **Day trips** to Bangkok, Rayong. **2-day trip** to Kanchanaburi.

Where to eat

P.I.C. Kitchen – Soi 5, North Pattaya. ☎ 038 428 374. Classical Thai-style dining, eclectic Thai and European menu using fresh produce.

Lobster Pot – 228 Beach Road, South Pattaya. ☎ 038 426 083. Open-air terrace restaurant by the sea. Seafood specialities.

Marco Polo – Montien Hotel Pattaya *(see below)*. ☎ 038 428 155/6. A fine establishment offering many Chinese specialities.

Where to stay

Budget

The Merlin Pattaya – 429 Moo 9, Pattaya Beach Road. ☎ 038 428 755-9, 02 255 7611-5; Fax 038 421 673, 02 254 8570; merlinpy@loxinfo.co.th; www.merlinpattaya.com; 2 200-2 700 Baht. A comfortable hotel with sea views, garden and good facilities a short distance from the beach.

Best Western Baiyoke Pattaya – 557 Moo 10, Thanon Prathamnak, South Pattaya. ☎ 038 423 300, 02 656 3000; Fax 038 426 124, 02 656 3905; bayokpattaya@baiyoke.co.th; 1 400-2 400 Baht. A fine modern hotel with sea views, garden and restaurants.

Island View Hotel – 410 Moo 12, Cliff Beach Road. ☎ 038 250 813-5, 02 249 8941/2; Fax 038 250 818, 02 249 8943; 950-1 200+Baht. Comfortable accommodation with pool, garden and sea views.

Moderate

Montien Hotel Pattaya – 369 Moo 9, Pattaya Second Road. ☎ 038 428 155/6; Fax 038 428 155; pattaya@montien.com; www.montien.com; 3 000-13 600 Baht. A pleasant modern hotel with restaurants, pool and garden, not far from the beach.

Amari Orchid Pattaya – 240 Moo 5, Beach Road, North Pattaya. ☎ 038 428 161, 02 255 3960; Fax 038 428 165, 02 655 5707, orchid@amari.com; www.amari.com; US$ 120-270. Excellent accommodation and facilities near the beach, beautiful gardens.

Siam Bayview Hotel – 310/2 Moo 10, Pattaya Beach Road. ☎ 038 423 871-7, 02 247 0120-30; Fax 038 423 879, 02 247 0178; siambayview @siamhotels.com; www.siamhotels.com; 2 500-10 500 Baht. Fine accommodation, sea views, restaurants, health club.

Sugar Hut – 391/19 Moo 10, Jomtien Road. ☎ 038 251 686-8; Fax 038 225 514; 2 500-5 000 Baht. Delightful Thai houses and restaurant in a luxuriant garden setting.

Expensive

Royal Cliff Beach Hotel – 353 Thanon Prathamnak. ☎ 038 250 421-40; Fax 038 250 511/513; info@royalcliff.com; www.royalcliff.com; 5 500-13 000 Baht. A smart hotel with private beach, magnificent sea views and superb facilities.

Dusit Resort Pattaya – 240/2 Pattaya Beach Road. ☎ 038 425 611-7, 02 636 3600 Ext 4521; Fax 038 428 239, 02 636 3571; pattaya@dusit.com; www.dusit.com; 2 800-16 000 Baht. A superb beach hotel offering luxury accommodation, health club, restaurants and gardens

Jomtien Palm Beach – 408 Moo 12, Jomtien Beach Road. ☎ 038 231 350-68, 02 254 1865-68; Fax 038 231 369, 02 254 1869; 3 200-20 000 Baht. An elegant beach hotel in a delightful setting with excellent facilities.

Ao PHANGNGA★★★

Phangnga

Michelin Atlas p 20 or Map 965 – M 3 – Local map see Phuket

The dramatic scenery of Phangnga Bay, which has been declared a national park (400sq km), ranks among the geological wonders of Southeast Asia. A multitude of spectacular limestone outcrops (over 40 islets) shaped by erosion jutting out of the shimmering waters arouses a sense of wonder; and a tour of the bay to discover sheer cliffs pitted with caves bristling with stalactites, jagged monoliths and strange animal shapes and arches carved by the sea, is a memorable experience. Abundant plant life and fauna thrive in the mangrove swamps and on the cliff faces.

TOUR ⊘ *1/2 day.*

Only some islands easy to visit are described below. Exciting discoveries await visitors with more time to spare.

As the boat glides along the river channel lined with lush mangrove, there is a splendid **view★★** north of the mountains framing the town.

Ko Tapu

On a cave wall **(Khao Khian)** near the river mouth, unusual **rock paintings** in black and ochre of crocodiles, fish, dolphins and humans are evidence of early occupation of the area. A natural arch gives access to **Tham Lot** *(in a side channel to the left behind Ko Panyi)* where curtains of stalactites hang from the vault.

Ko Machu is a fantastic rock formation resembling a small dog perched on a hilltop. A colourful Muslim fishing village (500 households) nestles at the base of **Ko Panyi**. The people show remarkable ingenuity in building their houses on stilts linked by wooden bridges. There is one school in the village, and a plot of land with a mosque and burial ground. Fishing and shrimp farming are the main activities and tourism is a profitable source of income. Restaurants offer delectable fare (seafood) and shops supply all necessities.

The twin islets of **Ko Nom Sao,** also called Ko Ok Meri, are outlined on the horizon. The eroded middle section of **Ko Talu** allows boats to pass through a cave filled with stalactites and emerge on the other side.

Ko Khao Ping Kan boasts towering cliffs including a massive rock split in two, one slab leaning precariously against the other. A staircase leads up to a cave and there is a fine beach.

With its narrow base and broad peak **Ko Tapu** is shaped like a spike, hence its evocative name Nail Island. The fantastic setting known to millions from the popular film, *The Man with the Golden Gun,* is overrun with visitors at certain times.

Ko Yao Yai – *2-hour boat trip from Phangnga Custom House.* Although the island is blessed with fine beaches and scenery, there are few facilities for tourists. The main activity is pearl farming.

ADDITIONAL SIGHTS

Phangnga Town – The pleasant town lies in a picturesque setting in a valley framed by limestone mountains. The old Chinese quarter by the river and the fine Sala Klang (Provincial Hall) off the main road are noteworthy.

The mountains in the vicinity are riddled with caves which have been turned into Buddhist shrines, and waterfalls tumble down the high cliffs.

Tham Russisawan – *2km before turning to Custom House.* A park gives access to a labyrinth of caves filled with dripstones guarded by a revered hermit formation near the entrance.

Tham Pong Chang – *Behind Wat Phra Pat Prajimkhet. Short tour in a dark tunnel with lamp.* The cave-shrine lies at the foot of Khao Chang (mountain of the elephants, named after its shape). Inside are statues of three sacred elephants. An underground stream surges behind the cave.

EXCURSIONS

★★ Tham Suwan Khuha – *Amphoe Takua Thung, 7km southwest by 4 from Phangnga or 30km northwest from Ban Khoke Kloi.* A palm-lined track leads past a modern temple to a spectacular cave-sanctuary lit from a natural opening and containing several statues. Near the entrance a **midden** provides a record of prehistoric settlement. Steps at the far end lead to a half-vaulted cave with an opening to the right. Beyond a small chedi a vast **chamber** opens out containing splendid concretions. Leave by the half-vaulted chamber and take a path through rocks and vegetation back to the main entrance.

Road No 4 to Krabi crosses Mae Nam Phangnga and climbs north then turns east to a pass, which gives a fine **view** (to the rear) of the valley and mountains. The road then dips through magnificent scenery of forest and dolomitic rocks. Further on are the Ao Luk limestone peaks, fantastically-shaped isolated outcrops rising above the forest.

25km from Phangnga take 4039 towards Laem Sak, a small fishing port. Past a bridge at Km 9 turn right into a laterite road, then left at brown sign to a pier. 20min boat trip to the caves.

Tham Lot – The boat trip is a pleasant run along the river lined with lush mangrove and limestone peaks to a vast vaulted cave with dramatic dripstones.

★**Tham Phi Hua To** – From the landing-stage climb up to the chambers which contain evocative **rock paintings** in black and ochre depicting animals, figures and two hands (one with five fingers, the other six). Prehistoric human bones have also been found. The cave overlooks the verdant scenery.

Prasat Hin PHANOM RUNG★★★
Buriram
Michelin Atlas p 14 or Map 965 – G 7 – Local map see Nakhon Ratchasima (Khorat)

Access: From Buriram about 80km south by 218 or 219 then left or right into 24, turn at Ban Ta Ko between Km 83-84, continue for 12km then take 2117 to Ban Ta Pek for 5.5km and 2221 for 7km.

In a dramatic **setting**★★ high up atop an extinct volcano, Prasat Hin Phanom Rung (the name means great mountain) dominates the forested landscape. The distinctive "stone castle" *(prasat hin)* is one of the most important Khmer monuments on the route between Angkor and Phimai; it is an architectural masterpiece, the most advanced to be found in Thailand. The craftsmanship and the narrative quality of the decorative elements (lintels, pediments, door-frames, mouldings, pilasters, antefixes) are outstanding.

Prasat Hin Phanom Rung

Prasat Hin
PHANOM RUNG

0 ————— 50 m

1	Naga bridge	5	Ruined prangs
2	Ponds	6	Mandapa
3	Gopuras	7	Antarala
4	Libraries	8	Garbhagrha

N→

3

Prang Noi — 8 **SANCTUARY ★★★**

3 7 3

5

6 4

4

★★EASTERN GOPURA

1

2

NAGA BRIDGE ★★

Avenue

Royal

Plabpla

ℹ️🅿️✕↓ Museum

214

Historical notes —

Inscriptions found on the site provide evidence that this was a place of worship for many centuries prior to the building of the temple in the 10C. It was remodelled and dedicated to Shiva and Vishnu in the 12C by the Khmer ruler Narendraditya, who became an ascetic and retired to the monastery, and by his son Hiranya. Steles and bas-reliefs record the ruler's campaigns during the reign of Suryavarman II (1112-52). Further additions were made in the 13C but it was abandoned at the fall of the Khmer empire.

A 17-year restoration programme — using the anastylosis method which consists of rebuilding with original material using original techniques — by Thai and foreign experts under the aegis of the Fine Arts Department was completed in 1988, when the site was officially opened as a historical park.

TOUR ⏱ 1 1/2 hours

Royal Avenue — The processional way (7m wide and 160m long), which dates from the 12C and is lined with sandstone columns crowned with lotus-bud finials, leads to a cruciform platform at the bottom of the steps to the temple. The galleried building to the north, known as the Plabpla (White Elephant Pavilion), is wrongly believed to be the king's stables but was probably used for robing.

Ascent — The great **Naga bridge★★** symbolises the link between the world of man and that of the gods. The balustrades are formed by the bodies of the nagas with the finely-carved crowned heads rising at the corners. Steps on the north and south also give access to the platform. Five sets of steps rise steeply to a wide terrace, which affords an extensive **view★★** of the vast plain to the north and of the wooded slopes of the Dong Rak range to the south. Four ceremonial ponds probably symbolise the four sacred rivers in the Hindu tradition. Another naga bridge has an unusual feature: the naga heads spout from the mouth of a fearsome makara whose body forms the balustrade.

Precinct – The walled galleries pierced by four entrances *(gopuras)* and divided into cells enclose the great sanctuary. In the large inner courtyard stand the imposing main sanctuary tapering in the shape of a lotus bud and crowned by a fine vase of plenty *(kalasa)*, two libraries *(northeast and southeast)*, two ruined 10C brick prangs *(northeast)*, and a small tower, Prang Noi, in the southwest corner.

Entrance – The cruciform eastern **gopura**★★ roofed with stone tiles and decorated with finials has three entrances; the central doorway was reserved for dignitaries while the other two entrances were for less important visitors. The remarkable eastern **pediment**★★ *(front)* features Shiva as an ascetic with female attendants, while the unfinished one at the back bears incised marks. A vivid battle scene between monkeys and yaksas from the Ramayana epic tale adorns the eastern gallery.

Pass into the large enclosure and walk to the main sanctuary.

★★★**Sanctuary** – The entrance with cruciform porches leads into an antechamber *(mandapa)* linked by a passageway *(antarala)* to the shrine *(garbhagrha)* above which rises the main tower.

Exterior – *Walk anticlockwise round the sanctuary.* The splendid **pediment**★★ above the entrance depicts Shiva with his ten arms fanned out in a cosmic dance; on the admirable **lintel**★★ below, Vishnu reclines on the back of the Naga king which is in turn lying on a dragon in the milky ocean; a lotus sprouting from his navel supports Brahma the creator; to the right are two finely carved parrots. The lintel, which had been stolen from the temple many years ago, came to light in America; it was returned to Thailand in 1988.

On the north side are depicted scenes from the Ramayana which are full of movement: a flock of birds flying above a monkey troop attacking demons (mandapa), the abduction of Sita and a mythical bird at the top (antarala).

Above the west door the pediment portrays the abduction of Sita in a chariot, which is a miniature replica of the central tower, carried on the backs of monkeys; on the lintel Rama and Lakhsmana are caught in the coils of the serpent Nagapasa.

An attendant guards the south portico which was probably the entrance to the inner sanctum. The pediments depict scenes of battles probably fought by the ruler Narendraditya, and above the southern entrance of the mandapa Shiva and his consort Uma riding on the bull Nandin, which has suffered much damage.

In the southwest corner **Prang Noi** is a square structure built of pink sandstone, with delicate floral motifs in the Khleang and Baphuon style on the lintels and pediment.

Interior – Lotus flowers adorn the door sill of the mandapa and on the interior lintel of the antarala five ascetics *(rishis)* guard the access to the shrine, which probably contained a Shiva linga. In the floor can be seen the *somasutra*, the pipe for draining lustral waters poured over the linga, which runs through the chamber and beneath the courtyard to emerge outside the gallery on the north side.

PHATTHALUNG★

Phatthalung – Population 124 578

Michelin Atlas p 22 or Map 965 – N 5 – Local map see Nakhon Si Thammarat

The Phatthalung plain is dominated by two towering cliffs honeycombed with caves – **Khao Ok Thalu** (mountain of the pierced heart) with a deep hole through it, and **Khao Hua Taek** (mountain of the split head) with one side split. The colourful names relate to a local legend, a sad story of jealousy and vengeance about a wife and a mistress who fought over an unfaithful husband (Khao Muang to the north); they were all turned to stone as a punishment.

East of the town a large freshwater lake separated from the Gulf of Thailand by a strip of land is a distinctive natural feature. Lush ricefields surround Phatthalung, the only rice-growing province in the south.

There are few sights of interest except for a colourful market *(turn left by a bank into Thanon Posarat)* in the small town which is the provincial capital but it is well worth exploring the surrounding area.

Phatthalung is famous for the original shadow play *(nang talung)* which survives here and in Nakhon Si Thammarat. A typical performance starts at midnight and lasts four to five hours – usually during temple fairs *(ngaan wàt)*.

Thale Noi

EXCURSIONS

Wat Khuha Sawan – *1km west by 4018 or 41 towards Khuan Khanun; by Thanon Khuhasawan from the railway station.* Behind the temple, steps lead to a cave lit by a natural arch and housing numerous seated or reclining Buddha statues under a copper bodhi tree. There is a smaller hermit cave nearby to the right. A hillside trail *(right of main cave)* leads to a chedi high up on the cliffs for a fine **view** of the mountains *(west)*, the rice fields in the plain, and Thale Luang *(east)*.

Tham Malai – *3km north. Access by boat from behind the railway station (15min) or take Thanon Nivas and continue by a laterite road to the foot of a hill. Take a torch.* Steps lead up to a platform with a shrine near which is a large cave with several chambers bristling with white concretions. Visitors will enjoy wonderful views of the picturesque limestone peaks.

★★**Thale Noi Waterfowl Park** – *32km northeast by 41 and 4048.* A shallow fresh-water lake and marsh (30sq km, depth 1-1.5m) which attracts over 100 species of water birds such as cormorants, herons, egrets, storks and ducks, and supports an abundant aquatic life; these are best viewed in the early morning (observation platform). There is a rich variety of reeds and water-lilies. Thale Noi is a glorious sight from March to May when the entire lake turns pink with water lilies. This birdwatchers' paradise is part of a non-hunting area which covers 457sq km. Near the park is a village where the craft of reed weaving is kept alive. Colourful bags and mats are on sale locally.

Wat Wang – *7km east by 4087.* The "palace" temple (the palace of a prince stood east of the wat; only the wall remains) is over 100 years old. An old chedi stands in the courtyard. The ubosot contains mural paintings dated *c* late 18C.
Opposite is **Wat Wihan Buk** which also has mural paintings of the same period.

Old Governor's Residence ⊙ – *A short distance further on the right.* The mansion stands in a pleasant garden setting overlooking a canal. The old palace *(near the entrance)* comprises a group of traditional Thai-style houses on piles, made entirely of wood and roofed with coloured glazed tiles. The new palace is built in a composite Thai-Chinese style and there is a sala by the canal.

Thale Luang – *15km east by 4047.* There is a fishing village on the banks of the lake at the northern end of Songkhla Lake. The long beach of Hat Sansuk which is lined with pine trees and has a fine view of the islands in the lake is a popular recreation area with food stalls and refreshments.

Thermal springs – *Khao Chaison 20km south by 41 and local road east.* Along the road south a detour can be made to several waterfalls. Hot (at the foot of a hill) and cold (nearby) springs *(1km from Amphoe Office)* are of interest.
Continue to the long sandy beach, Hat Khaï Tao, where giant tortoises lay their eggs in October and November each year.

PHAYAO★

Phayao – Population 129 625

Michelin Atlas p 3 or Map 965 – B 4

Although off the beaten track the peaceful town enjoys a pleasant location on the east bank of a large lake dominated by **Doi Bussarakam** (alt 1 856m) and is of great historical interest. The shallow lake is a great natural resource and is well-stocked with fish; the esplanade along the shore is a popular place for relaxation. Open-air restaurants and boat trips on the lake are added attractions.

Historical notes – Archeological evidence suggests that there was a Bronze Age settlement by the lakeside. In the 11C Phayao was a sovereign kingdom – a monument by the lake commemorates **King Ngam Muang**, a 13C ruler and a friend of King Mengrai of Lanna – which was annexed in 1338 to the Kingdom of Lanna and ruled from Chiang Mai. There are ruins of a 13C moated town, Wiang Lo, to the northeast near Chun. War with Burma caused the town to be abandoned until the mid 19C, when it was repopulated by migrants from Lampang and ruled by a prince of the Kavila dynasty. Phayao developed an artistic style which was classed until recently as a secondary trend of the Lanna school. It is now recognised as an independent school, perhaps the oldest typically-Thai school of art. The Buddha images carved from sandstone have pointed features, full lips and tight curls.

SIGHTS

★★**Wat Si Khom Kham** – *1km the north of the town centre.* It is one of the principal sanctuaries in Northern Thailand. A large building (1923) with a beautiful gable enhanced with carving, gilding, lacquer and glass mosaic replaces the original open vihara. A huge **Buddha image** (*c* 15C) sits directly on the ground probably following a tradition of the Phayao school. In the courtyard there is a collection of Buddha images of the Phayao school. A small sala *(in front of the vihara)* contains a twin **Buddha footprint★** (late-14C) carved in stone and noted for the very fine depiction of a celestial being.

To the west a bridge gives access to a new **ubosot★★** built in the modern Lanna style with the contribution of renowned Thai artists. The gable is decorated with intricate wood carving and glass mosaic. The slit windows and door panel were designed by Angkran Kalayanapong; he is also responsible for some of the delicate mural paintings, notably on the wall behind the altar. The exquisite **wall paintings★★** by Phabtawan Suwannakut depict the Buddhist Jataka executed in a composite Lanna-Bangkok style. The pure lines, bright colours and fine draughtsmanship break new ground by combining ancient values with a modern idiom.

Wat Doi Chom Thong – *1.5km north of Wat Si Khom Kham.* The temple atop Doi Chom Thong is notable for a white Lanna chedi on a high redented square base, an open vihara with a Lao-style Buddha image, and old lotus-shaped bai semas. Fine **view★** of Phayao nestling by the lake.

Phayao Lake

Wat Luang Ratcha Santhan – *Near the market.* Interesting buildings at the temple (*c* 12C) include a **vihara** with a two-tiered roof covered with terracotta tiles, massive pillars supporting the roof, and wooden shutters; and a white **chedi** on a stepped platform with an indented relic chamber pierced by gabled niches housing Buddha images.

Wat Si Umong Kham – *Thanon Tha Kwan.* Near the Lanna (Chiang Saen) chedi stands the ubosot which contains a very fine Lanna (Chiang Saen) **Buddha image**, the venerated Phra Chao Lan Toe.

EXCURSIONS

Wat Pa Daeng Bunnag – *Ban Rong Ha. North by 1 and turn right into a small road for access to the temple.* The oldest place of worship in Phayao comprises Wat Pa Daeng and Wat Bunnag. The Sinhalese-style **chedi★** stands on a high square base, and lotus-shaped bai semas mark the site of the cloistered vihara.

★ **Wat Analayo** – *33km northwest. Take 1 north for 20km then turn left into 1123 for 13km. Drive up to the car park.* A staircase flanked by a naga balustrade ascends to the top of Doi Bussarakam, crowned by a temple famous as a meditation centre. Excellent **views★★** of Phayao town and lake may be enjoyed from the summit.
Within the compound are several viharas and chedis in varied styles derived from Lanna, Sukhothai, India and China. A vihara contains a collection of gold regalia, offerings of the faithful. A large concrete Buddha image (18m high) is depicted in the pose of subduing Mara. There are also Chinese-style Bodhisattvas and a white chedi inspired from Bhod-Gaya in India.

Doi Luang National Park – *60km west by 1 and 120 and turn right into 1033 and continue for 25km* – The winding scenic route which skirts the southern end of the park affords wonderful **views** (viewpoint between Km 20-21) of Phayao lake and of the forested valleys and slopes. There are hot springs and waterfalls in the park which is a wildlife sanctuary.

PHETCHABUN

Phetchabun – Population 226 420

Michelin Atlas p 8 or Map 965 – E 6

The sprawling provincial capital is framed by forested mountain ranges which dominate the narrow valley watered by the Mae Nam Pasak. Its favourable location on an important trading route to the northern territories was recognised from the early days of the Sukhothai kingdom. The fertile alluvial soil is ideal for agriculture (tobacco, rice, maize, market gardening, fruit and flowers, cattle) which flourishes in the cool climate.

Town – **Wat Mahathat** *(Thanon Nikhon Damrung, opposite the Technical School),* which dates from the foundation of the town, boasts a tall Sukhothai-style chedi topped by a lotus bud, with two smaller chedis in front and a restored vihara. **Wat Trai Phum** *(Thanon Phetcharat, near the city moat)* houses a Lopburi-style Buddha image found in the Mae Nam Pasak and celebrated at a yearly festival. On the outskirts of the town, **Huai Pa Daeng Dam** *(north by 21, turn left into 2006 and continue for 8km)* and **Phra Muang Botanical Garden** are pleasant recreation spots in a beautiful mountain landscape.

EXCURSIONS

Tham Russi Sombat – *36km north by 21, turn left between Km 251-252 into 2011 and continue for 4km.* A cave bristling with dripstones and with a network of tunnels was the secret cache for the country's gold reserve, at the time of the Japanese occupation of Thailand during the Second World War.

Phu Hin Rong Kla National Park – *70km west by 12, turn right at Ban Yang junction into 2013 for 28km, then right again and proceed for 31km to the park headquarters.* The road affords spectacular **views★★** of the lush vegetation and undulating peaks. The park which straddles the boundaries of three provinces opened in 1984 after years of armed conflict (1968-72). Displays at a **Combat Museum and Tourist Information Centre** *(near the park office)* illustrate the ingenious methods used to overcome the hardships endured by recruits to the Communist Party of Thailand (CPT), which had established its headquarters and trained its army in the densely forested mountain fastnesses. A marked path *(time 2hr)* leads round the self-supporting camp *(3km southwest of the park)* set up on the cliff top. The village comprised a hospital, a water mill, a gaol, a machine repair shop, a political and military school, a cemetery and air-raid shelters, among other amenities.

Khao Kho – *13km north by 21, turn left at Na Ngu intersection between Km 236-237 and take 2258 for 30km. Or by 12 turn at Km 100 and take 2196 for 33km.* The lower Phetchabun range including Khao Kho (alt 1 174m), Khao Ya (1 290m) and Khao Yai (865m) is an isolated area with wonderful rugged scenery. The mountainous terrain was the scene of fierce battles with terrorist guerrillas.
A **memorial** *(at Km 23 on 2196)* commemorates the Nationalist Chinese Kuomintang volunteers recruited to the government cause. Turn right at Km 28 into 2323 and climb to Than Ithi, the stronghold of government forces, where a **museum** displays

weapons, gun emplacements, planes, helicopters and other artefacts used on the battlefield. A splendid **panorama**★★ of the surrounding peaks unfolds from the mountain top. 1km further stands a marble pyramid, the **Khao Kho memorial** to those who lost their lives in the armed conflict.

At **Si Dit waterfall** *(by 2196 turn at Km 18 and continue by 2325 for 10km)* the wheels of a hydraulic mill used to crush rice remain as evidence of terrorist ingenuity.

A beautiful garden enhances the unusual semicircular plan of the **Khao Kho Pavilion** *(at Khao Ya by 2196, at the Sa Dao Pong intersection turn right and take 2258, then turn left into a steep road)* which affords distant **views**★★ of the Khao Kho memorial and library, and of the rolling mountains.

Proceed to the **miracle mound** *(stop on the line at Km 17.5 on 2258)* to experience an unusual optical illusion.

The **scenic road**★★ (12) linking Khon Kaen to Phitsanulok winds through gently rounded summits clad with lush vegetation, and descends into a verdant plain passing Thung Phaya and **Thung Salaeng Luang,** a region of limestone hills with dense forest, meadows of savannah grass, waterfalls and exotic fauna and flora. The Hmong (Meo) have been settled in villages (alt 900-1 500m) along the road and are engaged in agriculture in an attempt to change their nomadic ways.

Further along at Km 68 a track *(left)* through the forest leads to the impressive three-tiered **Nam Tok Kaeng Sopha**★★ which cascades down huge limestone slabs. Another fine sight is Nam Tok Kaeng Song *(Km 44)*. Sakunothayan Botanical Garden *(Km 33)* by the Mae Nam Khek is a popular recreation spot with waterfalls (Nam Tok Wang Nok Aen), shady paths and picnic areas.

★Si Thep Historical Park

107km south by 21 from Phetchabun. At Km 100 turn right into 2211 and continue for 9km.

The ruined city girt by two concentric walls and moats first came to light in the late 19C, and was excavated in 1935 and again more recently. It lies in a strategic location in the Mae Nam Pasak basin, at a crossroads between the cities in the central plain and those in the north and northeast of the country.

The numerous sites and ponds inside and outside the city walls indicate that Si Thep was undoubtedly densely populated, from the early Dvaravati period in the 7C to the 13C when the Khmers deserted the city. The inner town is probably the older settlement which expanded outside the boundary.

Site – A naga bridge facing west gives access to the historical park. Near the entrance to the right stands the Chao Po Si Thep spirit shrine. A visitor centre displays photographs of the archeological survey and finds. Excavations at a **burial site** *(northwest of the visitor centre)* have uncovered five skeletons. The most complete is that of a woman wearing a bronze bracelet and cornelian necklace. Also on view are the bones of an elephant (2m long) which probably died in a ceremony or during the construction of the shrine. A wide **ceremonial way** paved in laterite leads to the temple buildings.

Small Prangs – The two west-facing structures built of brick without mortar (Prang Song Pi and Prang Nong) show the influence of Dvaravati Buddhism which flourished in the 7C-8C.

Prang Si Thep – The small square brick prang with a porch on each side on a cruciform sandstone base probably dates from the 11C-12C. It retains its original wooden beams, Khmer arch, and a triangular recess housing a wooden statue of Vishnu. The sandstone lotus-shaped crown lies nearby.

Khao Klang Nai – The large rectangular structure with steps on the east side was perhaps a warehouse for weapons, or a treasury. There are unusual **stucco motifs**★ along the base of the south wall. The most remarkable is a dwarf figure similar to one found at Ku Bua in Ratchaburi. A large Wheel of the Law fronts the ruined building to the east.

PHETCHABURI★★

Phetchaburi – Population 120 591

Michelin Atlas p 17 or Map 965 – H 4

A royal palace crowning Khao Wang, interesting temples of great artistic value from various periods and a lively atmosphere, as well as its proximity to the capital and easy access from the seaside resorts of Cha-am and Hua Hin on the road to the picturesque southern peninsula, all combine to make Phetchaburi an attractive destination. It is a pleasant town with wide, tree-lined avenues and fine traditional houses.

The Land of Diamonds – According to tradition the town derives its name from the sparkling diamonds which were to be found in the bed of the Mae Nam Phetchaburi. It was probably an important post on the trade route between India and China before being settled by the Mon (8C-11C). Religious monuments attest to the Khmer presence in the 13C until the founding of the Sukhothai kingdom, which was succeeded in the 14C-18C by the Ayutthaya empire. The latter enjoyed good trade relations with European powers. In the 19C-20C the healthy climate of Phetchaburi won special favour with Rama IV (King Mongkut) and Rama V (King Chulalongkorn), whose patronage is recalled by several imposing buildings.

★★PHRA NAKHON KHIRI ⊘

Access by cable-car or by a steep stairway from the Visitor Centre.

High up on the three peaks of Khao Wang, the Hill Palace (1859), where King Mongkut could escape the pressures of city life and enjoy his hobbies, comprises a temple *(east)*, a chedi *(centre)*, a mansion in neo-Classical style *(west)*, throne halls, an observatory, as well as a theatre, stables, guard-houses and ancillary buildings erected on the lower levels. The varied architectural styles are evidence of the eclectic royal interests. The site affords splendid **views★★★** over the town and of the lush landscape to the far horizon.

Phra Nakon Khiri

Valdin/ PHOTONONSTOP

Phra Nakhon Khiri National Museum ⊘ – The museum is housed in three royal pavilions: Phra Thinang Phetphum Phairot in neo-Classical style which was used as lodgings for royal guests; Phra Thinang Pramot Mahasawan, the royal suite, and Phra Thinang Wichien Prasat *(see below)*. Ceramics, sculptures and fine furnishings give a glimpse of the elegant way of life of the sovereigns.

Phra Thinang Wichien Prasat – Four ornate towers rise at the angles of the balustraded platform, on which stands a pavilion on a Greek-cross plan crowned by a small prang. It serves as a shrine and contains a bust and a statue of King Mongkut in formal dress. Stuccowork and gilded tracery ornament the gable and pediments.

Observatory – Walk past a large hall to the domed tower capped with a glass roof. Climb up the spiral staircase to the balustraded terrace where the king carried out his astronomical observations. The building served as a landmark for sailors.

Wat Phra Kaeo – Take the path leading to the east peak past an imposing **chedi** to the small harmonious temple which bears a resemblance to the royal temple in Bangkok. The doors and pediment of the **ubosot** are richly decorated. Also note-worthy are a fine chedi in grey marble, a prang in red sandstone and three pavilions. The terrace affords fine **views★★**.
The shady path back to the main entrance passes other residential and religious buildings and a theatre where entertainments were staged for the royal circle, dotted in the grounds.

TOWN CENTRE

★ **Wat Mahathat Worawihan** – *Thanon Damnoen Kasem.* The distinctive white prang of this temple which dates from the Ayutthaya period is visible from afar. The profusion of **stucco decoration** on the entrance doorway, the gables and the exterior of the viharas is remarkable. In the main courtyard note the base of a serene seated Buddha in U-Thong style highlighted in stucco and glass, and a redented chedi punctuated by niches housing Buddha images and crowned by four faces of Brahma at the base of the slim finial. A modern walking Buddha guards the entrance of **Wihan Luang;** vivid **mural paintings** adorn the interior. The tiered altar enshrines seated Buddha images and disciples – the largest is in the Ayutthaya style – and a Wheel of the Law. Fine **bai semas** of the U-Thong period housed in niches surround the chapel in the nearby courtyard. Pass into the enclosure dominated by the imposing Ayutthaya-style **prang**, framed by smaller prangs and guarded by demons. The niches and the gallery feature gilded Buddha images.

★★ **Wat Yai Suwannaram** – *Thanon Pongsuriya.* The 17C temple boasts fine wooden buildings of outstanding craftsmanship. The elegant raised **sala**★★ is noteworthy for its delicate roof brackets and decoration, and for its carved doors, one of which bears a gash from a Burmese attack. Rows of canted pillars support the roof; the interior retains traces of mural paintings. The harmonious wooden **ho trai** stands in the middle of a pond. The **mural paintings**★★ in the **ubosot** are renowned for their artistic and narrative quality and give a unique glimpse of 17C life in Ayutthaya and abundant details on the flora and fauna: the Buddha overcomes evil forces *(east wall)*, deities pay homage to the Buddha *(sides)*.

Wat Kamphaeng Laeng – *Thanon Phrasong. Continue past Wat Yai Suwannaram and turn right.* This ancient place of worship (12C) is the furthest point south of the Khmer sphere of influence in the country. A well-preserved **wall** surrounds a ruined central **prang** in the Lopburi style, preceded by a gopura and framed by three smaller prangs and minor structures. Few traces of the stucco decoration remain.

★ **Wat Ko Kaeo Suttharam** – *Thanon Boriphat, near the bridge.* A group of fine wooden buildings on stilts recalls traditional monastic scenes of olden times. Double **bai semas** surround the **ubosot** *(ask for the building to be opened)* preceded by a pillared porch. The gable and pediments are adorned with stucco floral motifs and celestial beings. The well-preserved 18C **mural paintings**★★ reveal great mastery and originality: Buddhist cosmology is unusually depicted on the east wall while the Victory over Evil fills the west wall. Some delightful scenes have a contemporary flavour and show Arab merchants, a Jesuit priest dressed as a Buddhist monk, and foreigners on horseback, among others.

Wat Yang – *Thanon Ratchadamnoen.* A row of redented **chedis** highlights the ubosot which is in the Ayutthaya style. Slender pillars capped by lotus capitals support the roof of the porch. Opposite is an elegant **ho trai** in a lotus pond. The temple has good modern buildings.

> The symbol of Phetchaburi is the sugar-palm tree. Its products are highly valued: palm sugar is essential for the delicious sweetmeats for which Phetchaburi is famous, the fruit is an important ingredient in Thai cuisine, the wood and leaves are used for furniture and craft items.
> Ban Khanom Thai, an establishment housed in a group of traditional buildings on the Phetchkasem Highway 4 *(east)*, is the place to taste these typical sweetmeats.

EXCURSIONS

★ **Tham Khao Luang** – *5km north from Khao Wang by 3173.* Steep steps descend into vast chambers bristling with wonderful concretions. A shaft of light illuminates an octagonal prang decorated with stucco, and a host of Buddha images including one in royal attire dedicated to King Mongkut by his son Rama V (King Chulalongkorn).

★ **Phra Ram Ratchaniwet** ⊘ – *South by Thanon Ratchadamnoen. Turn left at a sign.* Following the visit of Rama V (King Chulalongkorn) to Europe, he commissioned a summer palace in the neo-Baroque style modelled on the palace of the Kaiser; it was completed by Rama VI. The well-appointed audience halls and private apartments decorated in European style provided an elegant setting for the royal family.

★ **Khao Yoi** – *22km north by 4. Turn right to Wat Tham Khao Yoi.* The dolomitic hill is honeycombed by large caves with spectacular dripstones enshrining Buddha images in various postures in a dramatic setting. The principal cave, Tham Phra Non *(east cliff)*, is bathed in soft light and contains a huge reclining Buddha, a Buddha footprint and some 30 Buddha images. A steep stairway leads up to more caves.

Wat Kut Bang Khem – *20km north by 4. Make a U-turn after Km 130 then turn left into a lane for 800m. At an intersection turn right and proceed for 300m.* The wooden **ubosot★** of this village temple which probably dates from the 19C is an outstanding example of folk art. Floral motifs and scenes from the previous lives of the Buddha adorning the doors and wall panels are carved with great mastery and spirit. The wealth of detail imparts a sense of wonder.

★★**Kaeng Krachan Dam and National Park** ○ – *20km south by 4, at Tha Yang turn right at a sign and proceed for 49km to the park office and visitor centre by the lake. Easy access from Cha-am and Hua Hin. Allow 1 day.*

The road runs past fertile agricultural land and leads to two dams. Abundant streams and a river feed a vast lake which provides vital irrigation to the lowlands. Picturesque islands and a circle of rugged mountains add to its charm.

Thailand's largest national park (2 902sq km) extends to the Tenasserim range which culminates at 1 207m and is often wreathed in mist. It borders a wild tract of land in Myanmar and a wildlife sanctuary to the north, and is a successful conservation project initiated by King Bhumibol to protect this vital watershed from encroachments.

The park **scenery★★★** is spectacular: wild valleys, majestic peaks, dense rainforest, impressive **waterfalls** (Nam Tok Tho Thip, Nam Tok Pala-U) and caves. Abundant **wildlife** (banteng, gaur, barking deer, gibbons, pangolin, elephants, Asiatic black bears among others) thrives in the tropical forest, which resounds with the calls of rare birds such as hornbills, barbets, babblers, serpent eagles, etc. A sense of remoteness combined with the natural beauty make a visit to the park a wonderful experience.

Cha-am – *40km south by 4.* A popular resort with a long sandy beach fringed with sea-pines and ideal for relaxation. A temple at the north end boasts a monumental Buddha image, and further up the coast are typical fishing villages. To the south lies the elegant royal resort of **Hua Hin★★** *(see HUA HIN).*

PHICHIT

Phichit – Population 119 717

Michelin Atlas p 7 or Map 965 – E 5

The pleasant small town on the west bank of the Mae Nam Nan is a good touring base. It hosts a colourful **boat racing festival** *(first weekend in Sept)* at Wat Tha Luang *(below)*.

Wat Tha Luang ○ – *To the right of the Provincial Hall.* A balustraded pillared porch precedes the two entrances to the ubosot, which houses a serene Lanna-style (Chiang Saen) Buddha named **Luang Pho Phet** in the attitude of subduing Mara. Two attendants frame the statue placed high up on the altar against a delicate backdrop of celestial beings and mythical animals.

Bung Sifai – *1km west of Phichit market.* A vast swamp studded with aquatic plants is a haven for birdwatching. By the main gate a terracotta relief depicts a heroic legend with a crocodile as the main figure. There is also an aquarium.

EXCURSIONS

Old City Park – *Tambon Muang Kao. 8km south by 1068.* The road passes **Wat Rong Chang** *(left)*, which boasts large statues of the Buddha dotted in the grounds and a life-size one of an elephant near the ubosot.

Sculptures depicting characters from Thai literature are dotted in the shady park laid out as an arboretum, on the probable site of the old town of Phichit dating back 900 years to the Sukhothai period. A modern building *(right of the main alleyway)* houses the foundation stone (**lak muang**) with a statue of the founder in a cell below. A ruined Sinhalese chedi with a stepped square base and circular rings, and the foundations of a vihara and ubosot are all that remains of the moated **Wat Mahathat** *(left of the main alleyway)*.

In olden days the oath of allegiance ceremony was held in the old ubosot of **Wat Nakhon Chum** *(300m further)*. The elegant building with slim windows, tiled roof and pillared interior contains interesting Buddha images.

★**Wat Pho Prathap Chang** – *Tambon Pho Prathap Chang. 24km south by 1300, Klong Khachen-Lam Nam Kao Road, left.* The ancient monastery within a walled enclosure was built in the 17C by King Phra Phet Ratcha for his son Phra Chao Sua. A large seated Buddha high up on the altar built on an earlier brick base dominates the interior of the **ubosot**, which is lit by 14 windows (the stuccowork is still visible) and a tall balconied opening between two side entrances. The roof was supported by rows of square redented pillars. To the right of the ubosot stand small chedis pierced with niches which were probably lit by oil lamps. Beyond the wall is another ruined building which retains two rows of six square column bases and a doorway with a pointed arch.

Prasat Hin PHIMAI★★★

Nakhon Ratchasima (Khorat)

Michelin Atlas p 12 or Map 965 – F 7 – Local map see Nakhon Ratchasima (Khorat)

Access: From Nakhon Ratchasima (Khorat) 54km northeast by 2 and 206. Turn right at Km 49 and continue for 10km.

Although there is evidence of earlier settlements in the area dating back to the Neolithic era, the 11C-12C witnessed the golden age of Phimai at the heart of the powerful Khmer empire.

Phimai was an important centre on the road south to Angkor; the rectangular plan of the ancient walled town, on a strategic island site bounded by the Mae Nam Mun and Khlong Chakrai, formerly linked by a canal, is still traceable. Of the four town gates only the south **Pratu Chai** (Victory Gate) remains standing as well as parts of the outer wall, and various ruined monuments. A straight road gave access to the prasat and there are ponds dotted all around.

Decline set in after the defeat of the Khmer empire by the King Ramathibodi I of Ayutthaya in the 14C. At the fall of Ayutthaya to the Burmese in 1767, Phimai became the capital of a principality which was conquered a year later by King Taksin and annexed to the kingdom of Siam.

The modern town became a popular tourist centre after a major restoration of its monuments and the opening of the Phimai historical park in 1988.

Prasat Hin Phimai

HISTORICAL PARK ⓥ *Time 1hr*

Phimai is the most complete example of Khmer religious architecture in Thailand and it may pre-date Angkor Wat. The sanctuary, which has an unusual north-south orientation, combines Brahman and Buddhist traditions.

★★★ **Naga Bridge** – The raised terrace decorated with two simhas and naga crowns (seven heads), which symbolically connects the world with heaven, is a mark of the temple's importance.

To the left is the ruined Khlang Ngoen. Coins found on the site suggest that it may have been a treasury; however a lintel showing a figure pouring lustral water for Brahman priests supports the theory that it was a waiting chamber where rituals were performed.

South gopura – It is the largest of the four entrances, all in line with the main sanctuary, which pierce the second galleried curtain wall. Balustered windows, some of them blind, are placed at intervals. A Khmer inscription on the inner door-frame of the middle porch dates from the early 12C. Massive pillars in the three chambers give structural support.

Pass into the outer courtyard containing four **ponds** representing India's four sacred rivers, where rainwater was collected for use in the temple. Two stone pavilions to the west were probably royal lodgings. A causeway leads to the inner compound girt by a third galleried wall also punctuated by four porticoes.

Sanctuary – The roofed gallery and the finely proportioned white sandstone **prang**★★★ are the earliest parts of the sanctuary started by Jayavarman VI (1080-1107) and completed by Dharanindravarman I (1107-12). Stepped porticoes frame the skilfully articulated five-tiered tower crowned with a lotus bud and richly ornamented with stone carvings: petal motifs, naga antefixes, double pediments and lintels depicting scenes from the Ramayana epic and religious myths, pilasters with door guardians and foliage. Lotus-bud finials along the ridge of the arched tiled roof of the porches and turned bobbin windows highlight the admirable architectural monument.

Mandapa – The pediment of the south portico which opens into an antechamber *(mandapa)* features the dancing Shiva; the east pediment shows Hindu deities and their mounts *(left to right:* Brahma on a hamsa, Indra on Airavata, Vishnu on Ganesha and, above, Shiva and Uma on Nandin) and the lintel depicts Rama and his attendants in a boat after a victory in battle; on the unfinished west pediment a garuda flies to the help of Rama and Lakshmana who are shown tied up by a naga on the lintel with a grieving monkey host on the lower register.
The inner **lintels**★★★ are outstanding examples of Khmer craftsmanship. They relate the story of the Buddha and of the Bodhisattva: Buddha preaching *(west)*, the Trailokyavijaya deity *(east)*, a dancing deity framed by dancers and, above, a row of disciples *(north)*.
A windowless passageway *(antarala)* leads into the inner sanctum.

Prang – A copy of a fine 13C statue of the Buddha sheltered by a naga hood in the Bayon style has pride of place in the sanctuary, where the strict Mahayana Buddhist rites were performed. In the east corner may be seen the conduit channelling to the outside the sacred water poured over the statue.
In the north porch a lintel portrays the Vajrasattva, a meditating deity with three faces and six arms, with four other similar figures on the upper register and dancers on the lower register *(south)*.
The exterior of the tower bears vivid narrative carvings. Battle-scenes are featured on the pediments of the three porches and on the lintels: Krishna killing a giant with Rama and Sita on the left *(east)*, a deity *(north)*.

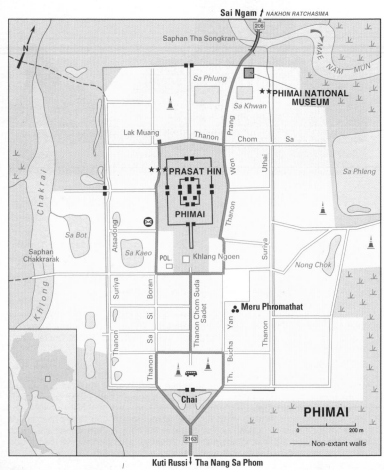

Minor prangs – Prang Phromathat, a redented tower in red laterite to the southeast, houses a replica of the very fine statue of Jayavarman VII modelled, unusually, from life, found on the site and now in Phimai Museum. To the southwest is Prang Hin Daeng built in red sandstone, and dated to the late 12C after Hinduism had given way to Buddhism; next to it stands a Brahman shrine of the same period.

Inner precinct – The southern **Pratu Chai** was the main gateway to the city, as it stood on the ancient highway to Cambodia. The square pavilion comprised three connecting chambers with a passage in the middle.

A street *(east)* parallel to the main street runs past the **Meru Phromathat,** a hill on which stands a ruined building where King Boromathat was probably cremated. His wife's cremation ceremony is thought to have been held on the smaller Meru Noi on the opposite side of the street.

Jayavarman VII

Outer area – The ruined **Tha Nang Sa Phom**, a cruciform laterite structure near Sa Chong Maew *(south)*, was probably the pier of Phimai. Nearby, **Kuti Russi** comprising a central prang with a portico *(east)*, a small west-facing vihara and a laterite wall pierced by a gateway to the east, is thought to be one of the hospitals *(Arokayasala)* built in the 13C all over the Khmer empire during the reign of Jayavarman VII.

★ Phimai National Museum ☉ – *Northwest of the town, on the right by bridge across the Mae Nam Mun.*

The well-presented collections provide a rewarding insight into the various cultural influences which have shaped the development of the northeastern provinces, in particular the Lower Isan region.

Upper floor – Exhibits explaining religious beliefs range from spirit houses and ancestor shrines to Buddhist scriptures. A Dvaravati standing figure dates from 1200. The Naga heads found in Khmer art reflect the worship of the serpent as ancestor (mother), while the Hindu lingam represents the three deities Brahma, Vishnu and Shiva. In the prehistorical section the trumpet-shaped vases are typical of **Ban Prasat★★** *(see NAKHON RATCHASIMA (KHORAT), Excursions),* while the shell bracelets indicate trading relations with coastal areas, and bronze ornaments the technical advances of early civilisations.

An inscription on a stele (AD 869) listing donations of cattle and slaves to monks dates from the Dvaravati Sri Chinasi Kingdom. A collection of Buddha images in various attitudes includes the only inclining Buddha from the Dvaravati period (8C-9C).

The Khmer civilisation is well illustrated by numerous artefacts found in the Isan region: lintel and pillar ornaments in Phrei Kmeng style (7C-8C) from Surin. The early round pillars were superseded by octagonal shapes. The early period of Hinduism is reflected in figurines, statues of **Ganesha** (symbolic of overcoming obstacles) and Hindu deities (Shiva, his wife Uma and the bull Nandin; Shiva as a hermit; Vishnu lying on the dragon Ananda). An inscription on a door frame from **Prasat Phanom Wan★** *(see NAKHON RATCHASIMA (KHORAT), Excursions)* which is dated AD 890 mentions the name of King Yasovarman I. Finds from **Prasat Hin Phanom Rung★★★** *(see Prasat Hin PHANOM RUNG)* include figures in contemporary dress, a head of Shiva featuring a third eye, and door guardians. The Bayon style (13C Bodhisattva **Avalokitesvara** with a kind smiling expression and a belt with eight-petal flower) marks the adoption of Mahayana Buddhism by Jayavarman VII. Among the bronzes found at Phimai are goddesses holding a lotus and a manuscript. The Ayutthaya Buddha images in stone and wood are portraits of real people, whereas those in Laotian style feature a round face. A Buddha footprint bears the distinctive auspicious symbols.

Lower floor – This section is devoted to the history and architecture of Phimai, which was built to celebrate the divine nature of the Khmer rulers. The exquisite gold ornaments of a Hindu deity are part of a very fine collection of Baphuon-style metalwork found at Thanon Hak. Also on display are ceremonial pieces and objects in gold and silver leaf and crystal, bronze palanquin ornaments, mirrors, perfume and betel sets, seals, musical instruments and ceramics.

Prasat Hin PHIMAI

The narrative quality of the stone carvings illustrating Hindu religious themes is out-standing. Among the remarkable **lintels★★★** found on Khmer sites the most important depicts Buddhist history for the first time: a demon army attacking the meditating Buddha. A 13C sandstone statue of **Jayavarman VII★★★** in meditation, probably a true likeness, and the serene 15C **Buddha** sheltered by a naga in Lopburi style rank among the museum's masterpieces. Fragments of lintels and pediments are on display in the courtyard.

Lintel

Sai Ngam – *Northeast. 3km from Amphoe Phimai.* Cross over a small dam and proceed along a shady road to an island in the middle of a reservoir formed by an irrigation dam on the Mae Nam Mun. An enormous **banyan tree** bristling with aerial roots covers a vast area. Local people pay homage to the tree spirit at the wooden shrines. Food stalls and picnic sites offer a pleasant respite.

Mu Ko PHI PHI★★
Krabi
Michelin Atlas p 20 or Map 965 – N 3 – Local map see Phuket

The exotic **islands** ⊘ blessed with a wonderful scenery of secluded coves, deserted beaches, clear waters, fine coral reefs and spectacular cliffs form part of a National Marine Park, which includes Hat Noppharat Thara *(see KRABI)*. Excessive commercial development, however, with the ensuing problems of litter, noise pollution and damage to coral reefs, is a threat to the fragile ecology of the islands.

Phi Phi Don – A narrow neck of land covered with coconut groves separates two crescent-shaped bays – admirable **views★★★** may be enjoyed from the viewpoint on the ridge *(30min climb by a steep trail east).* To the south, imposing cliffs and wooded hills frame Ao Ton Sai where boats dock and where there are restaurants, shops, diving agencies as well as a Thai Muslim village. The west of the island is uninhabited, while the Chao Le (Sea Gypsies) lead a traditional way of life on Laem Tong at the northern tip of the east coast. Along the east coast are idyllic beaches and deserted coves where relaxation and tranquillity are the order of the day. Ama-teurs of water-sports will enjoy good swimming, diving and snorkelling. Boat tours are a must to enjoy the exciting seascapes.

Birds' nests are highly prized as a delicacy in Chinese cuisine and are also believed to have aphrodisiac properties. Swiftlets build their tiny nests from thin strands of saliva which solidify when exposed to the air. The translu-cent strands which are similar to glass noodles are cooked in chicken broth. The lucrative licences to harvest the precious commodity are awarded to the highest bidder at an auction. Agile collectors perform hazardous feats by climbing up rickety bamboo ladders and scaffolding. They use special knives to collect the nests high up in hollows in the cliff face or in the caves.

Ko Phi Phi Don

Phi Phi Le – *1/2 day*. The craggy, indented outline of the limestone cliffs pockmarked with caves is silhouetted against the clear blue sky. **Tham Phaya Nak★★★** (Viking Cave – *east*) is a vast vaulted cave hollowed out at the base of the cliff by wave erosion. Swiftlets build their nests high up in hollows and collectors shin up precarious bamboo ladders to collect the lucrative bounty *(see above)*. On the wall to the right are **paintings** of sailing ships, hence the name, although these actually resemble Chinese junks. There is a fine stalactite near the entrance. Deep green bays – Ao Pilae, Lo Samah and Maya – hemmed in by sheer cliffs and fringed with fine sandy beaches beckon the dazzled visitor, who can indulge in swimming, diving and boating.

PHITSANULOK★

Phitsanulok – Population 268 182

Michelin Atlas p 7 or Map 965 – E 5

The modern town astride the Mae Nam Nan has developed as a commercial centre and is a major communications hub, with good roads radiating in all directions. It is also a university town with a lively student population. There are few traces of the old town destroyed by fire in 1957, and of its past historical importance. Tree-lined esplanades stretch along the fast-flowing Mae Nam Nan, where houses built on stilts and floating houses – some have been turned into restaurants or guesthouses – create a picturesque scene typical of Phitsanulok in olden times.

A royal seat – The foundation of the town probably pre-dates the glorious Sukhothai period, as there is evidence of the Dvaravati and Khmer civilisations in the vicinity. Phitsanulok which was an important town in the Sukhothai kingdom was conquered in the 14C by King **Ramathibodi I** (U-Thong) of Ayutthaya. King Luthai of Sukhothai recaptured the town soon after and ruled his kingdom from Phitsanulok. During his reign art, religion and politics flourished. After the decline of Sukhothai Prince **Ramesuan** was appointed ruler and in 1448 ascended the throne as King **Borommatrailokanat**. The town regained its importance and served as his capital until his death in 1488. In the 16C King **Naresuan the Great** also lived in the town and his declaration of independence from the Burmese is commemorated by a monument on the site of his former palace on the west bank. Phitsanulok later fell to the Burmese and after the destruction of the Ayutthaya kingdom it became part of a small principality which was absorbed in the late 18C by King Taksin.

SIGHTS

★★ Wat Phra Si Ratana Mahathat ⊙ – *East bank near Saphan Naresuan*. The principal temple in Phitsanulok which fortunately escaped fire damage was built in the late 15C by King Borommatrailokanat to assert the power of the Ayutthuya kingdom. It was restored in the 18C by King Borommakot and also in 1991 by the Fine Arts Department.

Vihara – A porch with a gilded, coffered pediment and slender pillars precedes the sanctuary. The ebony **doors★★** adorned with mother-of-pearl inlay and a floral and animal design are of admirable craftsmanship. Pillars highlighted in blue, red and gold and capped by lotus capitals divide the triple-aisled interior and support the coffered ceiling. The tiered, glazed roof sweeps low onto the side walls and creates an intimate setting for the serene **Phra Phuttha Chinarat★★★**, a masterpiece of late-Sukhothai art, which is given pride of place at the altar against a dark backdrop adorned with angels and stylised flowers. The bronze seated Buddha flanked by fine Buddha images and disciples is remarkable for the chased flame halo, terminating in mythical creatures framing the round face, the graceful curving arms and overlapped legs in the attitude of subduing Mara. The wall paintings which date from a later period depict the Buddha's enlightenment *(right)* and his renunciation of the world *(left)*. The finely carved **pulpits** are also of interest.

Cloisters – On either side of the vihara are small chapels, pavilions and the ubosot. The galleries house an array of fine Buddha images in various styles, and religious objects. In the centre rises the powerful Ayutthaya-style **prang**. The gilded upper part is visible from a distance, and a stairway leads to the crypt enshrining the relic of the Buddha.

At the rear of the cloisters are a ruined building and a huge standing Buddha which has been heavily restored. A chapel to the south contains a seated Buddha in the Sukhothai style.

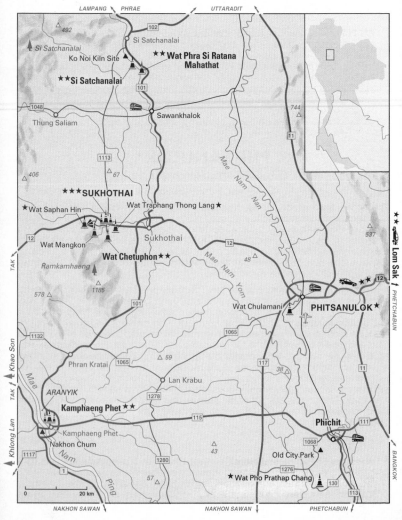

Phutta Chinarat

Front courtyard – A chapel surrounded by shops contains a small Buddha image named **Phra Lua★**, modelled from the gold remaining after the casting of three celebrated Buddha images, Satsada, Chinasri and Chinarat, by three artists from Chiang Saen, Sawankalok and Sukhothai. According to legend the god Indra assisted the artists in their task.

Phra **Wat Ratcha Burana** – *Opposite side of Saphan Naresuan.* Features of interest at this temple which also survived the fire are the imposing ruins of a stepped **chedi** and an **ubosot**, surrounded by double bai semas and adorned with 19C mural paintings depicting scenes from the Ramakien and finely-carved door panels.

★ **Folklore Museum** – *Thanon Visut Kasat. 2km south of the railway station.* The museum aims to present traditional country life and to foster a proud folk memory bank through an amazing array of agricultural and domestic implements, which are gradually disappearing as the use of modern tools and machines becomes the rule. The exhibits include ceramics, musical instruments, craftsmen's tools, coconut grinders, fish traps, hunting lures and cooking utensils.

EXCURSIONS

Wat Chulamani ⊙ – *5km south by 1063.* The temple probably dates from the Khmer period and later became an important Buddhist shrine, where in the 15C King Borommatrailokanat was ordained to the monkhood. A stele protected by wooden shutters at the back of a late-18C vihara near the prang bears an inscription marking the event.

The harmonious Khmer-style **prang★** has a stepped plinth, and doorways with exquisite stucco **friezes★** of geese and flowers on the sides. There is a fine seated Buddha image in the vaulted interior.

★★ **Scenic road to Lomsak** – *The route is described in reverse order under PHETCH-ABUN – Excursions.*

PHRAE★

Phrae – Population 128 414

Michelin Atlas p 7 or Map 965 – C 5

The Mae Nam Yom loops round the modern town with its wide avenues spread out on the east bank. The magnificent **wooden houses** in the old town attest to the town's prosperity derived from coal mining and the teak trade. Its temples reveal Burmese and Laotian influences, a legacy of the Burmese invasion and of the logging industry which attracted workers and merchants from Burma and Laos in bygone days. Agriculture is the mainstay of the fertile region which grows maize, sugarcane and tobacco; drying sheds are dotted all over the countryside.

SIGHTS

Old town – *West of the modern town.* The earthen wall and moat mark out the oval plan of the old town by the river which can be viewed from the road.

Wat Si Chum – *Thanon Kham Saen.* Three doors pierce the façade of the main **vihara** in the centre of the compound. The naive glass mosaic decoration, an ornate pulpit and a seated Buddha image with a flame glory in the Phra Phuttha Chinarat style *(see PHITSANULOK)* are of interest. A huge standing Buddha is enshrined in the vihara on the left. Other notable structures are a chedi and a small **ho trai** (library) on stilts and decorated with naive paintings.

Wat Luang – *Soi 1 off Thanon Kam Lu; west of Wat Si Chum.* One of the oldest temples in Phrae, it probably dates from the town's foundation (16C). The main **vihara** boasts a finely carved façade, decorated pillars and beams as well as a venerated Buddha presiding at the ornate altar. A Lao-style Buddha on the high altar and decorated shutters are the main features in the small vihara. Elephants and Buddha images in niches highlight the base of the octagonal stepped chedi in the Lanna (Chiang Saen) style. A small museum displaying religious art is housed in a modern sala.

Wat Phra Non – *Thanon Phra Non Nua near Wat Luang.* The vihara is noteworthy for its finely carved pediments, slim window openings and tiered roof. Nearby stands a library. The temple derives its name from the lacquered reclining Buddha covered in gold leaf in the small chapel *(left)*, which is lit by slit windows. The white chedi has a ringed finial.

Wat Phra Bat Ming Muang – *Thanon Charoen Muang.* Within the cramped precinct notable buildings include a canted stepped chedi and a charming **library** with decorated pillars.

Phraya Chaiyabun Monument – *4km from Phrae market.* It commemorates a governor of Phrae killed during a local rebellion (1902). Phraya Chaiyabun refused to sign a document conceding Muang Phrae to the rebels.

★★**Wat Chom Sawan** – *Thanon Yantaraket Koson (101).* Burmese and Shan influences are evident in the original architecture of this fine temple built by a Shan (Tai Yai). Two covered porches give access to the wooden **vihara** which presents a tiered roofline, an irregular floor level, partitions and coffered ceilings. The magnificent interior is graced by a Shan-style statue in a case to the left of the altar. The monumental Burmese-style chedi with its graceful crown has lost its stucco.

Wat Sa Bo Kaeo – *Thanon Nam Ku on the edge of the city moat.* Mythical animals and door guardians stand sentinel at the entrance to the walled enclosure. A tall white chedi framed by smaller chedis precedes the Burmese-style **vihara**, where a beautiful Buddha in translucent marble presides at an ornate altar.

Crafts

There is a strong craft tradition in Phrae which specialises in handwoven textiles – cotton and silk with intricate designs in Amphoe Long *(southwest)* and especially the blue **mohom** fabric used for the distinctive shirts worn by farmers and made in Ban Thung Hong *(northeast)*, rattan and wood furniture, knives, scythes, picks and spades.

EXCURSIONS

Ban Prathap Chai ⊘ – *Tambon Pa Maet. 10km west by 1023.* The imposing mansion built using 130 huge teak posts is a splendid example of a timber structure. Inside is a profusion of ornate furniture and decorative objects, some of which are very garish.

Wat Phra That Cho Hae – *Tambon Pa Daeng. 9km east. Turn left after 6km by 1022.* The name Cho Hae is derived from a satin cloth woven in Sip Song Panna (Yunnan) which is wrapped around the chedi by the villagers. Two naga stairways lead up to the temple which is an important pilgrimage centre. The seated Buddha

Phra Chao Than Chai *(in a shrine by the chedi)* is venerated by women with fertility problems. The gilded Lanna-style **chedi** and the cruciform plan of the vihara are of special interest. From the hilltop there are fine **views** of the landscaped grounds and the towering teak trees all around.

★★**Phae Muang Phi Forest Park** *– 18km east by 101, then take 1134 right for 6km and continue for 3km. Four-wheel drive vehicle essential at the site.* A fantastic landscape of earth pillars created by erosion similar to **Sao Din**★ *(see NAN)*. The area was previously covered with shrubs where the villagers often lost their way, leading them to call it "Phae Muang Phi", meaning the ghost village.

Mae Yom National Park *– 70km north by the old Song-Ngao road (101, 103, 1120, 1154).* The journey gives ample opportunity to enjoy the idyllic mountain scenery. The park encompasses vast tracts of land in Amphoe Song and Amphoe Ngao, including Dong Sak Ngam teak forest *(6km from the park office)* and Lom Dong pool *(10km).*

Wat Phra That Suthon Mongkhon Khiri *– Ban Huai Nam Phik, Tambon Den Chai. 30km southwest by 101 (3km from Amphoe Den Chai).* The modern temple founded in 1977 by a talented young monk is remarkable in that it marks a renaissance in Lanna art styles. A large teak-wood house on piles displays a collection of antique objects from the locality, old photographs depicting the story of Phrae in the 19C, Lanna musical instruments and lacquer ware.

The entrance to the cloister is guarded by two stucco statues of demons. The gallery is adorned with murals of Lanna fables and folk tales and 87 Buddha images in various styles. The interior of the ubosot features Khmer lintels, murals in both Ayutthaya and Bangkok styles, and granite flooring from Italy. A replica of the Phra Phuttha Chinarat Buddha image *(see PHITSANULOK)* cast locally by the venerable abbot has pride of place.

The multi-spired **Phra That Suthon**★ on a double base with its lotus mouldings, small bell-shaped chamber and slender finial derives from the early Lanna-Chiang Saen idiom. Buddha images are housed in niches along the base. The stuccowork is particularly fine. The **ho trai** (library) based on the remarkable libraries of **Wat Phra Sing Luang**★★★ *(see CHIANG MAI)* and **Wat Phra That Haripunchai**★★ *(see LAMPHUN)* reveals superb craftsmanship.

PHUKET★★★

Phuket – Population 138 785

Michelin Atlas p 20 or Map 965 – N 3

Phuket, the largest island in Thailand lapped by the sparkling waters of the Andaman Sea, wholly deserves all the superlatives which are lavished upon it to describe its success as a tourist destination. Its palm-fringed beaches of dazzling white sand, sheltered bays and coves, luxuriant rain forest, verdant hills and picturesque fishing villages are complemented by a rich history and a diverse cultural tradition. The climate is perfect with pleasant temperatures (28°-32°C) throughout the year and only intermittent tropical downpours during the monsoon season. The island has superb facilities to satisfy the most demanding traveller.

A bountiful land – In the past the island was visited by sailors sheltering from storms and was commonly known as "Junk Ceylon", a corruption from Malay. Its present name is probably derived from the Malay "Bukhit". The Moken, also known as Chao Le (Sea Gypsies), were among the early inhabitants along the south coast. They are famous for their sailing, diving and fishing skills.

The Thais arrived in the 13C to mine the rich tin lodes and the island became a port of call for Western ships on the trade route between India and China to escape the pirates who roamed the Andaman Sea. In the 16C, European trading posts were set up and prosperity flowed from a thriving trade in tin, pearls, ambergris and edible birds' nests. Chinese immigration boomed in the early 19C as workers attracted by the rich natural resources flocked to Phuket, which became part of the Thai kingdom under King Rama V (1853-1910).

A turn of fate – In the late 18C the explorer Captain Francis Light, who took a wife from Phuket, sought to secure the island for the East India Company. After the Thais had claimed sovereignty, British interest turned to the Straits of Malacca and he moved his operation to Penang which was the stepping-stone to colonisation of the Malay Peninsula by the British.

Development – Although the tropical paradise discovered by early travellers has changed as a result of commercial development, the beauty of the island remains a precious asset, and the authorities have become aware of the need for environmental protection and good management of tourism.

Tourism is now the main moneyspinner but tin and rubber were previously the major industries. The introduction of the dredger in 1909 made mining of the rich lodes a lucrative operation and was marked in 1969 by the **Sixty Years Pillar Monument** *(Thanon Phuket).* Tin is still dredged offshore. The introduction of rubber in the early 20C proved a boon for the economy. Large rubber plantations and sheets of latex drying in the sun are a common sight. Fishing and coconuts also contribute to the economic prosperity.

Out and about

Tourism Authority of Thailand – 73-75 Thanon Phuket, Amphoe Muang, Phuket 83000. ☎ 076 211 036, 076 212 213, 076 217 138. Fax 076 213 582.

Tourist Police – ☎ 1155, 076 217 517, 076 225 361.

Transport – There are regular domestic and international services to Phuket. **International Airport** ☎ 076 327 194, 076 327 246; **Thai International Airways** – 76 Thanon Ranong, Phuket Town; ☎ 076 211 195, 076 212 499; **Bangkok Airways** ☎ 076 225 033/5.
Buses also operate to and from Bangkok and other large towns. **Bus Terminal** ☎ 076 211 480.
Car and motorcycles for hire. Check the vehicles carefully and take note of insurance cover. Bicycles are also convenient to get around and are available at the various beaches. Take great care on the roads.

Sightseeing – **Boat Rental**: At Hat Patong and Rawai. Long-tail boats: 400 Baht for 3-4 persons.

Phuket Orchid Garden and Thai Village ⊙ – *3km west off Thanon Thepkasattri.* Folk dances, Thai Boxing, handicraft centre, elephant show and orchid farm.

Phuket Butterfly Garden and Aquarium ⊙ – Well presented display of tropical butterflies and fish species.

Cruises – In high season only. Information from TAT.

Watersports – Deep-sea fishing, sailing, scuba diving mainly from Hat Patong.

Phuket Cable Ski – Khatu area. ☎ 076 321 766/7.

Entertainment – Cabarets, bars, restaurants at Hat Patong.

Thai Boxing, Saphan Hin stadium, Fri, 8pm. 150-300 Baht. ☎ 076 214 690, 076 211 751.

Night market – In the Patong area.

Excursions – Ao Phangnga, Mu Ko Phi Phi, Mu Ko Similan.

Hotels and restaurants – Phuket is renowned for its excellent hotels in all categories and for its fine seafood and international restaurants all over the island.

Where to eat

Gung Café – Kata Beach. ☎ 076 330 015. Traditional Thai dishes with modern influences. Romantic ambience.

The Old Siam – Karon Beach Road. ☎ 076 396 090. Original Thai cuisine, spectacular décor, ocean view from the terrace, delightful atmosphere and gracious welcome.

The Boathouse Wine Bar & Grill – Kata Beach. ☎ 076 396 015. Delicious Thai specialities, succulent seafood and European dishes. Superb dining by the sea.

Patong Seafood – Patong Beach. ☎ 076 341 224. A well-established fish restaurant serving fresh seafood.

Where to stay

Budget

Phuket Island Pavilion – 133 Thanon Satun. ☎ 076 210 444; Fax 076 210 458; 800-1 600 Baht. A modern hotel with beach bungalows in a garden setting, sea views and near the entertainment centre

Patong Lodge – 61/7 Moo 5, Thanon Kalim, Patong. ☎ 076 341 020; Fax 076 340 287; 1 000-1 500 Baht. Comfortable accommodation, beach bungalows, garden. Convenient for entertainment centre.

Phuket Merlin Hotel – 158/1 Thanon Yaowarat. ☎ 076 212 866; Fax 076 216 429; 1 200-3 000 Baht. Good hotel in town centre. Restaurants, health club, tennis court, swimming pool.

Moderate

Dusit Laguna Resort – 390 Thanon Srisuntorn, Cherntalay. ☎ 076 324 320-32, 02 636 3600 Ext 4510; Fax 076 324 174, 02 636 3570; dlp@dusit.com; www.dusit.com; 4 000-12 000 Baht. A superior hotel with first-class facilities and lovely garden.

Sheraton Grand Laguna – 10 Moo 4, Thanon Srisoonthon, Ban Thao Bay. ☎ 076 324 101-7; Fax 076 324 108; sheraton@samart.co.th; www.lagunaphuket.com/sheraton; US$190-1 100. Fine accommodation with sea views, restaurants and sports facilities.

Novotel Coralia Phuket – Kalim Beach Road, Patong. ☎ 076 342 777, 02 237 6064; Fax 076 341 168, 02 333 1000; novotel@phuket.com; www.phuket.com/novotel; 4 600-10 700 Baht. An attractive hotel with excellent facilities in this popular resort. Restaurants and health centre.

Expensive

Banyan Tree Phuket – 33 Moo 4, Thanon Srisoonthon. ☎ 076 324 374, 02 285 0746/7; Fax 076 324 356, 02 285 0748; banyanrs@samart.co.th; www.banyantree.com; US$370-1 750. Luxury accommodation in Thai-style villas with sea views. Fine restaurants, fitness centre and landscaped gardens.

Cape Panwa Hotel – 27 Moo 8, Thanon Sakdidej. ☎ 076 391 123-5, 02 233 9560; Fax 076 391 177, 02 238 2988; kasemkij@ksc.th.com; www.capepanwa.com; 4 500-18 500 Baht. A splendid seaside hotel with Thai architectural features. Beach bungalows, restaurants and gardens.

Le Meridien Phuket – 8/5 Moo 1, Tambol Karon. ☎ 076 340 480-5, 02 653 2201-7; Fax 076 340 479, 02 653 2208/9; meridien@phuket.ksc.co.th; www.meridien-phuket.com; US$190-300. Elegant Thai-style buildings by the sea. Restaurants, health club and private beach.

★PHUKET TOWN

A stroll through the charming provincial capital built in the mid 19C to replace the old town of Thalang destroyed by the Burmese will reveal the varied architecture of the buildings, which reflects the cultural influences at play throughout its history.

In **Soi Rommani, Thanon Yaowarat, Deebuk** and **Phangnga**, the two-storeyed wooden buildings with arched skylights, balconies and arcaded galleries in Sino-Portuguese style are highlighted with stucco and wood carving. Around the town there are fine mansions decorated with faience, terracotta tiles and wood carving and set in large gardens, which were built by the rich from the proceeds of the tin and rubber industries.

The **Provincial Hall** and **Provincial Courts** *(Thanon Damrong)* as well as the **Old Governor's Residence** and **Law Courts** *(near Thanon Ranong)* are handsome buildings in the colonial style with pillars, galleries with fretwork and windows with shutters.

The typical market scenes *(Thanon Ranong, Phuket)* add a colourful note.

Put Jaw and Jui Tui Temples – *Thanon Ranong.* Chinese tradition is kept alive at the Taoist temples dedicated to Kuan Yin, the goddess of mercy, and Kiu Won In, a vegetarian god. Statues of the Taoist gods are housed in the buildings which are richly decorated with red-tiled roofs, ornate carving and green dragons.

Fishing Port – *East of the town.* A colourful scene unfolds as fishing boats put to sea or return with their catch. The small port is at its liveliest when the fish is unloaded.

Ko Sire – *Take the port road.* A bridge spans the channel to an islet. Follow a road running round the island to a Chao Le village with traditional thatched huts on stilts where the fisherfolk attempt to preserve their lifestyle.

Ao Makham – *South by 4023.* The wide bay is the ideal location for an important seaport where cargo and cruise ships berth. Ore smelting and storage plants are also sited in the vicinity.

★★**Aquarium** ⊘ – *9km south at Laem Panwa by 4023.* In a modern building on a headland overlooking a bay dotted with verdant islets with fine beaches, interesting species of fish, marine animals and shells are attractively displayed. An unusual exhibit is a fish which emits an electrical discharge. Among important research projects carried out by the Marine Biological Research Centre is the hatching of eggs laid by giant sea turtles which come ashore between October and February; the young are reared at the aquarium and released into the open sea (Turtle Festival at Songkran 13 April).

A **Vegeterian Festival** celebrated in October by the large Chinese population includes nine days of abstinence from eating meat for purification of mind and body. The participants in a trance pierce their skin with sharp objects such as blades, needles and spears and take part in processions, ritual dancing, walking on hot coals, and other events to the loud accompaniment of fire crackers. These practices which are akin to Hindu rituals are curiously unknown in China. The locals make offerings of tea, flowers, fruit, incense to the nine deities. Information about the festival is available from the Tourist Office.

NORTH OF THE ISLAND

Vast rubber plantations along the access road from **Saphan Sarasin** and **Saphan Thao Thep Kasetri** remain a source of wealth for the island. West of the airport is a conservation area comprising the Nai Yang National Park (Hat Nai Yang) and the deserted Hat Mai Khao where sea turtles lay their eggs from October to February. Rubber and coconut plantations flourish in this isolated area.

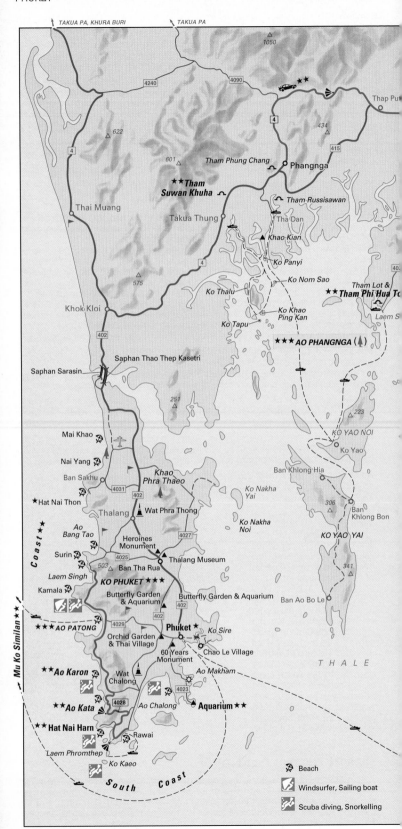

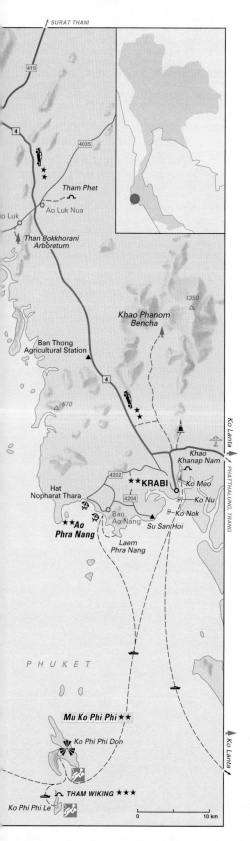

At **Wat Phra Thong** *(Km 20)* a half-buried statue in a vihara is revered by the locals. According to a curious legend all those who have attempted to move the statue have met with an untimely death.

Near **Ban Tha Rua** *(Km 12)* ruins of the ancient city, Muang Thalang – wall, forts, pond – recall ancient history.

Thalang National Museum ⓥ – The museum provides a valuable insight into the eventful history of Phuket. A diorama of the Battle of Thalang (1785) recalls this heroic event. Arms, jewellery, Chinese artefacts (photos, porcelain, furniture, wedding scene) recreate the life of the Chinese immigrants. Models of Chao Le boats and a display on a ceremonial boat launch into the sea *(twice a year – 6th and 11th months)* illustrate traditional culture. Examples of local dress feature brightly-coloured fabrics and embroidery. Other displays explain the processing of latex which involves the use of arsenic, and the complex procedures of tin mining and dredging. Finds from the prehistoric era include flints, axes, tools and pottery. A statue of **Vishnu** discovered at Takuapa as well as a stone inscription in the Dravidian language, which attest to trade links with India, are among the museum's prized exhibits.

Khao Phra Thaeo Wildlife Sanctuary – *3km east by 4027.* The dense jungle where flourishes the rare silver palm *(Karedoxa dolphin)* is all that remains of the rain forest which once covered the whole island. The teeming wildlife includes many species of tropical birds (crimson sunbird, paradise flycatcher), mammals (bears, wild boar, monkeys – gibbon project) and reptiles. Hiking trails lead through the shady recesses to waterfalls. **Nam Tok Ton Sai** *(300m from the car park)* is within easy reach.

Ko Naga Noi ⓥ – *2hr from Ao Por Pier. By 4087, turn right into a side road.* A pleasant excursion can be made to the pearl island, which also boasts a fine beach.

SOUTH COAST

From the pier in the sheltered small harbour *(12km southwest of Phuket Town by 4021 and left)* of **Ao Chalong**, boats can be hired for pleasant daytrips to offshore islands popular for diving and snorkelling.

The heroic deeds of two sisters is the stuff of legend. In the late 18C Phuket was under siege by the Burmese. On the death of the governor of Thalang, the main town, his widow Chan and her sister Mook, disguising themselves as male soldiers, fearlessly stepped into the breach to organise the defence of Phuket. They gathered troops, built stockades and repelled the invaders. King Rama I rewarded their bravery by conferring titles of nobility on the two heroines.

The **Heroines' Monument** at a major road junction (402, 4025, 4027) – bronze statues of two women in traditional costume and sword in hand – commemorates the sisters, who bore the titles Thao Thep Kasattri and Thao Si Sunthon.

Wat Chalong – *8km southwest by 4021 and right.* The Thai-style temple is dedicated to two revered hermit monks. A sala contains a statue of Luang Pho Chaem, a monk who helped to quell a rebellion of Chinese mine workers in the early 20C. Opposite stands a fine wooden Thai-style house on stilts. Modern additions include an ornate vihara.

Hat Rawai – *16km southwest by 4021 and 4024.* A fine beach lined with palm trees and Casuarina pines is famous for its Chao Le village, where the people eke out a living by fishing and trading with the locals. It is a good starting point for boat trips to islets in the bay. To the east is Laem Ka. Fishing boats, restaurants and hotels create a typical holiday scene.

Laem Phromthep – A shrine marks the southernmost tip of Phuket, which affords splendid **views**★★★ of tropical islands and the azure sea, especially at sunset.

Ko Kaeo – *30min boat trip from Hat Rawai.* On the island which lies off Laem Phromthep are a Buddhist chedi and a shrine housing a Buddha footprint. There are fine sandy beaches and coral reefs, as well as a restaurant.

★★ WEST COAST

All western beaches have strong tides and undercurrents.

★★ **Hat Nai Harn** – *15km southwest.* As the road descends and crosses a river and marshes there is a beautiful **view**★★ of the turquoise bay and sparkling white beach protected by two verdant headlands and three islands. The bay is the ideal venue for regattas organised by the Phuket Yacht Club. Swimming is dangerous during the monsoon season *(May-Oct)*.

The road from Nai Harn to Kata winds up and down hill. Stop at the viewpoint for spectacular **views**★★★ of three beaches with islands in the distance. Turn left for Kata Yai.

Ao Kata – *18km west.* The bay is fringed by the fine sandy beaches of **Hat Kata Yai**★★ and Hat Kata Noi sheltered by a rocky islet, Ko Pu.

Ao Karon – The long white beach of **Hat Karon Yai**★★ and the secluded cove of Karon Noi are ideal for relaxation.

West Coast, Phuket

Ao Patong – *13km west by 4029*. **Hat Patong**★★★ offers the longest and finest beach and excellent facilities for amateurs of water-sports. The resort is popular for its lively atmosphere – shops, restaurants, bars and nightclubs – and this may deter some visitors who prefer a more tranquil scene. It is now a far cry from the tranquil beach and unspoilt scenery which thrilled early visitors and made the fame of Phuket.

Hat Kamala – The road descends very steeply to the bay with its curving stretch of white sand. Tin dredging is carried out offshore. To the rear are rice fields. A circular road winds past a residential area and a small mosque which serves the Muslim community.
The coast road then climbs past several coves affording delightful **views**★★.

Laem Singh – *24km northwest by 4029 or 4025 and the coast road*. A narrow path leads down to a beautiful little sandy beach near the headland.

Hat Surin – The long beach backed by steep hills is popular with the local people. It has fairly heavy surf and offers good snorkelling.
Turn left at a golf course and continue north to the secluded **Hat Pansea** favoured by exclusive resorts (Pansea, Amanpuri).

★ **Hat Bang Tao** – The long, sandy beach is lined with elegant resorts (Pacific Island, Sheraton, Dusit Laguna) and a fishing village. An original feature is that the tin mines which disfigured the landscape have been turned into lakes.

Hat Nai Thon – *Turn left by Km6 on 4031 and continue for 3km*. The fine stretch of beach with a fishing village is a haven of tranquillity.

★★ Mu Ko SIMILAN ⊘ *at least 1 day*

An archipelago of nine idyllic islands (from the north Ko Bon, Ko Ba Ngu, Ko Similan, Ko Payu, Ko Miang, Ko Payan, Ko Payang, Ko Hu Yong), with crystal-clear waters, wonderful marine life and coral reefs, has been declared a national park. Its name derives from the Malay *sembilan* meaning nine. Huge boulders smoothed by erosion are a distinctive feature of the archipelago. The islands are popular with diving enthusiasts and amateurs of big-game fishing. The long journey on the open sea is exhilarating. The Park Office is on Ko Similan but there is no accommodation. There are camp sites on Ko Ba Ngu, Ko Similan and Ko Miang.

PHU KRADUNG National Park★★★

Loei

Michelin Atlas p 8 or Map 965 – E 6

Access – To reach the top of Phu Kradung ⊘ *(5.5km to the top from the park headquarters. Time: 4-6hr)*, a track climbs fairly gently at first through a sparsely forested area passing several scenic spots. Half way up it becomes steeper with more humid and dense forest cover and bamboo fences. The very steep last 100m stretch is managed by means of wooden steps and ladders emerging on a plateau. A path *(3km)* leads to the park office. *There are benches, shelters and food stalls along the trail.*

Geographical notes – Sheer cliffs emphasise the bell-shaped mass (Kradung means bell) of the flat-topped mountain or mesa; the undulating plateau (60sq km, elevation 1 360m) is a savannah dotted with groves of oaks, pines and conifers. The park cover comprises cloud forest, seasonal tropical forest and submontane evergreen forest. Streams meander through the plateau creating cool valleys, refreshing pools and waterfalls. There are rare varieties of flora (orchids, azaleas, rhododendrons, wild flowers, maples), and the abundant wildlife includes elephants, black bears, gibbons and barking deer as well as many butterflies and bird species (hornbill, forktail, oriole, Scops owl). The average temperature is 19°-29° (6° lower at the top than at the base of the mountain). The rainfall average is 122 days a year with the heaviest rainfall in October.

TOUR *allow 3 days*

There are 50km of marked trails *(maps available)*. Guides are compulsory for hikes into densely forested areas.

★★★ **Viewpoints** – A path leads east to **Liem Pha Nok Aen** (Swallow Cliff), named after the swallows which nest underneath. It affords spectacular views at sunrise and overlooks the plain and the surrounding mountains. Splendid views may be enjoyed from the south-facing Liem Pha Mak Duk and beyond Suan Sida (rhododendrons in season), from Liem Pha Ban Na Noi. Further along are Liem Pha Yiep Mek (literally, step-on-the-cloud – *5km from the park office*), jutting far

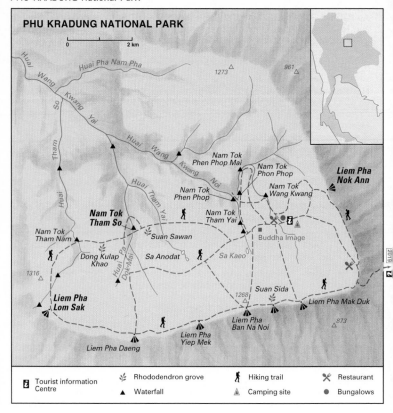

PHU KRADUNG NATIONAL PARK

0   2 km

[i] Tourist information Centre	☘ Rhododendron grove	🚶 Hiking trail	✕ Restaurant
▲ Waterfall		⛺ Camping site	● Bungalows

out from the plateau, Liem Pha Daeng and **Liem Pha Lom Sak,** a large overhanging sandstone block shaded by a pine tree – an ideal setting for photographs *(long queue in summer)* – which is the best spot for splendid views of the setting sun.

Waterfalls – Trails lead to the waterfalls which tumble down in full glory in the rainy season. To the north are Nam Tok Tham Yai, Phen Phop, Phon Phop and Phen Phop Mai, Wang Kwang. The trail to **Nam Tok Tham So** and Tham Nam, a cave through which runs a stream, further west passes Sa Anodat, a limpid pool enhanced by exotic flora, and rhododendron groves (Suan Sawan – Paradise Garden, Dong Kulap Khao) which are a riot of colour in season.

PRACHINBURI

Prachinburi – Population 112 388

Michelin Atlas p 17 or Map 965 – G 6 – Local map see Khao Yai National Park

Important archeological sites – Si Mahaphot and Si Mahosot – in the vicinity of Prachinburi, a tranquil town on the banks of the Mae Nam Prachin, attest to its power as a city state in the 1C-5C AD, and later as a Dvaravati trading centre in the 6C-11C on the route to Cambodia. A majestic statue (near Chakkrapongse Camp) of King **Naresuan** commemorates a royal visit in the 17C while on his way to confront the ruler. of Lawaek (Cambodia). The fertile land all around is crisscrossed by canals.

SIGHTS

Town – A wide esplanade along the south bank of Mae Nam Prachin offers riverside restaurants. An unexpected sight further east along the south bank is the early-20C **mansion** of Chao Phraya Apai Phubet *(in the grounds of a hospital)* in French Renaissance style and with fine stuccowork built for a royal visit.
A Royal Handwriting Monument (Amphoe Si Mahaphot – *take 3070 east and at Km 14 turn left)*, a small mondop built on the site of a Khmer monument and set in landscaped grounds, commemorates King Rama V's visit in 1908. Further along the road turn right along a track to view **Phan Hin**, a chedi with a stepped laterite base on a cross plan and a round pedestal which was probably the base of a tall statue.

Museum ⓥ – *200m southeast of the City Hall.* On the ground floor the museum exhibits masterpieces from archeological sites: a regal four-armed **Vishnu★★★** (7C-8C) is a beautiful example of Hindu sculpture; a Dvaravati **stele★★** (7C-11C) depicts the Buddha seated in meditation – the curved eyebrows, the stupa and bodhi tree decoration and the realistic foot are noteworthy. Also of interest are a linga from Lopburi, a Wheel of the Law, small sculptures and bronzes, terracotta heads and votive tablets as well as admirable Khmer **lintels★★** – vivid scenes from the Jataka and a reclining Vishnu in a cosmic dream – including those from Prasat Hin Khao Noi *(see below)* near Sa Kaeo which are among the earliest examples of Khmer carving in Thailand (*c* mid 7C). On the first floor are presented artefacts and pottery recovered from sunken ships in the Gulf of Thailand.

EXCURSIONS

Wat Kaeo Phichit – *2.5km south.* The unusual architectural style of this 100-year-old monastery combines European and Oriental elements: stucco garlands, peristyle with fluted columns, filigree doors, Chinese dragons at roof level, Khmer gopura and basement, and Thai plan and roof. Cupolas, a gallery and fluted columns adorn a school building.

Si Mahaphot – *South by 319, turn left into 3070 and continue to Ban Sa Koi then take a track to the right.* The excavation site has yielded many Hindu and Buddhist sculptures of great artistic value (sandstone lingam, 7C-8C standing Buddha, 6C-7C Ganesha, statues of Vishnu); most are displayed in the National Museum in Bangkok. Traces of ruined temples remain, as well as a dam built in the 13C by Jayavarman VII. A sluice has been identified northwest of the site. Decorative features (lions, nagas, etc) are also on view.

Wat Si Maha Pho – *22km south by 319, turn right at Km 129 and continue for 3.2km.* This important monastery boasts the oldest bodhi tree in the country grown from a seedling brought over from Bodh Gaya in India. A seated Buddha is placed nearby and objects found in the area are displayed around the plinth. On the opposite side of the road stand a Shiva linga and laterite columns.

Si Mahosot – *Entrance opposite the Provincial Office.* The moated site of a Dvaravati settlement is clearly identifiable. A track *(1km)* leads past **Sa Kaeo★**, a large reservoir with remarkable animal carvings along the sides. Further along are the foundations of eight small shrines. *Return to 319, continue south and turn left near a hospital for 300m.* On display are a Buddha footprint surrounded by lotus pillars and a wall, and Wheels of the Law. A short distance further is a small temple museum; nearby shimmers an emerald pond.

Nakhon Nayok – *18km northwest by 320 and 33.* Among the attractions of the small town on the edge of the rich and fertile plain (rice fields, orchards) watered by streams against a backdrop of forested hills is the fine **Wang Takrai Park** *(19km east, branch right at Km 12 into 3049 for 7km, entrance on the left)*, through which babbles a stream. Near the entrance is a statue of Prince Chumphot who laid out the gardens and planted rare species. Continue 1km to the nine-tiered **Nam Tok Namrong** which cascades from pool to pool in beautifully landscaped grounds (picnic sites, viewing areas). **Nam Tok Sarika** *(15km east, branch left at Km 12 into 3050 for 3km)* tumbles spectacularly down the cliff side, especially in the rainy season.

Also noteworthy is the site of **Dong Lakon** *(southwest)*, an ancient 11C-12C Dvaravati trading centre which was close to the sea at the time and has yielded interesting artefacts (terracotta, Persian porcelain, beads, bronze hamsa). A sanctuary and a mill site have been uncovered.

The popular **Khao Yai National Park★★★** *(see KHAO YAI National Park)* is within easy reach of Nakhon Nayok.

★**Scenic road to Aranyaprathet** – *140km southeast by 33.* It is an easy drive through the flat verdant landscape to the Cambodian border. In the vicinity of Sa Kaeo, **Prasat Khao Noi** (Wat Khao Noi Si Chomphu, Tambon Krong Nam Sai – *turn left into a minor road at Km 11; 250 steps and a track to the right*), which probably dates back to the 7C and towers high up on a hill overlooking the Cambodian plain, is worth a visit. The middle one of the three brick prangs has been rebuilt and reproductions of fine lintels lie nearby (the originals are displayed in Prachinburi National Museum – *above*).

The Pang Sida National Park *(27km by a branch road from Sa Kaeo market)* which adjoins the Thap Lan National Park forms a wildlife haven with many natural attractions for visitors (trails, waterfalls, rock formations).

Large crowds flock to the vast border **market** at Aranyaprathet where an amazing array of goods is traded. The Thai and Cambodian authorities have recently signed an agreement to facilitate communications between the two countries, and the area is scheduled for development.

An additional tour may be made to **Prasat Sadok Kok Thom** *(Ban Klong Takhian, 33km north by 301)*. The ruins of the border temple – gopura, wall, libraries, prang – are evocative of past times when the population moved freely. The prasat is best known for an important inscribed **stele** *(now in Bangkok National Museum)* dated 1052, which gives detailed information on Khmer history and beliefs.

PRACHUAP KHIRIKHAN

Prachuap Khirikhan – Population 85 546

Michelin Atlas p 19 or Map 965 – J 4

At the entrance to the town is **Khao Chong Krachok,** a hill pierced by a natural arch and crowned by a Buddhist temple *(398 steps)* besieged by a horde of monkeys, from which may be enjoyed fine **views** of the town, bay and mountains.

This small provincial capital boasts the long curved coastline of Ao Prachuap with to the north the rocky headland Khao Mong Lai; the road runs behind the fishing village of Ban Ao Noi. From a hillside temple, a path *(10min)* to the left of the naga staircase leads to a cave sanctuary, **Tham Khao Khan Kradai.** To the south are the high rocky cliffs of Khao Lom Muak. The natural harbour is alive with the activity of the fishing fleet. A pungent smell from the fish drying on frames permeates the air. Boat trips may be made to three islets in the bay.

EXCURSIONS

★ **Scenic coast** – The highlights of the picturesque coastline to the south include the beautiful bay of **Ao Manao** *(5km),* the deserted beaches of fine white sand of **Wa Ko** *(12km, turn left at Km 335)* – the area is being turned into a scientific research compound – and **Hat Wanakon** *(22km, turn left at Km 345 and proceed for 3.5km following signs to Huai Yang Arboretum),* and the half-moon bay *(over 6km long)* at **Bang Saphan** *(77km south, accommodation, restaurant)* with to the north the verdant headland of Khao Mae Ramphung and to the south the islands of Ko Thalu, Ko Sing and Ko Sang which offer colourful reefs and tropical fish. Beyond Bang Saphan the landscape becomes more fertile and tropical – pineapple fields, palm groves, rubber plantations, wooded hills and green plains.

Myanmar border area – In the past, old caravan routes cut across Maw Daung Pass to Mergui. A road *(west at Km 330)* to Dan Singkorn is the narrowest point (12km across) between the Gulf of Thailand and the Myanmar border. Further south is the impressive **Nam Tok Huai Yang** (120m) 35km from Prachuap *(27km south, at Km 350 turn right and continue for 8km)* in Thap Sakae district.

An astronomer king

The expertise of King Rama IV (Mongkut) as an astronomer was confirmed as he assembled many Thai and foreign guests to view an eclipse which he had accurately predicted would occur on 18 August 1868. Lavish hospitality was laid on at an elaborate camp set up at **Wa Ko** *(see above)* and the successful event confounded the sceptics. A tragic outcome, however, was that the enlightened monarch contracted malaria and died two months later.

RANONG

Ranong – Population 76 610

Michelin Atlas p 20 or Map 965 – L 3

Its geographical proximity to Myanmar, and a strong Chinese influence as the area was originally settled by Hokkien Chinese, make the busy port town and provincial capital an interesting stopover. The pleasant site at the mouth of the estuary is backed by mountains.

Tin mining was once an important industry in the province; nowadays kaolin is extracted for the manufacture of porcelain.

For information on access to Ko Surin (below) and Mu Ko Similan (see PHUKET) from Ranong – see Practical Information.

Town – Two-storeyed **wooden houses** with galleried passages at ground level in Sino-Portuguese style add an exotic note to the main street. Thanon Tha Muang leads to the bustling new fishing port of Saphan Pla where boats can be chartered for **day trips** to the fine white beaches of nearby islands (Ko Chang, Ko Phayam), which are inhabited by the Chao Le (Sea gypsies) and where pearl farming is an important activity.

On the outskirts are three **hot mineral springs** *(2km east near Wat Tapotharam)* with water temperatures around 65 °C, and an arboretum. A shrine is dedicated to the spirit of the well. A nearby hotel pipes water from the springs to a jacuzzi.

Near Hat Som Paen *(7km further along the river),* a former tin mining village, the white silt and the gouged cliff faces are ugly scars on the landscape. Women use wooden bowls to pan tin from the river. At Wat Hat Som Paen there is a stream teeming with sacred black carp.

Paknam Ranong

EXCURSIONS

Paknam Ranong – *9km, north by 4, turn left at a crossroads, proceed straight ahead and turn first right.* The road runs past wooded hills and passes in front of the Koh Su Chiang **mausoleum**, dedicated to a Chinese governor of Ranong. Nai Khai Ranong on the northern edge of the town is now a clan house and shrine and is well worth a visit.

Opposite the old fishing port are traditional houses on stilts. Restaurants along the mouth of the river offer delicious fare (fish, seafood).

Hat Chandamri *(10km northwest of Ranong)* affords wonderful **views**★★ *(from Jansom Thara Resort)* of Victoria Point and of the picturesque wide estuary of Mae Nam Kra Buri (also known as Pak Chan – mud flats), especially at sunset.

★★**Scenic road to Phuket** – *170km south by 4. Allow 1 day.* The unspoilt natural attractions along the coast make for a very pleasant drive.

A waterfall cascading down the mountain side is visible from afar and is one of the highlights of **Nam Tok Ngao Forest Park** *(12km south).*

The **Laem Son National Park** (315sq km) – *turn right at Km 657 and proceed for 10km* – extends over 100km of coastline and some 20 islands. Mangrove swamps teem with birds, deer and monkeys. **Hat Laem Son** *(3km north)* is a fine deserted beach with no facilities. From the long sandy beach lined with Casuarina pines at **Hat**

> In the first millennium AD Takuapa was a port frequented by Indian traders who settled on the Malayan coast when the region was called **Suwannaphum**, Land of Gold. Archeologists have found traces of the original town (Ban Thung Tuk) built by ancient Indian settlers, which was located in Tambon To Kho Khao *(15km from Amphoe Khura Buri district office)*. Hindu statues found at Phra Narai Hill (Tambon Leh, Amphoe Kapong) – now in museums in Phuket and Nakhon Si Thammarat – are fine stone carvings of the deities Vishnu, Shiva and Uma and are considered to be the oldest works of art (8C-9C) found in the province of Phangnga.

Bang Ben (park office, restaurant, bungalows) boat trips can be arranged to several islands – Ko Kam Yai, Ko Kam Nui, Ko Kang Kao, **Ko Phayam** *(above)* – which boast good beaches, clear waters and fine coral reefs and are ideal for swimming and diving.

The small town of **Takuapa** has a fascinating history *(see above)*. Some distance from the modern town with its wide avenues is the **old town** where houses with galleried arcades and stucco decoration and remains of the town wall are nostalgic reminders of bygone days.

Proceed to **Hat Ban Sak** *(13km south)*, a long sandy beach lined with sea pines. The road then climbs *(viewing point)* and descends through wooded hills.

Hat Khao Lak *(35km south from Takuapa, take a short track to the right)* boasts a fine sandy beach framed by rocks and shaded by tall trees *(steep path)*. There is a fine **view**★ of the splendid surroundings from the viewpoint near a restaurant.
Past the **Thai Muang Beach National Park** *(65km from Takuapa)* is a conservation area where turtles come to lay their eggs on the long sandy beach in season, before reaching **Phuket**★★★ *(see PHUKET)*.

Ko Surin ⊘ – Five islands 53km from the mainland are grouped as a national park. The Park office on Ko Surin Nua has some beach accommodation. A small Chao Le fishing community inhabits Ko Surin Tai. The granitic islands are covered with evergreen and deciduous trees as well as mangrove. The best season to visit is from December to March or early May at the latest. The seas are rough during the monsoon from May to November. Game fishing, diving, good beaches with coral reefs provide ample entertainment.

RATCHABURI★

Ratchaburi – Population 189 475

Michelin Atlas p 17 or Map 965 – H 4 – Local map see Kanchanaburi

Agriculture and trade are the two main activities which have brought prosperity to Ratchaburi. The sea has receded as the estuary of the Mae Nam Mae Klong silted up, and the fertile land produces abundant rice harvests. To the west lie rugged limestone mountains riddled with caves.

A long history – Owing to its favourable location by the Mae Nam Mae Klong the region has attracted settlements through the ages. The whole area including Ku Bua *(below)* was part of the Dvaravati Suwannaphum kingdom later ruled by the Khmers. It then came under the aegis of the Sukhothai and Ayutthaya kingdoms and was subsequently overrun by the Burmese. After King Taksin's victory over the Burmese in the 18C Ratchaburi became part of the new kingdom. King Rama V delighted in the beautiful scenery and in the late 19C built a palace on a hill. The population is an interesting mix of natives of central Thailand, Thai Yuan from Chiang Saen, Mon from Burma, and Lao who were moved from the northeast in the course of Thai history. The Karen tribe settled in the area some 200 years ago.

SIGHTS

Town centre – Ratchaburi is famous for its jars in brown glazed ceramic with dragon and floral motifs which are exported throughout the land. Jars of all sizes piled up along the river bank awaiting collection on barges are a typical sight. The jars are used to collect water or for decoration. From the bridge there are good views of the busy town which has a clock tower and fine Law Courts.

★ **National Museum** ⊘ – *Thanon Woradet*. The former town hall, a harmonious pink building with wooden shutters, houses the museum which traces the history of the region. The geographical section explains the topography of the area and its rich

Ceramic Jars

P. de Wilde

mineral resources. Prehistoric settlement is illustrated by a burial site, stone tools, earthenware vessels, a model of a house based on post holes, and precious ornaments including a six-spar tortoise-shell **bracelet**. Terracotta bas-reliefs, a rare silver medal with a Sanskrit incription (7C), copper and silver coins are evidence of the mysterious Dvaravati kingdom. In the 11C-13C the Lopburi-Khmer influence was dominant: richly-decorated Buddha images, powerful irradiating **Lokesvera** in stone, bronzes, glazed ceramics. Boundary stones and ceramics and coins recovered from the Mae Nam Mae Klong mark the Ayutthaya period (14C) when conflicts raged with Burma. There are also exhibits on the ethnic groups, folklore and crafts which flourish in the province.

Wat Phra Si Ratana Mahathat – A majestic prang dominates this ancient monastery built during Khmer rule. Buddha images crown the walls of the compound, and a serene seated Buddha in pink sandstone graces the cloister. Three smaller structures frame the prang which has a remarkable stucco decoration of floral motifs, demons and celestial beings, and ornate gables and pediments. The advanced main chamber boasts mural paintings in the Ayutthaya style depicting figures of past Buddhas.

EXCURSIONS

Caves – *West by 3087*. Many caves in the limestone hill Khao Ngu *(7km)* are shrines housing powerful Buddha images in the Dvaravati style, including a seated Buddha in **Tham Russi**, a reclining statue with disciples in **Tham Fa Tho**, and two seated Buddha images in **Tham Chin**. A quarry nearby is being turned into a park with a large pond. **Tham Khao Bin** *(20km – turn left)* in the Khao Bin range has remarkable concretions including an eagle spreading its wings. In the grounds of a shady arboretum *(north side of the road)* is Tham Chumphon where stalactites and stalagmites frame a reclining Buddha.

Ku Bua – *11km southwest by 4 and 3339*. Within the precincts of Wat Ku Bua and Wat Khlong are extensive ruins of an 8C chedi and a 7C vihara with steps and moat, all that remains of an important Dvaravati settlement.

Photharam – *20km north by 4*. In a pleasant site on the west bank of the Mae Nam Mae Klong, Photharam has some interesting temples which are worth a visit if time allows. The buildings of **Wat Khong Kharam**, Wat Photharam and **Wat Sai Arirak** *(follow the railway track north)* are ornamented with fine mural paintings and wood carving.

Ban Pong – *40km north by 4 and 323*. In the grounds of Wat Muang, an old Mon temple on the west bank of the river, stand a distinctive Burmese-style chedi and a well-presented **museum** featuring the history, lifestyle and heritage of the local community which comprises Thai, Chinese and Lao as well as a majority of Mon origin. Stone tools, earthenware, bronze ware, beads and bangles provide evidence of early human settlement in the Mae Klong basin. Mural paintings and religious objects illustrate local traditions and beliefs. There is also a section on the economic development of the region and its social consequences.

RAYONG★

Rayong – Population 181 631

Michelin Atlas p 17 or Map 965 – I 6 – Local map see Pattaya

The idyllic coastline of white sandy beaches fringed with sea pines and a string of beautiful islands are the main attractions of the small town of Rayong, through which meanders the Mae Nam Rayong. The bustling **Paknam Rayong** with its fishing fleet and the nearby Wat Pak Nam, a landmark for sailors, present a colourful spectacle on the estuary. Si Muang Park is the focal point for popular celebrations.

Rayong has good tourist facilities and fine restaurants serving delicious seafood. It is also noted for its fish sauce *(nam pla)* and shrimp paste *(kapi)*, the essential condiments for many Thai dishes.

Fun and games

Boat races and folk spectacles are held during an annual religious festival *(Nov)* at Phra Chedi Klang Nam.

The **Rayong Fruit Fair** *(May or Jun)* celebrates the region's abundant fruit production (pomelo, rambutan, durian, etc). Local growers sell fruit from their orchards, spectacular floats decorated with fruit and flowers parade through the streets and there are beauty pageants, fruit contests and displays of handicrafts and agricultural produce as well as cultural and folk shows.

Resort – Long white beaches (Hat Saeng Chan, Laem Charoen) are the pride of Rayong and are very popular with local people.

To the west stretch the secluded Hat Takhuan, Hat Sai Thong *(boat trip to Ko Saket, 15min)*, Hat Phayun and Hat Phala. Further along between **U-Taphao** airport and the naval base at **Sattahip** is Ban Chong Samae San with its small fishing harbour sheltered by rocky headlands, and Ko Raet and Ko Samae San and a string of islets which can be explored at leisure.

The east coast to Laem Mae Phim offers beautiful views and beaches (Hat Saen Chan, Laem Charoen, Hat Mae Ramphung, Khao Laem Ya) and is ideal for leisure activities. In the **Sobha Botanical Gardens** *(by 3 at Km 238)* are a sala and 3 Thai houses complete with typical furnishings and utensils as well as art objects and antiques.

Ban Phe *(by 3, at Km 231 turn right for 5km)*, a busy fishing port, is the departure point for boats to **Ko Samet★** *(see below)*. The shops sell local products such as dried fish, shrimp paste, etc as well as useful essentials for visits to the islands – sun tan lotions, insect repellents and mosquito coils. **Suan Son** Pine Park *(5km from Ban Phe by the beach road)* is a shady haven. Further along, **Hat Wang Kaeo** is dominated by a promontory affording bird's eye **views★★★** along the coast. On the horizon off Laem Mae Phim lie the **Ko Man** group of islands *(boat trips)*.

Proceed for 15km north by 3161 to Ban Khram where a memorial park celebrates **Sunthorn Phu**, Thailand's greatest poet (1786-1856) and brings to life the characters of his most famous work *Phra Aphaimani*.

Phra Aphaimani

The romantic epic poem by the celebrated 19C poet **Sunthorn Phu** relates the story of a prince who was banished by his father and condemned to live in the sea with a she-monster. The prince escapes with the help of a beautiful mermaid; the she-monster follows in pursuit but she dies as he plays his magic pipe. The prince then marries the mermaid. The action takes place on Ko Kaeo Phisadan which is based on the island of Ko Samet where resided the poet.

EXCURSIONS

Khao Chamao – Khao Wong National Park – *71km northeast by 3 and 3377 (at Km 274)*. The Khao Chamao granite massif culminates at 1 028m above the dense forest surrounded by fertile agricultural land. Many species of fauna (gibbons, serow, sambar, gaur, tiger, black bear) prosper in the wild, and bird species include the crested serpent-eagle, the silver pheasant, hornbills and bay owls. The air is cooled by several waterfalls; **Nam Tok Khao Chamao** *(2km by trail from the park office)* is the most beautiful. Another spectacular feature is the **Khao Wong Caves** *(6km further by 3; at Km 286 turn left and proceed for 12km)* which comprise 80 chambers bristling with concretions.

★Ko Samet

Ko Samet ⊘ the main island of the **Ko Samet National Park** established to protect the fragile environment from over-development, has a distinctive hilly outline covered with dense vegetation and tapering to a long deserted headland indented, with secluded bays and palm-fringed beaches on the sheltered east coast. There is only one beach, at Ao Phrao on the rugged west coast. The wind sweeps over the scrub but the cliffs afford stunning **views** at sunset.

A poetic setting – The beautiful island which takes its name from the samet tree, traditionally used for boat building, has a legendary character. As Ko Kaeo Phisadan it is the scene of some of the action of the epic poem *Phra Aphaimani* by Sunthorn Phu.

Tour – *Allow 1 day*. **Hat Sai Kaew★★** (Diamond Beach) lives up to its name with its long stretch of sparkling white sand, and the delightful coves separated by steep headlands are havens of solitude for those who wish to escape the crowds of visitors from the capital who flock to the island at weekends and during holidays. The clear waters and fine coral reefs offshore and the outer islands (Ko Plai Tin, Ko Kham, Ko Kruai, Ko Kudi, Ko Khangkhao, Ko Thalu) attract snorkelling and diving enthusiasts.

ROI ET

Roi Et – Population 151 220

Michelin Atlas p 13 or Map 965 – E 8

A picturesque lake, known as Bung Phalan Chai *(near the provincial hall)*, with an island linked by two bridges and on which stands the city pillar, is the centrepiece of this moated town (three of the channels remain) which is a growing provincial capital. Take a stroll to enjoy the lively atmosphere of the area with its excellent restaurants and bustling markets.

Other interesting sights include **Wat Burapharam** *(east Thanon Phadung Phanit)* with a huge standing Buddha in the Dvaravati artistic tradition *(see MAHASARAKHAM)*; and Wat Klang Ming Muang *(north, Thanon Phadung Phanit)* with its colourful murals illustrating the legend of Prince Wessanthon, which dates from the late-Ayutthaya period and was used for the official ceremony of taking the oath of allegiance to the Siamese king.

Thung Kula Rong Hai – The name given to the flat land comprising Roi Et, Mahasarakham, Surin and Buriram, meaning The Weeping Field of the Kula (a nomadic people known for their qualities of endurance and patience), aptly describes its harsh environment with scorching dry summers and flooding in the rainy season. The topography and fossil evidence suggest that the area was an inland sea. A land reform scheme has been introduced to encourage agricultural production in this poor arid region which has no natural water resources.

EXCURSIONS

Prang Ku – *Wat Si Rattanaram, Amphoe Thawat Buri. 8km east by 23. Turn right at Km 8 and continue for 800m by a laterite road.* A ruined main prang, a library surrounded by a low laterite wall and a doorway are all that remains of this Khmer healing house, under the auspices of Buddha Bhaishajyagon Vaduryaprabha the healer, built by Jayavarman VII (AD 1121-1210). To the southeast of the wall are scattered decorative carvings including a lintel depicting Vishnu on Nandi with a kala and foliage.

Ku Phra Ko Na – *Wat Ku Phra Ko Na, Ban Ku, Mu 2, Tambon Sa Ku, Amphoe Suwannaphum. 60km south by 214, turn right between Km 6-7 and continue for a short distance past a rubber tree plantation.* A laterite wall pierced by a sandstone doorway on four sides surrounds the

Standing Buddha

three east-facing prangs made of brick on a sandstone base which lie north to south. The architectural features suggest that the reliquary *(ku)* dates from the Baphuon era (11C).

The tiered middle **prang** (restored 1928) is enhanced with niches enshrining Buddha images and a stucco crown. A building in front houses a Buddha footprint. The **pediment** of the northern structure illustrates scenes from the Ramayana, and the lintel carvings represent a Reclining Vishnu *(east door)* and Shiva riding on Garuda *(west on the ground)*. A celestial being, sword in hand, with a kala on the lower part adorns the lintel over the north false door, and Shiva riding the bull Nandin is depicted on the fallen lintel in front. The sanctuary was probably linked by a naga bridge to a lake *(baray)* 300m away.

245

SAKON NAKHON

The large agricultural market town lies on the southern edge of the fertile Sakon Nakhon basin, which is rich in traces of prehistoric settlement and archeological remains of the Dvaravati and Khmer civilisations. According to tradition the town was built after the original Khmer town sited near Nong Han lake collapsed to the lake bottom.

The town gained fame as a religious centre when a famous meditation master, Phra Achan Mun Phurithatto, was based at Wat Pa Sutthawat *(opposite the town centre)*.

SIGHTS

Ancient Bridge – Near the city pillar shrine *(Km 161 on the left side of road 22 east)* is an ancient Khmer bridge, part of the city wall, the only one of its kind in Thailand.

★**Wat Phra That Choeng Chum** – *Thanon Charoen Muang*. Built on top of a 10C prang with an 11C Khmer inscription, the phra that is a simple white **chedi** on a high superimposed base, with a false door (half open to reveal the laterite and sandstone monument inside) and a portico on all sides and a bud-shaped relic chamber. The tiered spire on a pedestal is crowned by a royal parasol made of pure gold. To the east of the chedi is a vihara enshrining a large seated Buddha called Phra Chao Ong Saen. A gate *(open by special permission)* behind the statue gives access to the inner chamber housing the Khmer prang.
A Buddha footprint *(opposite the chedi)*, an unusual two-storeyed octagonal library surrounded by water, and a large Isan wooden bell fashioned from a tree trunk may be viewed in the temple grounds.

Nong Han Lake – *No bathing*. The largest lake (123sq km, average depth 8-10m) in Thailand located in a large basin is a popular recreation area. It is fed by 13 streams and is the source of the Mae Nam Kam. There are fishing villages all round the lake, and production of fish sauce and fish paste *(Phan La)* is a local activity.

Suan Somdet Phra Sri Nakarin – *Tambon Choeng Chum, 1km from town*. A public park founded in 1989 encloses an ancient pond, Sra Pang Thong, believed to date from the foundation of Phra That Choeng Chum (11C). It offers beautiful landscape.

EXCURSIONS

★**Wat Phra That Narai Jaeng Weng** – *Ban That. 6km northwest near the junction to 22, left at Km 156*. Legend has it that the Baphuon-style 11C Khmer sanctuary was built by women in competition with the men who had undertaken to build Prasat Phu Phek *(see below)*. The latter stopped work when they mistook a lamp lit by the women for the star Phek and the women won the contest.
Walk round the monument to admire the finely carved scenes from Hindu (Brahman) mythology: the dancing Shiva surrounded by minor gods with rare folk elements *(east pediment)*, Vishnu reclining and a realistic naga *(north pediment)*, Krishna fighting two lions *(north lintel)*. There is a rare example of a *somasutra*, the conduit through which runs lustral water used in ceremonies inside the sanctuary, by the north false door; it is adorned with a fine head of a makara.

Phra That Dum – *Tambon Ngui Don. 5km past the town hall, turn left at sign and continue for 400m by a laterite road*. The north and south sides of the boundary moat still frame a ruined 11C Baphuon-style brick prang (8m high), and the laterite bases of two other collapsed structures. The false south door features a kala, garlands, prancing lions and elephants, and floral motifs; decorative elements include a pink sandstone lintel and a Buddha image.

Phra That Phu Phek – *Tambon Na Bor, Amphoe Phanna Nikhom. 34km west by 22, turn left at sign and continue for 14km. 3km on foot, steep climb (491 steps)*. In a leafy setting on top of Phu Phek rises the unadorned Khmer **prang** with a redented square base, probably built at the same time as Phra That Narai Jaeng Waeng *(see above)*. Staircases give access to the terrace which affords a panoramic **view** of the landscape.

Wat Pa Udon Somphron – *Amphoe Phanna Nikhom 37km west by 22. Turn right at Km 123 and continue for 3km*. A peaceful forest temple where lived a revered meditation monk, Phra Achan Fan. A modern **chedi** – tiered lotus-petal base with terracotta scenes of the monk's simple life, bud-shaped spire with gold mosaic decoration – houses a museum enshrining the monk's relics and personal effects and works. A fine **view** may be enjoyed from a large stone platform *(access by steps from the parking area)*.

Phu Phan National Park – *25km southwest by 213*. The winding road affords good **views** of the Sakon Nakhon plain and of the forested area. The nature reserve's attractions include many species of birds and wildlife (barking deer, sambar, monkeys). From the park headquarters, trails lead to scenic spots (Pha Nang Moen, Lan Sao Ae, Yot Phu Khieo), waterfalls (Tat Ton, Huai Yai, Kham Hom, **Pricha Suksan**) and caves (Tham Seri Thai). The mountainous area provided shelter for the Free Thai liberation movement against the Japanese in the Second World War.
The **Phu Phan Ratchaniwet Palace** *(14km by 213)* is a modern house with a fine garden used during royal visits to Isan. Near the entrance is the handicraft training centre where villagers learn new skills.

Ko SAMUI★★★

Surat Thani – Population 34 792

Michelin Atlas p 21 or Map 965 – L 4

The paradise island of Ko Samui ⊘ is the jewel of the **Mu Ko Ang Thong**. The archipelago is a chain of 80 islands with palm-fringed beaches, tranquil coves and rocky headlands lapped by the limpid turquoise waters off the coast of Surat Thani. In the 1970s the island was the preserve of a few adventurous travellers, drawn by its natural beauty and easy atmosphere far from the commercial pressures of the modern world. Nowadays Ko Samui is among the most favoured holiday destinations with a wide range of tourist facilities which blend into the natural environment, but it retains much of its tropical charm and peaceful ambience to soothe away the cares of weary travellers.

A wind of change – Early settlers were fishermen seeking rich fishing grounds in the Gulf of Thailand. According to ancient chronicles the island was also on the trading route between China and India during the 16C. The proud population which has a distinctive ethnic identity and local culture remained aloof from the mainland for centuries.

Besides fishing, coconut palms, an intrinsic feature of the tropical scenery, contribute to the economic prosperity. Coconuts are exported in vast quantities to the mainland to flavour delectable Thai dishes, and the by-products (copra, fibre, shells, timber from the trees) are processed locally. A curious sight is that of trained monkeys used to bring down the coconuts from the trees.

Another important activity is the cultivation of exotic fruit (mangoes, durians, rambutans, papayas, bananas, cashew nuts). As a result of the tourist boom many islanders have become very rich from the sale of unproductive land along the coast, previously thought to be of little value but now greatly prized by developers.

The highest peak Khao Yai (alt 636m) dominates the mountainous interior clad in luxuriant vegetation through which tumble picturesque waterfalls.

When to go

The best time to visit is from February to June for the clear sky and calm sea. At other times until the monsoon season (Oct-Dec) the climate may be cloudy with occasional downpours and rough seas.

Motorbikes and jeeps are the ideal means of transport to explore the recesses of the island. Besides all the pleasures of sand and surf, Samui offers excellent facilities for water-sports (sailing, scuba diving, snorkelling, windsurfing) and other activities (fishing, hiking, parasailing, go-karting).

TOUR *1 day*

A good road skirts the island with easy access to the main sights, which are described in a clockwise order. Drivers should take great care on the road. There are numerous resorts and restaurants along the way offering refreshments and other facilities.

Na Thon – The town which is the principal arrival point by boat from Surat Thani is the main commercial centre where are located post office, banks, information centre, travel agencies and other essential services, as well as bars, restaurants, craft and souvenir shops.

Big Buddha

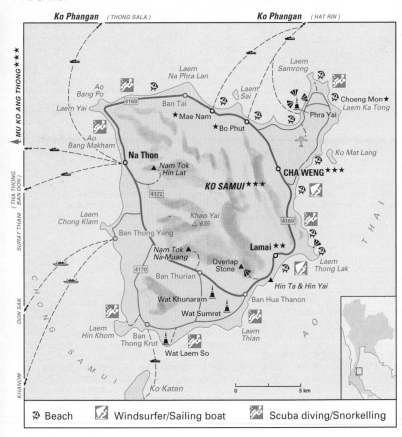

🏖 Beach	🏄 Windsurfer/Sailing boat	🤿 Scuba diving/Snorkelling

North coast – The road north runs along Ao Bang Makham fringed with a coral reef and a rocky shore. From Laem Yai to Laem Na Phralan there are good beaches, and the coral reefs along Ao Bang Po are ideal for snorkelling. Branch off at Ban Mae Nam to admire the white sandy beach of **Hat Mae Nam★** stretching to Laem Sai

with clear views of Ko Phangan to the north. Continue 2km east and take a side road to the quaint fishing village of Ban Bo Phut, the oldest settlement on the island. The long sandy stretch of **Hat Bo Phut★** offers good swimming and water skiing.

Road 4171 leads to the peaceful **Hat Phra Yai** (Big Buddha Beach) named after a major landmark of Samui, a tall seated statue of Buddha (12m) which dominates a nearby temple, Wat Phra Yai, situated on an islet linked by a causeway. The meditation temple is worth a visit. Climb up the staircase lined with a naga balustrade to the base of the statue to enjoy **panoramic views★★★** of the coast and of Ko Phangan.

Further along, the road skirts the headland where pleasant resorts nestle in the secluded coves. Elegant hotels – note the curious boathouses, formerly squat rice barges – enjoy a splendid location on a fine beach, **Hat Choeng Mon★** which curves around the bay. The road then runs a short distance from the rocky coast through rugged scenery.

Hat Lamai

Hat Cha Weng – The long beach (7km) of sparking white sand, stretching from Laem Son with Ko Mat Lang in the distance to the steep Laem Thong Yang (Coral Cape) which affords wonderful **views* of the coast and the bay, comprises three sections with a varied appeal. The best stretch of beach is in the central section which is framed by a more rugged area to the north and a steep cape to the south. Besides water-sports, visitors will also enjoy plenty of lively entertainment in the numerous bars, clubs and restaurants.

**Hat Lamai – The road dips down to another delightful bay lined with resorts accessible by side roads. Visitors flock to the extensive central beach to enjoy water-sports and a lively night-life which attracts a young crowd.

At the south end of the bay are two curiously graphic rock formations named **Hin Ta** and **Hin Yai** (Grandfather Stone and Grandmother Stone) sculpted by wind and water and facing the rising sun. Asian visitors consider these suggestive shapes as auspicious fertility symbols according to the Eastern concepts of *yang* and *yin* forces.

From Lower Lamai a steep road *(four-wheel drive vehicle or park half way up and walk up the last very steep 1km section)* climbs inland to the **Overlap Stone,** a huge boulder perched precariously on a rise from which fine **views** of Ao Lamai may be enjoyed.

The road (4169) south hugs the coast to Ban Hua Thanon, a picturesque Muslim fishing village, then veers right back to Nathon passing a trail leading east to two ruined Coral Buddhas lost in the vegetation. An old temple **Wat Khunaram** which boasts some traditional wooden buildings is also worth a visit. Further on **Nam Tok Na Muang** tumbles down a sheer cliff into a cool green pool. A short distance (3km) to the south of Na Thon is another picturesque waterfall, **Nam Tok Hin Lat.**

To visit the south coast, branch left into 4170 past Ban Hua Thanon. Further along on the right is the shady compound of **Wat Sumret.**

South coast – From Laem Set to Ao Phanka, elegant resorts nestle along the rocky shore lapped by shallow waters ideal for snorkelling but not for swimming.

Wonderful sunsets may be

Events and Festivals

Many traditional festivals – Songkran (Thai New Year, *Apr*), Loy Krathong *(Nov)* – are celebrated throughout the year.

Buffalo Fighting, a popular sporting event where two water buffaloes lock horns in an arena, is now held only on special occasions such as Songkran. For some time before the contests the beasts are fed extra rations and are pampered. There are several stadiums around the island. The fights draw crowds and although gambling is not allowed, there is enthusiastic betting.

enjoyed from the capes and bays reached by dirt tracks. The secluded coves lined by coconut groves afford peace and quiet for those seeking a relaxed environment. At **Wat Laem So** a restored ancient **chedi** stands in a pleasant seaside setting washed by the waves, and from Ban Thong Krut boats may be hired to Ko Katen and smaller offshore islands. The coast road rejoins 4169 a short distance from the side road to Thong Yang Pier on the way back to Na Thon.

Le Monde/ HOA QUI

Ko PHANGAN ⊘

The unspoilt atmosphere of Ko Phangan draws visitors who shun the amenities of Ko Samui. The splendid pristine beaches and scenic bays are best reached by boat as the dirt roads plied by songtao taxis and motorbikes are difficult. **Thong Sala** is the island hub where there are shops, banks, travel and rental agencies. Resorts are strung along white sandy beaches and pretty coves along the east coast which affords good swimming, while the best coral reef for snorkelling is on the west coast.

Hiking *(guides advisable)* is the best way to explore the mountainous interior cut by fast-flowing streams and waterfalls (Nam Tok Than Sadet). An occasional temple crowns a hilltop and trails lead to viewpoints dominating the rugged limestone slopes and the luxuriant jungle vegetation. Fishing is the main activity of the population which numbers some 9 000 inhabitants, although tourism is gaining ground.

> Backpackers congregate in large numbers at full-moon parties which have become a tradition over the years on Ko Phangan. These raves which are famous for loud music, wild dancing and unihibited behaviour are mostly fun occasions; however, excessive drinking and drug taking can have serious consequences.

Ko TAO ⊘

The remote "Turtle Island" is famous for the huge golden boulders smoothed by wind and water strewn along the shoreline, and for the slow pace of life reminiscent of the early days before Ko Samui and Phuket were put on the tourist map. The small resident population is dependent on coconuts for its livelihood. There are simple facilities on the island which boasts long stretches of sandy beach and coral reefs.

One kilometre northwest of Ko Tao is the picturesque **Ko Nang Yuan** comprising three tiny islets connected by a sand bar.

★★★ Mu Ko ANG THONG NATIONAL PARK ⊘

The marine park created in 1980 to protect the unspoilt environment comprises some 40 limestone outcrops, with a thick forest cover exotically outlined against the deep blue sky, and the sparkling waters of the Gulf of Thailand. The sheltered coves edged with pristine white beaches, the shimmering lagoons and towering cliffs make for an idyllic experience. The highlight of the tour is **Ko Mae** (Mother Island) which features an emerald salt-water lake, **Thale Nai** *(15min by boat from the visitor centre and an easy trail)*, surrounded by sheer cliffs. **Panoramic views★★★** of the islands are ample reward for a steep hike to a hilltop (240m high). On the trip there are many opportunities for snorkelling to admire the coral reefs and marine life.

SAMUT SAKHON

Samut Sakhon – Population 201 398

Michelin Atlas p 24 or Map 965 – H 5

The busy town has evolved from a fishing community at the mouth of the Mae Nam Tha Chin which is linked by Khlong Mahachai to the Mae Nam Chao Phraya. Orchards (coconuts, pomelo, guavas, grapes) and vegetable and flower (orchids) plantations thrive on the rich alluvial land, and shrimp farming and salt production are important activities along the coast. The landscape is changing fast as the area is being developed as a centre for light industry, with the ensuing problems of pollution and traffic congestion.

Town centre – From the esplanade the **harbour** with fishing boats leaving their moorings or landing their catch is a lively spectacle. The **market** near the pier is also very picturesque. Samut Sakhon boasts excellent fish restaurants. In front of the City Pillar Shrine and Provincial Hall are placed cannons from the ruined **Wichian Chodok Fortress** nearby, built in the 19C to prevent enemy invasion.

EXCURSION

Boat trips – It is well worth hiring a boat to see the sights and the beautiful scenery. **Ban Tha Chalom**, a picturesque fishing village with houses built on stilts, is situated on the west bank downriver. **Wat Sutthiwat Woraram** *(near Tambon Tha Chalom, on the west bank opposite the town)* is an ancient monastery built in the Ayutthaya period with a monument to Rama V in a garden. The ubosot of **Wat Yai Chom Prasat** *(near Tambon Tha Chin, on the west bank upriver – also accessible by road)*, a royal temple also dating from the Ayutthaya period, has beautiful carved door panels.

SAMUT SONGKHRAM

Samut Songkhram – Population 106 973

Michelin Atlas p 24 or Map 965 – H 5 – Local map see Kanchanaburi

A network of canals crisscrosses the marshy terrain of the estuary of the Mae Nam Mae Klong where Samut Songkhram is situated. The fertile land supports lush **orchards** (vines, guavas, litchis, coconuts). A boat trip is a delightful way to explore the countryside and admire the typical wooden houses lining the banks of the Mae Nam Mae Klong and the canals.

Damnoen Saduak★ *(see DAMNOEN SADUAK)* is the most famous of the **floating markets** in the vicinity of Tambon Amphawa. Owing to its proximity to the sea, the area is also devoted to **salt production** and lobster farming.

Salt flats

SIGHTS

Salt flats – The flat landscape along the road no 35 (Thonburi to Pak Tho) is a patchwork of salt pans punctuated by windmills which pump the sea-water. Workers toil under the hot sun through the various stages of evaporation and finally rake the salt into sparkling white mounds.

Don Hoi Lot – *At the mouth of the Mae Nam Mae Klong. Boat hire at the market landing.* The mud-flats uncovered at low tide are a rich hunting ground for razor clams, a local delicacy served in restaurants on the sea front. A bar formed by worm shells is visible in the dry season *(45min by long-tail boat)*.

Wat Phet Samut Wora Wihan – The main attraction of this large temple is a revered Buddha image enshrined in the ubosot. According to tradition the statue found floating in the river *(see CHONBURI – Excursions Chachoengsao)* is one of three revered by fishing communities. There are performances of classical music and dance at the request of the faithful.

EXCURSION

★King Rama II Memorial Park ⊘ – *6km south by 325.* The area was the fief of powerful families including the queens of Kings Rama I and Rama II, as well as the birthplace of the latter. Five traditional **wooden houses** which serve as a museum and a library are charmingly grouped in the beautiful grounds planted with tree species found in Thai literature. Porcelain, puppets, furnishings evoke the royal owner. Walk to the sala by the waterway for a pleasant **view**.

SARABURI

Saraburi – Population 113 439

Michelin Atlas p 24 or Map 965 – G 5

Low hills and limestone crags mark the northeast boundary of the fertile central plain with its undulating rice fields. Saraburi which was founded in the 16C is a provincial capital and serves as a gateway to the Khorat plateau.

Saraburi is a good base from which to explore many natural attractions (waterfalls, caves, Phu Khae, Khao Sam Lan and Muak Lek nature parks) in the area, but it is renowned for its important religious centres which attract large numbers of pilgrims. There are several Chinese temples 4km north of the small town of Hin Kong. **Wat Tham Krabok** *(25km north by 1)* has won great acclaim for its unorthodox herbal treatment of drug addiction.

A pleasant **excursion** by long-tail boat *(from Chalerm Phrakiat Bridge near district hall of Khaeng Khoi 15km east by 2; 30min)* can also be enjoyed going up the Mae Nam Pasak to Pha Sua and Pha Mi, cliffs resembling a tiger and a bear with dark caves at water level.

EXCURSIONS

Wat Phra Phuttha Chai – *5km south by 1, turn right at Km 102 and continue for 4km*. The temple is located on a site where according to tradition a hermit saw the Buddha's shadow on a sheer cliff wall; a natural outline is visible on the rock face. A steep staircase hewn out of the rock leads to the top of the hill. Fine views complement the peaceful setting.

Muak Lek Arboretum – *45km east by 2 and a minor road to the left*. The clear waters of a small river cut through the arboretum which specialises in species from central Thailand, in particular *phyllocarpus septentrionalis*. A waterfall, shady paths and picnic areas provide cool havens for recreation.

★★Wat Phra Phutthabat – *28km northwest by 1*

The temple is one of the holiest shrines in Thailand. A chronicle relates that in the late 16C-early 17C a group of monks on a royal mission to religious sites in Ceylon learned that according to a Pali inscription a sacred Buddha footprint existed in

Wat Phra Phutthabat

Siam. The king carried out a fruitless search until a hunter stumbled on a well shaped like a footprint and filled with fresh water, which healed the hunter's wounded quarry and cured him of a skin disease. The king built a temple on the site which was later destroyed by the Burmese after the fall of Ayutthaya (18C). The present buildings were erected by King Rama I and his successor.

Pilgrims from all over the country converge on Phra Phutthabat at two annual festivals *(early-Feb and mid-March)* when the stalls at the base of the temple do brisk business in amulets and other religious objects.

★★★ **Mondop** – An imposing triple stairway lined with five-headed nagas leads up to the marble terrace, where the elegant mondop, a masterpiece of Thai architecture and built over the footprint soars to the heavens. The pyramidal gilded roof is finely articulated and supported by slender columns capped with lotus capitals. Large bronze bells aligned in the balustraded enclosure are rung by pilgrims to gain merit.

Interior – The ornate **door panels**★★ inlaid with mother-of-pearl and based on Ayutthaya designs, the elaborate coffered ceiling and the fine silver floor covering are of special interest. A canopy resting on decorated pillars surmounts the large **footprint**★★ – 150 x 50 x 30cm – bearing the 108 auspicious signs and covered in gold leaf.

Monastic buildings – A museum displaying votive gifts is housed in the large **Wihan Luang**★, formerly used as lodgings for members of the royal family and visiting monks. Royal emblems adorn the door panel and windows, and similarly those of the ubosot. Its gable depicts Vishnu and Garuda.

Several wihans are also of note within the temple compound. **Wihan Phra Phutthabat Si-Roi** *(north)* contains four superimposed footprints in line with the Buddhist belief that four Buddhas have already visited this world. At the foot of the main staircase stands a **pavilion** (restored) where the king changed his attire before going up to worship the holy relic.

SATUN

Satun – Population 94 405

Michelin Atlas p 22 or Map 965 – O 5

The remote capital on the estuary of Mae Nam Satun of the southernmost province of Thailand has two ports accessible at high tide by small fishing boats and is the departure point for boats to Kuala Perlis and Langkawi Island which are part of Malaysia. Under the Anglo-Siamese agreement of 1909 part of the territory came under British rule to diffuse British territorial ambitions. 80% of the population is Muslim and speaks Yawi and the Sea Gypsies or Chao Le also have settlements on the outlying islands. The traditional character of the town and the natural attractions of the environs give Satun a certain charm.

Town – Interesting features in the town include the Governor's Mansion in a distinctive Western style with Muslim architectural elements, the Central Mosque *(Thanon Satun Thani)* and row houses with Italianate arches and wooden Venetian windows *(Thanon Buri Wanich)*.

Khao Phaya Wang, a limestone outcrop 30m high to the west of the provincial office *(by Thanon Kuha Praves)* affords views of the waterways and the fertile rice fields and coconut groves. A pleasant boat trip may be enjoyed from Laem Tanyong Bo, a headland jutting into the Andaman Sea, where there is a fishing village and a long white beach lined with coconut trees, Hat Sai Yao.

EXCURSIONS

Duson Dam – *22km north by 406, turn right and continue for 2km.* The dam lies in a pleasant setting at the foot of cliffs and is ideal for an excursion.

★ **Thale Ban National Park** – *30km north by 406 and 4184. Park Office and Visitor Centre.* The last remnants of the glorious rain forest (102sq km) which once covered the southern peninsula extend on either side of the Malaysian border, and comprise the Khao Chin range culminating at 740m. The superb scenery is exhilarating: huge buttressed trees and luxuriant vegetation, limestone crags framing a vast **lake** *(by the park office)* in the valley floor, and magnificent **waterfalls** (Yaroi, Huai Jingrit) tumbling down sheer cliffs into deep pools. The teeming wildlife includes elephants, tigers, sun bears as well as rare birds – narcissus flycatcher, bat hawk, booted eagle. The **Sakai,** a primitive tribe of hunter-gatherers which once roamed the forest, have set up camp within the park.

★Mu Ko Tarutao

Departure from Pak Bara north of Satun. Allow at least 2 days.

The natural beauty of the remote islands of the Andaman Sea untouched by commercial interests remains a precious asset. The **Mu Ko Tarutao** ⊙, an archipelago of 51 islands covering 1 490sq km, was declared the first marine national park in 1974. It remains an unspoilt tropical paradise with excellent beaches, tranquil coves, and stunning scenery of craggy peaks, dense jungle and mangrove swamps.

For centuries the islands were the lair of pirates who scoured the Andaman Sea. Shipping remained under threat until the 1960s. From 1939 to 1946 Ko Tarutao became a penal colony for political prisoners. Tarutao, Adang, Rawi, Lipe and the Ko Klang group are now inhabited by the Chao Le (Sea Gypsies) and park officials, but the rest are deserted.

Ko Tarutao – *Harbour and Park Office at Ao Phante Malaka.* The main island boasts long sandy beaches, tranquil bays and capes, dramatic limestone pinnacles and cliffs, luxuriant vegetation and fine coral reefs. Upstream of Khlong Phante Malaka is **Tham Chorakhe** (Crocodile Cave), which extends about 1km under the limestone mountain (dangerous at high tide). A 12km trail bisects the island passing the remnants of the prison camp at Ao Talo Wao *(east)* and Ao Talo Udang *(south).* Nature lovers will delight in the rich wildlife which includes many protected species – green turtles, dolphins, dugong. Hornbills, herons, wagtails and terns are common on the island.

Ko Adang, Ko Lipe and Ko Rawi – *Park Offices.* The stunning beauty and wild character of the islands as well as a sense of isolation will appeal to the adventurous traveller. Clear waters and splendid coral reefs surround the granite hills which have a dense forest cover.

SINGBURI

Singburi – Population 55 850

Michelin Atlas p 11 or Map 965 – G 5

At the junction of busy roads which cut through the flat rice-growing central plain lies the main town of a small province. The typical landscape reflects the seasons and the rhythm of agricultural work.
Singburi has a place in Thai history for the bravery of its people against the Burmese invaders in the past.

EXCURSIONS

Inburi National Museum ⊙ – *20km north by 311, turn right at Km 15.* Exhibits include a greenstone Buddha image, shadow play characters, ecclesiastical fans, a royal palanquin and agricultural machinery.

Wat Phra Non Chaksi – *3km west by 3032, turn left.* The peaceful temple enshrines a huge reclining Buddha (46m long) of some artistic merit in spite of restoration. It is probably of ancient origin.

Wat Na Phra That – *400m further west.* All that remains of the monastery is a fine **prang** from the early-Ayutthaya period. Steps lead up to the shrine which contains a seated Buddha. The prang retains stucco garudas and guardian demons, and standing Buddhas in niches. Other buildings lie in ruins.

Khai Bang Rachan Park – *15km west by 3032.* The shady park *(both sides of the road)* is a perfect setting for a replica of a fortress and a monument celebrating the valour of the local people, who in 1765 withstood repeated assaults before being defeated by the invading Burmese army. The monks of Wat Pho Kao Ton *(in the enclosure)* played an important part in the resistance. A vihara with a keel-shaped base houses a statue of a Buddhist monk who led the villagers.

SI SA KET

Si Sa Ket – Population 134 688

Michelin Atlas p 15 or Map 965 – F 9 – Local map see Ubon Ratchatani

The town, formerly known as Muang Khu Khan, probably dates back to the Khmer period. The majestic Dong Rak mountain range to the south forms the border with Kampuchea (Cambodia). Impressive Khmer sanctuaries all over the province testify to its historic past.
From Si Sa Ket a day-excursion can be made to the splendid **Preah Vihear** *(see below)* which is among the best examples of Khmer religious architecture. It is now in Cambodian territory following a dispute arbitrated by the International Court. Visitors were not allowed in previous years owing to the civil war in Cambodia which ended in 1991. As the situation at the border is now less unstable, it is possible to gain access. The site can be reached by road only from Thailand.

Town – Places of interest include **Wat Maha Phuttharam** *(near the north end of Thanon Khukhan)* which boasts a marble Buddha image, Luang Pho To, (knee span width 3.5m and height 6.8m) in the subduing-Mara stance and believed to date from the Khmer period; and on the outskirts the **Suan Somdet Phra Sri Nakharin** (Princess Mother Park – *at Si Sa Ket Agricultural College, Thanon Kasikam, Tambon Nong Khrok, 1km west of town*), which has remnants of the original forest and wildlife (rabbit, wild cock) and the Lamduan tree species which bears a yellow flower *(Oct-Nov)* adopted as the symbol of the province. **Si Sa Ket Zoo** *(Non Nong Kwang, Tambon Nam Kham, 4km south)* situated in a forest park has many wild animals – tigers, bears, monkeys, deer and birds.

EXCURSIONS

Prasat Hin Wat Sa Kamphaeng Noi – *Ban Klang, Tambon Kayung, 8.7km west by 226, turn right.* The remains of a prang, a library and a pond with a stepped rim, all surrounded by a wall, stand on a rise. The plan is typical of the healing-houses built in the 13C by Jayavarman VII. There are some fine lintels above the doorways.

★ **Prasat Hin Wat Sa Kamphaeng Yai** – *40km southwest of Si Sa Ket. 2km from Amphoe Uthumphon Phisai by 226, turn left or right at Km 81 and continue for 1km by a laterite road.* The large Khmer temple, which probably dates from the reign of Suriyavarman in the 10C, was first built as a Brahmanic sanctuary and altered to a Mahayana Buddhist temple in the 13C.
A gallery surrounds the complex which comprises a main stupa flanked by two smaller brick structures, with another brick stupa at the back and two brick libraries to the east. The monumental gateway has three entrances; an inscription in ancient Khmer script on the courtyard side of the main gate refers to a dedication of the land to Shiva in 1042. The carved doorways, lintels and pediments are of great artistic value: the south pediment of the central prang features Shiva seated on the bull Nandin with his wife Uma sitting on his lap, and various attendants; the interior lintel depicts Indra riding an elephant above a kala flanked by simhas spouting foliage; on the inner lintel of the north library Vishnu reclines on a crowned naga with his wives seated next to him. In the modern chapel is a fine 13C statue of the Buddha seated under a naga, and other sculptures excavated at the sanctuary.

Prasat Ban Prasat – *Wat Ban Kamphaeng, Tambon Muang Chan, Amphoe Uthomphon Pisai. 20km further west by 226; at Ban Huai Thap Than turn right and cross the railway line, after 8km turn right at sign.* A wall surrounds three tall brick prangs with a lotus-bud crown aligned north to south on a laterite base. Some of the sandstone door-frames are still standing. The east doorway of the middle prang has an unfinished lintel featuring a divinity standing over a kala spouting garlands. The smaller prangs are much restored; a lintel on the ground near the south prang depicts the churning of the sea of milk.

Prasat Prang Ku – *Amphoe Prang Ku. 60km southwest by 220, 2167 and then 2234 for 10km in the direction of Ban Pok.* The moated Khmer sanctuary comprises three brick prangs, each with a door to the east, with beautiful carved decoration. Lintels and other elements are scattered throughout the site. There is a large pond to the east.

Preah Vihear ⓥ – *About 90km southeast by 221 and minor road. Information pavilion on the Thai side.* The temple dramatically perched on a rocky plateau is dedicated to the Hindu god Shiva and was built between the 11C and the 13C. A majestic naga staircase rises steeply to the main sanctuary. The decorative features of the ruined buildings are noteworthy although in a state of dilapidation: gopura (gateways) with superb carved lintels, pediments and antefixes; Buddha images and carved reliefs.

Mor Daeng Cliff – *Near Preah Vihear (1km). 220m steep climb from the carpark at the foot of the cliff.* The viewing-point affords the best view of the temple and of the Cambodian plain. On the south face of the cliff there is a bas-relief dating from the 9C, probably the oldest in Thailand, and rock paintings.

B. Davies

Prasat Hin Wat Sa Kamphaeng Yai

SI SATCHANALAI★★

Sukhothai

Michelin Atlas p 7 or Map 965 – D 4 – Local map see Phitsanulok

The imposing ruins of Si Satchanalai, Sukhothai's twin city founded in the 13C, nestle in a tranquil wooded setting bounded by a line of hills and the Mae Nam Yom. The overall plan of the settlement reveals the ingenuity of the founding fathers in taking full advantage of the topography. The peaceful atmosphere invites visitors to roam at leisure and explore the monuments, which mark the earliest expression of the Thai independent spirit.

The modern town (Population 94 648) is located some 10km to the north of the historical area.

A royal seat – Prior to the founding of the kingdom of Sukhothai there was a Khmer outpost at **Chaliang** in a bend of the river, which owed its importance mostly to its connections with other townships through both land and water routes. After the Thais had asserted their independence Si Satchanalai became the seat of the viceroy of Sukhothai, and the 15C during the rule of King Li Thai as viceroy marked the peak of the progress of Buddhism and art. Stone inscriptions relate that upon accession to the throne he built and restored many temples in Sukhothai and its secondary towns. Between 1460 and 1474 Si Satchanalai was occupied by Chiang Mai; in the 17C when it came under Ayutthaya's rule it declined in importance and was finally deserted in the 18C.

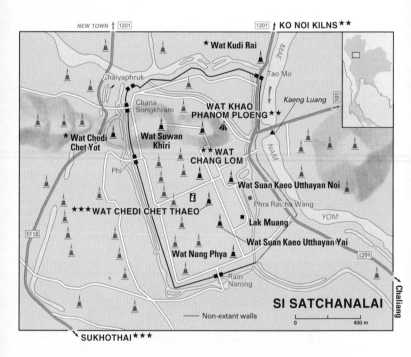

Site – The original centre at Chaliang expanded, probably in the 15C, to the walled enclosure to the northwest which comprises 42 ruined sites of religious sanctuaries. Outside the walls there are about 95 ancient sites including those on the mountain ranges. The sensitive restoration of the deserted site which was overgrown with dense scrub has preserved the mystical atmosphere as well as the verdant environment, and thus Si Satchanalai has deservedly been classed among the World Heritage Sites by UNESCO.

HISTORICAL PARK ⊘ 3 hr

According to the typical plan the two main sanctuaries Wat Chang Lom and Wat Chedi Chet Thaeo form the central axis of the town, along which are aligned smaller temples with the **Lak Muang** to the northeast. Further east are traces of the ruler's palace (Phra Ratcha Wang); the wooden buildings fell into ruins a long time ago. Only parts of the town walls remain. The moat is being dug anew to recreate the setting. Temples crowned the hilltops which afford fine **views** of the historic site.

Inner area

★★ Wat Chang Lom – Its central feature is a large Ceylonese bell-shaped **chedi★** with stucco elephant sculptures projecting from the base. The next level is pierced by niches housing **Buddha images★** which although damaged retain traces of their beauty. The finest image is on display in the Ram Kamhaeng National Museum in Sukhothai. In front of the chedi which is believed to contain relics of the Buddha stand columns of a vihara.

The wat originally stood within a large moated enclosure at the centre of the town and was thought to have been founded by King Ram Kamhaeng (13C) on the evidence of a stone inscription, but archaeological investigation suggests a later date. The imposing monument evokes a sense of power and reverence.

★★★ Wat Chedi Chet Thaeo – The literal meaning of the name is a temple with seven rows of chedis, and is prompted by the numerous **chedis★** in the compound which enshrine the relics of members of the ruling family – seven is an auspicious number used instead of the actual number which stands at 32. The structures exemplifing all the artistic styles of Sukhothai chedis mark the cultural zenith of the new kingdom and probably date from the reign of King Li Thai (15C).

The harmonious lotus-bud crown of the **principal chedi★★** is distinctive of the Sukhothai style. Aligned with the chedi is a vihara, with rows of smaller chedis behind and along the main axis in an orderly pattern. There are still traces of stucco decoration including a fine **Buddha** in meditation raised on a coiled naga on the outer face of a small chedi (behind the main one) which retains **mural paintings**; these have suffered from exposure to the elements. However, reproductions exhibited in the National Museum in Sukhothai show the previous lives of the Buddha and scenes of dignitaries wearing decorations and costumes from the Sukhothai period.

Wat Suan Kaeo Utthayan Yai – The temple dates from the mid-15C before the annexation of Si Satchanalai to the Kingdom of Ayutthaya. There are only traces of the moated enclosure, the ruined chedi, and the base and columns of a vihara.

Wat Nang Phya – This large temple which also dates from the mid-15C boasts an elegant bell-shaped chedi preceded by a ruined vihara to the east. The south wall of the latter retains splendid decorative **stuccoes★** with graceful floral and botanical designs evidently inspired by Lanna art with its strong Chinese influence, and also reminiscent of Muslim art.

Lak Muang – The unique feature of the sanctuary which stands at the centre of the compound is its indented and tiered square structure. To the east stands a small vihara.

Wat Suan Kaeo Utthayan Noi – A charming small shrine roofed in stone and a slender chedi resting on a square base and terminating in a lotus-bud crown are noteworthy.

★★ Wat Khao Phanom Ploeng – A steep stairway leads up to this important temple built on a small hill, forming a backdrop to Wat Chang Lom and affording fine **views★★** of the compound. Dotted over the site are the columns of a vihara, a seated Buddha and a ruined **chedi**. To the rear is an elegant small **vihara**. Walk down the slope to view the temple on the opposite hilltop.

Le Monde/ HOA QUI

Wat Chedi Chet Thaeo

Wat Suwan Khiri – A harmonious chedi on a terraced square base dominates the site. Buddha images were placed in the extensions on all four sides. Around the base of the bell shape is a row of high-relief figures in walking postures, symbolising the procession of worshippers. The chedi is framed by a vihara in front and a small chedi within a low enclosure. Excellent **views★★** of the scenery of Si Satchanalai may be enjoyed on all sides.

Outer area

The road (1201) north passes the **Kaeng Luang** rapids.

★**Wat Kudi Rai** – The small temple compound outside the northeast entrance gate comprises two elegant and well-proportioned buildings: a small **vihara** and an **ubosot** marked out by stone slabs. The thick laterite walls lean gradually from the base to support the roof structure. In front stand the base and columns of two structures where religious rituals were probably held.

★**Wat Chedi Chet Yot (Kao Yot)** – Steps lead up to this ancient monastery built at the foot of a hill. Its popular name is derived from the number of spires of its principal chedi, although the actual number is not seven (chet) but nine (kao). The imposing principal **chedi★** is on a square plan with an inner chamber; the central spire is framed by eight smaller spires. In front are the ruins of a vihara including its base and columns, and the plinth of a statue of the Buddha.

★★**Ko Noi Kilns** ⊙ – *5km northeast by 1201.* Archeologists have uncovered more than 20 kiln sites at Pa Yang village but four kilometres further on was the largest production site of Ban Ko Noi, where 150 kilns were found by the Mae Nam Yom. Some were visible at ground level, some were buried underground and others were constructed upon even older kiln sites. The major sites include **site no 42★** and **site no 61★** which give a glimpse of this important activity.

A **museum** ⊙ displays objects of great artistry and craftsmanship.

From kiln site no 42 a road leads to **Had Sieo** which is a well-known centre of production and sale of local textiles.

King **Ram Kamhaeng** of Sukhothai invited Chinese potters to instruct local craftsmen, who previously produced rough brown wares from the hard clay found in the area but soon mastered the art of glazed ceramics.

"**Sangkalok**" refers to pale blue or off-white porcelain. The decorative patterns such as floral, foliage or fish motifs reveal the Chinese influence. There were also Sangkalok products for architectural decoration as well as art objects such as dolls known as "Sangkalok dolls".

Sangkalok ceramics were exported from Sukhothai to foreign lands as far as Borneo, the Philippines and Japan. Finds from sunken junks in the Gulf of Thailand are evidence that the export trade was carried out along important sea routes.

In the late 15C the craftsmen moved to San Kamphaeng on the outskirts of Chiang Mai.

Chaliang

Wat Chao Chan – Evidence of Khmer culture is provided by a square **prasat** with an entrance doorway to the front, opening into a chamber which contained a sacred Buddha image for worship, fake openings on three sides and a terraced upper structure. A later vihara lies to the east and a square building to the north. There are excavation sites to the west of the compound.

Wat Chom Cheung – An air of piety pervades this large temple in its riverside setting comprising a roofed mondop, a ruined vihara with weathered seated Buddhas and a Khmer-style chedi. Burial pits provide useful information on contemporary culture.

★★**Wat Phra Si Ratana Mahathat** – This remarkable temple located to the east outside the town walls in a picturesque bow of the Mae Nam Yom probably dates from the founding of the Sukhothai kingdom, and presents artistic elements from the early-Sukhothai period with traces of Khmer influence. A massive **wall** made up of thick round columns surrounds the compound. **Stuccoes★** depicting the four faces of the Hindu god Brahma adorn the small prasat structure forming the top of the entrance doorway. These are typical of the Khmer Bayon style (late 12C-early 13C).

A fine seated Buddha dominates a ruined vihara which retains its canted pillars. Also of note are a standing Buddha *(left)* half-embedded in the ground, and in particular an admirable **walking Buddha★★** in high-relief stucco which is among the masterpieces of the Sukhothai period. A niche *(northeast)* contains a **meditating Buddha** beneath a naga hood of fine craftsmanship.

The imposing 15C Ayutthaya-style **prang★** resting on a recessed base typical of the Sukhothai era is a potent symbol of Khmer culture, which flourished on the site and was revived during the Ayutthaya period. A small **vihara** *(west)* houses a Buddha footprint.

Pass into the west sanctuary, which includes a vihara enshrining seated Buddha statues and a **mondop** containing a large standing statue.

SONGKHLA★

Songkhla – Population 154 919

Michelin Atlas p 23 or Map 965 – N 5 – Local map see Nakhon Si Thammarat

The picturesque town of Songkhla situated on a peninsula between Thale Sap (Songkhla Lake) and the Gulf of Thailand retains much of its charm, with its traditional architecture complemented by excellent beaches and beautiful scenery. The natural harbour, protected by a headland planted with sea pines (Laem Son On), presents a colourful scene with the movement of small coastal vessels and fishing boats. Larger boats anchor off Ko Nu and Ko Maeo as the town is used as a base for offshore oil exploration. The local economy is based on fishing and fish processing and the export of fish products. The area which is popular with visitors from Malaysia has fine hotels and coastal resorts.

A troubled history – Little is known of the early history of Songkhla which bore the name Singhora prior to the 8C. Archaeological evidence from the ancient site of **Sathing Phra** *(north)* reveals that it was part of the powerful Srivijaya empire which ruled southern Thailand from the 8C to the 13C and controlled the sea trade routes. During the Ayutthaya period the province became a dependency under appointed governors and paid tribute to the sovereigns. European trading companies won the right to open posts in the south to trade with Ayutthaya. During the 17C Ayutthaya's internal dissensions and conflicting interests over relations with the Malay states led to frequent rebellion by Songkhla and its neighbours against the central authority. After the fall of Ayutthaya the southern states were governed by local rulers.

In the late 18C the Burmese posed a serious threat to the south and Rama I set about imposing Bangkok's authority. A Chinese governor reporting to Bangkok was appointed and until the late 19C Songkhla was ruled as a quasi-autonomous principality. After a boundary dispute had been settled with the British in Malaya the south became integrated within the Thai state.

Songkhla's distinctive character has been shaped by Chinese immigration, which originally provided labour for the tin mines of the south.

Original site – The old town was originally at the foot of Khao Hua Daeng on the north bank of the lake where there is now a large fishing village, Ban Na Sop. In the ancient cemetery are the tombs of the Na Songkhla family, former rulers of Songkhla. There are also remains of the fortifications built by a sultan who rebelled against Ayutthaya. The town was destroyed and later rebuilt on the south bank in the early 19C.

Beaches

Laem Samila and **Hat Samila** *(north of Thanon Ratchadamnoen 3km from Songkhla market)* lined with sea pines, good for swimming, restaurants. Boat trip to Ko Nu and Ko Maeo.

Hat Kao Seng *(Thanon Kao Seng 3km south of Laem Samila)* – A long sandy beach dotted with large rocks. Muslim fishing village with market, restaurants and brightly painted korlae boats.

Hat Son On *(northeast of Laem Samila)* is a long shady beach on the narrow peninsula. Ferry *(pier on west side)* to north bank.

Hat Kaeo *(7km north by 408; turn right at sign and continue 2km by asphalt road)* – a dazzling white beach 3km long. Resort.

SIGHTS

Town – The streets parallel to the waterfront – Thanon Nang Ngam, Nakhon Nai and Nakhon Nok – will reveal charming examples of traditional architecture combining Chinese, Malay and Portuguese influences. Piers and warehouses line the waterfront which presents a lively scene with the fish market and the noise of fishing and long-tail boats.

Mermaid

B. Davies

Two hills dominate the town. At the foot of **Khao Noi** *(Thanon Ratchadamnoen near Laem Samila – surfaced road to the top)* is a pleasant landscaped garden, Seri Park (topiary). **Khao Tang Kwan** *(west of Khao Noi, naga staircase to the top near Wat Laem Sai)* is crowned by a harmonious chedi, Phra Chedi Luang, renovated in 1862 by King Mongkut, and a royal pavilion (Sala Wihan) built in 1888; there are extensive **views**★★ of the lake and town.

Paknam Laem Sai Fort *(along Thanon Laem Sai from Khao Tang Kwan, in the grounds of the Port Authority and the Police compound)* which dates from the early 1800s – the guns have been replaced – is a reminder of more turbulent times. In the bay are the aptly-named **Ko Nu** and **Ko Maeo** (Mouse and Cat islands opposite Hat Samila).

A **bronze mermaid** (1965) perched on a rock *(opposite Samila Hotel)* is the symbol of Songkhla.

Songkhla Lake – The only natural lake in Thailand (80km long, 20km wide, total area 974sq km) comprises four parts from north to south: Thale Noi, Thale Luang, Thale Sap and Songkhla Lagoon where the water is brackish and prawns are plentiful. Take a **tour** ⊘ of the lake by long-tail boat to discover the flora and birdlife and to explore the islands.

★ **Songkhla National Museum** ⊘ – *Thanon Chana.* The museum is housed in a late-19C Chinese-style **mansion**★ with a double staircase, wood carvings and inner courtyard. which belonged to Phraya Suntharanurak (Naet Na Songkhla), and later served as the Governor's official residence.

It presents the art and archeology, ethnology and folk art of the lower south of Thailand from the prehistoric era to the Bangkok period. The displays include Chinese art, folk crafts and art objects from the Na Songkhla family collection. Among the prized exhibits note a **Shiva linga**★, a Buddha votive tablet from Pattani *(ground floor)*, elegant Chinese furniture *(first floor)*, and a beautifully-carved wooden door panel *(second floor)*.

Opposite the museum stands a **wall** which marks the limit of the old town, all that remains of the rectangular wall (400m wide, 1 200m long) constructed by Phraya Wichian Khiri, governor of Songkhla in 1842, and later demolished.

★★ **Wat Matchimawat** – *Thanon Saiburi.* The 400-year-old monastery is the oldest and most important in Songkhla. The ubosot *(centre)*, established during the reigns of Rama III and Rama IV, is decorated with an ornate ceiling and beautiful **mural paintings**★★ (1863) of 19C life in Songkhla and scenes from the Jatakas (previous lives of the Buddha); a venerated marble Buddha was commissioned by Rama III. The outer gallery supported on square pillars features stone **bas-reliefs**★ imported from China, which illustrate a Chinese epic called the Romance of the Three Kingdoms.

A **museum** ⊘ *(north of the ubosot)* displays the collection of a former abbot, including artefacts found in Amphoe Sathing Phra and Amphoe Ranod: prehistoric hand-axe and painted pottery, and clay votive tablets, Buddha images, Hindu gods in various styles and Chinese porcelain.

The **vihara** *(left)* has Thai and European architectural features. Also of interest is the arcaded **Sala Russi** *(left in the courtyard)* decorated with lively **mural paintings** depicting hermits practising yogic exercises.

A tale of hidden treasure

According to legend Kao Seng, a rich patron, laid anchor in Songkhla in a boat laden with treasure intended for the construction of Wat Mahathat in Nakhon Si Thammarat. On learning that the temple had been completed, he buried his treasure and held his breath until he died; his spirit is said to guard the treasure, estimated at 900 000 Baht. A large boulder balanced on top of a cliff and known as Hua Rung is believed to mark the site at Hat Kao Seng.

Ko Yo – *Access by road (408) or by boat from the market pier.* The two spans of **Saphan Tinsulanonda,** the longest bridge in Thailand (1984, total length 2640m – scenic **viewpoints** at the bridgeheads and along its length), have improved access to Ko Yo in the lagoon.

The wooded island is famous for its traditional colourful cotton fabrics *(on sale at roadside stalls)* and two picturesque temples – Wat Khao Bo *(north)* and Wat Thai Yo *(west).* There are good seafood restaurants along the coast.

EXCURSIONS

★**Folklore Museum** ⊙ – *10km west near Ban Ao Sai (north).* The museum, established in 1978 and run by the Institute of Southern Thai Studies, occupies a picturesque site affording **views**★★★ of the lake to the distant horizon. The complex includes 17 **Thai houses** with pitched roofs in modern and local styles connected by paths and stairs. On display are interesting collections of local art, handicrafts, metal objects, terracotta, textiles and porcelain. Local and medicinal plant species are planted in the delightful gardens.

Sathing Phra – *30km north by 408.* The area is interesting for remains from the Srivijaya empire. Excavations have revealed bronze sculptures (8C-12C), some displaying Javanese influence, others in the Khmer style *(now in museums in Bangkok or Songkhla).* At Wat Sathing Phra is a Srivijaya-style **chedi** (Phra Chedi Prathan) with a square base and niches on three sides, and a staircase to the upper platform. The bulbous chedi is crowned by a spire. **Wihan Phra Non** nearby contains a fine reclining Buddha, fine stuccowork on the pediment and doors, and frescoes in blue and yellow from the Ayutthaya period on the walls.

Wat Pha Kho – *45km north by 408 (14km north of Sathing Phra). Turn left at Km 110 and continue for 1km.* The temple high up on a hill surrounded by rice fields is dominated by an old **chedi,** resting on a three-tier square base with a covered gallery highlighted by elephant stucco reliefs and decorated with small chedis. In the niches are **seated Buddhas** in bronze in the Ayutthaya and Bangkok styles.

A modern vihara contains mural paintings and a statue and relic of Phra Luang Pho Tuat, a venerated monk who was captured by pirates. He took pity on his abductors who were dying of thirst, and turned the sea into fresh water around the pirate boat. The old **ubosot** with its decorated roof is an interesting structure.

Khu Khut Bird Sanctuary ⊙ – *50km north by 408 at Mu4 Tambon Khu Khut, Amphoe Sathing Phra. Turn left between Km 125-126 and continue for 3km to the park headquarters. Or ferry trip to Hua Khao Daeng and continue for 73km by 4083 to Amphoe Ranot; turn left at the access road branching off at Km 33 and continue for 3km to Ban Khu.*

The wetlands within the park area (25sq km) are the habitat for 140 species of **waterfowl** including herons, fishing eagles, kites, hawks, cormorants, storks, sandpipers, terns and kingfishers. The best time for bird-watching is in the mornings and late afternoons in the cool season between November and February.

SUKHOTHAI★★★

Sukhothai – Population 115 787

Michelin Atlas p 7 or Map 965 – D 4 – Local map see Phitsanulok

The northern region of the Central Plain bounded by mountain ranges and drained by the Mae Nam Yom witnessed the birth of Thai civilisation. Sukhothai was the capital of a powerful empire which shaped the political and cultural ethos for nearly 200 years (mid 13C to mid 15C). Its dominance extended as far as Vientiane in Laos, Pegu in Burma and Nakhon Si Thammarat in the south, and it also established diplomatic links with the Chinese empire. Its remarkable achievements in the fields of art and architecture combining Khmer, Mon and Sinhalese influences endure to the present day. Sukhothai and its secondary towns of Si Satchanalai and Kamphaeng Phet have been accorded world heritage status by UNESCO.

The new town *(12km east by 12)* on the east bank of the Mae Nam Yom was rebuilt after being destroyed by fire in 1968. It offers good facilities for visitors.

"The Happy Dawn" – There already existed in the 11C-12C densely populated communities in the lower part of present-day northern Thailand. These early settlements close to communication routes grew in importance and subsequently formed the Thai kingdom of Sukhothai, the "happy dawn", in about 1235.

Sri Indrarathit was among the Thai leaders who co-operated in driving out the Khmer overlords. He became the first king of Sukhothai and took the name **Intradit.** His son, **King Ram Kamhaeng the Great,** ruled the kingdom from 1279 to 1298 during its golden age. This able monarch devised a Thai alphabet, promoted Buddhism and expanded the kingdom. This spiritual and material flowering, especially in art and culture, was at its peak when King Li Thai (1347-*c* 1368) came to the throne.

Li Thai's rule was politically weak and as his kingdom shrank the king moved to Phitsanulok, a major southern outpost, to resist the encroaching influence of Ayutthaya, another Thai kingdom established in 1350 in the lower Chao Phraya river valley. Ayutthaya's forces gradually weakened Sukhothai, and finally in the reign of Mahathammaracha IV (*c* 1419-38), the last king of the Sukhothai dynasty, the kingdom was annexed by King Borommatrailokanat of Ayutthaya; however, this event led to direct confrontation between Ayutthaya and Chiang Mai, another strong Thai Kingdom. A ten-year war ensued which was occasionally interrupted by negotiations relying on their common Buddhist faith as a medium for peace. Sukhothai thus became a vassal state, which owed allegiance to the Ayutthaya kingdom and suffered the same fate at the fall of Ayutthaya.

In the late 18C, interest in Sukhothai's glorious heritage was revived when Rama I, the first monarch of the Chakri dynasty, assumed power in Bangkok. Numerous statues were taken from the ruins to adorn the temples built in the new capital.

HISTORICAL PARK ⊙ *Allow 1 day*

The Sukhothai Historical Park launched in 1976 covers an area of 70sq km and includes 193 ruined sites. Under a major restoration programme started in 1960 by the Fine Arts Department, almost all the ruins have been carefully restored or rebuilt; ancient objects from the site are on display in the Ram Kamhaeng National Museum. The site has been divided into five zones charging separate admission.

The sites described are only a selection to guide visitors who have limited time. It is, however, a wonderful experience to wander in the remote corners of the park and discover minor temples hidden in the vegetation.

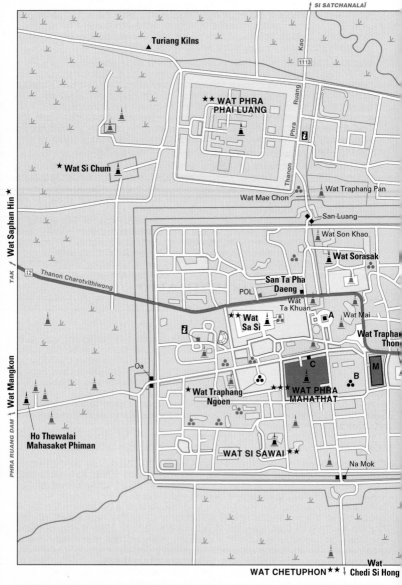

| A | Statue of King Ram Kamhaeng | B | Royal Palace | C | Lak Muang |

Site – Moats and ponds have been cleared of silt, revealing the distinctive plan of the city girt by three defensive earthen walls, which symbolises a sacred centre comparable in Buddhist belief to heavenly peace and happiness. Four main gates give access to the moated enclosure. As Sukhothai was located some distance from a river, the moats probably served as water supply and conservation systems for water diverted from sources in a nearby mountain range. Such innovative techniques attest to the great ingenuity and engineering skills of the people.

Traces of historic Sukhothai include brick or laterite ruins of religious sanctuaries and monuments such as chedis and pagodas. The tiled roofs supported by wooden structures as well as all royal residential buildings and dwellings of the population which were traditionally made of wood are no longer extant.

Inner city

Near the main entrance *(by the museum)* a bronze **statue** (**A**) of King Ram Kamhaeng on a throne is given pride of place. The royal palace (**B**) where the king dispensed justice stood in pleasant grounds to the east of Wat Phra Si Ratana Mahathat; only the foundations remain. The **Lak Muang** (City Pillar) (**C**) is situated to the west of the king's monument.

SUKHOTHAI

0   500 m

Mae Nam Ramphan

Wat Chang Lom

Kamphaeng.Hak

Khlong

Mae Ramphan

PHITSANULOK ↓ NEW TOWN

12

★ Wat Traphang Thong Lang

hlong Sao Ho

M Ram Kamhaeng National Museum

★★★ **Wat Phra Si Mahathat** – The shrine was the town's religious centre. An inscription indicates that it was probably founded in the early years of the Sukhothai kingdom. The important sanctuary (200 x 200m), built of laterite and enclosed by walls and a moat, was renovated and expanded all through the Sukhothai period. It comprised a principal vihara, an ubosot, 10 viharas and about 200 chedis. All these ruins have been restored.

Principal Chedi – The Si Mahathat believed to contain the Buddha's relics is the largest and tallest of all the structures and is surrounded by eight satellite chedis. The streamlined shape is crowned by a **lotus-bud finial** characteristic of Sukhothai's simple but elegant architectural style. Four of the satellite chedis (facing the cardinal points), built of brick, represent a Khmer-prasat style simplified to suit the Sukhothai taste, whereas the style of the other four chedis on the sides is inspired from Lanna art. Niches of the minor chedis house Buddha statues, and the **stucco decoration★** depicts major episodes in Buddhist history including the birth and nirvana (death) of the Buddha. The beautiful patterns and animal shapes are reminiscent of Sinhalese and Burmese art forms which derive from Theravada Buddhism. There is a fine stucco frieze of Buddhist pilgrims at prayer at the base of the chedi.

In front of the chedi stand gigantic columns, all that remains of the main vihara which is reputed to have enshrined the **Phra Si Sakyamuni,** a large and elegant bronze statue of the Buddha which was moved by King Rama I to the ubosot of Wat Suthat in Bangkok. Further west are the ruins of a later vihara built in the Ayutthaya period on a raised platform and housing a large seated Buddha.

Two huge standing Buddhas protected by walls flank the main chedi. Also of interest are a vihara *(north)* and a large stepped structure *(south)* with lively stucco figures at the base.

Wat Phra Si Mahathat

★★ **Wat Si Sawai** – *South of Wat Mahathat.* A Hindu shrine (*c* 12C) dedicated to Shiva and bearing a bas-relief of Vishnu was left unfinished when the Khmers were driven out in the 13C. Twin walls surround three **tower chedis** (Khmer-style prangs) adorned with stuccowork. The middle tower is connected to the vihara *(south)* built when the shrine was converted to a Buddhist sanctuary in the Sukhothai period.

★ **Wat Traphang Ngoen** – *West of Wat Mahathat. Access by a path to the north.* In a beautiful natural setting a graceful lotus-bud **chedi**, echoing that of Wat Mahathat and preceded by the columns of a ruined vihara, forms a romantic picture reflected in a "Silver Lake" (Traphang Ngoen) filled with lotus blossoms. On an island in the centre is a large seated Buddha in a vihara in front of a ruined ubosot.

★ **Wat Sa Sri** – *Northwest.* A bridge *(west)* gives access to this attractive temple on an island in a pond (Traphang Trakuan) covered with lotus blossoms. A Sinhalese-style **chedi** with a square base, bell-shaped dome and slender finial is flanked by a small chedi with niches. Three rows of columns divided the nave of a large **vihara** *(east)* which enshrines a seated Buddha.

San Ta Pha Daeng – *Left of the road to the north gate.* An east-facing 12C Khmer **tower** with a square cell and four porticos is the oldest religious monument on the site and was probably used as a Hindu sanctuary. Five Khmer-style stone sculptures of deities found inside have been moved to the Ram Kamhaeng National Museum.

Wat Sorasak – *Near the north gate.* The square base of the Sinhalese-style **chedi** features 24 elephant buttresses. The sandstone columns of a vihara are in marked contrast to the laterite columns of other monuments.

Outer area: north

★★ **Wat Phra Phai Luang** – The late-12C temple girt by a moat was probably the principal sanctuary of the Khmer settlement before the Thais moved the town centre further south.
This important temple was originally a Khmer Hindu shrine later converted into a Buddhist temple. Of the three east-facing **prangs** only the northern one remains in fairly good condition and retains some of its decorative stuccos (the Buddha and his followers on the gable of the false door).
In front are the ruins of a vihara (outside wall, four rows of columns) and a square chedi. The niches which were previously bricked up contained Buddha images unfortunately damaged or removed by thieves. Fine fragments of stuccoes and statues of disciples and celestial beings discovered on the site are on display at the Ram Kamhaeng National Museum.
Near the entrance stands a brick **mondop** with traces of large high-relief stucco Buddha images in standing and walking postures. Further east lies a ruined reclining Buddha, and to the north a seated Buddha presides amid the ruins of a vihara.

Turiang Kilns – *North of Wat Phra Phai Luang.* Near the Mae Chon moat may be seen the restored remnants of 39 ceramic kilns including the fire area, baking oven and flue. Sangkhalok porcelain *(see SI SATCHANALAI)* was one of Sukhothai's major exports and had a great impact on its economy and trade relations with other lands far and near. Potters were brought over from China in about the late 13C to impart their skills to the native craftsmen.

Return to the road along the moat west of Wat Phra Pai Luang and continue to a modern **vihara** with beautiful gilded doors and pediment, lotus capitals and slim windows. Naga heads adorn the stepped roofs.

Next to the vihara is a large modern hall used as an information centre by the TAT: diorama of the historical park.

★**Wat Si Chum** – *West of Wat Phra Phai Luang.* Three rows of columns with holes in which the roof beams were inserted, remain of a small vihara in front of the mondop, a large windowless building.

The roof (pyramidal wooden superstructure or bell-shape brickwork) has disintegrated exposing to view a huge stucco seated Buddha, the serene **Phra Achana**, which occupies the whole space within the enclosing walls. Steps in the thickness of the south wall lead to the top of the structure, giving rise to speculation that the statue was used for propaganda purposes. The ceiling of the cavity was lined with 50 **slate slabs** *(not on view)*, incised with remarkable drawings and inscriptions from the Jataka (stories of the former lives of the Buddha) and dated back to the mid 14C from the character and artistic style of the designs.

North of the compound are the ruins of a small vihara and a seated Buddha in a brick building.

Outer area: west

The western part of the outer city embraces the forest monasteries *(Aranyik)* of Sukhothai where Buddhist monks sought spiritual tranquillity through meditation. Romantic ruins evoke the pious tradition of bygone days.

★**Wat Saphan Hin** – A stone track *(east)* leads to the top of a hill dominated by a roofless vihara with brick and laterite columns, enshrining a tall stucco **Buddha**★ (12.5m) in a standing posture raising his hand in a forgiving gesture. A statue of this size was built in accordance with the traditional belief that the Buddha was very tall. Fine **views**★ of the historical park.

Wat Mangkon – In a secluded wooded area the temple, which derives its name from the discovery of porcelain with a *mangkon* (dragon or mythological animal) pattern, included several bell-shaped chedis. The crown of the restored principal **chedi** lies next to the structure, and the vihara retains its columns. The low walls marking the compound feature glazed white terracotta banisters. Boundary stones are dotted all around.

A road branching to the right leads to an earthenwork **dam** in a pleasant setting. The dam referred to in a Sukhothai inscription attests to the advanced irrigation system which supplied the old town. Return to the road round the ruins.

Ho Thewalai Mahakaset Phiman – The base of a square brick building supports eight tall columns with holes for the insertion of roof beams. The overall shape of the structure is uncertain. A stone inscription (1316) indicates that the temple housed a statue of Shiva commissioned by King Li Thai, a devout Buddhist. The shrine was associated with the Hindu religious tradition as its name evokes agricultural fertility and progress.

Outer area: south

★★**Wat Chetuphon** – The largest temple in the area which was probably founded *c* 1417 lies in a moated enclosure against a backdrop of mountains. A tall square structure probably roofed in the past and adorned with stucco Buddha images in different postures on two sides is a unique feature of Sukhothai art, which later spread to secondary towns such as Kamphaeng Phet (*see KAMPHAENG PHET – Wat Phra Si Iriyabot★*).

Wat Si Sawai

Ruins of a vihara are found outside the walls built of large slate slabs surrounding the shrines which included a row of chedis to the west. Entrance gates pierce the north, west and south walls. The slate slabs forming the walls and gate frames are held together by shouldered tenons similar to those used in carpentry. There is no other Sukhothai construction of this kind.

Wat Chedi Si Hong – The temple is remarkable for the remnants of fine **stucco** motifs of lions mounted on elephants, and deities holding vases of flowers ornamenting the base of a small bell-shaped brick chedi. The spire of the chedi lies on the ground. The temple has been plundered by thieves.

Outer area: east

★**Wat Traphang Thong Lang** – Four rows of columns of a vihara precede the arched doorway of a square building in which the holding base and traces of a large Buddha statue remain. Of outstanding interest are the high-relief **stucco Buddhas** in niches on the outside walls representing different episodes of Buddhist history: the Buddha descending from heaven after preaching to his mother *(south)*, the Buddha teaching his wife *(north)*, the Buddha and his father *(west)*. The elegant beauty of these works of art makes it possible to date them from King Li Thai's reign when Sukhothai art was at its peak. The south stucco, which is the least dilapidated, depicts the Buddha walking down a glass staircase laid before him by a mighty god. According to the story, the deity also provided two more flights of steps, one made of gold and the other of silver, for the heavenly beings accompanying him on his way down to earth. Copies of the stuccos are exhibited in the Ram Kamhaeng National Museum.

Wat Chang Lom – A stone inscription dates the large moated temple to the late 14C. Elephant buttresses jut out around the base of the main bell-shaped **chedi** extending to the east into a vihara along which lies a row of eight chedis. The **ubosot** is within a separate moated enclosure further east.

★★Ram Kamhaeng National Museum ⊘ (**M**)

The museum presents the evolution of Sukhothai art, ranging from the influence of Khmer culture to the flowering of Sukhothai art and the later dominance of the Ayutthaya style. In the annexe there is an interesting photo exhibition tracing the stages before and after the restoration of the monuments.

In the annexe by the entrance, photographs trace the renovation of the site and a copy of King Ram Kamhaeng's alphabet has pride of place. The first **stone inscription** (1283) describes the king's auto-biography and the Sukhothai kingdom in his reign. On display are art objects, stucco decorations and statutes of divinities.

Elephants were animals of high status suited to kings. They often figure in Buddhist literature; it was related for instance that when the Buddha was staying in the forest he was attended by an elephant. According to Thai traditional belief, elephants not only signify patronage for Buddhism as exemplified in the story but also represent royal prestige and power. White elephants – in reality animals with lighter patches – are highly prized.

Ground floor – The jewel of the collection is a bronze statue of the **walking Buddha★★★** (14C-15C), the only example of sculpture in the round in Thailand. The graceful posture, serene expression and harmonious features convey the perfect state of enlightenment of the Buddha. In the left corner are displayed a stone fragment believed to be a Khmer turned into stone; footprints of the four Buddhas (14C); a sandstone lintel of Vishnu in Lopburi style (13C), a 14C kala and votive tablets.

Further along are 14C statues of Hindu gods, graceful **divinities** from San Ta Pha Daeng shrine, and fine **stucco decoration** and art objects from Wat Phra Phai Luang. Recent finds at Wat Mahathat include small Buddha statues from the chedis and two Buddhas placed face to face *(display case centre)*. A copy of an admirable 14C **stucco** of the descent of Buddha from Tavatimsa heaven attests to the artistry of Sukhothai craftsmen.

On the right, interesting exhibits include copies of statues from other historical sites, lingas and inscriptions in Pali and Thai script.

First floor – Examples of Sangkalok ware (13C-14C) comprise water jars, nagas and yaksas. Stucco heads from Buddha images and angel heads are noteworthy. In the centre are prehistoric finds from Si Thep (coins, shells) and a collection donated by the abbot of Sukhothai. The progress of irrigation is illustrated by terra-cotta water pipes *(left)*.

Also of note are a reproduction of a vihara *(left)* complete with decorative elements, finely carved **door panels** depicting guardian angels in the Ayutthaya style (17C-18C), weapons including large decorative arms, and an Ayutthaya-style **crowned Buddha** in meditation (15C-16C – *back*).

Grounds – A pleasant stroll in the garden will reveal many interesting items: Dvaravati finds from **Si Thep★** *(see PHETCHABUN)* – Wheel of the Law (7C-11C), Shiva linga (11C-13C), bell stone (7C-11C), finial of sanctuary tower (12C-13C); elephant buttresses from Wat Chang Rob; a ceramic kiln.

East of the museum stands **Wat Traphang Thong** set in the middle of a "Golden Lake" and forming a pendant with Wat Traphang Ngoen *(see above)*.

King Ram Kamhaeng's inscription is regarded as the earliest written document in Thai. The script is based on Sanskrit and Khmer characters.

The **Suphasit Phra Ruang** (Maxims of King Ruang) paint a glowing picture of the powerful Sukhothai kingdom that ruled over a vast territory including many vassal states, and of a happy people living in a prosperous land blessed by nature and ruled by a benevolent king. The people were free to tend their land and cattle or engage in trade and pass on their wealth to their heirs. They had easy access to the king, who was the just arbiter of all disputes regardless of rank and riches. Theravada Buddhism was the guiding principle of the kingdom.

There are theories that this account of a golden age was primarily intended to instil a sense of identity into the people of the new Siamese kingdom, after centuries of authoritarian Khmer rule.

EXCURSION

★**Sangkhalok Museum** ⊙ – *By 12 east, then north to junction of 101 and bypass.* Sangkalok ceramic is typical of the Sukhothai era and this modern museum presents an excellent display of artefacts (vases, plates, utensils and other decorative objects) illustrating the early beginnings to the artistic peak of this craft as the technique was refined. The ceramic wares were exported by land and sea throughout East Asia. There is also a fine ceramic collection from the northern kingdom of Lanna.

SUPHAN BURI

Suphan Buri – Population 157 553

Michelin Atlas p 11 or Map 965 – G 5 – Local map see Kanchanaburi

The prosperous town situated on the east bank of the Mae Nam Tha Chin in a rich rice- and sugarcane-growing region is served by an excellent road network. A leisurely **boat trip** on the river allows visitors to admire the traditional houses, the temples and the lush countryside.

A chequered history – Several ruined monuments in the area attest to the town's ancient origin. The old town founded in the 9C on the west bank of the river was moved to various sites over the centuries, before the present settlement was consolidated in the early 20C in the reign of King Rama VI. It was involved in many battles owing to its strategic location on the invasion route from Burma. In the late 16C King Naresuan fought a decisive battle against the Burmese in the area.

SIGHTS

Tower – This distinctive landmark set in well-tended grounds affords a splendid **panorama**★★ of the fertile countryside. Paintings in a gallery relate the exciting story of the battle waged by King Naresuan.

Wat Pa Lelai – *West bank.* Several monarchs have restored the colossal statue of **Buddha**★ (23m tall) over the years. This accounts for variations in style ranging from the square Dvaravati jaw-line to the early-Ayutthaya features. The present posture differs from the original preaching attitude. The gable bears the insignia of King Rama IV who built a roof over the vihara.

Lak Muang – *West bank by 321.* Two statues of the Hindu god Vishnu in greenstone are unusually enshrined in a gaudy Chinese pavilion.

Wat Phra Si Ratana Mahathat – *West by 321 – 200m from the bridge over the river.* Niches and stucco figures are interesting features of a tall **prang** enshrining relics of the Buddha, which probably dates from the mid 14C or early 15C. Nearby are the bases of two smaller prangs as well as two ruined chedis. Unusual boundary stones *(bai sema)* frame the old vihara. There are also two small viharas with slit windows and decorated gables.

Wat No Phutthangkun – *Turn first left beyond the above and proceed for 3.3km.* The old ubosot is decorated with fine **mural paintings**★★ *(under restoration).* Scenes from the life of the Buddha are highlighted with gilding and floral bands. The gable and pediment are also noteworthy.

Wat Pratu San – *West by 321 and 3318.* The restored ubosot features a porch with square pillars capped with lotus capitals and an ornate gable. Twin doors give access to the interior, which boasts fine **mural paintings**★★ by the same talented artist responsible for Wat No Phutthangkun.

Wat Phra Rup – *West by 321 – opposite the market on the west bank. Ask to view the Buddha footprint on the first floor of the sala.* The monastery which is of ancient foundation includes a finely-proportioned ruined **chedi** on a tall redented square base, and a large reclining Buddha. Its most precious possession is a rare wooden **Buddha footprint**★★ with vivid scenes finely carved on both sides. The front depicts Buddhist cosmology with Mount Meru in the centre surrounded by seven rings of continents within which are inlaid the 108 auspicious symbols. At the back the Buddha is guarded by the four guardians of the earth.

EXCURSIONS

Don Chedi – *31km northwest by 322. Turn right at Km 23-24.* The fine white **chedi** with a canted base, bell shape and ringed finial is built over a monument erected by **King Naresuan the Great** to mark his decisive victory over King Maha Uparacha of Burma in single combat fought mounted on elephants. In front of the chedi stands a statue of King Naresuan and his signalman holding his feathers aloft on the back of an elephant.

Tha Sadet Bird Reserve – *Northwest by 322. Make a U-turn at Km 6-7 then turn left after a second bridge and continue for 2km. Viewing platform.* In the evening large flocks of birds such as storks, herons, cormorants and ibises home in on the trees.

SURAT THANI

Surat Thani – Population 148 057

Michelin Atlas p 20 or Map 965 – L 4

Surat Thani, the capital of the largest province in southern Thailand, is situated on the Tapi estuary in a fertile plain watered by two rivers, Mae Nam Tapi and Khlong Phum Duang. Idyllic islands fringe the coast, while the picturesque hinterland to the west is dominated by a high plateau and dolomitic outcrops covered with dense forest. Fishing, shipping, agriculture and forestry bring prosperity to the region.

The town is served by a good road network and is the gateway to the south as well as the departure point for the renowned holiday island of **Ko Samui**★★★ *(see Ko SAMUI).*

A rich heritage – Several prehistoric sites reveal human occupation in the Stone Age. In the first millennium the town's commercial links with Takuapa *(see RANONG)* on the strategic trade route between India and China flourished, and the culture of the region was shaped by Indian influences as merchants settled in the area. Investigation of important archeological sites (Chaiya – *north,* Muang Wiang Sa – *south)* in the province has yielded finds which rank among the country's oldest and finest art treasures *(now in the National Museum, BANGKOK)*: imposing 7C statues of **Vishnu** (Muang Wiang Sa and Khao Si Wichai, Amphoe Phunpin); harmonious 7C-8C **Bodhisattva sculptures** (Chaiya and Muang Wiang Sa). Wat Kaeo and Wat Long (AD 857) in Amphoe Chaiya *(see CHAIYA)* are also important architectural monuments which date back to the Srivijaya period (7C-13C).

Town – The pleasant town presents a lively spectacle with its busy market, colourful fruit and food stalls and the bustling harbour on the north bank of Khlong Phum Duang. There are excellent restaurants along the riverside where discerning diners will enjoy delicious fare. **Wat Phathanaram** *(Thanon Na Muang)* boasts an ubosot decorated with mural paintings dating from the reign of King Rama V.

A leisurely excursion by boat *(from the market pier)* is the best way to enjoy the verdant scenery along the khlongs on the north bank of Mae Nam Tapi.

Festivals

A **Rambutan Fair** *(Aug)* with exotic floats decked with the prickly fruit, displays of local products and various activities and the **Chak Phra and Thot Phapa Festival** *(Oct)*, which mark the end of the Buddhist Lent, are occasions for popular rejoicing. At Thot Phapa celebrated at sunrise Buddha images are carried in water borne procession or are pulled on land by the local people. Afterwards saffron robes are offered to the monks and donations made to temples at Chak Phra. Cultural events and music enliven the proceedings.

EXCURSIONS

Monkey Training School ⊘ – *Amphoe Kanchanadit. East by 401; turn right between Km 22-23 after a bridge, take the road via Ban Bo Chalok and continue for 2km.* Pig-tailed monkeys have proved remarkably adept at picking coconuts which are produced in large quantities locally. The school founded over a decade ago has devised an unorthodox training programme which lasts three months. Visitors are welcome to attend a training session when the agile and highly intelligent animals are put through their paces *(contact local TAT for appointment)*.

★★**Tham Kuha** – *Amphoe Kanchanadit. 16km east by 401, turn right between Km 30-31 and proceed for 2km.* A limestone hill dominates a temple standing in a shady compound. The major interest of the site is a cave shrine: high up on the wall (left) near the entrance is a clay-and-stucco **moulding** of seated Buddha images surrounded by small meditating Buddhas, Bodhisattvas and small chedis in the Dvaravati style dating from the late 9C-10C. Further back a **low-relief** stucco of the Buddha protected by a naga (13C-14C) reveals the influence of Khmer art. The focal point is a large **reclining Buddha** image framed by numerous statues in red sandstone and stucco.

Khun Talay Swamp – *South by 410 and 4009; at Km 1 turn left and continue for 4km by laterite road.* A freshwater lake (2km long and 800m wide) is a wintering-ground for migrating birds. The beautiful setting and views will appeal to nature lovers.

Khao Tapet Wildlife Study Centre – *6km south by 4009.* The centre which is situated at 210m above sea-level affords a panoramic **view** of the Ban Don area and bay, and of the winding course of the Mae Nam Tapi.

★**Scenic road to Takuapa** – *150km west by 401. 4hr.* A majestic scenery of rugged mountains and dense forest unfolds as the road cuts across the ridge which sweeps down the peninsula. Adventurous travellers can make a rewarding detour to the impressive **Chieo Lan Dam** ⊘ or Ratchaprapha Dam (95m high, 700m long) – *west by 401; turn right between Km 52-53 and continue for 14km)* with its vast lake (165sq km) dotted with islands. The peaceful atmosphere and spectacular landscape add to the interest of the excursion.

Khao Sok National Park ⊘ – *109km west by 401 – 35km from Takuapa.* Khao Sok peak culminating at 815m dominates the park, which covers 646sq km and is connected to four other nature reserves in the region. Craggy limestone cliffs soar above the densely forested area. Trails lead to dramatic caves, tinkling streams and picturesque waterfalls along the course of Khlong Sok and Khlong Saeng. The wide expanses support rare wildlife including 25 mammal – bears, tigers, banteng, gaur – and 170 bird species – hornbills, storks.

SURIN

Surin – Population 251 527

Michelin Atlas p 14 or Map 965 – G 8

To the south of the Khorat plateau this quiet little town with a rich Khmer heritage comes into its own at the Elephant Round-up Festival. Silk weaving is an important activity in this dry region.

The town was founded when Ban Muang Thi was moved to the present site in 1763 and surrounded by a double moat and wall (a part is still visible along Thanon Krung Sri Nok to the west). It was renamed Surin in 1786 after a governor appointed in the reign of Rama I.

Town – A bronze **statue** of a man in traditional costume with a mahout's hook in his right hand and a pair of swords on his back commemorates the governor, Phraya Surin Phakdi Si Narong Chang Wang *(Thanon Phakdi Chumpon)*. The **San Lak Muang** *(Thanon Lak Muang 500m west of the Provincial Hall)* is a 3m-high wooden pillar carved from laburnum wood from Kanchanaburi, erected in 1974.

A small **museum** *(Thanon Chao Bamrung)* displays a collection of Khmer artefacts (10C-12C) found in the area: lintels, sculpture and pottery.

Two notable **Buddha images★** are enshrined in Wat Burapharam *(Thanon Krung Sri Nai, near the city pillar shrine)* which dates from the foundation of the town.

EXCURSIONS

★★ **Prasat Hin Sikhoraphum** ⊘ **Prasat Hin Sikhoraphum** – *Ban Prasat, Tambon Ra Ngaeng, Amphoe Sikhoraphum. 34km east by 226, turn left at Km 36 and continue for 800m.* A large pond surrounds the Khmer sanctuary which was renovated in the 17C as a Buddhist temple, according to an inscription by the doorway.

Four three-storey **brick towers** frame the main stupa which has five storeys in an unusual plan which is probably of symbolic importance. A door guardian and a female deity holding a lotus flower on the columns guard the entrance of the **main stupa**. The remarkable **lintel★★★** portrays the dancing Shiva on a pedestal supported by three birds, resting in turn on a kala shown grasping the lower legs of two rampant lions. Amid the foliage six small figures ride a crested dragon, with four deities above: Uma with a human-headed sceptre, Vishnu with four arms, Brahma playing the cymbals, and Ganesha beating the drums.

Prasat Ban Phluang ⊘ – *Ban Phluang, Tambon Kang Aen, 4km from Amphoe Prasat. 30km south by 214 turn left between Km 31-32 and continue 600m by surfaced road.* The tranquil setting enhances the charm of the 11C Baphuon-style prasat built of sandstone, brick and laterite but left unfinished; it was restored in 1970. Ponds line the path leading to a single **stupa** rising from a trilobed high base.

Elephant Round-up

Its decorative carved elements are noteworthy: Krishna lifting the Govardha Mountain to protect herdsmen and cattle from the might of Indra's rain on the east **pediment**★; Indra on his mount Airavata on the lintel below; door guardians (unfinished) in the southwest corner.

★ **Prasat Phum Phon** – *Ban Phum Phon, Tambon Dom, Amphoe Sangkha. 40km southeast by 2077 and 2124.* The oldest ruin in Surin forms an evocative picture. The 7C-8C Khmer temple in the Prei Kmeng style comprises a brick **prang** with sandstone door-frame, colonnettes and lintels. The basement of a building lies to the west and and there is another ruin further away.

Prasat Yai Ngao – *Ban Sangkha, 4km southeast of Amphoe Sangkha by 24, turn right between Km 190-191 and continue for 800m along a dirt road.* Two ruined redented brick **prangs** (12C) on a low laterite base and with a sandstone door-frame at the main entrance are noteworthy for their remarkable brickwork, and for the unusual shallow naga **carving**★ in the Angkor Wat style (south pediment of the main prang).

Elephant Round-up Festival

Elephants converge on Surin *(Amphoe Muang)* for the spectacular yearly round-up in November. The festival which lasts several days includes games, races and demonstrations of skill and obedience, and usually ends with an awesome presentation of elephants in battle formation.

At other times visitors can see a few elephants at Ban Ta Klang *(Tambon Krapho, Amphoe Tha Tum 51km north by 214)*, which is renowned for the skill of its elephant trainers and mahouts whose ancestors originally hunted wild elephants near the Thai – Cambodian border. The number of elephants is decreasing because of mechanisation and scarce natural environment and resources. The noble animals now earn their keep by performing for the entertainment of spectators in tourist centres such as Bangkok, Chiang Mai and Pattaya. The village boasts an elephant **museum** and training ground.

★★ **Prasat Ta Muen Thom** ◷ – *70km south by 214, turn right at Km 35 and continue for 12km by laterite road.* This is one of the finest stone temples on the road between Angkor and Phimai. It has been extensively damaged during the recent war in Kampuchea (Cambodia) and further pillaged by thieves. A massive laterite staircase leads down from the south entrance to a stream marking the border with Kampuchea.

Four doorways *(gopuras)* punctuate the gallery surrounding the temple, with the main entrance to the south. The redented **main prang** built of pinky-grey sandstone contains two unusual features: a *Syayambhu* (a natural rock linga) on a stepped pedestal hewn from the bedrock; and a long *somasutra*, a conduit for draining the lustral waters built along a natural fissure from the antechamber to the northeast gallery wall. Two prangs also built of sandstone rise to the north; the west structure boasts a unique example of a **false door**★ carved from a single block of stone. Two laterite buildings frame the sanctuary: the rectangular structure near the east wall faces south, while the square cell by the west wall opens to the west.

Prasat Ta Muen Toch – *Tambon Bak Dadi, Amphoe Kap Choeng, 12km from Ban Ta Miang or 100m south of Prasat Ta Muen.* The 13C Bayon-style Khmer temple was a chapel to a hospital, as indicated by an inscription found on the site which has been restored and cleared recently. This was the first hospital to be visited by travellers across the border. The east gate is divided into three passages and has shallow porches to the front and back. The **sanctuary** is unusual as the body of the prang, the entrance, the pediment and the finial were built of sandstone.

Crafts

Ban Khwao Sinarin and Ban Chok *(north by 214; turn right between Km 14-15 and continue for 4km)* which formerly produced only hand-woven silk have diversified into silverware (beads and other ornaments).

In **Ban Bu Thum** *(14km northeast by 226)* basketry provides additional income for the villagers during the period not taken up by agricultural tasks.

There are specialised craft shops along the road in the villages.

Prasat Ta Muen – The restored chapel to a resting-place is built of laterite whereas the door-frames, lintels, tower crown and roof ornaments are of sandstone. There are windows on the south side of the long entrance.

Prasat Tapriang Tia – *Wat Thep Nimit. Mu 5 near Ban Nong Pet, Tambon Chok Nua, King Amphoe Lam Duan. 7km southeast by 2077.* The four-tiered brick monument is crowned by five lotus-bud pinnacles and is adorned with a carving of a three-headed elephant. The Lao architectural style is noteworthy and the structure dates from the late-Ayutthaya period.

Phanom Sawai Park – *Tambon Na Bua, Amphoe Muang. 22km north by 214, turn right between Km 14-15 and continue for 6km.* In a peaceful setting high up on the three peaks of a small mountain range, the park comprises Wat Khao Phanom Sawai and the Phra Phuttha Surin Mongkhon Buddha image (on Yot Khao Chai – man peak 300m high), a medium-sized Buddha image enshrined on Yot Khao Ying (woman peak 228m high), a sala and a Buddha footprint on Khao Kok, as well as a white chedi.

TAK

Tak – Population 97 600

Michelin Atlas p 6 or Map 965 – E 4

The remote town is laid out on a grid pattern with a wide esplanade on the east bank of the Mae Nam Ping which is spanned by a suspension bridge. The surrounding mountainous scenery is spectacular with to the west the peaks of the Thanon Thong Chai range bordering Myanmar outlined on the horizon.

The province presents distinctive cultural influences with its many hill-tribe settlements. In recent years clashes between the Burmese army and the Karen National Union have led to an influx of Karen refugees into Thailand. Cross-border trade, sometimes illegal, accounts for the province's prosperity.

A royal connection – Tak is renowned as the fief of **King Taksin** (1767-82), the son of wealthy Chinese merchants, who rose from being a royal page to the highest honour. He became governor of Tak and Kamphaeng Phet. Later after the fall of Ayutthaya to the Burmese in 1767 he rebuilt the army; within seven years he had regained the lost territory and claimed the throne. He established his capital at Thonburi *(see BANGKOK Environs)*.

SIGHTS

Town – It is worth exploring the area west of Wat Tha Sima Muang to admire some fine traditional **wooden houses** which add a touch of elegance to the busy modern town.

San Somdet Phra Chao Taksin Maharat – *Near the provincial highway division north of the town.* A **shrine** houses a seated statue of King Taksin with a sword lying on his lap, greatly venerated by the people.

The road which skirts the grounds runs past three temples with noteworthy features: **Wat Khok Phlu** has a slender ringed prang on a stepped tiered base framed by four smaller prangs; **Wat Pathum Khiri** is dominated by a bulbous Lao-style chedi on a raised platform; and **Wat Doi Khiri** is graced by an octagonal white chedi and an old vihara with ornate gables.

★**Wat Bot Mani Sibunruang** – *Turn right off 104 past King Taksin's shrine.* The temple has some interesting buildings. Near the entrance is an elegant white **chedi** fronted by a porch and housing a Sukhothai Buddha. The chedi rests on an unusually wide base and tapers to a slim finial surmounted by a gilded crown. On the left at the far end stands an old wooden **vihara** with a finely carved gable. Inside are delicate mural paintings which have suffered some deterioration, a Lanna-style Buddha presiding above the altar, and a tiered wooden pulpit.

EXCURSIONS

Wat Phra Boromathat – *Ban Tak. 25km north by 1107 and 1175 west.* The road along the west bank of the Mae Nam Ping affords views of the fertile valley. Ban Tak with its houses built on stilts by the river occupies the site of an earlier settlement, of which traces remain.

High up on a hill soars a gilded octagonal **chedi** crowned by a slim finial and framed by similar small chedis. The square base is decorated with lotus petals; stucco and glass motifs highlight the small chapels. An old wooden vihara contains Buddha statues; the ubosot (north) and the vihara (west) bear rich carvings.

Phra Chedi Yutthahatthi – *As above.* The Sukhothai-style **chedi** on a stepped square base is crowned by a lotus bud. It is believed to commemorate a victory over the Burmese by King Ram Kamhaeng in the 13C. Nearby is a large swamp covered with lotus and other water-plants.

Bhumibol Dam – *Amphoe Sam Ngao. 70km north by 1, at Km 464 turn left and continue for 17km.* The largest dam in Thailand, rising to 245m and describing an elegant curve across a narrow stretch of the Mae Nam Ping, was built in 1953-64 to alleviate flooding and to provide irrigation in the valley. However, this has caused the destruction of important habitats. The hydro-electric plant feeds the national grid. Excursions on the lake (304sq km) ringed by craggy mountains (highest peak alt 1 238m) offer spectacular **scenery★★** and opportunities for water-sports. The upper section of the lake is part of the Mae Ping National Park which borders two wildlife sanctuaries. The best time to visit is October to May. Highlights of the park include the 7-tiered Ko Luang waterfall *(20km from park headquarters, accessible by car)*, the Huai Tham scenic point, high cliffs and caves *(accessible only on foot)*. The park supports many endangered species of wildlife.

★ **Road from Tak to Mae Sot** – *80km west by 105*. The picturesque drive affords spectacular **views★★** as the road cuts through a forested area. The **Lan Sang National Park** *(at Km 12-13 take 1103 left and continue for 3km)* which encloses steep granite peaks offers wildlife, waterfalls, hiking trails and verdant scenery. Then the road climbs steeply through luxuriant landscape *(turn left at Km 25-26 for the Taksin Maharat National Park)*, and beyond the pass it winds through dense teak and pine forest.

Along the way there are several hill-tribe settlements (Meo, Lisu, Lahu), including the **Doi Musur** Hill Tribe Development and Welfare Centre, which offers an insight into their rustic lifestyle. An experimental project aims to encourage the hill-tribes to change from the practice of slash-and-burn agriculture and the cultivation of the opium poppy to the production of exotic plants, flowers and vegetables suited to the cool climate. Crafts and local produce are on sale in the village and at roadside stalls *(Km 29)*.

After crossing a valley the road climbs to another pass hemmed in by limestone crags past the San Chao Pho Phawo **shrine** *(Km 62-63)* with a bronze statue commemorating a brave Karen leader who fought to the death against the Burmese.

TRANG

Trang – Population 143 199

Michelin Atlas p 22 or Map 965 – N 4

The pleasant town laid out over a series of small hills *(khuans)* replaces the original town built at the mouth of the Mae Nam Trang, where flooding and invasion from the sea were constant threats.

In ancient times Trang was an important trading centre and seaport for ships plying the seas from the Straits of Malacca. Known as Krung Thani and Trangkhapura when the Srivijaya Empire held sway over the peninsula, it was a stopping-point between the east coast and Sumatra. During the Ayutthaya period Trang was frequented by western seafarers who then travelled by land to Nakhon Si Thammarat or Ayutthaya.

Extensive rubber plantations in the undulating countryside have brought prosperity to a large Chinese population who gives the town its special character. Dense forests and jagged mountains riddled with caves are now important conservation areas (**Khao Pu – Khao Ya National Park** – *60km north by 4, 403 and 4151*).

Town – Near the Clock Tower *(Thanon Rama VI)* are the fine buildings of the Governor's House, Provincial Hall and courthouse *(east)*. Chinese temples *(west between Sois 1 and 2 off Thanon Visetkun)* are the scene of a colourful vegetarian festival *(late Oct)*. **Phraya Rattanu Pradit Park** *(1km south, Thanon Phatthalung)* commemorates the civic leader who introduced rubber to the province. Nearby a picturesque pond covered with lotus blossom is the focal point of Kaphang Surin Park.

> Trang is famous for its wickerwork and fabrics with an intricate diamond pattern *(wholesale market in Thanon Thaklang – north)* as well as for its traditions including bullfighting and shadow puppet theatre.

EXCURSIONS

West coast – The unspoilt beauty of the indented coastline is a delight: the long sandy beaches in Amphoe Sikao *(39km northwest by 4046, 4162)*, Kantang *(50km west by 403)* and Palian *(40km south by 404)*. Picturesque offshore islands include Ko Libong (fishing villages), Ko Muk, Ko Ngai and Ko Sukon.

Khao Chong Forest Park – *20km east by 4, turn right*. The park is situated within an army compound. A track *(1km)* leads through dense forest to a waterfall with several pools (Ton Noi). Cross a wooden bridge and continue 1.5km (bad road). A path shaded by tall trees runs along the river up to another impressive waterfall which drops from a great height (Ton Yai).

Road to the waterfalls – *East by 4 and south along 4122*. Bird-lovers will stop at **Khlong Lamchan Waterbird Park**, a large swamp which attracts several species of waterfowl including teals.

The scenic road passes near numerous waterfalls created by the meeting of the Trang and Palian rivers or their tributaries and the Khao Banthat Mountains: Sai Rung, Phrai Sawan, Lam Plok, Chong Banphot, Ton Tae *(46km)* and Chao Pha.

TRAT

Trat – Population 90 480

Michelin Atlas p 18 or Map 965 – I 7

Trat, an unremarkable commercial town with few attractions, is the gateway to Kampuchea (Cambodia) and the departure point for Ko Chang and lesser-known islands, which attract discerning visitors in search of deserted beaches and beautiful scenery. A pleasant excursion is to take a leisurely boat trip *(from the canal pier)* on the canal and the estuary.

A favourable outcome – In the late 19C Trat was an important pawn in Rama V's attempts to counter French designs on Thailand. The king ceded Trat in exchange for the withdrawal of French forces from **Chanthaburi** *(see CHANTHABURI)*. In 1906, however, Trat and its nearby islands regained their Thai identity under another territorial accord.
The people have close cultural and trading links with neighbouring Kampuchea.

EXCURSIONS

Wat Bup Pharam – *Mu3, Tambon Wang Krachee. 2km southwest. Take a side road west near the bus station.* The fine old temple which dates from the late-Ayutthaya period (18C) has many interesting buildings set in large grounds: an elegant ubosot, several mondops and viharas decorated with wall paintings, a bell-tower, a wooden sala on stilts, and traditional monastic cells *(kutis)*. There is also a museum at the far end of the compound.

Gem mining

The town grew prosperous from the open-cast mining of rubies and sapphires in the districts of Khao Saming and Bo Rai. The Red Ruby, "Tab Tim Siam", is particularly famous. The heady times of instant fortune are long gone as economic reality bites, and there is little activity as in Chanthaburi. A word of caution – visitors should beware of tempting offers unless they are gem experts.

Scenic road to the Cambodian border – *95km south by 318.* This is a fine excursion for those who enjoy travelling off the beaten track. For most of the way the picturesque road is hemmed in between the deserted sandy beaches (Hat Sai Ngam Km 41, Sai Kaeo Km 41-42, Mai Rut Km 57, Ban Cheun 18km before Amphoe Khlong Yai Km 59-60) with their fishing villages, and the Buntud mountain range in Cambodian territory. Stop at a viewing-area at Km 70 to admire the glorious scenery. The narrowest point *(sign)* is between Km 81-82. Ban Hat Lek is a quiet border village, the crossing point for Kampuchea *(by land and ferry to Ko Kong)*.

Laem Ngop – *17km west by 3148.* The road runs past a typical Muslim fishing village *(Km 12-13)* to the pier. Make a small detour *(turn right near the marine police station for 800m)* to visit the **Naval Battle Memorial** shaped like a battleship. In 1941 the Thai Navy saw off a French squadron but lost three warships in a border conflict. A **museum** is devoted to the history of the navy.

Ko Chang

Boats depart from the pier to Ko Chang and other destinations in the **Ko Chang National Park** Ⓥ which comprises 47 islands. Besides Ko Chang, the most beautiful which will appeal to those searching for peace and tranquillity and have facilities are Ko Kut, Ko Mak, Ko Wai, Ko Ngam, Ko Khlum, Ko Kradat. All boast secluded sandy beaches, beautiful corals and luxuriant vegetation.

★★ **Ko Chang National Park** – The charm of the island with its white sandy beaches, secluded bays and crystal-clear waters is enhanced by coconut groves, lush orchards and the densely forested peaks and cliffs. The main harbour is in Ao Khlong Son and trails give access to all the beaches *(buses and motorbikes)*. The ferry also stops off the best beaches on the west coast (Hat Sai Khao, Hat Khlong Phrao, Laem Chaiyachet, Hat Kai Bae, Ao Bang Bao) and passengers transfer to a small boat to reach their resort *(not in the monsoon season)*. A surfaced ring road allows pleasant excursions to deserted coves and to the Khlong Phlu, Nang Yom, Nonsi and **Than Mayom** waterfalls which make the stay all the more enjoyable.

UBON RATCHATHANI★★

Ubon Ratchathani – Population 220 445

Michelin Atlas p 15 or Map 965 – F 9

The bustling town, located on the north bank of the Mae Nam Mun, is the provincial capital and stands at an important crossroads where Khmer, Lao and Thai influences merge; its monuments are, however, fairly recent. It has good tourist facilities and is a fine base for exploring the many sights in this border area.

The emblem of Ubon is a blooming lotus, reminiscent of Nong Bua Lamphu (a lotus pond) *(see UDON THANI, Excursions)*, to which the ancestors of the local people migrated after war with Vientiane (Laos) in 1773.

Candle Festival

In July at the start of Buddhist Lent, local temples take part in a colourful procession of floats bearing huge candles and wax carvings and accompanied by music and dance. The candles and floats are crafted with great artistry into wonderful compositions by the local artisans who devote much time and care to the undertaking. The candles of various shapes and sizes are presented to the local temples.

Festivities lasting several days are held at Thung Si Muang *(Thanon Uparat)*, an open space reserved for public celebrations since the reign of Rama V. A statue of a nobleman in official costume and sword in hand commemorates Thao Kham Phong, the founder of the city, and a big rectangular stone slab with an inscription was built by alliance countries during the Great East Asian War (waged during the Second World War) to represent the links between the people of Ubon.

SIGHTS

★★ **National Museum** Ⓥ – *Thanon Khuan Thani, Amphoe Muang, Ubon Ratchathani 34000.* A fine **building★**, formerly the provincial governor's residence in Rama V's reign, houses the museum presenting the history and culture of the region. In front of the building stand *bai sema* of the Dvaravati period (mid 8C-9C) and a 7C Pallava stone inscription.

There are sections on the geology of the Khorat Plateau (fossils, gems) and on prehistory (tools, bronze drum *c* 2500-2000, rock paintings). The historical displays highlight the Hindu – Khmer influences of the Chenla, Baphuon and Angkor eras (mid 7C-8C **Ardhartsvara★** – half Shiva,

B. Davies

Candle Festival

half Uma – 10C Ganesha, 11C-13C jars, 12C lintels). A serene group of two stand-ing Buddhas in the attitude of dispelling fear is a fine example of Laotian art *(Room 5)*. In the next room fine gilded and lacquered Buddhas with typical fea-tures, ornate dress and enigmatic expressions illustrate Thai – Lao culture, show-ing the strong influence of the Vientiane school of art in the 18C-19C and of the Bangkok school in the 19C-20C. Other rooms feature displays on textiles, folk crafts and music as well as administration and religion.

Around the courtyard, exhibits include a unique **bai sema★** with a lotus base and two parrots, a majestic 11C Khmer Baphuon-style singha, a late-10C **stele★** depicting nine Hindu divinities, seven mounted on animals and two on pedestals, in the Khmer Khleang style, and red sandstone inscriptions – one in ancient Khmer script (AD 1032) and another in northeastern Thai letters in the Thai and Pali language (mid 18C-19C) – as well as a Thai wooden gable (19C-mid 20C) with floral decor-ation and a celestial being painted red and yellow.

Nearby stands the City Pillar Shrine (San Lak Muang – *to the south of Thung Sri Muang*) which is in the Bangkok style.

Wat Thung Si Muang – *Thanon Luang*. The temple built in the reign of Rama III (1824-51) boasts two interesting buildings. A wooden **ho trai★★** (library) in a mixed central and Isan style is beautifully decorated in gilded lacquer; on the lower part of the side wall are carvings of 12 astrological animals. The roof is adorned with *chofa* (stylised bird) and *bai raka* (roof supports) motifs, and the gables bear clas-sical Lao-style designs. **Mural paintings★** depicting stories from the life of the Buddha and scenes of local daily life decorate the pillared interior of the elegant **ubosot.**

Wat Sri Ubon Rattanaram – *Thanon Uparat near the Provincial Hall*. The small seated Buddha image, **Phra Kaeo Busarakham**, made of topaz, was transferred from Laos by the founders of Muang Ubon and is enshrined in the pillared temple; the stepped roofline is similar in style to the Wat Benchamabopit in Bangkok. Finely carved window and door panels add a touch of elegance to a vast wooden sala.

Wat Maha Wanaram – *Thanon Suppasits*. Also known as Wat Pa Yai – the great forest temple – this important ancient temple dates from 1820. A low boundary wall surrounds the ubosot (1976), and the vihara (facing south) built by the ruler of Muang Ubon, Phra Prathum Wonarat Suriyawong, houses the revered Buddha image, **Phra Chao Yai Inthara Plaeng**, which has an ancient stone inscription at the base.

Wat Supattanaram – *Thanon Promthep*. The architectural style of the temple built in 1853 by Rama IV on the bank of the Mun is an unusual combination of Khmer, Thai and European elements. Realistic nagas frame the pediment of the **ubosot★★** with a chedi in the middle of its ornate foliage motif; the Thai-style roof is covered with orange glazed tiles. A pillared gallery with orange lotus capitals surrounds the building. The bas-reliefs decorating the low boundary wall are derived from Khmer lintel motifs, and the interior of the hall also has Khmer elements. Near the front stands a giant wooden bell made from an entire log.

Fine carved stone boundary markers *(bai sema)* are placed all round an interesting **museum** *(left of the ubosot)* which presents weapons, Buddha images, sculpted figures of the god Ganesha and female deities. A Khmer sandstone **lintel★** (AD 607-57) depicts two makaras facing inward at each end and two arches meeting at the centre as a medallion with a simha figure. Another lintel fragment dates from the late 6C.

Forest temples

There are several important meditation temples in the region which have attracted many foreign disciples.

A small museum near the entrance of **Wat Nong Pa Phong** *(4km southwest from Amphoe Warin Chamrap by 2178, turn right at Km 54 and continue for 2km)* explains the daily life in a forest temple and displays the personal belongings of the Venerable Achan Cha. A terracotta bas-relief on one side of the wall depicts the life of the abbot. In its densely wooded setting are dotted the monks' cells, the white ubosot with a terracotta wall relief illustrating the abbot's wander-ings to the forests of Isan and Laos, and a graceful Lao-style chedi.

Wat Pa Nanachat *(Tambon Bang Wai, Amphoe Warin Chamrap, 12km west by 226, turn right and continue for 500m)* is known for its strict rules.

EXCURSIONS

★Ban Wang Kan Luang – *Wat Ban Kan Luang, Tambon Kham Yai northeast by 2050, turn left at Km 1-2*. Several prehistoric sites reveal the archeological import-ance of the area. The open-air museum on high ground near a swamp comprises a burial site with skeletons and pottery (globular earthenware jars, cream-coloured pottery either cord-marked or painted) dating from *c* 500-100 BC. Prehistoric and Dvaravati artefacts recovered include bronze axes, bronze ornaments (bangles cast by the lost wax technique).

Wat Nong Bua – *Thanon Chayangkul. 3km north by 212, turn left into a branch road and continue for 800m.* The temple founded to provide facilities for pilgrims comprises a distinctive **chedi**★ built in 1957 to celebrate the 25th century of Buddhism, on the model of Bodh Gaya in northeast India which has been widely copied. Bodh Gaya is where Lord Buddha attained enlightenment under the tree of wisdom which was enclosed in a simple shrine by the Emperor Ashoka; by the 19C this had turned into a tower shaped like a truncated pyramid. Lotus petals decorate the square base and the top section of the chedi, whereas the lower part bears reliefs inspired from Bodh Gaya and niches containing standing Buddhas. A small gilded chedi crowns the pyramid. Smaller towers rise at the four corners of the court.

★**Wat Phu Khao Kaeo** – *Amphoe Phibun Mangsahan. 43km east by 217, turn left at Km 42.* From the bottom of the steps leading up to the modern

Wat Nong Bua

Tourism Authority of Thailand

ubosot the design represents a boat, recalling the vessel carrying all animals across the Samsara in the Buddhist tradition. Belfries with Khmer decorative elements in the gable and pillars and covered entirely with glazed ceramic tiles stand at the four corners. The window and door panels are decorated with Khmer-style carvings of deities. Inside the **ubosot** are mural paintings featuring the Phra That Chedis (enshrining relics of the Buddha) in Thailand. Stars highlight the ornate red and gold ceiling and on the gilded ship-shaped altar are three black Buddha images. Downstairs the large sala is decorated with Khmer-style lintels carved in wood and contains a collection of pottery found in the area. A vast sala stands in the grounds.

Wat Sa Kaeo – *Mu 3 Ban Thai, Amphoe Phibun Mangsahan (near Kaeng Saphu). 45km east by 217, turn right before the bridge.* Also known as Wat Tai, its name is derived from a large pond to the north of the temple boundary. Excavations have brought to light artefacts including deities, lintels, Bai Sema and a sandstone Dharmachakra (Wheel of the Law), many of which have been transferred to the museum in Ubon. The temple museum displays a 7C **lintel**★ decorated with foliage and garlands in the Prei Kmeng style, which is the biggest and the most unusual example of this period found in Thailand.

Rapids – At **Kaeng Saphu** *(45km east by 217, turn right before the bridge and continue for 400km opposite the temple)* an outcrop of hard sandstone beds forms a series of rapids which can be viewed in the dry season. Continue further downstream to **Kaeng Tana** *(Amphoe Khong Chiam – by 217 east from Ubon and 2222 then at Km 13 turn right and continue for 2km by a laterite road)* to enjoy a spectacular view of rocks and rapids near which the swirling gravel and sand have created curious potholes. These are part of the Kaeng Tana National Park.

Khong Chiam – *80km east by 217 and 2222.* This eastern district on the Mekong river enjoys the earliest sunrise in Thailand;

Beaches

To the south of Ubon is **Ko Hat Wat Tai**, a small island with beaches in the Mun River. **Hat Ku Dua** *(take 23 south then turn right to the ring road for 11km, then turn left and continue for 2km to Ban Ku Dua)*, a white sandy beach on the Mun river with restaurants and floating bamboo huts, is a popular recreation spot.

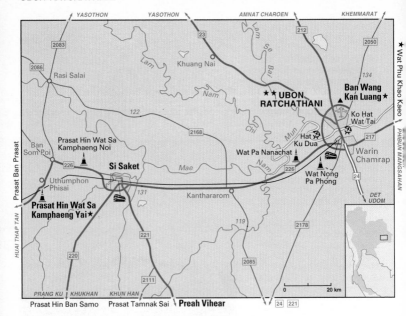

Yasothon · Yasothon · Amnat Charoen · Khemmarat

★ Wat Phu Khao Kaeo

★★ UBON RATCHATHANI

Rasi Salai · Khuang Nai

Ban Wang Kan Luang ★

Ban Som Poi

Prasat Ban Prasat

Prasat Hin Wat Sa Kamphaeng Noi

Si Saket

Ko Hat Wat Tai

Hat Ku Dua · Wat Pa Nanachat

Warin Chamrap

Uthumphon Phisai

Prasat Hin Wat Sa Kamphaeng Yai ★

Kanthararom

Wat Nong Pa Phong

HUAI THAP TAN

PHIBUN MANGSAHAN

DET UDOM

Prang Ku | Khukhan | Khun Han

Prasat Hin Ban Samo · Prasat Tamnak Sai · **Preah Vihear**

0 · 20 km

pleasant restaurants line the riverside. From Wat Tham Khuha Suwan there is a fine **view**★★ of the Mekong River. Sightseers can take a boat trip to **Mae Nam Song Si** (meaning Two-coloured river, near Ban Woen Buk) where the waters of the muddy Mekong and the clearer Mun merge amid beautiful verdant scenery and against a mountainous backdrop on the Laotian bank.

Sao Chaliang – *11km from Amphoe Khong Chiam. 95km east from Ubon by 217, 2222, 2134, at Km 57 turn right into 2112 and proceed for 11km, then turn right into 2368 and continue for 3.5km further and bear left.* Curious mushroom stone outcrops are dotted over a large area which geologists believe to be a dried-up sea, from the large amount of shells found in the stone texture.

★★★**Pha Taem** – *98km from Ubon. As above, 3km further from Sao Chaliang entrance. A trail (500m – 45min Rtn) to the right of the viewing area leads down to the rock paintings.* From the cliffs formed by the erosion of thick sandstone beds by the Mekong River, there are superb bird's-eye **views**★★★ of Laos across the river. Protected by the overhanging cliff, prehistoric **rock paintings**★★★ at Pha Taem (400m in length, the longest painted area in Southeast Asia – *illustration see INTRODUCTION, Art*), dating back 2 000 to 3 000 years and featuring human figures, hands, catfish, fish traps, elephants, geometric forms and farming symbols, provide an amazing insight into contemporary beliefs and activities. Kok Hin, a circular rock formation situated above Pha Taem, is believed to have been used in fertility cults in the late-prehistoric era and is perhaps related to the rock painting below. The cliffs **Pha Kham** and **Pha Mon** also afford wonderful views.

Chong Mek – *90km east by 217.* This border post is the only point where it is possible to cross into Laos by land and continue 3km to Muang Pakse. The first road linking Phibun to Chong Mek was constructed by prisoners of the Great East Asian War. There is an amazing variety of goods for sale at the bustling border market.

Sirinthon Dam – *Amphoe Phibun Mangsahan. 71km east by 217, turn right between Km 71-72 and continue for 500m.* The dam completed in 1971 has a production capacity of 36 000cu m or an annual 13.5 million units of electricity. This vast stretch of water is surrounded by beautifully landscaped grounds and there are facilities for visitors.

Wat Sri Nuan Saeng Sawang Arom – *Ban Chi Tuan, Amphoe Kuang Nai. 30km northwest by 23.* There is a **pulpit**★★ (thammat) in a characteristic prasat style believed to have been made by travelling Vietnamese craftsmen. The singha and the body of the pulpit are made of concrete while the top is decorated with fretwork. The stairs to the pulpit are carved in the Naga design.

Crafts

The province specialises in fabrics, basketry, and silver and bronze ware (lost wax method) especially betel-nut containers and accessories from Ban Pa Ao *(18km northwest by 23, turn right at Km 273 and continue for 3km).*

UDON THANI

Udon Thani – Population 388 476

Michelin Atlas p 8 or Map 965 – D 7

At an important crossroads on the Friendship Highway (Road no 2) near the Thailand – Laos border, this large market town, which serves the neighbouring agricultural provinces, experienced an economic boom when American army bases were set up in the province during the Vietnam War. Many foreigners have taken up residence in the town, which provides modern amenities (hotels, cinemas, department stores, airport). The original settlement, Ban Dua Mak Kang, grew in the mid 19C during the campaign against French colonisation of Vientiane (Laos), as under the terms of a treaty the Thai army withdrew 25km south from the Mekong River.

Town – The Nong Prachak lake *(northwest)* is a popular recreation area (flower garden, stage for entertainment, restaurants, fitness park). Near the railway station is a large Chinese shrine, Pu Ya Shrine (literally grandfather and grandmother shrine), which houses a Golden Dragon (99m long). There is a pleasant garden near the Nong Bua swamp.

EXCURSIONS

Wat Tham Klong Phen – *West by 210, after 13km turn left at Km 90-91 and continue for 2km.* A meditation forest temple in a rocky setting riddled with caves. The monuments include a slim white chedi dedicated to a revered former abbot and teacher, and a mondop built on a rock platform overlooking the Phu Phan forest. There is also a small museum.

Nong Bua Lamphu – *46km west by 210.* This is a famous town of ancient foundation in Thai history. In the Thonburi period (late 18C) two Laotian noblemen crossed the Mekong with their troops and settled here, thus escaping a political crisis in Vientiane and placing themselves under the protection of the Siamese king. After successive attacks by Vientiane and Burmese forces, they later moved to Don Mot Daeng *(near UBON RATCHATHANI)*.
King Naresuan stopped with his troops on his way to attack Laos in 1574. Opposite the provincial hall, a **monument** portrays the king in traditional garb and standing, sword in hand.

★★ Phu Phra Bat Historical Park ◷ – *68km northeast by 2, at Km 13 turn left into 2021 in the direction of Amphoe Ban Phu for 42km, then left opposite hospital take 2348 to Ban Tiu, after 11km turn right and continue for 2km by a laterite road. Visitor Centre. Time: 2hr.*
There is rich evidence of early human settlement dating from the prehistoric period amid the amazing rock formations in the park, which covers an area of 580sq km and is located in the Phu Phan Kham range. A trail passes **Khok Ma Thao Barot** (Prince Barot's Stable), **Ho Nang Usa** (Usa's Tower), Wat Po Ta (Father-in-law's Temple), Wat

Phu Phra Bat Historical Park

Luk Kei (Son-in-law's Temple) which are associated with a local legend of a king who disapproved of his daughter's union and lost his life in a contest with his son-in-law. Large mushroom-shaped sandstone slabs balanced on a smaller rock (Ku Nang Usa) and surrounded by bai semas found throughout the park suggest a religious site. Two rock shelters are decorated with realistic **mural paintings** of cattle (Tham Wua), and eight human figures engaged in a ritual dance (Tham Khon). Marked trails meander past caves, a pond, cliffs and shrines through the fascinating scenery.

Wat Phra Phutthabat Bua Bok – "Bua Bok" – terrestrial lotus – is a wild flower with leaves like those of a lotus, found in the area. Huge boulders rise near the elegant white chedi in the distinctive style of That Phanom highlighted with blue and green mosaic motifs, which is built over a Buddha footprint discovered by a monk. The superimposed square base supports an elongated relic chamber crowned by a spire on a receding lotus pedestal, and a golden parasol. There is a cave shrine near the entrance and a smaller *that* of more ancient origin on a rock platform.

> The town is famous for a new type of scented orchid "Miss Udon Sunshine" from which is extracted the first perfume from pure orchid in the world. The heady scent is highly prized locally and in Laos.
> Crafts include textile weaving – **khit** – from Na Kha village *(16km north by 2)*.

UTHAI THANI

Uthai Thani – Population 54 148

Michelin Atlas p 11 or Map 965 – F 5

The small town was founded in the reign of Rama I in a pleasant site on the banks of the Mae Nam Sakae Krang to the east of an old settlement. Prehistoric paintings (Khao Pla Ra) attest to human occupation in the western region. There are also impressive caves in the limestone hills.

SIGHTS

Wat Sangkat Ratana Khiri – The temple *(access by stairway – 450 steps or take a side road to the right off 1090 to the town)*, which dominates the town from the summit of Khao Sakae Krang, is a pilgrimage centre. An imposing mondop houses a Buddha footprint and a seated Buddha presides in a large vihara.

Wat Phichai Puranaram – *Thanon Si Uthai*. Interesting buildings include an old vihara and a smaller one containing fine Buddha images.

Wat Ubosotharam – *In a bend on the east bank*. This temple is notable for a precious Buddha image made of silver.

U-THONG

Suphan Buri – Population 102 497

Michelin Atlas p 11 or Map 965 – G 4 – Local map see Kanchanaburi

The modest town located in the middle of rice fields against a mountainous backdrop to the west is of great historical importance.

An ancient settlement – Its origin probably dates back to the prehistoric era and it was an important Mon settlement at the heart of the Dvaravati kingdom (8C-11C) until the 11C, when it came within the Khmer sphere of influence. The Mon site has been identified in the museum area.

It is a matter of great debate among historians whether the kingdom of Ayutthaya originated in U-Thong in the mid 14C, but the most common theory is that the local sovereign, styled King U-Thong after the name of the kingdom, moved his capital to Ayutthaya to escape an outbreak of cholera caused by a water shortage. The ruler was later crowned King of Ayutthaya and took the name of **Ramathibodi I.** The deserted town was repopulated in the late 18C by displaced people from Laos.

★ **National Museum** ⊘ – *Right of Amphoe office on 321*. A distinctive art style, in particular as regards sculpture, evolved in U-Thong. The early period combines Mon-Dvaravati and Khmer elements, while art historians now ascribe the later school to the early Ayutthaya period.

Prehistoric finds (stone tools, utensils) from excavations in the area date back to 3000 BC. The exhibits trace the Indian influence (*c* 5C-6C) and the Dvaravati legacy (*c* 8C-11C): painted bricks, **terracotta reliefs and heads**, stucco figures and divinities, a Wheel of the Law, Shiva lingas and votive tablets. A **Roman coin** and Dvaravati silver pieces are evidence of a thriving trade. Bronzes and a **Sanskrit text** inscribed in South Indian consonants are also noteworthy.

UTTARADIT

Uttaradit – Population 159 670

Michelin Atlas p 7 or Map 965 – D 5

The pleasant modern town was built in 1967 on the west bank of the Mae Nam Nan after the destruction of the old town by fire. Its prosperity is derived from agriculture which flourishes in the fertile plain, especially after the building of the Sirikit Dam on the mighty Mae Nam Nan to the northeast. Although Uttaradit is off the tourist circuit it offers many fine sights and excursions. The annual **Langsat Fair** *(early Sept)* is a popular event.

Historical notes – There are traces of ancient settlements all over the province: Muang Lap Lae *(9km northwest)*, Muang Fang *(50km east)*, Wiang Chao Ngo succeeded by Muang Thung Yang Kao *(5km west)*, which have not yet been extensively investigated. A bronze monument *(in front of the Provincial Hall)* commemorates a gallant soldier, Phraya Phichai Dap Hak, who fought valiantly alongside King Taksin in the 18C and successfully repelled attacks by the Burmese invaders. He became ruler of the province. Uttaradit was an important fluvial port and the gateway to the eastern part of northern Thailand and to western Laos, before river transport was superseded by modern road developments.

SIGHTS

Uttaradit Cultural Centre – *Opposite the Governor's residence.* A handsome wooden building enhanced by fretwork presents ancient artefacts from the province.

Wat Tha Thanon – *Between the river and the railway station.* An ancient Lanna-style (Chiang Saen) seated **Buddha image**★, framed by two standing Buddhas – one in royal apparel in late-Ayutthaya style and the other in Sukhothai style – presides at the altar of a Chinese-style vihara. The bronze statue was moved in 1900 by order of King Rama V to the Marble Temple in Bangkok, but was returned to Uttaradit 10 years later. Within the temple precincts stand elegant monastic buildings in Chinese and colonial style.

Wat Yai Tha Sao – *North by 1045.* Steps lead up to the ancient ubosot. The windows and the twin **doors**★ finely decorated with floral motifs have stucco frames. The unusual tiered roof is enhanced by a wooden gable adorned with swirling garlands and a deity.

Wat Thammathipatai – *Thanon Samranreun.* The highlight of the temple is a pair of massive 17C **door panels**★★ which belonged to the main vihara of Wat Phra Fang *(below)*. The exquisite floral design enhanced with glass mosaic and framed by deities in adoration illustrates the mastery of Ayutthaya craftsmen. The Lanna (Chiang Saen) Buddha image and the mural paintings depicting Buddhist legends are of interest.

EXCURSIONS

Wat Phra Boromathat – *5km west by 102, near Thung Yang market.* The main vihara boasts front and back **porches**★ with a sweeping roof and wood panelling and pediments exquisitely carved with vivid scenes. The ubosot is less elaborate but also beautifully decorated. A stepped base with small corner pagodas supports the **chedi**. Niches housing Buddha images punctuate the main body; above it rises the bulbous relic chamber ringed with lotus motifs and capped by a moulded finial.

Wat Phra Thaen Sila-At – *6km west by 102.* The hilltop temple is renowned as a pilgrimage centre which was visited in 1740 by King Borommakot. Interesting elements include a stone Buddha footprint in the modern vihara, four **footprints** in bronze in the small vihara, a small Chinese temple, and a vast two-storeyed wooden **sala** supported on tall pillars.

Wat Phra Yun Phutthabat Yukhon – *Next to above.* A unique feature of this ancient temple is the elaborate five-tiered roof of the colonnaded **mondop**★★ built by Chiang Saen craftsmen. The small vihara houses two seated Buddha images made of gold, silver and bronze flanked by attendants against a colourful backdrop.

Wat Phra Fang – *Mu 3, Ban Phra Fang, Tambon Pha Chuk. 25km east by 1045, 2km south by 11, then left and proceed for 14km.* On the south bank of the Mae Nam Nan in the grounds of a modern temple are the interesting **ruins** of an old monastery. The roof of the vihara which houses a large seated Buddha image is supported by massive pillars capped with capitals. Mouldings adorn the body and the finial of the fine chedi rising from a square base. Behind it stands an elegant vihara roofed with wooden tiles; its windows are decorated with stuccowork.

Sirikit Dam – *Amphoe Tha Pla. 60km east by 1045.* The dam (169m high, 800m long) inaugurated in 1977 was built to harness the Mae Nam Nan for energy and irrigation. The lake is stocked with fish and provides recreation facilities in a beautiful landscape.

Ton Sak Yai Forest Park – *81km east. As above then turn right and proceed for 11km by 1146, turn right at Km 56 and continue for 2km by a laterite road.* Visitors will marvel at the sight of a gigantic **tree** – 47m high, about 10m in circumference – about 1 500 years old, which is the pride of the arboretum. Although damaged by lightning it is claimed to be the biggest teak tree in the world.

YASOTHON

Yasothon – Population 131 648

Michelin Atlas p 14 or Map 965 – F 9

The town is of ancient foundation. Its principal monument is Wat Mahathat which is graced by a tall Lao-style white **that** and an elegant **library** delicately decorated with black lacquer and gold leaf.

Wat Thung Sawang *(near the market east of the town)* is worth a visit for its unusual **stupa** culminating in a lotus-bud design.

The traditional craft of silk and cotton handweaving is kept alive in Ban Si Than *(Amphoe Pathiu 20km east by 202, turn right between Km 18-19 and continue for 3km by a laterite road)*.

EXCURSIONS

Phra That Kong Kow Noi – *Tambon That Thong, Amphoe Muang southeast by 23 for 8km, turn left at Km 196 and continue for 600m by a track.* The ancient monument in a mixed Lao and Lanna style stands in the middle of rice fields. A wall surrounds the restored brick and stucco stupa dating from the Ayutthaya period and next to it is a small square structure with a curved roof.

According to tradition it was built by a poor rice farmer in atonement for treating his mother harshly and causing her demise because she had brought him only a small amount of food after all his hard morning's toil; however, after her death he was unable to finish the food in spite of his great hunger.

Phra Phutthabat – *Ban Nong Yang. 25km southeast by 23 to Amphoe Kham Kuan Kaeo, turn right into 2083 to Amphoe Maha Chana Chai and right again for 6km.* A site in the middle of a sandy island in Mae Nam Che bears a Buddha footprint, a Khmer-style Buddha image and a laterite inscription, which were transferred from Ayutthaya in 835.

Ban Song Puei – *25km southeast by 23 to Amphoe Kham Kuan Keo, turn right into 2083 and continue for 5.5km.* The ancient Khmer archeological site **Muang Toei** *(1km south of Ban Song Puei)* with its ruined temple, city wall and pond was probably a town of the Chenla-Dvaravati period.

A **museum** exhibits an interesting collection of artefacts found at Muang Toei – stele, bed of the ruler of the settlement. A chedi built on top of an ancient one contains earth from major Buddhist sites in India. There is also a Buddha footprint (1955).

Amnat Charoen – *60km east by 202.* It is the administrative centre for the growing population and is also a gateway to the Laotian border.

Phuttha Utthayan Khao Dan Phrabhat (Buddhist Park) – *3km north by 212. The site is on the left.* The shady park is dominated by the huge Buddha, **Phra Mongkhon Ming Muang** in the posture of subduing Mara, in gold mosaic tiles; it was designed by an Isan artist Chit Buabut and inaugurated in 1965.

Wat Phra Lao Thep Nimit – *45km south by 212, turn left between Km 35-34 into 2049 or 20km south by 212 turn right into 2134 to Amphoe Phana and continue for 2km.* This old temple is remarkable for the admirable decoration of the **bot**★ especially the base with a lotus stucco motif and the fine gilded wood-carving on a red ground above the pillared doorway with a mythical monster Rahu in the middle of the floral motifs. Pride of place is given to a splendid gilded and lacquered **Buddha image**★★ in the attitude of subduing Mara which dates back to 1724 and is notable for its fine workmanship. Next to it is a Lao-style structure.

Don Chao Pu Forest Park – *45km south by 212, turn left between Km 35-34 into 2049 and turn right between Km 25-26. Or 20km south by 212, turn right into 2134 to Amphoe Phana and bear right between Km 25-26.* A pleasant forest park with many species over 100 years old and a large number of monkeys. The locals revere an old wooden shrine where Chao Pu (the spirit of grandfather) is believed to reside.

Rocket Festival

Yasothon is famous for its annual Ngan Bun Bang Fai festival *(second week in May)* held at the end of the dry season to propitiate the rain god Phaya Thaen. The rockets (traditionally made of bamboo canes filled with saltpetre and charcoal) are taken in a colourful procession of floats with music and dance to the launching ground in a pleasant public park, Suan Phaya Thaen *(Thanon Chaeng Sanit near 23)*, and are fired, to the great delight of the spectators.

World Heritage List

In 1972 the United Nations Educational, Scientific and Cultural Organization (UNESCO) adopted a Convention for the preservation of cultural and natural sites. To date, more than 150 States Parties have signed this international agreement, which has listed over 500 sites "of outstanding universal value" on the World Heritage List. Each year a committee of representatives from 21 countries, assisted by technical organizations (ICOMOS – International Council on Monuments and Sites; IUCN – International Union for Conservation of Nature and Natural Resources; ICCROM – International Centre for the Study of the Preservation and Restoration of Cultural Property, the Rome Centre), evaluates the proposals for new sites to be included on the list, which grows longer as new nominations are accepted and more countries sign the Convention. To be considered, a site must be nominated by the country in which it is located.

The protected cultural heritage may be monuments (buildings, sculptures, archeological structures etc) with unique historical, artistic or scientific features; groups of buildings (such as religious communities, ancient cities); or sites (human settlements, examples of exceptional landscapes, cultural landscapes) which are the combined works of man and nature of exceptional beauty. Natural sites may be a testimony to the stages of the earth's geological history or to the development of human cultures and creative genius or represent significant ongoing ecological processes, contain superlative natural phenomena or provide a habitat for threatened species.

Signatories of the Convention pledge to co-operate to preserve and protect these sites around the world as a common heritage to be shared by all humanity.

Some of the most well-known places which the World Heritage Committee has inscribed include: Australia's Great Barrier Reef (1981), the Canadian Rocky Mountain Parks (1984), The Great Wall of China (1987), the Statue of Liberty (1984), the Kremlin (1990), Mont-Saint-Michel and its Bay (Great Britain and Ireland, 1979), Durham Castle and Cathedral (1986).

UNESCO World Heritage sites in Thailand are:

Historic Town of Sukhothai and Associated Historic Towns
Historic City of Ayutthaya and Associated Historic Towns
Ban Chiang Archaeological Site

Admission Times and Charges

As admission times and charges are liable to alteration, the information printed below - valid for 2001 - is for guidance only. The sights are listed below in the same order as in the Sights Section of the guide.

⊙ - Every sight for which times and charges are listed below is indicated by the symbol ⊙ after the title in the Sights section.

Dates *- Dates given are inclusive. The term holidays means religious and national holidays.*

Admission *- Ticket offices usually shut 30min before closing time.*

Charge *- The charge given is for an individual adult.*

Prices *- Prices are given in Thai Bahts. Student rates are available with international student card. Lower rates apply for Thai nationals.*

Tourist Information Centres ▣ *- The addresses and telephone numbers are given for the Local Offices of the Tourism Authority of Thailand (TAT) which provide information on sights, accommodation and transport. TAT offices: open 8.30am-4.30pm*

Temples *- Temples are usually open from sunrise to sunset. Ask the custodian to open the main buildings (ubosot, vihara) if closed. Dress properly and avoid visits during services.*

National Parks *- The parks are accessible from sunrise to sunset. Park rangers are usually on duty.*

Photographs *- It is courteous to ask permission to take photographs of people and religious shrines.*

A

AYUTTHAYA
▣ Thanon Si Sanphet; ☎ 035 246 076/7. Fax 035 246 078.

Historical Park - Open daily, 8.30am-4.30pm. 20 Baht per zone; 180 Baht combined ticket to all sites

Wat Na Phra Men - Same opening times as for the historical park. 20 Baht.

Wat Chai Wattanaram - Same opening times as for the historical park. 20 Baht.

Wat Yai Chai Mongkon - Open daily, 8.30am-4.30pm. 20 Baht.

Chao Sam Phraya National Museum - Open Wed-Sun, 9am-4pm. Closed Mon, Tues and national holidays. 30 Baht. ☎ 035 241 597.

Ayutthaya Historical Study Centre - Open daily, 9am-3pm (4.30pm Sat, Sun). 100 Baht. ☎ 035 245 123/4.

Chandra Kasem National Museum - Open Wed-Sun, 9am-4pm. Closed Mon, Tues and national holidays. 30 Baht. ☎ 035 245 586.

B

BAN CHIANG

National Museum - Open Wed-Sun, 9am-4pm. Closed Mon, Tues and national holidays. Combined ticket for museum at Wat Pho Si Nai 30B. ☎ 042 261 351.

BANGKOK
▣ Le Concorde Plaza, 202 Thanon Ratchadapisek; ☎ 02 694 1222-302. Fax 02 694 1361.

372 Thanon Ratchadamneon Nok; ☎ 02 282 9773-6. Fax 02 282 9775.

Grand Palace - Open daily, 8.30am-3.30pm. 150 Baht. Ticket also valid for Phra Thinang Vimanmek. ☎ 02 222 0094, 02 222 6889.

Wat Po - Open daily, 8am-5pm. 30 Baht.

Wat Phra Kaeo, Bangkok

SUPERSTOCK/ HOA QUI

National Museum - Open Wed-Sun, 9am-4pm. Closed Mon, Tues and national holidays. 40 Baht. ☎ 02 224 1370; Fax 224 9911.

Phra Thinang Vimanmek - Open daily, 9am-4.30pm; last admission 2.40pm. Guided tours. 50 Baht or combined ticket with Grand Palace. **Royal Elephant National Museum:** 5 Baht. ☎ 02 281 1569, 02 280 5928.

Wat Traimit - Open 9am-5pm; 10 Baht.

Snake Farm - Open 8.30am-4pm (12 noon Sat, Sun). Demonstration: weekdays 10.30, 14.00; weekends 10.30 only. 70 Baht. ☎ 02 252 0161-4.

Jim Thompson's House - Open daily, 9am-5pm. Guided tours only (in English, French). 100 Baht. ☎ 02 216 7365, 02 612 3744; www.jimthompsonhouse.com

Suan Pakkard Palace - Open Mon-Sat, 9am-4pm. Closed Sun and public holidays. 80 Baht. ☎ 02 245 4934.

Ban Kamthieng - Open Mon-Sat, 9am-4pm. Closed Sun and national holidays. 100 Baht. Guided tour for groups by appointment. ☎ 02 661 6470/75.

BANGKOK Environs

Boat services - Express boat and ferries from the piers at Tha Orienten, Tha Maharaj and River City. Fares 5-15 Baht. Long-tail boats are available for private hire. Apply at River City pier. 500-1200 Baht depending on type of craft and duration.

Wat Arun - Open daily 8.30am-5.30pm. 10 Baht.

Museum of Royal Barges - Open daily, 9am-5pm. 20 Baht. ☎ 02 424 0004.

Crocodile Farm - Open daily, 7am-5pm (6pm Sat, Sun). 300 Baht, child, student 200 Baht. Shows every hour from 9-11am and 1-4pm; additional shows at weekends 12noon and 5pm. ☎ 02 703 4891/5, 02 703 5144/8.

Muang Boran - Open daily, 8am-5pm. 50 Baht; and 50 Baht per car. ☎ 02 323 9253. Allow 1 day. Tour by car or bicycle.

BANG PA-IN

Tour of the Palace - Open daily, 8.30am-3.30pm. 50 Baht. ☎ 035 261 044, 02 281 548.$

Wat Niwet Thamapravat - Access by cable-car. No charge.

BURIRAM
Excursions

Prasat Muang Tham - Open daily, 8.30am-4.30pm. 20 Baht. ☎ 044 613 666.

C

CHAI NAT

Chai Nat Muni National Museum - Open Wed-Sun, 9am-4pm. Closed Mon, Tues and holidays. 10 Baht. Guided tours by appointment. ☎ 056 411 467.

CHAIYA

Chaiya National Museum - Open Wed-Sun, 8.30am-4pm. Closed Mon, Tues and national holidays. 30 Baht. ☎ 077 437 1066.

CHANTHABURI
Excursions

Oasis Sea World - Shows daily, 9am-6pm. 60 Baht, child 30 Baht. ☎ 039 363 238/9.

Nam Tok Phliu National Park - Open daily, 8am-5pm. 10 Baht.

CHIANG MAI
🚹 105/1 Chiang Mai-Lamphun Road. ☎ 053 248 604, 053 248 607, 053 241 466. Fax 053 248 605.

National Museum - Open Wed-Sun, 8.30am-4pm. Closed Mon, Tues and national holidays. 30 Baht. ☎ 053 221 308.

Hill Tribe Research Institute - Open Mon-Fri, 8.30am-4pm. No charge.

Chiang Mai Arboretum - Open daily, 8.30am-4.30pm. No charge.

Chiang Mai Zoo - Open daily, 8am-5pm. 30 Baht. ☎ 053 221 1179, 053 222 2283.

Excursions

San Kamphaeng Hot Springs - Open daily, 8am-5pm. 10 Baht.

Tang Dao Elephant Camp - Demonstration daily, 9am and 10am. 30 Baht. ☎ 053 298 553.

Tham Chiang Dao - Open daily, 8am-4pm. 10 Baht. Lamp Service: 50 Baht.

Tha Ton to Chiang Rai by boat - Departure daily at 12.30pm, arrival in Chiang Rai at 5pm. 160 Baht.

CHIANG RAI
🚹 448/16 Thanon Singhakhlai. ☎ 053 717 433, 053 744 674/5. Fax 053 717 434.

Excursions

Market, Doi Mae Salong – 5am-8am. Charter of minibus from 500 Baht.

House and Garden, Doi Tung - 100 Baht; **Garden**: 20 Baht.

CHIANG SAEN

Visitor Centre - Open daily, 8am-4.30pm. ☎ 053 777 030.

Wat Pa Sak - Open daily, 8am-4.30pm. 30 Baht.

National Museum - Open Wed-Sun, 8.30am-4.30pm. Closed Mon, Tues and national holidays. 30 Baht. ☎ 053 777 102. Slide and video shows, information leaflet.

Opium Museum - Open daily, 8am-4.30pm. 30 Baht.

CHONBURI
Excursions

Aquarium, Bang Saen - Open Tues to Sun, 8.30am-4pm (5pm national holidays). Closed Mon. 10 Baht.

Khao Khieo Open Zoo - Open daily, 8.30am-6pm. 20 Baht; and 20 Baht per car. ☎ 038 298 187/8.

Ko Si Chang - Ferry services from Ko Loi pier or Tha Charin pier in Si Racha from 7am. Last return trip from the island at 7pm. 50 Baht Rtn. Boat charter from 1200 Baht.

CHUMPHON
Excursions

Boats to Ko Tao from Paknam Chumphon - 2 services daily: 7.30am, time: 1hr 30min; midnight, time: 6hr. 400 Baht.

Tham Rab Ro and Tham Phra – Open daily, 8am-5pm.

D - H

DAMNOEN SADUAK

Access - By bus from Southern Bus Terminal : every 20min from 5am. Reduced time-table on Buddhist holidays, Chinese New Year. Amphoe Office ☎ 032 421 204, 032 254 976; Changwat Office ☎ 032 337 890.

Wat Phra That DOI SUTHEP

Cable car - Donation 5 Baht.

Phuping Palace and Gardens: Open Fridays, Sat, Sun and public holidays except when the Royal Family is in residence.

HUA HIN
Excursions

Phra Ratcha Niwet Marukatayawam - Open daily, 8am-4pm. Donation.

K

KAMPHAENG PHET

Historical Park - Open daily, 8.30am-4.30pm. 20 Baht per zone.

National Museum - Open daily, 8.30am-4pm. 30 Baht. ☎ 055 711 921.

KANCHANABURI   🛈 Thanon Saeng Chuto. ☎/Fax 034 511 200.
Excursions

Excursion by rail - Trains at 6am, 11am, 4.35pm. 17 Baht. Steam Train services: 10.25am, 11am, 4.35pm. Time: 2hr 30min. ☎ 034 511 285.

Kanchanaburi War Cemetery - Open daily, 8am-5pm.

JEATH War Museum - Open 8.30am-6pm. 20 Baht.

Ban Kao Museum - Open Wed-Sun, 8.30am-4.30pm. Closed Mon, Tues and national holidays. 30 Baht. ☎ 034 654 058.

Prasat Muang Sing - Open daily, 8am-4pm. 20 Baht.

Sai Yok National Park - 25 Baht.

KHON KAEN   🛈 15/5 Thanon Prachasamoson. ☎ 043 244 498/9/Fax 043 244 497.

National Museum - Open Wed-Sun, 8.30am-4.30pm. Closed Mon, Tues and national holidays. 30 Baht. ☎ 043 246 170.

Excursions

Khuan Ubonrat Dam - Open daily, 8.30am-6pm.

KRABI
Excursions

Mu Ko Lanta - Boats from Ban Hua Hin to Ko Lanta Noi and small boat on to Ko Lanta Yai (2hr) or from Ban Bo Muang (1hr). The crossing is dangerous in rainy season. Access also from Krabi town.

L

LAMPANG
Excursions

Elephant Conservation Centre - Show times daily 9.30am, 11am (also 2pm Sat, Sun). Closed Wed. 30 Baht.

LAMPHUN

Haripunchai National Museum - Open Wed-Sun, 8.30am-4pm. Closed Mon, Tues and national holidays. 30 Baht. ☎ 053 511 186.

LOEI

Excursions

Phu Luang Wildlife Sanctuary - Open Oct-May. Closed Jun-Sept. Reservation of basic accommodation (bungalows) in advance to Loei Administration Office, ☎ 042 811 776, 042 812 033. Take own food supplies.

LOPBURI

🛈 Thanon Narai Maharat. ☎ 036 422 768/9. Fax 036 422 769.

Phra Narai Ratcha Niwet - Open Wed-Sun, 8.30am-4pm. Closed Mon, Tues and public holidays. 30 Baht. ☎ 036 411 458.

Wat Phra Si Ratana Mahathat - Open daily, 9am-4pm. 30 Baht. ☎ 036 412 510.

Prang Sam Yot – Open daily, 8.30am-4.30pm. 30 Baht. ☎ 036 411 458.

Vichayen House - Open daily, 9am-6pm. 30 Baht.

M - N

MAE HONG SON

Excursions

Padong Village - 250 Baht.

Tham Lot - Open 8am-5pm. Guide service recommended for safety reasons. 200 Baht including lamp. Time: 1hr 30min.

NAKHON PATHOM

Phra Pathom Chedi - Open daily, 7am-6pm.

Museum – Open Wed-Sun, 9am-4pm. Closed Mon, Tues and national holidays. 30 Baht.

Excursions

Rose Garden - Open daily, 8am-4pm. 10 Baht. Show 2.45pm. 300 Baht. ☎ 034 322 544-7.

Samphran Elephant Village - Open daily 8am-6pm. Shows Mon-Sat, 12.45pm, 2 20pm; Sun and national holidays, additional shows 10.30am. 300 Baht, child 200 Baht. ☎ 02 429 0361/2.

Thai Human Imagery Museum - Open Mon-Fri, 9am-5.30pm; Sat, Sun and national holidays. 8.30am-6pm. 200 Baht, child, student 100 Baht. ☎ 034 332 607, 034 332 061.

NAKHON PHANOM

🛈 184/1 Thanon Soontomvijit. ☎ 042 513 490/1.
Fax 042 513 492.

NAKHON RATCHASIMA (KHORAT)

🛈 2102-2104 Thanon Mittraphap.
☎ 044 213 030, 044 213 030. Fax 044 213 667.

Maha Werawong National Museum - Open daily, 8.30am-4pm. 30 Baht; 100 Baht combined ticket to all sites in the province. ☎ 044 471 167.

Excursions

Prasat Hin Phanom Wan – Open daily, 8.30am-4.30pm. 30 Baht.

Ban Prasat – Open daily, 9am-4pm. Donation.

Prasat Hin Muang Kaek – Open daily, 9am-4pm. 30 Baht.

NAKHON SI THAMMARAT

🛈 Sanam Na Muang, Thanon Ratchadamnoen.
☎ 075 346 515/6. Fax 075 346 517.

Ho Phra Phuttha Sihing - Open daily, 8.30am-4pm.

Wihan Khien - Open daily, 8am-4.30pm.

National Museum - Open daily, 8.30am-4pm. 30B. ☎ 075 341 075.

NAN

National Museum – Open daily, 8.30am-4pm. 30 Baht. ☎ 054 710 561.

NARATHIWAT

🛈 102/3 Moo 2, Narathiwat-Tak Bai Road. ☎ 073 516 144, 073 522 411. Fax 073 522 412.

Excursions

Sungai Golok - Border post open 5am-5pm (6am-6pm on Malaysian side) but may close early. Hotels, restaurants.

NONG KHAI

Friendship Bridge - Immigration Office open 6am-6pm; in Laos office closes from 11.00 to 14.00.

P

PATTANI

Pattani Central Mosque - Open daily, 9am-3pm.

PATTAYA

🛈 609 Moo 10, Thanon Phra Tham Nak, Tambon Nongpue. ☎ 038 427 667, 038 428 750. Fax 038 429 113.

Excursions

Mini Siam - Open daily, 7am-7pm. 200 Baht, child 100 Baht. ☎ 038 421 628, 038 424 232; Fax 038 421 555.

Million-Year Stone Park - Open daily, 8am-4pm. Shows 10.15am, 3pm, 3.45pm. 300 Baht, child 125 Baht. ☎ 038 249 347/9.

Wihan Sian - Open daily, 8am-5pm. 30 Baht.

Suan Nong Nooch - Open daily, 8am-4pm. 20 Baht, child 10 Baht. Shows 10.15, 3pm and 3.45pm. 250 Baht, child 100 Baht. ☎ 038 429 321, 038 422 958, 02 252 1786.

Ao PHANGNGA

Tour - Boats from Tha Dan Pier on Khlong Khao Thalu (7km west of Phangnga Town by 4144), Amphoe Muang or Sarakun Pier in Amphoe Tukua Thung. From 900 Baht for up to 4 passengers.

Excursions

Tham Suwan Khuha - 10 Baht.

Prasat Hin PHANOM RUNG

Open daily, 8.30am-4.30pm. 30 Baht. ☎ 044 613 666.

PETCHABUN

Excursions

Si Thep Historical Park - Open daily, 8.30am-4.30pm. 30 Baht.

PHETCHABURI

🛈 500/51 Thanon Phetkasem, Amphoe Cha-Am. ☎ 032 471 005/6. Fax 032 471 502.

Phra Nakhon Khiri - Visitor centre. Admission and funicular 40 Baht.

Phra Nakhon Khiri National Museum - Open daily, 8.30am-4.30pm. ☎ 032 428 539.

Excursions

Phra Ram Ratchaniwet – Open Wed-Sun, 9am-4pm. Closed Mon, Tues and national holidays. 30 Baht.

Kaeng Krachan Dam and National Park - Tour of the park by four-wheel drive vehicle or park vehicle at set times morning and afternoon as trails are suitable for only one vehicle. 20 Baht and fee (from 600 Baht) for vehicle. Guides essential for trekking. Fee. ☎ 032 459 291.
Boat trips arranged at the park office: from 500 Baht.

PHICHIT

Wat Tha Luang - Open daily, 9am-4pm.

Mu Ko PHI PHI

Access by boat from **Krabi** and **Ao Nang** (1hr 30min). **Phuket** (2-3hr).

Prasat Hin PHIMAI

Historical Park - Open daily, 8.30am-4.30pm. 40 Baht. ☎ 044 471 568.

Phimai National Museum - Open daily, 8.30am-4.30pm. 30 Baht. ☎ 044 471 167.

PHITSANULOK

🛈 209/7-8 Surasi Trade Centre, Thanon Boromtrailokanat. ☎ 055 252 743, 055 259 907. Fax 055 252 742.

Wat Phra Si Ratana Mahathat - Open 7am-5pm. 10 Baht. Proper dress required. Photography permitted.

Folklore Museum – Open 9am-4pm. Donation.

Excursions

Wat Chulamani - Open daily, 8.30am-4pm. No charge.

PHRAE
Excursions

Ban Prathap Chai - Open daily, 8am-4pm. 20 Baht.

PHU KRADUNG National Park

Open Oct-May and closed annually Jun-Sept.
Advance reservations for accommodation to Reservation Service, National Park Division, Royal Forestry Department. ☎ 02 561 4292 Ext 724/5. Private accommodation available at Ban Pak Phu Kradung - ☎ 02 270 0488, 02 270 0861.
Porters are available to carry bag or food to the top at 20 Baht per kg. Contact Park Headquarters.

PHUKET

🛈 73/75 Thanon Phuket. ☎ 076 211 036, 076 212 213, 076 217 138. - Fax 076 213 582.

Aquarium - Open daily, 8.30am-4pm. 10 Baht, child, student 5 Baht.

Thalang National Museum - Open Wed-Sun, 9am-4.30pm. Closed Mon, Tues and national holidays. 30 Baht. ☎ 076 311 426.

Ko Naga Noi - Open all year.

Phuket Orchid Garden and Thai Village - Open daily, 9am-8pm. Shows 11am, 5.30pm. 230 Baht. ☎ 076 214 860/1

Phuket Butterfly Garden and Aquarium - Open daily, 8am-5pm. 100 Baht. ☎ 076 210 859.

Excursions

Mu Ko Similan -Boat trips from **Phuket** (8hr by regular boat or 3hr 30min by fast boat) or from Chumphon Pier, Ban Hin Lad, **Khura Buri** (3-5hr).

PRACHINBURI

🛈 182/88 Thanon Suwannason, Nakhon Nayok. ☎ 037 312 282, 037 312 284. Fax 037 312 286

National Museum - Open Wed-Sun, 9am-4pm. Closed Mon, Tues and national holidays. 30 Baht. ☎ 037 211 586.

R - S

RANONG
Excursions

Boat trips - To **Ko Surin** : from Chumphon Fishing Pier in Ban Hin Lad, Amphoe Khura Buri. 4-5hr one way.
Mu Ko Similan : from Chumphon Pier, Amphoe Khura Buri. 3-5hr one way; from pier in Thap Lamu. 3hr.

RATCHABURI

National Museum - Open Wed-Sun, 9am-4pm. Closed Mon, Tues and national holidays. 30 Baht. ☎ 032 321 513.

RAYONG

153/4 Thanon Sukhumvit. ☎ 038 655 420/1. Fax 038 429 113.

Ko Samet – Access: Boats leave from Ban Phe in Amphoe Rayong to Na Dan and Ao Wong Duan from 6am-5pm and more frequently at weekends. Fare: 30 Baht. Boats can also be chartered for groups. From the harbour at Na Dan access to the beaches round the island is by truck or on foot. National Park: 50 Baht.

Ko SAMUI

Access: Day express (2hr 30min, passengers only) from Tha Thong Sala northeast of Surat Thani. Night ferry (4hr to Samui or 5hr to Ko Phangan, passengers only) from Ban Don. Vehicle ferry (1hr 30min) from Don Sak 60km east from Surat Thani or 1hr from Khanom 80km east. Regular air services from Bangkok.

Excursions

Ko Phangan - **Access** by express boat from Na Thon Pier twice daily and boat service daily from Bophut Pier depending on weather conditions. Also night ferry from Ban Don Pier, Surat Thani. Enquire locally.

Ko Tao - Access by boat (5hr) from Paknam Chumphon or Surat Thani via Ko Phangan. Enquire locally.

Mu Ko Ang Thong National Park - Day trips daily in high season. Enquire locally.

SAMUT SONGKHRAM

Excursions

King Rama II Memorial Park - Garden: open daily, 9am-5pm. 10 Baht, child 5 Baht. Museum and Library: open Wed-Sun, 9am-5pm; closed Mon and Tues. 10 Baht. ☎ 034 751 666.

SATUN

Excursions

Mu Ko Tarutao – Access - Regular boat services (2hr) in season (Nov-May) from Pak Bara harbour, Amphoe Langu, ☎ 074 711 199. 60km north of Satun by 406 to Chalung, 4078 left to Langu and local road. Also boat hire from Satun piers. Accommodation and camping must be booked in advance from the Marine National Park Division in Bangkok. ☎ 02 579 0592. Fax 02 579 1154.

SINGBURI

Inburi National Museum – Open Wed-Sun, 8.30am-4.30pm. Closed Mon, Tues and national holidays. 30 Baht.

SI SA KET

Preah Vihear - Check with Tourist Office in Ubon Ratchathani (below) or Provincial Office - accessible from the Thai side at Khao Mor E Deang.

SI SATCHANALAI

Historical Park - Open daily, 8.30am-4.30pm. 30 Baht per zone; 150 Baht combined ticket to all sites in Si Satchanalai and Sukhothai. ☎ 055 641 813.

Museum – Open Wed-Sun, 8.30am-4.30pm. Closed Mon, Tues and national holidays. 30 Baht.

Ko Noi Kilns – Open daily, 8.30am-4.30pm. 30 Baht.

SONGKHLA

Soi 1, Thanon Niphat Uthit 3, Hat Yai. ☎ 074 231 055, 074 238 518, 074 243 747. Fax 074 245 986.

Songkhla Lake - Tour: boat hire from the market pier on Thanon Chana or behind the post office.

Songkhla National Museum - Open Wed-Sun, 8.30am-4.30pm. Closed Mon, Tues and national holidays. 30 Baht. ☎ 074 311 728.

Wat Matchimawat - Open Wed-Sun, 9am-4pm. Closed Mon, Tues and national holidays. 10 Baht. ☎ 074 311 728.

Excursions

Folklore Museum - Open daily, 9am-4pm. 5 Baht.

Khu Khut Bird Sanctuary - Boat hire for sightseeing (1hr 30min) in the early morning. 150-200 Baht.

SUKHOTHAI

Historical Park - Open daily, 8.30am-4.30pm. 40 Baht per zone and fee per car. Access by minibus or tuk tuk from the new town. Bicycles for hire near park entrance. Guided tours by appointment. Visitors should be properly dressed and remember that the monuments are sacred. ☎ 055 611 110.

Ram Kamhaeng National Museum - Open Wed-Sun, 8.30am-4.30pm. Closed Mon, Tues and national holidays. 30 Baht. Tel 055 612 167.

Excursion

Sangkhalok Museum – Open daily, 10am-6pm (8pm Sat, Sun). 250 Baht. Restaurant, shop and special events in plaza.

SURAT THANI
🛈 5 Thanon Talat Mai, Ban Don. ☎ 077 288 818/9. Fax 077 282 828.

Excursions

Monkey Training School - Information from the local TAT. ☎ 077 282 828, 077 288 818/9.

Chieo Lan Dam - Accommodation from EGAT. ☎ 042 44 794 or 077 311 542.

Khao Sok National Park - 30 Baht. Fee for tours and rafting trips organised by rangers. Accommodation from National Parks Division.

SURIN

Excursions

Prasat Hin Sikhoraphum – Open daily, 8.30am-4.30pm. 30 Baht.

Prasar Ban Phluang – Open daily, 8.30am-4.30pm. 30 Baht.

Prasat Ta Muen Thom - The temple is under the control of special border police and army patrols. Enquire about safety conditions from TAT Office in town. Information also from the Fine Arts Division, Phimai. ☎ 044 213 666. 044 213 030; Fax 044 213 066.

TAK
🛈 193 Thanon Taksin, Tambon Nong Luang. ☎ 055 514 341/3. Fax 055 514 344.

TRAT
🛈 100 Mu 1, Tambon Laem Ngop. ☎ 039 597 255, 039 597 259/260. Fax 039 597 255.

Excursions

Ko Chang National Park – Boat services from Laem Ngop every hour in season (every two hours out of season) from 8am-5pm. Fare 50 Baht. Bus fare on Ko Chang: 30 Baht. Information about accommodation from TAT Office.

U

UBON RATCHATHANI
🛈 264/1 Thanon Khaun Thani. ☎ 045 243 770/1. Fax 045 243 771.

National Museum - Open Wed-Sun, 8.30am-4.30pm. Closed Mon, Tues and national holidays. 30 Baht. ☎ 045 255 071.

UDON THANI
🛈 16/5 Thanon Mukmontri. ☎ 042 325 406/7. Fax 042 325 408.

Excursions

Phu Phra Bat Historical Park – Open daily, 8.30am-4.30pm. 30 Baht.

U-THONG

National Museum - Open Wed-Sun, 8.30am-4.30pm. Closed Mon, Tues and national holidays. 30 Baht.

Index

Fang . . . . Towns, sights and tourist regions followed.
Chiang Mai . . . . by the name of the district (amphoe) or province (changwat).

Isolated sights (historical parks, temples, islands) are listed under their proper name. Figures in bold indicates main entry

Ram Kamhaeng, King People, deities, events, religious traditions, artistic styles, general themes

Elephant Kraal . . . . Sights of important towns

293

N

T

Notes